PLANET NARNIA ✦

PLANET NARNIA

*The Seven Heavens in the Imagination
of C. S. Lewis*

MICHAEL WARD

OXFORD
UNIVERSITY PRESS

2008

OXFORD
UNIVERSITY PRESS

Oxford University Press, Inc., publishes works that further
Oxford University's objective of excellence
in research, scholarship, and education.

Oxford   New York
Auckland   Cape Town   Dar es Salaam   Hong Kong   Karachi
Kuala Lumpur   Madrid   Melbourne   Mexico City   Nairobi
New Delhi   Shanghai   Taipei   Toronto

With offices in
Argentina   Austria   Brazil   Chile   Czech Republic   France   Greece
Guatemala   Hungary   Italy   Japan   Poland   Portugal   Singapore
South Korea   Switzerland   Thailand   Turkey   Ukraine   Vietnam

Published by Oxford University Press, Inc.
198 Madison Avenue, New York, New York 10016

www.oup.com

Oxford is a registered trademark of Oxford University Press

Library of Congress Cataloging-in-Publication Data
Ward, Michael, 1968–
Planet narnia : the seven heavens in the imagination of C.S. Lewis / Michael Ward.
    p. cm.
Includes bibliographical references and indexes.
ISBN 978-0-19-531387-1
1. Lewis, C. S. (Clive Staples), 1898–1963—Criticism and interpretation.
2. Lewis, C. S. (Clive Staples), 1898–1963—Religion. 3. Lewis, C. S.
(Clive Staples), 1898–1963—Knowledge and learning. I. Title.
PR6023.E926Z945 2007
823'.912—dc22   2007014919

9 8 7 6 5 4 3 2 1
Printed in the United States of America
on acid-free paper

To James G. Levine
expert in atmospheric chemistry

The spacious firmament on high,
with all the blue ethereal sky,
and spangled heavens, a shining frame,
their great Original proclaim.
The unwearied sun from day to day
does his Creator's power display;
and publishes to every land
the work of an almighty hand.

Soon as the evening shades prevail,
the moon takes up the wondrous tale,
and nightly to the listening earth
repeats the story of her birth;
whilst all the stars that round her burn,
and all the planets in their turn,
confirm the tidings, as they roll
and spread the truth from pole to pole.

What though in solemn silence all
move round the dark terrestrial ball?
What though no real voice nor sound
amid their radiant orbs be found?
In reason's ear they all rejoice,
and utter forth a glorious voice;
for ever singing as they shine,
"The hand that made us is divine."

—Joseph Addison, 1712 (after Psalm 19)

There then comes to you a person, saying, "Here is a new bit of the manuscript that I found; it is the central passage of that symphony, or the central chapter of that novel. The text is incomplete without it. I have got the missing passage which is really the centre of the whole work." The only thing you could do would be to put this new piece of the manuscript in that central position, and then see how it reacted on the whole of the rest of the work. If it constantly brought out new meanings for the whole of the rest of the work, if it made you notice things in the rest of the work which you had not noticed before, then I think you would decide that it was authentic.

—C. S. Lewis, 'The Grand Miracle'

PREFACE ✑

It is to be hoped that this book reaffirms the worth of implicit communication; not everything that needs to be said needs to be said outright. Some
things, indeed, cannot be directly told: like happiness which 'writes white'
they vanish when put into words. Thankfulness, however, is usually not such a
thing and often finds itself only in the act of articulation. Let me therefore
discover the nature and extent of my gratitude as I acknowledge the help and
kindness of the following people:

The Reverend Professors Jeremy Begbie and Trevor Hart of the University
of St. Andrews, who supervised the doctoral thesis in which this book originated and who made the seminars at the Institute for Theology, Imagination
and the Arts such profitable occasions. My thanks also to my colleagues in ITIA
(rhymes with *idea*), especially Kirstin (and Greg) Johnson, Julie (and Matt)
Canlis, and Tony Clark.

For funding my research I thank the Whitefield Institute (now the Kirby
Laing Institute for Christian Ethics) and the Ministry Division of the Arch-
bishops' Council of the Church of England; also Mr and Mrs Otto Stevens for
their generous support. I am grateful for the award of the 2006 Clyde S. Kilby
Research Grant from the Marion E. Wade Center, Wheaton College, Illinois.

Mr Christopher Holmwood and the Rt Revd Simon Barrington-Ward
deserve special mention for their parts in the discovery which provided the focus
for that research and, in turn, for this book.

For their professionalism and efficiency I thank the staff of the Bodleian
Library, Oxford; the library of Magdalene College, Cambridge; the library of

New Hall, Cambridge; the Wade Center, Wheaton College, Illinois; the Warburg Institute, London.

Mr Andrew Cleland, the Revd Nigel Dawkins, Ms Antonia Irvine, the Revd Dr Michael Thompson, and Dr Steven Young for technical support and assistance.

Miss Pauline Baynes for responding helpfully to my enquiries.

Lord Harries of Pentregarth, Mrs Rachael Howorth, Mrs Kay Stevenson, and the Most Revd Rowan Williams, for supplying me with documents or copies of documents in their possession.

Dr Walter Hooper, Dr Christopher Mitchell, and Dr Andrew Cuneo for their scholarly advice and encouragement.

Dr Charles Weiss, Dr Arend Smilde, and the Revd Henk van Wingerden for help in the sourcing of quotations; Mr Alex Ingrams, Mr Anish Lakhani, and Mr Matthew Woodcraft for joining in the ichneutic effort.

Dr Mari Jones, Professor Ted Kenney, and the Revd Dr John Yates III for linguistic advice.

Dr Clare Baker, Dr Berthold Kress, Miss Libbi Lee, Mr Quentin Maile, and Miss Catherine Tabone for assisting with the illustrations.

All of these people have contributed directly to the content or the production of this book, and though I am indebted to them all I owe them none of the errors that may appear in what follows; they, of course, are my own responsibility.

'By indirections seek directions out.' For indirect helps too various and numerous to particularise, I thank Adam Barkman, Mike and Emma Blanch, Erika Cuneo, Liam and Pip Cuttell, Colin Duriez, Charles Hart, Chris and Cath Hayhurst, Ruth Holmwood, Don King, Andrew Lazo, Sean Lip, Wayne and Nita Martindale, Marjorie Mead, Sebastian Nokes, Barnaby Perkins, Ben Quash, Jerry Root, Alessandro Scafi, Kevin Taylor, Guy Treweek, David Whalen, and Emma Young.

The indirect help which must be particularly noted is that of my parents, Keith and Olive Ward, whose loving influence (*influence* is a key term in what follows) exerts itself invisibly on every page of this book. But here words fail and Mercury must take wing, bearing his message through what is not said. Sometimes silence is, as Shakespeare put it, 'the perfectest herald.'

ACKNOWLEDGMENTS

'The Planets,' 'A Pageant Played in Vain,' 'Noon's Intensity,' 'Scazons,' and 'The Birth of Language' quoted from *Collected Poems* by C. S. Lewis copyright © C. S. Lewis Pte. Ltd. 1994; material quoted from chapter 15 of *That Hideous Strength* by C. S. Lewis copyright © C. S. Lewis Pte. Ltd. 1945; material quoted from chapters 11 and 12 of *The Lion, the Witch and the Wardrobe* by C. S. Lewis copyright © C. S. Lewis Pte. Ltd. 1950. Reprinted by permission.

Material quoted from chapter V of *The Discarded Image* by C. S. Lewis copyright © Cambridge University Press 1964. Reprinted by permission.

Illustrations by Pauline Baynes copyright © C. S. Lewis Pte. Ltd. Reprinted by permission.

Mural of Mars reproduced from *The Gardens of Pompeii: Herculaneum and the Villas Destroyed by Vesuvius* by Wilhelmina F. Jashemski, Caratzas Bros., New Rochelle, New York, 1979.

Photograph of the statue of Mercury, Christ Church, Oxford, taken by the author with the permission of Christ Church.

Painting of Venus holding an apple reproduced from *Venus, Vergeten Mythe* by Ekkehard Mai, Koninklijk Museum Voor Schone Kunsten Antwerpen, 2001.

CONTENTS ✐

A photo gallery follows page 126

PLANET NARNIA

ONE

Silence

As is proper in romance, the inner meaning is carefully hidden.
—Letter to Arthur Greeves (18 July 1916)

An enquiring mind is likely to find that C. S. Lewis's Chronicles of Narnia present certain problems. Solving these problems matters because stories such as these that are popular and accessible to children have a good claim to being the most important kind of imaginative literature. As the father of philosophy wrote in *The Republic:* 'The beginning is the biggest part of any work, and therefore it is of supreme importance, in that work which is the construction of the human person, that children should hear good fables and not bad.'[1] Western philosophy has been called a series of footnotes to Plato, and one prominent contemporary footnoter, the British philosopher Alasdair MacIntyre, in his influential *After Virtue,* has closely echoed the view of his ancient Greek master: 'It is through hearing about wicked stepmothers, lost children, good but misguided kings . . . that children learn or mislearn what a child and what a parent is, what the cast of characters may be in the drama into which they have been born and what the ways of the world are.'[2] The problems presented by the Narnia Chronicles throw into question whether they are good fables or bad and whether they teach their readers to learn or mislearn the ways of the world.

There are three problems.

First, a problem of occasion. Why were they written at all? What was it that led a childless academic in his fifties suddenly to branch out into so-called 'children's literature'? Was it a crisis of belief, as some critics have suggested, caused by the attack on his most serious work of Christian apologetics, *Miracles,* from the philosopher Elizabeth Anscombe? Are the Chronicles therefore the products of a mind in retreat, an embattled psychology withdrawing into fantasy?

Second, a problem of composition. Why is the series not uniformly allegorical? Three of the books seem to be clearly based on biblical source material while four of them have no obvious scriptural foundation. And it is not just the series which is uneven: the individual titles also seem to be constructed out of very disparate elements, so that, for example, we find wedged into the first Chronicle, *The Lion, the Witch and the Wardrobe,* Father Christmas from popularised hagiography, a Snow Queen out of Hans Andersen, English children fresh from E. Nesbit, and 'high style' diction reminiscent of Sir Thomas Malory. And why is there so much controversial violence in the tales—militarism in *Prince Caspian,* corporal punishment in *The Silver Chair,* massacring of children in *The Last Battle?* Is there any imaginative logic governing these compositional choices?

Third, a problem of reception. Why have these stories become so extraordinarily successful? For over half a century they have continually found devoted readers among not just the young, but also the adult; not just the simple, but also the highly educated; not just the Christian, but also the non-Christian, including non-Christians such as the self-styled 'liberal, feminist, agnostic' Sarah Zettell, who says she 'loves' Narnia *because* of her personal views, not despite them.[3] What makes these books appeal so widely? Given the problems of occasion and composition, is it not strange that the Chronicles should have acquired such huge popularity, a popularity, it must be added, that is only likely to be increased as they are adapted into a franchise of major international feature films? Modern merchandising techniques are now geared up to impress these titles upon markets all over the globe, making it the more important that their problems of occasion, composition, and reception should be addressed.

The problems may be summarised in the following question: How is it that seven such stories, authored by an unlikely novice and possessing little apparent coherence in design, should have become some of the best-selling and most influential fables in the world?

This book attempts to answer that question. I will suggest that the Chronicles were indeed occasioned by Lewis's debate with Elizabeth Anscombe, but that they were a deliberate engagement with, rather than a retreat from, her critique of his theology. I will argue that the Chronicles do not lack coherence, either as a series or when considered as seven individual texts, and that their 'controversial' elements are to be understood within the context of that coherent imaginative strategy. And I will contend that they have found such a large readership because they communicate seven ancient archetypes in a manner which is artistically and theologically suggestive.

What these arguments amount to is a large and bold claim, which is this: I think I have stumbled upon the secret imaginative key to the series. I know full well that finding secret codes is a favourite pastime for obsessives, conspiracy-theorists, charlatans with an eye to the main chance, *et hoc genus omne;* it has been unwittingly satirised in Dan Brown's blockbusting thriller, *The Da Vinci Code.* Occasionally, however, a sober critic, paying close attention to a text, will make an interpretative discovery and produce a *bona fide* 'code-breaking' work. In 1960, for instance, Kent Hieatt revealed in *Short Time's Endless Monument* that the stanzas of Spenser's *Epithalamion* represent the twenty-four hours of midsummer's day, a cryptic theme which had remained unnoticed by scholars for nearly four hundred years. I believe that I also have discovered a genuine literary secret, one that has lain open to view since the Chronicles were first published, but that, remarkably, no-one has previously perceived. I am not claiming to have unearthed a hitherto unknown document in which Lewis divulged this secret, nor am I relying on previously unpublished testimony from one of his friends or relatives. My case rests on an intellectual basis—that is, literally, a 'reading between' basis. By reading between the Chronicles and the rest of Lewis's writings, I think it is possible to discern a hidden meaning deliberately woven into these seven fairy-tales or romances.

I am aware, of course, that Lewis had a low view of literary critics who attempted to discover inner meanings in his works; but I think his view of them was low because they missed their target, not because there was no target to aim for. The arguments presented in this book have sufficient explanatory power, I trust, to be regarded as a hit.

Assuming for a moment that these arguments do indeed turn out to be correct, the question is immediately raised as to whether Lewis ever told anyone that the books were written to a plan. (The sort of plan I have in mind is an incremental plan, for we know that he did not have the whole series of seven books mapped out when he began to write the first.) As far as I know, he made no such disclosure. Although he hinted at it a couple of times—and these hints will be mentioned in due course—Lewis never apparently communicated this plan either to paper or to a confidant. Of those surviving colleagues, friends, and relatives of his who might conceivably have been told—people such as Pauline Baynes, Walter Hooper, Douglas Gresham—none recalls any mention of it ever having been made. If Lewis did happen to intimate it to his wife, his brother, or a friend such as Owen Barfield or Arthur Greeves or George Sayer, none of them revealed it further.

This fact is, on the face of it, an objection to the very possibility of the arguments that I am going to advance. Lewis, it may be pointed out, was not a secretive or deceitful person, but bluff, honest 'Jack' (his self-chosen nickname), matter-of-fact and down-to-earth. Although he kept his network of close friends fairly small, he was, within that circle, a candid man. Sayer records: 'We talked in the frankest way as friends should. I have never known a man more open about his private life.' And although Lewis's friendship with Sayer may not have been built upon a shared interest in literary composition, we could reasonably expect a similar degree of openness with, say, Roger Lancelyn Green, to whom Lewis related very deeply on literary matters, especially the writing of the Chronicles. But Green never even implies that the Narniad (as the series has been called) contains a literary secret. If Green was unaware of it, is it likely to exist?

It will be worth addressing this question at the outset because, if the idea of a literary secret is considered *prima facie* implausible, I do not expect to win an attentive hearing for the substance of the argument itself. I will show in the remainder of this chapter that secretiveness was a recurrent feature of Lewis's behaviour; that many critics have already sensed that the Chronicles contain a secret; and that the evidence points in a particular direction.

A Secretive Man?

First, we must consider whether the view of Lewis as invariably and wholly candid is accurate. His was a complex personality, even a mysterious one. J.R.R. Tolkien regarded him as unfathomable.[4] Owen Barfield said that 'he stood before me as a mystery as solidly as he stood before me as a friend.'[5] Malcolm Muggeridge felt there was about Lewis 'an element of mystery' and that it included 'some evasion he is hiding from us.'[6] Stephen Medcalf has written illuminatingly about his various personae.[7] And if Lewis presented many fronts to other people, he did no less to himself, for he was able to identify his own 'postures' and 'multiple factions.'[8] The very fact that he gave himself the name 'Jack' is an aspect of this complexity, and his interest in masks, self-deception, and the difficulty of achieving identity issued ultimately in what he regarded as his best work, *Till We Have Faces*.

A multi-faceted and impenetrable personality does not necessarily mean that Lewis was secretive, still less that he was dishonest; however, there is plenty of evidence to indicate that Lewis could be both secretive and dishonest. Before his conversion to Christianity he often lied to his father, and he later admitted as much.[9] More significantly (from his eventual Christian point of view), he was sometimes content to be less than frank even after his conversion, when he would have had additional, religious motives for transparency. The same Sayer who praises Lewis's openness also recognised the opposite strain in his friend and goes so far as to say that 'Jack never ceased to be secretive.'[10] The various omissions from *Surprised by Joy* (for example, Mrs Moore, his adoptive mother, is never even acknowledged) led one of his circle, Humphrey Havard, to joke that it would have been better entitled *Suppressed by Jack;* and Sayer shared that view, commenting that only those who knew him very well would have been able 'to penetrate the smoke screen.'[11] Lewis kept his Civil Marriage to Joy Gresham concealed for the best part of a year and the way in which he finally disclosed it to Maureen Moore was described by his brother as a '*suggestio falsi.*'[12] He supported lying if it protected a friend and reportedly practised it in order to defend his students from the suspicions of colleagues.[13] The clearest evidence that he was not always Washingtonian in his candour is the occasion when he deliberately misled a fox hunt: 'He cupped his hands and shouted to the first riders: "Hallo, yoicks, gone that way," and pointed to the direction opposite to the one the fox had taken. The whole hunt followed his directions.'[14]

Opinions will differ as to the justifiability of these examples of secretiveness or deception. They do not require to be examined further here for it is not by any means the intention of this book to build its case on the claim that Lewis was habitually untrustworthy. Though continuingly mysterious and complex, Lewis was undoubtedly, in the second half of his life, by most normal measurements, a man of integrity. But it is no less indubitable that a thoroughly maintained secretiveness about the imaginative underpinnings of the Narnia Chronicles would rank as entirely consistent with what is recorded about many of his actions and habits. He valued privacy and saw no need to decompartmentalise the various segments of his life. Oxford friends, for instance, may never have heard mention of his Belfast friends.[15] His benefactions were hidden from nearly all his intimates and the gifts themselves were almost always made anonymously.[16] He kept his own identity camouflaged in certain publications, using four different *noms de plume* in the course of his career: 'Clive Hamilton' for *Spirits in Bondage* and *Dymer;* 'N. W.' for most of his poems; 'Anonymous' for a few of his poems; and 'N. W. Clerk' for *A Grief Observed*, which he wrote, so he said, using 'stylistic disguisements all the way along.'[17] He lent *Dymer* to a friend without revealing that he himself was the author and he kept up the façade as 'N. W. Clerk' in private correspondence.[18]

Given that Lewis was occasionally willing to be economical with the actualité, even about a matter of such legal, moral, and personal importance as marriage, it need come as no surprise that, in the relatively minor matter of a literary code, he should have kept his own counsel. No artist is obliged to unveil his every strategy and, as we will see below, Lewis had long-held views about the importance of 'hiddenness' in literature.

With regard to the Narnia Chronicles and the sheer practical possibility of keeping such a secret, it must be borne in mind that, according to Carpenter, they were never read aloud to his group of friends, the Inklings, and that they therefore did not undergo the same scrutiny of that inquisitive and perceptive group as did much of Lewis's corpus.[19] Tolkien was given a private reading of the first book, but so disliked what he heard that 'he soon gave up trying to read them':[20] there was to be no meeting of minds in that direction. Green, the young protégé, responded more sympathetically and discussed the early drafts with their author in some detail, but seems to have been deliberately steered away from conversation that might have led toward the covert theme (as we will note in chapter 7). Pauline Baynes was given free rein to illustrate the books as she thought fit: Lewis carefully examined her finished drawings but did not control their composition.[21]

Contending that Lewis was psychologically and practically capable of keeping such a secret is different, of course, from showing that the secret actually existed, but it is worth registering how many critics have sensed that there is more to the Chronicles of Narnia than meets the eye, and have therefore worried away at the series, trying to find a key to its idiosyncrasies. This leads us toward a consideration of the second of the three problems outlined at the head of this chapter.

A Secret Theme?

Of the three problems listed above, the one that has most troubled critics has been the second, the problem of composition. Are the books really without coherence or is there a level of coherence that remains to be uncovered?

Tolkien was the first to voice the view that the Chronicles are a hodge-podge, and his opinion has rumbled on in critical assessments of the series ever since. To Tolkien, the wide range of literary traditions upon which Lewis drew was not an acceptable heterogeneity, but evidence of imaginative confusion. Sayer reports that Tolkien 'strongly detested [Lewis's] assembling figures from various mythologies. . . . He also thought they were carelessly and superficially written.'[22]

That this should have been Tolkien's view is to be expected, for he was one of the most minutely painstaking authors ever to take up a pen: he laboured for decades over the legendarium from which *The Hobbit* and *The Lord of the Rings* were culled, and Lewis likened his work-rate to that of a coral insect.[23] Since Lewis was prodigious in his output, critics have found it easy to set up the two writers in sharp contrast to each other. Adey is typical: 'As novelists, the perfectionist Tolkien and the boyishly eager Lewis represent opposed extremes.'[24] With every passing study the opposition becomes starker and invariably to the detriment of Lewis. For instance, Wilson (who follows and intensifies Carpenter[25]) regards Tolkien's imaginary world of Middle-earth as 'finished' and 'complete,' with 'never an intrusive moment.' The Narnia books, on the other hand, are a 'jumble,' a 'hotch-potch,' they are 'full of inconsistencies, and by his standards are not even particularly well written. He frequently repeats epithets.'[26] Wilson does not give examples of these inconsistencies or cite any of the epithets which Lewis repeats; nor does he explain why repetition, a common enough artistic device, should be a sign of bad writing. He also fails to reflect on the improbability of the situation he describes. Is it at all likely that tales so fadged up should have achieved the status of classics in their genre? How can it be that works hastily concocted out of such disparate materials should have been read and enjoyed by even a single generation of readers, let alone three or four?

One has to conclude that Wilson, like certain other critics, has allowed Tolkien's view of the Chronicles to set the agenda and has not considered Lewis's works with his own eyes. It must be emphasized that Tolkien's literary tastes were quite extraordinarily narrow (he read little in English literature after Chaucer) and not only did he dislike most modern literature in general, he also disliked the majority of Lewis's writings. Although Lewis loved Tolkien's work (*The Lord of the Rings* was largely written to keep Lewis quiet[27]), that esteem was virtually never reciprocated. Almost every time Tolkien mentions Lewis's books in his correspondence it is to find fault with them, and Sayer suspects that his motives for being so critical were not entirely disinterested, that he envied Lewis's fluency.[28] With these considerations in mind, we should not be surprised that Tolkien dismissed the Narniad; his approval would have been the more remarkable reaction.

Second, there is evidence to suggest that the process of composition was lengthier and more careful than Tolkien assumed. Even before we consider the new arguments made in this book about the imaginative gestation of *The Lion, the Witch and the Wardrobe*, we know that its manuscript origin can be traced to a story begun probably in 1939 and thence to pictorial images which had been entertained by Lewis's inner eye since 1914. It was written in earnest in 1948 and published in 1950. In other words it could be said to have been growing in Lewis's mind for thirty-six years. It is not known how many drafts he wrote because he usually threw away his roughs. However, early work on *The Voyage of the 'Dawn Treader'*, *The Silver Chair*, and *The Magician's Nephew* has survived that shows the composition process for these three books to have been far from facile and instantaneous. And as late as 1953, when five of the seven books had been written, Lewis could still say that the Chronicles were taking 'all my imagination.'[29]

Third, it must be asked: why compare Tolkien and Lewis at all? It is not as if the Chronicles were composed during the heyday of their friendship in the 1930s; they were written during the late 1940s and early 1950s, when the long and gradual cooling of their relationship was setting in. Even if they had been written during the 1930s, it would nonetheless remain important to recognise that their author was a unique individual and not one half of a pair of conjoined twins. Lewis and Tolkien were not competing with each other for the same vital literary organs. The two men must be allowed to attempt different things in different ways and each deserves to be assessed on his own peculiar merits, irrespective of the other's opinion and the other's tendency toward slower or faster habits of working. Lewis is not Tolkien quickened any more than Tolkien is Lewis prolonged.

Most readers have not been persuaded by Tolkien's dismissive attitude to his friend's work and have felt that the series hangs together well enough despite its apparent heterogeneity: there might be mishmash on display, yes, but it is good and enjoyable mishmash. For instance, Brown writes approvingly, 'Narnia is intentionally a hodgepodge collection of widely diverging elements, often with no relation to each other, giving it a dreamlike quality.' Mueller notes that 'Lewis wrote with deliberate complexity and richness'[30] and is content to leave it at that.

However, many critics have been dissatisfied with such an unreflective position and have attempted to unify the Chronicles under a head, working on the assumption that the books' apparent stew-like qualities mask a deeper coherence. They have tried to solve the problem of composition by demonstrating the series' underlying simplicity or thematic unity.

Myers, for instance, argues that the seven books may be best understood as a miniature version of Spenser's *Faerie Queene*.[31] She does not claim that her reading is definitive, which is just as well, given that elsewhere she connects them to what she calls the stages of Anglican commitment.[32]

Pietrusz, overlooking the fact that Lewis was an Anglican, links the Chronicles to the seven Catholic sacraments.

King and Hulan have both made the case for reading the Narniad as a commentary on the seven deadly sins, but they assign different sins to different books.

Trupia relates the first three published tales to the theological virtues of love, faith, and hope (in that order) and the last four to the cardinal virtues.

Schakel sees 'a special imaginative relationship' between *Mere Christianity* and the images and stories of Narnia.[33]

Huttar finds value in the description of the Chronicles as 'a sort of Bible.' He thinks the term 'is accurate enough as a label of the genre: a loose collection of varied material structured to highlight the climactic events of world history, beginning, middle and end.'[34]

Montgomery claims that the theme unifying the Chronicles into 'an integrated single conception' is that of redemption through Christ.

Manzalaoui invites us to note 'the basic governing pattern of every one of the Narnia stories—closeness of the supernatural, the divine, to the mundane, the everyday, the humdrum.'[35]

Christopher concentrates on the Chronicles' supposed indebtedness to Tolkien (an irony, if ever there was one).

Wilson, despite his own assessment of the books as jumbled and full of inconsistencies, thinks that faerie land itself provides the series with 'unity.'

Spufford also has it both ways; he suggests that 'the Narnia books are unmistakably unified by Lewis's common delight in all the heterogeneous stuff he knocked it up from.'

This present work will not be making any attempt to challenge the various theories listed above. It would, in any case, be all but impossible to disprove some of them, so unspecific are they. It is enough to point out that none of them has been advanced in a fully serious way, nor has any one of them commanded general acceptance or even the support of a substantial minority of critics.

One is tempted to conclude that the search for a unifying thread is the search for the rainbow's end. Perhaps there simply is no governing idea and the problem of composition is insoluble. Lewis revealed in a letter to a schoolboy called Laurence Krieg that he did not have the whole series planned out in his mind when he began the first story. Maybe therefore they are just random.

Yet he never admitted they were *random*, and one does not need to have a deep acquaintance with the contours of Lewis's mind to know that randomness is not a characteristic feature of it. Anyone familiar with his poetry will know that it manifests an almost staggering degree of phonetic and metrical complexity, and the poems which look as if they are free verse are actually in the most complicated metres of all. 'Intricacy is a mark of the medieval mind,'[36] Lewis wrote; and as a medievally-minded writer himself, intricacy marks much of his own corpus, the Narniad not excluded: though it looks superficially chaotic, there is an organising intelligence at work. And, indeed, occasionally Lewis was prepared to give his readers reasons to believe that there was some sort of underlying plan. We will now consider the evidence that indicates he had a controlling idea.

A Fully Worked Out Idea

Could it be its Christological dimension that provides the key to the Narniad's unity? In a letter to a young girl named Anne Jenkins, Lewis wrote, 'the whole Narnian story is about Christ'; and in *The Horse and His Boy* he makes Shasta observe that Aslan 'seems to be at the back of all the stories.' A Christocentric reading has a good deal to recommend it because Aslan, the Christ-figure, is the only character who appears in all seven books. But in the précis of the series which Lewis provides for Anne we are reminded that Aslan, in fact, has definitively Christological roles to play in only three of the seven stories:

The Magician's Nephew tells the Creation and how evil entered Narnia.

The Lion etc the Crucifixion and Resurrection.

Prince Caspian restoration of the true religion after a corruption.

The Horse and His Boy the calling and conversion of a heathen.

The Voyage of the 'Dawn Treader' the spiritual life (especially in Re-epicheep).

The Silver Chair the continued war against the powers of darkness.

The Last Battle the coming of the Antichrist (the Ape). The end of the world and the Last Judgement.[37]

Aslan is creator in the Narnian genesis (*The Magician's Nephew*); redeemer in the Narnian gospel account (*The Lion, the Witch and the Wardrobe*); and judge in its version of the apocalypse (*The Last Battle*). These books make up less than half the sequence. What Christocentric explanation can account for Aslan's roles in the remaining four books? One might reasonably expect parallels to the annunciation, the nativity, the boyhood, and the ascension of Christ; his sending of the Holy Spirit at Pentecost might receive a treatment. That would be the natural way of proceeding if Lewis was intending to produce a Christological series. Instead, Aslan in these other four books represents no particular Christological office or stage of Christ's incarnation or the *missio dei*. His appearances are very various and irregular: he is mistaken for two lions in *The Horse and His Boy;* he flies in a sunbeam in *The Voyage of the 'Dawn Treader';* he enters the story among dancing trees in *Prince Caspian;* and in *The Silver Chair* he does not appear bodily within Narnia at all, but is confined to his own high country above the clouds. There seems to be no rhyme or reason, Christologically speaking, for these stories.

Perhaps we should simply bite our critical tongues and accept this trilogy-plus-quartet analysis. Chad Walsh is content to do so. He identifies the three 'Biblical' books and categorises the others as taking place within 'Act IV' of the Narnian drama, between the resurrection of Aslan and the end of the world. Aslan's role in these other four books, Walsh argues, is 'relatively marginal.'[38] But it is not marginal. In every one of these four books Aslan is mentioned earlier than in either *The Lion* or *The Magician's Nephew;* his first appearance and his first words occur earlier in these four books than in either *The Lion* or *The Last Battle;* and his overall involvement in these stories is at least as substantial as in the trio of books dealing with what Walsh calls 'grand, cosmic deeds.' And if *heilsgeschichte* is meant to be our interpretative grid, why is there no indication that Aslan's mode of appearance in *The Lion*—where he is 'incarnate'—is any different from his appearances elsewhere, which would be the Narnian equivalent of Christophanies? Should we not expect his appearances in 'Act IV' to relate to Church history in some way? Should we not at least expect his appearances in 'Act IV' to betray a family likeness? As it is, Aslan's roles in these stories show no uniform features nor any discernible link to particular historical or prophesied events between Christ's ascension and second coming. Rather than presenting his theory as '3 + 4,' Walsh ought to admit it is '3 + 1 + 1 + 1 + 1.'

In short, we have to conclude that, if the whole series is 'about Christ,' it is so in a way that neither scriptural source material nor the major events of salvation history can make sense of.

We find ourselves in this dead-end as a result of attaching too much significance to Lewis's letter to Anne Jenkins. The summaries given there are so brief and general as to be of little explanatory use. For instance, to say that The 'Dawn Treader' is concerned with 'the spiritual life' does almost nothing to distinguish it from any of the other six books. This letter is best understood as an example of Lewis's avuncular and pastoral interest in one small child (one among hundreds to whom he wrote over the years); it is not a serious piece of literary self-disclosure. Anne is being given a broad and breezy welcome to the series, not a key to its internal workings.

This is not to imply that Aslan is not the most important character in the series, nor is it to deny that Lewis had serious Christological purposes at heart: we will look at those purposes later in this book. However, it is to say that, in attempting to find the Narniad's unity, we must move away from the assumption that the Christology it displays is chiefly based on biblical passages that have been reimagined for the purposes of a 'suppositional' world.[39] Since four out of the seven stories do not accord with such a scheme, plainly it is not the solution to the problem of composition.

Setting aside Lewis's remarks to Anne Jenkins, we bring forward for examination his comments to Charles Wrong, who had been his pupil in the 1930s, to whom he indicated that there was another governing theme, apparently connected not with Christology, but with numerology. (This I take as the first of the two recorded hints Lewis dropped about the secret.) According to Wrong, Lewis 'happened to have had an idea that he wanted to try out, and by now, having worked it out to the full, he did not plan to write any more.' Wrong reports Lewis as adding, 'I had to write three volumes, of course, or seven, or nine. Those are the magic numbers.'[40]

This evidence is highly intriguing. If Lewis felt he 'had to write' at least three books (in order to make a magic number), what did he mean when he told Laurence Krieg that, at the outset, he did not know that he was going to write more than one book? And if his idea had been worked out 'to the full' after seven books, why did he mention to Wrong the number three and the number nine?

I suspect that Lewis was deflecting Wrong from asking questions about this 'idea' that originally issued in a single story but that, upon further reflection, required seven outworkings for its completion. When writing about the Chronicles in public he took care never to draw attention to such numerological considerations. For instance, in an article in *The New York Times Book Review*, he said that the imaginative process began with seeing pictures in his mind's eye (a faun carrying an umbrella, a queen on a sledge, a magnificent lion), pictures that gradually resolved themselves into a story with a particular form. That was what 'the Author' in him did. Then 'the Man' set to work and gave to this form the desired Christian orientation. But he says nothing about needing at least three volumes.

Similarly, in an article for the Junior Section of the *Radio Times*, he reveals that the one thing he is sure of is that the Chronicles 'began with seeing pictures in my head,' but he makes no reference to an idea that might require to be expressed, say, ninefold. Instead, rather curiously, he tells his young audience, 'you must not believe all that authors tell you about how they wrote their books.'[41] Then, because this statement has an obvious implication, he straightaway goes on to add: 'This is not because they mean to tell lies. It is because a man writing a story is too excited about the story itself to sit back and notice how he is doing it.'

This comment about the blinding effects of excitement is somewhat disingenuous. Of course, Lewis is right: in the heat of inspiration, authors will not primarily be observing their own thought processes. However, there may well be other reasons that an author would not be able, or would not choose, to reveal all the details of the process of composition. One reason is forgetfulness, and Lewis acknowledges this. And yet another reason, a more fundamental reason that he does not mention, though he would surely have accepted it, is that authors who talk about the origins of their stories are not under oath. Why should they expose the coordinates of every highway and byway that their imaginations have traversed? To do so would inevitably lessen the impact of their creative work. In his articles for *The New York Times* and the *Radio Times* Lewis had not solemnly sworn to tell the truth, the whole truth, and nothing but the truth.

In laying a false trail (or at any rate, a trail that was not completely dependable), Lewis would have been following the example of one of his greatest poetic inspirations, Edmund Spenser, who once penned an account of his purposes in writing the *Faerie Queene* that Lewis regarded as 'most misleading' and 'demonstrably untrue.'[42] We should not be surprised that he equivocates in his turn. For instance, he tells the young readers of the *Radio*

Times that Aslan arrived in his imagination after he had been having 'a good many dreams of lions,' whereas four years earlier in a private letter to an adult he wrote that 'the whole thing took its rise from *nightmares* about lions which I suddenly started having' (Lewis's emphasis).[43]

So we see that his testimony about the conception and composition of the Chronicles was not simple or unvarnished; he said different things to different people at different times. No doubt some of these inconsistencies are to be expected and can be explained by the vagaries of memory, editorial requirements, the nature of his various audiences, and so on. However, when one factors in the problem of composition, one hesitates. Is it not possible that there is something else going on here too? Can all those critics who have spent so much time and effort looking for hidden themes really have been mistaken? 'Jack never ceased to be secretive.' The judgement of George Sayer, who knew Lewis for nearly thirty years, counts for a good deal. To hear *Surprised by Joy* retitled *Suppressed by Jack* is an amusing piece of wordplay, but amusement should not obscure the fact that Lewis really was capable of putting up a smoke screen. And if he was capable of it in his spiritual autobiography, why not also in Narnia? Christology, numerology, mental pictures of fauns in snowy woods, dreams or nightmares of lions, planlessness and plans that need to be worked out sevenfold: these several accounts are not just incomplete explanations, they are also diversionary tactics. As such, they have been successful. Like Lewis's 'Yoicks!' to the fox hunt, they have thrown critics off the scent of the real quarry.

Literary Reasons for Secrecy

Lewis's temperamental secretiveness and his discrepant testimony about the origins of the Narniad should give us pause. And as we pause, we notice a most striking thing: Lewis actually declared himself to be interested in imaginative 'hiddenness'; it is a major element in his thinking as a literary critic.

In 1940 he gave an address to the Martlets, the literary society of University College, Oxford, entitled 'The Kappa Element in Romance.'[44] 'Kappa' he took from the initial letter of the Greek word κρυπτόν, meaning 'hidden' or 'cryptic.' Lewis later reworked the talk as the essay 'On Stories,' published in 1947, and although he dropped the term 'kappa' from 'On Stories,' the hidden thing itself was still his main concern. By this stage in his career he tended to call it by a number of different terms, of which 'atmosphere' is the most common.

'Atmosphere' is a somewhat inadequate word to describe what Lewis was concerned with, but then he once complained how his critical interests 'have no vocabulary.' Historical criticism and character criticism had, in his view, by long practice perfected their own terminology, aided by the fact that their concerns were those that people were accustomed to handling in the everyday business of life. 'But the things I want to talk about have no vocabulary and criticism has for centuries kept almost complete silence on them.'[45] He mentions certain pioneering studies in the field—Caroline Spurgeon's *Shakespeare's Imagery and What It Tells Us* and Maud Bodkin's *Archetypal Patterns in Poetry*—and also names Wilson Knight and Owen Barfield among those scholars who are attending to the same sort of critical terrain, but he brings no terms out of their works, nor does he forge any permanent terms of his own.

He uses a variety of words in his efforts to catch his meaning. They include: 'the *ipseitas*, the peculiar unity of effect produced by a special balancing and patterning of thoughts and classes of thoughts'; 'a state or quality'; 'flavour or atmosphere'; 'smell or taste'; 'mood'; 'quiddity.' In a comic poem that he wrote with Barfield he tries to summarise it thus:

> Q is for Quality—otherwise 'Whatness'—
> The gauntness of Ghent and the totness of Totnes.[46]

Again and again, in defending works of romance, Lewis argues that it is the quality or tone of the whole story that is its main attraction. The invented world of romance is conceived with this kind of qualitative richness because romancers feel the real world itself to be 'cryptic, significant, full of voices and 'the mystery of life.''[47] Lovers of romances go back and back to such stories in the same way that we go 'back to a fruit for its taste; to an air for . . . what? for *itself*; to a region for its whole atmosphere—to Donegal for its Donegality and London for its Londonness. It is notoriously difficult to put these tastes into words.'[48]

That this atmospheric quality is virtually inexpressible leads Lewis to speak of it at times as a spiritual thing. For instance, it is 'the vast, empty vision' of *Hamlet* that is, in his view, Shakespeare's chief accomplishment—the sense that 'a certain spiritual region' has somehow been captured by the use of images such as night, ghosts, a sea cliff, a graveyard, and a pale man in black clothes. Within the mesh of these images the mysterious epiphenomenal flavour of *Hamlet* is caught and communicated to the attentive reader or theatregoer.[49] Likewise, in David Lindsay's *Voyage to Arcturus*, the planet Tormance is so described that it amounts to an encapsulation of 'a region of the spirit.' The net of the story—the events, the characters, the background descriptions—has temporarily ensnared, as if it were an elusive bird, a sheer state of being; and for the duration of the read, this bird's plumage may be 'enjoyed.'[50]

'Enjoyment' is almost always used by Lewis in a particularly significant way, and here I must digress briefly to clarify the importance that the term had for him.

'Enjoyment,' for Lewis, was to be distinguished from 'Contemplation,' a distinction he first encountered in 1924 in the work of the philosopher, Samuel

Alexander, and which was important enough for him to record in his diary: 'I took Alexander's *Space, Time and Deity* out of the Union and went to Wadham [College] where I sat and walked in the garden reading the introduction, enjoying the beauty of the place, and greatly interested by my author's truthful antithesis of enjoyment and contemplation.' He was later to describe this antithesis as 'an indispensable tool of thought' and Hooper does not claim too much when he says that Alexander's book was 'of overwhelming importance to Lewis.'[51] He applied what we might call 'the Alexander technique' to many departments of life in addition to literary criticism and he thought it so useful that he eventually wrote his own essay on the subject, 'Meditation in a Toolshed,' in which he recast 'Contemplation' and 'Enjoyment' as follows:

> I was standing today in the dark toolshed. The sun was shining outside and through the crack at the top of the door there came a sunbeam. From where I stood that beam of light, with the specks of dust floating in it, was the most striking thing in the place. Everything else was almost pitch-black. I was seeing the beam, not seeing things by it.
>
> Then I moved, so that the beam fell on my eyes. Instantly the whole previous picture vanished. I saw no toolshed, and (above all) no beam. Instead I saw, framed in the irregular cranny at the top of the door, green leaves moving on the branches of a tree outside and beyond that, ninety-odd million miles away, the sun. Looking along the beam, and looking at the beam are very different experiences.[52]

'Looking along the beam' is what Alexander had called 'Enjoyment' (participant, inhabited, personal, committed knowledge) and 'looking at the beam' is what he had called 'Contemplation' (abstract, external, impersonal, uninvolved knowledge). For Lewis, this distinction was so fundamental that he was prepared to divide conscious knowledge accordingly: 'Instead of the twofold division into Conscious and Unconscious, we need a three-fold division: the Unconscious, the Enjoyed, and the Contemplated.'[53] Like the ancient Persians who debated everything twice (once when they were sober and once when they were drunk), we should try out every question in both lights, the light of Enjoyment (similar to the French *connaitre*) and the light of Contemplation (similar to the French *savoir*).

The digression is now over and we return to 'On Stories.' When Lewis writes there that the elusive, atmospheric state of being that may be captured in romance is to be 'enjoyed,' he means it not only in the normal sense of being appreciated or welcomed, but also in the Alexander sense: the atmosphere should be entered into so that it comprises our whole imaginative vision. If we attempt not to Enjoy, but rather to Contemplate, the deathliness of *Hamlet* or the 'redskinnery' of *The Last of the Mohicans* (which is the opening example of *kappa* provided in 'On Stories') we will find the quality going dead and cold in our hands, because we will have stopped 'living the story.' For this atmosphere is not one of the abstractions of literary criticism, but a description of 'concrete imagination' in practice, the full tasting of a work of art on the imaginative palate. If we are properly to Enjoy it, we must 'surrender ourselves with childlike attention to the mood of the story.'[54]

It is for this reason that 'atmosphere' is so difficult to put into words, for really, in any given work of art, it is that whole work and its total effect, not any desiccated critical account of it, which is the thing Lewis is trying to categorise. If the atmosphere could have been communicated in any briefer way than the whole work, presumably the artist would have done so. Since the artist has not done so, we must be content to accept that every part of the story is necessary for the intended effect on our literary taste-buds. We must attempt to be inclusive and not discriminate between what we imagine to be the 'important' and 'unimportant' aspects of the work:

> A child is always thinking about those details in a story which a grown-up regards as indifferent. If when you first told the tale your hero was warned by three little men appearing on the left of the road, and when you tell it again you introduce one little man on the right of the road, the child protests. And the child is right. You think it makes no difference because you are not living the story at all. If you were, you would know better. *Motifs,* machines, and the like are abstractions of literary history and therefore interchangeable: but concrete imagination knows nothing of them.[55]

And since this atmosphere has to be Enjoyed rather than Contemplated, it is, in a sense, invisible. When, in his 'Meditation in a Toolshed,' Lewis looked *along* the beam, he saw no toolshed and (above all) no beam. Likewise, the inner meaning of a romance cannot be flagged up by the author without altering its true nature. It has to remain hidden, woven into the warp and woof of the story so that it comprises not an object for Contemplation but the whole field of vision within which the story is experienced. The kappa element is more like seeing than it is like something seen. Just as one cannot take out one's eyeballs and turn them round in order to look back at one's optical organs, so one cannot jump out of this 'state of being,' this mode of Enjoyment consciousness. It is, by its very nature, though knowable, not explicit.

It took Lewis until 1940 to coin the term 'kappa element,' but he had valued the thing itself for over two decades before that date. In the early years of his correspondence with Arthur Greeves we may note several straws in the wind that indicate the future trajectory of his literary critical interests. Writing to Greeves in 1916, he praises the Gawain poet's 'power of getting up atmosphere' and enthuses about the magical use of words in William Morris and George MacDonald that, like a composer's orchestration of a melody, 'fill the matter by expressing things that can't be directly told.'[56] In that same year he composed a story called 'The Quest of Bleheris' and sent it to Greeves for his comments, which were not initially very positive. Lewis was not abashed. He wrote: 'You will like the main gist of the story even less when you grasp it—if you ever do, for as is proper in romance, the inner meaning is carefully hidden.'[57] *The inner meaning is carefully hidden.* At this point in his life, Lewis was still callow enough to draw attention to a silence. By the time he wrote Narnia, he knew better than to make a noise about his implicit purposes.

Precedents for Secrecy

Lewis's interest in hiddenness, then, precedes his composition of the Narniad by many years. However, it is not just to his own work that we should look for precedents in this regard; we should also consider the work of those writers whom he read and studied most closely. Manifestly, Lewis was attempting to convey numerous aspects of medieval life in the Narnia Chronicles: language, dress, polity, geography, cosmology, and cartography are all presented so as to communicate a sense of the Middle Ages.[58] Once we arrive at the possibility of a secret and silent theme, we should continue to bear this medievalism in mind. Might Lewis have wished to draw not only upon the matter, but also on the compositional conventions, of medieval and renaissance times in his construction of the Narniad? Secrecy and polysemy were important features of the literature of that period.

For instance, Spenser disguised Venus in the *Faerie Queene* (so Lewis argues in *Spenser's Images of Life*) because he was drawing on the tradition of neo-Platonic thought which deemed it proper that 'all great truths should be veiled,' should 'be treated mythically (*per fabulosa*) by the prudent.'[59] It is for the same reason that the good 'is (usually) hidden'[60] in Spenser and that the *Faerie Queene* is 'dangerous, cryptic, its every detail loaded with unguessed meaning.'[61] And as with the romance, so with the masque: 'The iconography of masques could be extremely sophisticated. In fact, much of the effort in writing them must have gone into subtle finessing on the well-known iconographical types, into progressively lightening the touch in pursuit of the ideal of *multum in parvo*.'[62] One particular element that was hidden or finessed by these techniques was divine presence. 'In the medieval allegories and the renaissance masks, God, if we may say so without irreverence, appears frequently, but always *incognito*.'[63] Sir Philip Sidney neatly expressed the prevailing aesthetic temper of the period when he wrote: 'there are many misteries contained in Poetrie, which of purpose were written darkly, least by prophane wits it should be abused.'[64] In an age long before universal schooling and mass communication, and when the idea of using the vernacular instead of Latin for religious purposes was still a relative novelty, it was customary to think in such categories. To a typically modern sensibility there can only be precious and élitist reasons for such exclusiveness, but in earlier times the distinctions which these habits of thought maintained would have been felt to be real and valuable. Since both pearls and swine were believed to exist, it was important not to throw the former before the latter.

But the pearls of Christian wisdom which suppositionally underlie Narnia are obvious, are they not? Did not Lewis happily discuss them in numerous letters and articles? We might therefore well ask: where is the truly hidden, medieval sense of these works? Lewis's professional life was largely given over to nurturing the relevance of the mindset which operated in the literature of medieval and renaissance Europe; he determinedly held the line against intellectual currents that would equate 'high style' and discernible organisation with empty pretence. Wordsworth, in the preface to *Lyrical Ballads*, might outline a manifesto for preferring 'natural' speech to elevated poetic diction; Joyce and Woolf might, in their turn, abandon received novelistic structures; functionalism, brutalism and absurdism might become the height of fashion and even buildings might eventually be constructed with their innards showing. None of these artistic movements (or their adumbrations) meant much to Lewis. His models remained Dante, Spenser, Sidney and others of their kind who practised literary formality and self-control, and who considered rhetorical maskings and layerings valuable. If, from a literary point of view, we are trying to find out *why* Lewis had an interest in hiddenness, we need look no further than his admiration for the example provided by these writers.

Not, of course, that he had to reach all the way back to medieval and renaissance times to find authors who could be cryptic or oblique within an ordered, deliberated, 'builded' aesthetic. From time to time he applauded the use made of silence by writers as contemporary as Walter de la Mare and John Galsworthy.[65] He also had a devout respect for the works of George MacDonald who provided him with an especially good precedent for keeping quiet about his artistic intentions. In a Socratic dialogue on the fantastic imagination, MacDonald wrote:

'But surely you would explain your idea to one who asked you?' 'I say again, if I cannot draw a horse, I will not write THIS IS A HORSE under what I foolishly meant for one. Any key to a work of imagination would be nearly, if not quite as absurd.'[66]

Lewis provided a key, in the form of chapter headlines, to the third edition of his earliest work of fiction, *The Pilgrim's Regress*, but did so with 'great reluctance' and only because he considered the allegory in that book to have failed. If he thought such explanation inadvisable in an avowed allegory, how much more inadvisable would it have been for him to explain a secret theme embedded in his Narnian romances?

Of course, I have not yet demonstrated that such a secret exists and I must not put the cart before the horse. However, it is instructive to survey the many occasions on which Lewis praised the indirect approach in communication. He believed that success in writing comes about by 'secretly evoking powerful associations'; that expressions should 'not merely state but suggest'; that the mechanism in poetry by which its effects are obtained should not be 'too visible'; that 'what the reader is made to do for himself has a particular importance'; that 'an influence which cannot evade our consciousness will not go very deep'; that silences could be 'dialectical'; that silences could make certain things 'audible.'[67] It is to silences, suggestions and secret associations that we need to be attuned if we would discern the hidden inner meaning of the Chronicles.

Two Kinds of Silence

For Lewis there were two kinds of silence, the good and the bad. The bad kind features in the title of the first volume of his Ransom Trilogy (1938–1945), *Out of the Silent Planet*. The silent planet is Earth, out of which comes the hero of the trilogy, Dr Elwin Ransom, on a journey to Mars. He discovers that, in the language of Mars, Planet Earth is known as *thulcandra*. Earth is *thulc* ('silent') because she does not join in the music of the spheres. Earth's presiding intelligence (or *oyarsa*) is 'the Bent One' who has nothing to say or sing to the other planetary angels. Earth's silence is a dumb silence, a dead silence.

Mars and all the other planets are also silent, as far as the inhabitants of Earth are concerned, but for a different reason. It is not because these other planets are sullenly mute that they are not heard. On the contrary, they are not heard because their singing is perpetual. As Lewis explained in an address entitled 'Imagination and Thought in the Middle Ages':

> [The music of the spheres] is the only sound which has never for one split second ceased in any part of the universe; with this positive we have no negative to contrast. Presumably if (*per impossibile*) it ever did stop, then with terror and dismay, with a dislocation of our whole auditory life, we should feel that the bottom had dropped out of our lives. But it never does. The music which is too familiar to be heard enfolds us day and night and in all ages.[68]

In the pre-Copernican model of the cosmos the planets were silent and sounding at the same time: their music was not heard on earth because it was always heard. And it is this sort of silence, a pregnant silence, resonant with significance, that I believe Lewis was attempting to encapsulate in the Narnia Chronicles. He told Sayer that he was concerned with the 'atmosphere'[69] of the adventures in Narnia, and we will do better in our attempt to understand the Chronicles if we approach them holistically, if we focus more on their gestalt flavour, their total effect on our imaginative palate, their kappa element, than in trying to find Biblical parallels or moral 'points.' We must remember that each Narnia story is 'something made' (*poiema*) as well as 'something said' (*logos*). Too often critics (both friendly and hostile) have treated the Chronicles as if they were principally works of propaganda and have exchanged their poetry for a pot of message.

This critic works on the assumption that their poetry *is* their principal message. It is silent, but only because it is heard in every part of the story, as the music of the medieval spheres was to be heard in every part of the cosmos. That old cosmology fascinated Lewis; it appears continually throughout his corpus and throughout his life. And one particular facet of the pre-Copernican model of the heavens deserves our closest attention: it contained seven planets.

When pressed about the length of the Narnian series and why there were only seven tales, Lewis tended to daff away the question with some light comment about not wishing to tire his readers: was it not better to stop while they still wanted more?[70] Yes, certainly, but what about the 'idea' that he mentioned to Charles Wrong? What sort of idea would make seven neither too many nor too few for its full outworking? We know that the number seven, to this medievalist, was 'numinous,'[71] and seven is certainly a very prominent number within the Chronicles themselves.[72] As I observed above, critics have already tried, without success, to link the series to the seven virtues, the seven sacraments, and the seven deadly sins. Astonishingly, no one has ever considered whether Lewis might have built the Narniad upon what Donne called 'the Heptarchy, the seven kingdoms of the seven planets.'[73]

It is time to do so.

TWO

The Planets

The characters of the planets, as conceived by medieval astrology, seem to me to have a permanent value as spiritual symbols.
—'The Alliterative Metre'

In *The Discarded Image*, Lewis's introduction to the medieval worldview, he repeatedly encourages his readers to take a stroll under the sky at night. Looking up at the heavens now, Lewis argues, is a very different experience from what it was in the Middle Ages. Now we sense that we are looking out into a trackless vacuity, pitch-black and dead-cold. Then we would have felt as if we were looking into a vast, lighted concavity. In the nearest part of the sky our eyes would have seen—or, rather, seen through—the transparent sphere in which the Planet Luna revolves, then the larger sphere of Mercury, then the still larger one of Venus, and so on through the spheres of Sol, Mars, Jupiter, and Saturn, each sphere rotating more rapidly than the last and each exerting a peculiar influence upon mundane people and events, and even upon the metals in the Earth's crust. Beyond Saturn's sphere we would have seen the heaven of the fixed stars, the *Stellatum*, and, beyond that, the *Primum Mobile*, the sphere which conveys movement to all the other, lower spheres. Further than the *Primum Mobile* we would not have been able to see, for that would take our sight outside the created order into the Empyrean, the very home of God and all the elect (see figure 23 in the photo gallery). One of God's titles was 'The Unmoved Mover' because He moved the *Primum Mobile* 'by being loved, not by loving; by being the supremely desirable object.'[1] It is in this sense, Lewis says, that we should understand Dante's immortal line, the final words of *The Divine Comedy*: '*L'amor che move il sole e l'altre stelle*'—'The love that moves the sun and the other stars.'

To Lewis, this ceaseless dance of singing spheres around the home of God represented the revelry of insatiable love:

> We are watching the activity of creatures whose experience we can only lamely compare to that of one in the act of drinking, his thirst delighted yet not quenched. For in them the highest of faculties is always exercised without impediment on the noblest object; without satiety, since they can never completely make His perfection their own, yet never frustrated, since at every moment they approximate to Him in the fullest measure of which their nature is capable.... Run your mind up heaven by heaven to Him who is really the centre, to your senses the circumference, of all; the quarry whom all these untiring huntsmen pursue, the candle to whom all these moths move yet are not burned.
>
> The picture is nothing if not religious.[2]

But religious in what way? Lewis was conscious that this picture of the universe, in which God is not so much the lover as the beloved and humanity is peripheral, might be thought incompatible with the Christian picture in which God proactively seeks out the lost sheep who is the centre of divine concern. However, Lewis reckoned there to be no absolute contradiction between the two pictures because the love of the spheres for God exhibits the perfect natural order of the uncorrupted translunary realm, while God's searching love for humanity represents the action of divine grace toward fallen, sublunary creatures.

Lewis makes no effort to hide the pleasure he derives from this view of the cosmos. He remarks that the human imagination has seldom entertained an object so sublimely ordered; the medieval universe was 'tingling with anthropomorphic life, dancing, ceremonial, a festival not a machine.'[3] Its tingling quality is especially worth noting for Lewis is here drawing on his knowledge of Old English. As he wrote to his father in 1922: '[Anglo-Saxon] gives the impression of parodied English badly spelled. Thus...TINGUL for a star...think of 'Twinkle, twinkle little star.''[4] Almost invariably when the word appears in his subsequent works it comes loaded with astrological significance. For instance, 'tingling sounds' are heard in Ransom's rooms on the night the planets descend in *That Hideous Strength*; and in *The Voyage of the 'Dawn Treader'* when Lucy lays her hand on the book of spells in the house of Coriakin, the fallen star, 'her fingers tingled when she touched it as if it were full of electricity.'

As these quotations from his fiction indicate, Lewis's delight in this old picture of the heavens was not confined to his professional academic life as a literary historian; he also had a much more personal and imaginative investment in it. He told Green that he liked 'the whole planetary idea as a *mythology*,'[5] and in *Surprised by Joy* he reports that, at the age of ten, 'the idea of other planets exercised upon me then a peculiar, heady attraction,' a coarse curiosity quite different from his romantic interest in 'joy.' He adds that 'my own planetary romances have been not so much the gratification of that fierce curiosity as its exorcism. The exorcism worked by reconciling it with, or subjecting it to, the other, the more elusive, and genuinely imaginative impulse.'[6]

The planetary romances which he refers to here are *Out of the Silent Planet* (1938) in which the hero, Ransom, goes to Mars; *Perelandra* (1943) in which he goes to Venus; and *That Hideous Strength* (1945) in which he stays on earth but acts as a bridge across which five of the seven planetary intelligences pass as they come down to earth to bring about the dénouement of the story. In this trilogy the planets are given new names, as follows: Sulva (Luna), Viritrilbia (Mercury), Perelandra (Venus), Arbol (Sol), Malacandra (Mars), Glund or Glundandra (Jupiter), and Lurga (Saturn). These and the other heavenly bodies overwhelm Ransom with their beauty as he floats among them at the beginning of the first book during his journey to Mars: 'the stars, thick as daisies on an uncut lawn, reigned perpetually with no cloud, no moon, no sunrise, to dispute their sway. There were planets of unbelievable majesty, and constellations undreamed of: there were celestial sapphires, rubies, emeralds and pin-pricks of burning gold.' As Ransom marvels, he becomes aware that there is a 'spiritual cause for his progressive lightening and exultation of heart':

A nightmare, long engendered in the modern mind by the mythology that follows in the wake of science, was falling off him. He had read of 'Space': at the back of his thinking for years had lurked the dismal fancy of the black, cold vacuity, the utter deadness, which was supposed to separate the worlds. He had not known how much it affected him till now—now that the very name 'Space' seemed a blasphemous libel for this empyrean ocean of radiance in which they swam. He could not call it 'dead'; he felt life pouring into him from it every moment. How indeed should it be otherwise, since out of this ocean the worlds and all their life had come? He had thought it barren; he saw now that it was the womb of worlds, whose blazing and innumerable offspring looked down nightly even upon the Earth with so many eyes—and here, with how many more! No: Space was the wrong name. Older thinkers had been wiser when they named it simply the heavens—the heavens which declared the glory—the

    'happy climes that ly
Where day never shuts his eye
Up in the broad fields of the sky.'

    He quoted Milton's words to himself lovingly, at this time and often.[7]

It is significant that Ransom should quote from Milton, for Milton was not just one of those 'older thinkers' who understood 'space' as 'the heavens,' he was also the first writer (so Lewis opines in *The Discarded Image*) to use the word 'space' in the modern sense.[8] Milton straddled the old and new views of the cosmos; he marked the transition to the new disenchanted model of the universe from the traditional one which stretched back to time immemorial. The Ransom trilogy, which we will examine in depth as this book progresses, is in large part an attempt to rehabilitate that traditional conception.

And in Lewis's poetry, too, the celestial bodies, as understood by the pre-modern mindset, receive frequent treatment. 'The Planets,' an alliterative poem of 122 lines, is only the most obvious example, and it, like the Ransom trilogy, will be a major object of our attention in the course of this book. We must also note here, in this preliminary survey, 'The Turn of the Tide,' a complex poem about the birth of Christ, in which not just the planets but several of the zodiacal houses ('Crab,' 'Bowman,' 'Maiden,' 'Lion,' etc.) play a significant role. Other short poems that make use of astrological or astronomical imagery include 'The Star Bath,' 'Hesperus,' 'Science Fiction Cradlesong,' 'My Heart is Empty,' 'The Meteorite,' and 'Prelude to Space.' His narrative poems show the same level of interest in such imagery: for example, 'The Nameless Isle' ("My love's looking is long dimness / And stars' influence") and *Dymer* ('between two clouds appeared one star. / Then his mood changed'). But the subject is pervasive, for Lewis's whole imaginative outlook was enamoured of the medieval, or Ptolemaic, or Aristotelian, view of the heavens.[9] In reading his poetry we need to be alive to the astrological significance of even so small a word as *air*. Lewis comments in *The Discarded Image* that the planetary influences do not work upon us directly, but by first modifying the air of the earth's atmosphere: 'Hence when a medieval doctor could give no more particular cause for a patient's condition he attributed it to "this influence which is at present in the air." If he were an Italian doctor he would doubtless say *questa influenza*. The profession has retained the useful word ever since.'[10] When Lewis writes a seemingly innocent phrase such as 'the air / Burns as with incense' (in 'The Small Man Orders His Wedding') we should be aware that he means more by it than might at first appear. The air is heavy with incense not because a joss-stick is aglow, but because 'the dynasts seven incline from heaven.'

Despite Lewis's imaginative pleasure in this old cosmology, he recognises that it had a serious defect: 'it was not true.' Nicolaus Copernicus, the Polish astronomer, had exposed its untruth in the mid-sixteenth century with his epoch-making work, *De Revolutionibus Orbium Coelestium* ('On the Revolutions of the Heavenly Spheres'). There were not seven planets and they did not go round the Earth. The Sun was the centre and it was orbited by six planets: Mercury, Venus, Earth (with its moon, Luna), Mars, Jupiter, and Saturn. By the time Lewis wrote 'The Planets,' astronomers had added to the list three further celestial bodies: Uranus, discovered in 1781; Neptune, discovered by the mind of John Couch Adams in 1845 and by the observations of Johann Galle the following year; and Pluto, discovered in 1930. Lewis ignored these developments. Why? Given that the Ptolemaic picture of the cosmos had been shown to be inaccurate, what reason could there be for Lewis to immerse himself so wholeheartedly within this discarded image?

Reasons to Be Interested in the Seven Heavens

If he had lived long enough to witness the relegation of Pluto to the status of a dwarf planet in 2006, Lewis would have been quietly pleased. He would have taken it as confirmation of his view that 'a scientific fact' is not necessarily the immutable, universal truth that it is popularly believed to be. The glory of science is to progress as new facts are discovered to be true, and such progress means that 'factual truth' is a provisional human construct. Which is why the wise man does not think only in the category of truth; the category of beauty is also worth thinking in. And it was because he thought it beautiful that Lewis so revelled in the pre-Copernican cosmos.

Lewis admits that, from a purely aesthetic point of view, 'the procession of the gods round the sky' has to him a spontaneous appeal greater than that of Christianity,[11] just as his imaginative preference was not only for Norse, but also for Irish and Greek mythologies, over the poetry of his believed religion.[12] Following his conversion, Lewis naturally considered pagan religions to be less true than Christianity; but, regarding them without reference to questions of truth, he felt that they possessed the superior beauty. Beauty and truth could be, and ought to be, distinguished from each other, and both from goodness. One of the reasons he objected to the school of criticism associated with F. R. Leavis was that he thought it contained no notion of the specifically literary good: all literature had to be judged according to how well it reflected the critics' idea of what was good simply. However, in Lewis's view, one could, for example, enjoy the work of D. H. Lawrence for the artistry with which it captured certain sensations, even if one thought it morally muddled or even pernicious, and likewise one could approve of Ovid's pornography for stylistic reasons without approving of pornography as such. So with cosmology; it could be approached from an aesthetic perspective, regardless of whether it was true or whether it would do one any good. The Ptolemaic cosmos might not satisfy one's appetite for solid, reliable, useful, Gradgrindian fact, but that was no reason for not tasting it at all. It might satisfy other appetites, and Lewis found that it did indeed slake his thirst for certain pleasures of form and pattern. He enjoyed it because it raised formal regularity to the level of universal comprehensiveness, because it everywhere deployed the principle of *idem in alio* ('the same in the other'), and because it consisted of a perfectly graded hierarchy in which small and great were equally at home.

But a much more substantial reason for Lewis's love of the Ptolemaic cosmos, despite its factual inadequacy, has to do with some of his most deeply held religious beliefs. As a boy he had been told by his schoolmasters that Christianity was 100 per cent correct and every other religion, including the pagan myths of ancient Greece and Rome, was 100 per cent wrong. He found that this statement, rather than bolstering the Christian claim, undermined it and he abandoned his childhood faith 'largely under the influence of classical education.' It was to this experience that he owed his 'firm conviction that the only possible basis for Christian apologetics is a proper respect for Paganism.'[13]

Therefore Lewis was not troubled by the similarities between, for instance, the pagan Jupiter and the Hebrew Yahweh. He takes pleasure in pointing out, in *Miracles*, that 'God is supposed to have had a "Son," just as if God were a mythological deity like Jupiter.'[14] The resemblance ought to be present, given that God works through human myths as well as through His own true myth, the historical story of Jesus Christ.[15] Since God is the Father of lights, even the dim and guttering lights of paganism could be ascribed ultimately to Him. Christians should feel no obligation to quench the smouldering flax burning in pagan myths: on the contrary, they should do their best to fan it into flame. Lewis, with Spenser, believed that 'Divine Wisdom spoke not only on the Mount of Olives, but also on Parnassus.'[16] Of course, the Parnassian wisdom was not as complete or as sufficient as that offered in Christ, but it should be honoured as far as it went.

Lewis's religion was not a upas tree in whose shadow nothing else could grow. If paganism could be shown to have something in common with Christianity, Lewis concluded 'so much the better for paganism,' not 'so much the worse for Christianity.' He did not want merely to instrumentalise paganism, like the ancient Hebrews plundering the spoils of the Egyptians: rather, like St. Paul quoting Aratus's poem about Zeus (Acts 17:28), he wanted to respect and redeem and accommodate it within a new, larger worldview, even though it was superficially at odds with his faith. And if he was prepared to adopt such an inclusive stance with respect to pagan divinities, it is to be expected that he would be all the more inclusive with respect to a cosmology that had once been considered fully consonant with Christianity.

For it must be emphasised that the pre-Copernican model of the cosmos was a Christian model despite its acceptance of astrological influence. As Lewis points out in *English Literature in the Sixteenth Century*, astrology and astronomy were not really distinguishable until the Copernican revolution and no Christian theologian before that time denied the general theory of planetary influences or the significance of constellation.[17] The planets were not to be worshipped[18] or regarded as determinative in their influence,[19] and the lucrative and politically undesirable practice of astrologically grounded predictions was to be avoided,[20] but within these parameters the Church was content to sanction what we would now call 'astrology.' After all, the Bible appeared to support the belief that there were seven planets and that they possessed influences. The author of the Book of Judges (5:20) records, 'They fought from heaven; the stars in their courses fought against Sisera.' (Lewis alludes to this verse in *Out of the Silent Planet:* 'The stars in their courses were fighting against Weston.') The author of the Book of Job as translated in the King James Version mentions the 'sweet influences of Pleiades' (38:31). (Lewis glances at this verse in his poem, 'My Heart is Empty,' with its reference to the heaven shedding 'sweet influence still on earth.') And throughout the Bible the stars are seen as 'signs'—most notably at Bethlehem, signifying the birth of Christ[21]—and sometimes as a celestial court or angelic choir.[22] Christ himself is shown in the Book of Revelation (1:16, 20; 2:1) holding the seven stars—that is, the seven wandering stars, the planets—in his right hand, a vision that Austin Farrer, Lewis's close friend and an expert in apocalyptic imagery, understood to be a portrayal of Christ's lordship over time, 'for it is after these seven that the weekdays are named.'[23] Saturn gives Saturday its name, the Sun Sunday's, the Moon Monday's, and so on.[24]

Following the Copernican revolution, astronomy and astrology became gradually distinct and the former prospered while the latter fell on hard times. *Astronomy* is now the name of a respectable science. *Astrology,* in sharp contrast, has become the label of a subject that is generally thought to deserve no serious consideration. Academics are apt to dismiss it as foolish superstition or, at best, trivial entertainment, and academics who are Christians may also regard it as potentially or actually dangerous to spiritual health, recalling only the scriptural condemnations of astrological practice and not bearing in mind that there is also in the Bible, as there once was in the Church, a much more positive view of the same. *Astrology* is now therefore a dangerous word, it connotes all sorts of things that the academic and the Christian mainstream find ridiculous or objectionable. But to Lewis, as a scholar of the sixteenth century, it would have meant something very different, and he was not content to be dismissive or condemnatory. He was not prepared to write off a view of the cosmos, as his schoolmasters had written off paganism, simply because it had been shown to be factually inadequate; ideas could be entertained for their beauty, not just their truth. In 1935 he declared his hand with the publication of his poem 'The Planets,' which appeared as part of a learned article on medieval alliterative poetic metre. He introduced it with these words:

In order to avoid misunderstanding I must say that the subject of the following poem was not chosen under the influence of any antiquarian fancy that a medieval metre demanded medieval matter, but because the characters of the planets, as conceived by medieval astrology, seem to me to have a permanent value as spiritual symbols—to provide a *Phänomenologie des Geistes* which is specially worth while in our own generation.[25]

Lewis here makes three high claims on the behalf of the medieval planets. First, that they are 'spiritual symbols.' Second, that they possess 'permanent value.' Third, that their value is 'specially worth while' at the time of his writing. His reason for regarding them as timely for his own generation will be explored below in chapters 3 and 9. Whether he was right to regard them as permanently valuable will be touched upon in chapter 11. My principal objective in the rest of this chapter is to examine what Lewis means by describing the seven planets as 'spiritual symbols.' I will analyse both terms, taking them in reverse order.

Lewis's Definition of 'Symbol'

Lewis equated 'symbolism' roughly with 'sacramentalism' and distinguished both from 'allegory.' In a work of allegory, the allegorist takes something immaterial (love, for instance) and provides for it a material representation (as in the form of a god called Amor disporting himself in a beautiful garden). In symbolism, the symbolist works the other way round:

> If our passions, being immaterial, can be copied by material inventions, then it is possible that our material world in its turn is a copy of an invisible world. As the god Amor and his figurative garden are to the actual passions of men, so perhaps we ourselves and our 'real' world are to something else. The attempt to read that something else through its sensible imitations, to see the archetype in the copy, is what I mean by symbolism or sacramentalism.[26]

This distinction between allegory and symbolism is similar to the distinction between 'magistral metaphor' and 'pupillary metaphor' which Lewis made in a seminal essay, 'Bluspels and Flalansferes.'[27] An allegorist is a 'master,' knowing the data—the passions of love—and consciously choosing to talk about them under the form of bodies that were 'confessedly less real,' the fiction of the god and the garden. A symbolist is a 'pupil,' inspecting the data—the world with its visible gardens and invisible passions—in order 'to find that which is more real,' the realm of archetypal Forms from which the data derive and in which they may participate. The symbolist uses the data heuristically: they are indispensable to the meaning arrived at. But the allegorist may at any time strip off this rhetorical vesture and 'show the true sense.' Symbolism, then, is 'a mode of thought,' determining what may be expressed, while allegory is 'a mode of expression'[28] undetermined by what has been thought.

Allegory and symbolism represent convenient ways of talking about opposite ends of a spectrum, but the two methods are not utterly discontinuous. Between the master's and the pupil's metaphors come 'an endless number of types, dotted about in every kind of intermediate position.' Lewis does not bother to define points on this middle-ground, and neither will I. I will only observe that Lewis had doubts about the merits of pure allegory; he was never an uncritical admirer of the genre even as he did so much to rehabilitate it in *The Allegory of Love*. There he acknowledged that it was natural to prefer symbolism to allegory, and that allegory could easily turn into a 'disease of literature' if the equivalences were 'purely conceptual' and did not 'satisfy imagination as well.' And elsewhere he lamented the fact that, since Spenser's time, allegory has often been little more than 'a literary toy.'[29]

Spenser, like all great allegorists, had satisfied imagination as well as the intellect by ensuring that his allegorical images were not excessively pure; he had allowed an admixture of symbolism into the images, making it difficult for the reader to treat them as ciphers that automatically required, or were easily susceptible of, decoding. The more that allegory admitted symbolism in this way, so as to inhibit the felt need for decryption, the more the critic (or, for that matter, the allegorist) had to be wary of thinking that the kernel could be distinguished from the husk, the tenor from the vehicle, or that 'the true sense' was superior to, or quickly separable from, the rhetorical sense. A good allegory, though magistrally formed, has a symbolic charge which will be found to be practically all but indispensable. Thus, Humiliation really is like Bunyan's green valley: the valley is not merely a convenient token of Humiliation.[30] Spenser's Truth and Grace are like Una, not vice versa.[31] For, controverting Croce, Lewis maintained:

> Allegory is not a puzzle.... We must not sit down to examine [*The Faerie Queene*] detail by detail for clues to its meaning as if we were trying to work out a cipher. That is the very worst thing we can do. We must surrender ourselves with childlike attention to the mood of the story.[32]

If we have to choose between calling Lewis an allegorist or a symbolist, it is safer to call him the latter. In the twenty-three years between his first and last published works of fiction, there is a steady move away from magistral toward pupillary metaphor. *The Pilgrim's Regress* (1933) is an 'allegorical apology,' while

Till We Have Faces (1956) is a 'myth retold.' These two works may be taken respectively as the most allegorical and most symbolical parts of his corpus, with the Ransom Trilogy, *The Great Divorce,* and the Chronicles of Narnia falling somewhere in between. Intelligent response to imagery in Lewis's writings depends on knowing in which work it appears. Indeed, one needs constantly to adjust one's critical antennae even within a given work. This is especially true of the Narnia Chronicles which are, as we will discuss in chapter 11, a complex mix of allegory and symbolism.

Lewis's Definition of 'Spirit'

Having come to a working definition of symbolism as a mode of thought that may be more or less combined with a magistral mode of expression, we now turn to clarify what Lewis meant by 'spirit' and 'spiritual.' In *Miracles* Lewis distinguishes five senses of these words. Two of them (the chemical and the medical senses) need not detain us. The other three are:

Sense 1: the opposite of 'bodily' or 'material,' including emotions, passions, memory, and imagination. This immaterial but wholly natural dimension of human nature may, Lewis thinks, be usefully termed 'soul.' It can be good or bad.

Sense 2: the rational element in human nature. Lewis considers reason to be 'relatively supernatural.' That is, reason is not rigidly interlocked with all other events in space and time, but has a certain independence from them. However, it is still a created faculty, and can be either good or bad. Lewis regards the words 'spirit' and 'spiritual' as useful terms for this second sense.

Sense 3: the life which is imparted to those who surrender in Christ to the divine grace of God the Father. This new life or *novitas* is absolutely supernatural to the Christian's created being, and is always and only good. It is not a faculty separate from the other parts of the person, but a redirection of them all: body, soul, and spirit (that is, reason).

When Lewis in 1935 described the seven planets as 'spiritual symbols,' he seems to have had in mind principally the first of these three meanings. Nearly every line of 'The Planets' has to do with emotions or passions of one kind or another (the changeableness of Luna, the sexuality of Venus, the jocundity of Jupiter, et cetera), and 'soul' itself is directly mentioned in a couple of places ('soul's darkness,' 'soul in secret'). Sense 2 (rationality) and Sense 3 (*novitas*) are less obviously identifiable. They are present, but not throughout the whole poem; rather, they are linked to particular planets. Rationality is linked to Sol; *novitas* is linked to Jupiter.

Symbols of Spirit (Sense 2)

In order to explain how rationality is communicated in 'The Planets' by means of Sol, we must go a long way round and turn back to an earlier, and somewhat overlooked, work in Lewis's corpus, a short story entitled 'The Man Born Blind.'[33]

Lewis wrote 'The Man Born Blind' during his 'Great War,' the long philosophical dispute that he had in the 1920s with his friend, Owen Barfield, a dispute that Lewis described as one of the turning points of his life. No attempt will be made to sketch the 'Great War'; that has already been done by the hand of Lionel Adey. Adey, however, omits discussion of 'The Man Born Blind,' a regrettable gap in his study. We know its relevance to the subject on the testimony of Barfield himself, who wrote that 'the story has always remained closely associated in my mind with the Lewis of the so-called "Great War."'[34]

The story is the earliest piece of prose fiction that we have from the adult Lewis and the only one that antedates his conversion to Christianity. It is brief (less than 2,000 words in length) and tells the tale of how the eponymous protagonist, whose name is Robin, regains his sight after surgery. When the bandages have been removed from his eyes, Robin expects to be able to see the marvellous thing that he has heard about all his life—light. No one can show it to him. He begs his wife to tell him where it is, but she cannot explain to his satisfaction: her attempts to do so only confuse him further. At first she seems to equate light with everything visible, then only with the bulb hanging from the ceiling, then only with what comes from the bulb. In despair at these contradictions, Robin leaves the house and walks up to the lip of the local quarry where the rising sun is burning through the morning mist. There he finds an artist who, pointing at the swirling vapour, tells Robin that he is trying to catch the light. The next moment the artist is alone on the quarry edge. Robin has taken a dive into the bright fog and has fallen to his death.

From the *poiema* point of view, the story is unimpressive: the prose style jerks, the characterisations are paper-thin, the climax is too sudden. But these defects are irrelevant since, as John Fitzpatrick observes, 'Lewis was concerned with the *argument* of his story.'[35] One way to understand that argument is by reference to *Surprised by Joy,* where Lewis gives a history of his intellectual development in the 1920s, including what he believed he had learnt from Barfield during the 'Great War.'

One of the things Barfield convinced him of was 'that the positions we had hitherto held left no room for any satisfactory theory of knowledge.' Their positions had been those of realists, by which Lewis means those who view 'as rock-bottom reality the universe revealed by the senses.' Yet at the same time they maintained that abstract thought, if obedient to logical rules, gave indisputable 'truth' and the possibility of 'valid' moral judgement. Barfield, who had advanced beyond realism some time before his friend, taught Lewis that, if thought were purely a subjective event, these claims for abstract thinking would have to be abandoned. Lewis was not willing—indeed, not able—to abandon them. Their abandonment would lead, he thought, to behaviourism in logic, ethics, and aesthetics; and behaviourism was to Lewis flatly 'unbelievable,' a position that his mind found impossible to adopt. He now saw that a realist philosophy that admitted only sensory perception would be effectively solipsistic, but that if solipsism were true it could not know itself to be true. The cerebral physiologist who says that thought is 'only' tiny physical movements of grey matter must be wrong, for how could he think that thought truly except by participating in the medium which the logic of his statement denies? 'The inside vision of rational thinking must be truer than the outside vision which sees only movements of the grey matter; for if the outside vision were the correct one all thought (including this thought itself) would be valueless, and this is self-contradictory.'[36]

Something more fundamental, more 'rock-bottom' than the ability to derive information through the senses must exist. Lewis had wanted Nature to be quite independent of his observation, something other, indifferent, self-existing. 'But now, it seemed to me, I had to give that up. Unless I were to accept an unbelievable alternative, I must admit that mind was no late-come epiphenomenon; that the whole universe was, in the last resort, mental; that our logic was participation in a cosmic *Logos.*'[37] (*Logos* as a pervasive spirit of rationality is of course to be distinguished from *logos* as a work of art's message or point.) Lewis was moving toward an idealist philosophy. To be more precise, he was recognising that his present position already entailed idealism.

'The Man Born Blind' is a cautionary tale about pursuing to its end the logic of realism as represented by the 'stupidity' of Robin's wife and the 'savagery' of the painter. They have had their sight since birth, yet they cannot explain to a formerly blind man that light is not something you see but something you see by. They keep pointing Robin to things that the light comes from, or that catch the light, or that are in the light, but never tell him that light itself is invisible. To adopt terms from a later work by Lewis, their world is 'all fact and no meaning.'[38] Robin's tragic end is a demonstration of Lewis's new-found agreement with Barfield, an agreement that realism left no room for a satisfactory theory of knowledge. Robin fails to learn what Lewis had recently learnt, that thought depends upon a cosmic *logos,* symbolized here by invisible but ubiquitous light. Robin fixes his mind only on light's products in 'Contemplative,' as opposed to 'Enjoyment,' consciousness (to use Alexander's terms outlined in the previous chapter).

This argument against realism represented one of the principal philosophical consequences of 'the Great War' in Lewis's thinking. That thought was immersion in a cosmic spirituality called Reason became for Lewis the linch-pin of his case for idealism, which in turn supported his belief in theism, which in turn supported his belief in Christianity. Some twenty years or so after writing 'The Man Born Blind,' Lewis would be making fundamentally the same point in his most ambitious work of Christian apologetics, *Miracles*, where he attacks 'the self-contradiction of the Naturalist'[39] and contends that 'supernatural Reason enters my natural being . . . like a beam of light which illuminates.'

It is important to clarify what Lewis means here by 'supernatural.' Rational thought is supernatural because it is 'cosmic or super-cosmic. It must be something not shut up inside our heads but already "out there"—in the universe or behind the universe . . . a rationality with which the universe has always been saturated.'[40] But it is supernatural only in relation to us, not absolutely: 'human thought is not God's, but God-kindled.'[41] However, it was only a small step to theism. Indeed, Lewis admits in *Surprised by Joy* that he cannot now understand how he ever regarded his idealism as 'something quite distinct from Theism.'[42] Rather, 'idealism turned out, when you took it seriously, to be disguised Theism.'[43] He considered Berkeley's account of idealism 'unanswerable'[44] and, when asked what school of philosophy God might support, he replied, 'God is a Berkeleyan idealist.'[45] It was for this reason that, as a Christian apologist, Lewis attached such importance to his defence of idealism. Any effective critique of his defence—such as that made by Elizabeth Anscombe at the Socratic Club—was, for Lewis, a serious matter.

Returning to 'The Planets,' we can now understand how that poem also symbolises the rational spirit by means of Solar imagery. Although Sol, the poem tells us, emits 'beams' that foster 'soul in secret,' which suggests Spirit Sense 1, Sol also wields a 'sword of light,' directing his 'arrow' through 'mortal mind' so that 'mists are parted' and 'wisdom' is born—all of which activity suggests Sense 2. Since Sol's sphere was regarded as the heaven of philosophers and theologians, this is exactly what we should expect.

Having shown that 'The Planets' conveys Spirit (Sense 1), the psychological sense, and Spirit (Sense 2), the rational sense, let us now examine how it conveys Spirit (Sense 3), the regenerate sense.

Symbols of Spirit (Sense 3)

Spirit (Sense 3) is communicated in 'The Planets' most clearly through the symbolism of Jupiter, who brings about 'wrath ended and woes mended,' 'winter passed and guilt forgiven'; he makes 'men like the gods' and imputes 'righteous power.' The illumination provided by Sol might be partly understood as a regeneration of the mind as well as a rational clarification of it; Sol's 'paradisal palm' might support such an interpretation, but it is a weak nod toward *novitas*, if that. The connection between the other five planets and 'new life' is even weaker. Luna, Mercury, and Venus appear to have no connection to it whatever; Saturn is able to give a 'blessing' of an unspecified kind; and it is under Mars that Christ is said to have been crucified, but that is the extent of it. In short, there is no clear indication in the poem that any planet other than Jupiter symbolises regeneration of the Spirit (Sense 3).

However, as Lewis continued his imaginative involvement with the planets, he gradually came to use more than just Jupiter to symbolise *novitas*. Moving on from 'The Planets' (1935) to *That Hideous Strength* (1945), we can see a development in the symbolic value Lewis attached to Mercury, Venus, Mars, and Saturn; they, as well as Jupiter, are deployed in the final Ransom book in a way that suggests supernatural renewal. Sol and Luna do not come down upon Ransom and his company of heroes at St. Anne's-on-the-Hill in Chapter 15 ('The Descent of the Gods'), but the arrival of the other five planets is strongly reminiscent of the coming of the Holy Spirit at Pentecost as recorded in Acts 2. There are three main ways in which this resemblance is suggested.

First, the descent of the planetary gods occurs in a story that draws much of its imagery from the Babel myth. The title of *That Hideous Strength* is taken from the sixteenth-century writer, David Lyndsay, and is an allusion to the Tower of Babel whose shadow (the 'shadow of that hideous strength') is said to be more than six miles in length. The story's villains, who run the N.I.C.E. (the National Institute for Co-ordinated Experiments), plan to build a tower that 'would make a quite noticeable addition to the skyline of New York,' a project which we are meant to understand as a modern manifestation of the pride of the men of Babel. Traditionally, the descent of the Holy Spirit at Pentecost, which empowered the disciples to speak in other tongues, is understood as an undoing of the confusion of languages brought about by the Babel curse (Gen. 11:6–9); the descent of the planets likewise overthrows the power of the N.I.C.E.

Second, there are implications that the heroes at St. Anne's are intoxicated: 'A stranger coming into the kitchen would have thought they were drunk, not soddenly but gaily drunk.' In Acts 2:13–15, the apostles are accused of being 'filled with new wine,' an accusation Peter rebuts: 'these men are not drunk, as you suppose, since it is only the third hour of the day.'

Third, there is extensive use of wind imagery throughout the book and, in particular, on the night of the descent. Camilla exclaims, 'How it's blowing! They [the Planets] might come to him [Ransom] tonight.' They do indeed descend on a 'Wet and Windy Night' (the title of chapter 12), for 'the wind had risen,' there is 'wind and starlight'; a 'Bay of Biscay gale.' These comments are meant to put us in mind of Acts 2:2, 'And suddenly a sound came from heaven like the rush of a mighty wind, and it filled all the house where they were sitting.'

In all these ways, then, the descent of the planetary gods in *That Hideous Strength* is reminiscent of the birth of the Church, the first and foundational regeneration. Lewis may have been influenced to think of Pentecost in connection with the planets as a result of reading George Herbert's poem, 'Whitsunday,' in which the dove of the Spirit is said to have kept open house at Whitsun so that 'th'earth did like a heav'n appeare' and 'The starres were coming down to know / If they might mend their wages, and serve here.' Lewis made this underlining in his copy of Herbert's poetry which is now in the Wade Center at Wheaton College.[46]

However, the descent of the gods is only allusively, not allegorically, linked to Pentecost, and Carnell is wrong to state baldly that 'the Holy Ghost descends' in chapter 15.[47] Lewis makes it clear that the planetary intelligences are 'created powers' which must not be worshipped.[48] They are rather, as Fiddes points out, 'an extension on to the cosmic scale of the biblical idea of 'the sons of God' who are assigned by Yahweh as guardian angels to the nations on earth.'[49] The passage in which they descend is an example of Lewis the prose stylist working at the height of his powers,[50] but the subjects of his pen are not themselves of highest significance.

And this should not surprise us, for the Holy Spirit and the *novitas* He brings are exceptionally difficult to symbolise. As Lewis wrote:

> In one sense there is nothing more in a regenerate man than in an unregenerate man, just as there is nothing more in a man who is walking in the right direction than in one who is walking in the wrong direction. In another sense, however, it might be said that the regenerate man is *totally* different from the unregenerate, for the regenerate life, the Christ that is formed in him, transforms every part of him: in it his spirit [Sense 2], soul [Sense 1] and body will all be reborn.[51]

Spirit (Sense 3) thus means both nothing and everything. How is such a paradoxical situation to be symbolised?

One might answer, in the case of an author such as Lewis, who considered himself 'regenerate,' that it could be achieved by examining his own 'new life' and seeing what sorts of symbols it suggests to him. Lewis, however, was extremely wary of anyone who claimed to be able to make the Holy Spirit an object of conscious Contemplation. He suspected that,

> save by God's direct miracle, spiritual experience can never abide introspection. If even our emotions will not do so . . . much less will the operations of the Holy Ghost. The attempt to discover by introspective

analysis our own spiritual condition is to me a horrible thing which reveals, at best, not the secrets of God's spirit and ours, but their transpositions in intellect, emotion and imagination, and which at worst may be the quickest road to presumption or despair.[52]

The impossibility of inspecting one's spiritual life (Sense 3) arises from the simple fact that one cannot step outside it, for 'He is above me and within me and below me and all about me';[53] 'He is inside you as well as outside';[54] 'He is always both within us and over against us.'[55] There is an inescapable participatory aspect to the Christian's relationship with God and 'looking along the beam' of that participation means inevitably that the beam is invisible.[56] Lewis applied Alexander's category of Enjoyment as much to Spirit (Sense 3) as to Spirit (Sense 2): 'In the Christian life you are not usually looking *at* Him [the Holy Spirit] . . . you have to think of the third Person as something inside you, or behind you.'[57]

The typically insensible nature of the Holy Spirit's operations presumably accounts for why Lewis makes the startling statement that 'there can be no plausible images of . . . the Spirit.'[58] This is startling because there are certain images of the Third Person which are sanctioned by scripture and tradition, notably *dove, breath,* and *fire.* Lewis is naturally aware of these, and uses them himself in various places when wanting to evoke something of the Holy Spirit's presence. But these moments are when Lewis is content, as it were, to atomise the Spirit and symbolise His transpositions into sensible awareness. Properly understood, however, the Spirit is just as present when un-sensed as sensed; and His insensible presence is the more usual experience for the Christian, in Lewis's view.[59] Be that as it may, it is in any case 'the actual presence, not the *sensation* of the presence, of the Holy Ghost which begets Christ in us. The *sense* of the presence is a super-added gift for which we give thanks when it comes, and that's all about it.'[60]

This picture is further complicated by the fact that the Holy Spirit is not present in the regenerate individual alone; rather 'He speaks also through Scripture, the Church, Christian friends, books etc.'[61] Because of this, 'we may ignore, but can nowhere evade, the presence of God. The world is crowded with Him. He walks everywhere *incognito.*'[62] Considered on this large scale, how is a writer to symbolise a universal and usually imperceptible spiritual presence? If God is present everywhere *incognito,* how can His presence be brought to cognitive effect without changing its nature? The difficulty of such representation explains Lewis's remark that 'the Holy Ghost is not matter for *epic* poetry.'[63] In *Paradise Lost,* for example, the absences of the Third Person of the Trinity are not noticed until they are pointed out. In lyric poetry, however, which may try to encapsulate discrete moments of spiritual intensity where Enjoyment is raised (or lowered?) temporarily to Contemplative consciousness, the Spirit may be more easily depicted.[64] But to symbolise Him in 'the big picture' is a much harder task for the poet to accomplish.

In the big picture, *novitas* is not confined to moments of special intensity, but to all moments, special and ordinary, individual and universal: *theosis,* the sharing in the divine life, means sharing them all. This was Lewis's settled view and therefore, although Kort may be right in one sense to say that Lewis's work is 'without strong doctrines of . . . the Holy Spirit'[65] (for it is true that he writes very little about the Spirit doctrinally in his apologetics), we must not assume that the Spirit's apparent symbolic absence from his work is the same as a real absence or that it betokens a lack of interest in Pneumatology. Lewis had his own very strongly held belief in the difficulty, even the impropriety, of Contemplating one's *novitas,* and an equally strong belief in the presence of the Spirit flooding and transvaluing every part of a Christian's life. In other words, his doctrine of the Spirit (Sense 3) was that He could and should be Enjoyed, and as fully as possible. The possibility of full Enjoyment was great because, in his view (which he took from MacDonald), 'that which is best [God] gives most plentifully, as is reason with Him. Hence the quiet fullness of ordinary nature; hence the Spirit to them that ask it.'[66]

'Quiet fullness' is a good description of the presence of the planets in the Narnia Chronicles. In chapters 3 to 9 I will be arguing that, in the Narniad, building on his efforts in 'The Planets' and 'The Descent of the Gods,' Lewis employs planetary imagery so that each Chronicle is quietly full with it. The imagery is 'quiet' in the sense that it draws no attention to itself: it is not something one looks at as one reads each tale, but something one looks along. And the imagery is 'full' in the sense that it determines the overall shape and feel of each story, governing the architectonics of each narrative, the incidental ornamentation, and also, most significantly, the portrayal of the Christ-like character of Aslan and the Spirit (Sense 3) that he imparts. In the tenth chapter I will further contend that Lewis may well have originally conceived the first Chronicle as a way of symbolising Spirit (Sense 2) by the same quiet means, that is, by means of Enjoyment consciousness, getting his readers to inhabit, but not Contemplate, a Reason-saturated world. Before we come on to those questions, we must first look at the smaller issue of how, in the Narniad, Lewis depicts the planets themselves in a Contemplatable fashion.

Contemplating the Planets in the Chronicles of Narnia

Jupiter is the only one of the seven medieval planets to be directly named in the Chronicles; it is seen, apparently in 'our' universe, as Digory and Polly are being whirled between worlds in *The Magician's Nephew.* Within the subcreated world of Narnia itself, we are given to understand that the heavenly bodies are different; they are 'the bright Narnian stars,' 'nearer than stars in our world,' which include 'the Ship, the Hammer and the Leopard' and various other constellations. The Narnian North-Star is 'brighter than our Pole Star' and is called 'the Spear-Head': Jill, who knows 'her Narnian stars perfectly,' can guide by it. The Narnian Moon 'is larger than ours'; it is called 'Zardeenah' in Calormen and appears in every Chronicle except *The Magician's Nephew*. The Narnian Sun, which appears in all seven books, is 'younger' than ours: 'fireflowers' grow on its mountains and 'fire-berries' in its valleys; birds fly from these valleys and the sun itself can be sailed right up to at the eastern edge of Narnia. There is a Narnian 'morning star,' but its name is Aravir, not Venus: it appears in three of the stories. Even the dying world of Charn seems to have an equivalent of the morning star.

As well as being nearer, brighter, larger, and younger, the Narnian stars differ from ours by being a kind of people, 'the great lords of the upper sky' who 'tread the great dance'; we meet two of them by name in *The Voyage of the 'Dawn Treader'* (Coriakin, complete with orreries and astrolabes, and Ramandu). These great lords sing at their creation in 'cold, tingling, silvery voices': 'One moment there had been nothing but darkness; next moment a thousand, thousand points of light leapt out—single stars, constellations, and planets, brighter and bigger than any in our world.' They are all 'called home' by Aslan at the end of *The Last Battle*.

In addition to this Narnian 'astronomy,' there is a good deal of 'astrology' in the series. In *Prince Caspian* Dr Cornelius interprets the conjunction of 'two noble planets, Tarva and Alambil'; and later in that book, Glenstorm, 'a prophet and star-gazer,' tells Caspian that the heavens augur well for an attack on Miraz. In *The Last Battle*, Roonwit informs Tirian that there are 'disastrous conjunctions of the planets' and that 'the stars never lie.' In *The Horse and His Boy*, Rabadash believes that things come about by 'the alteration of the stars.' In *The Voyage of the 'Dawn Treader,'* Lucy thanks 'her stars.' In *The Silver Chair* two centaurs tell Jill and Eustace about 'the influences of the planets.' The 'air' of Narnia often has effects, making people feel younger in *The Magician's Nephew*, for instance, and stronger in *Prince Caspian*.

This brief overview of the explicit astronomical and astrological elements in the Chronicles does not require analysis. Our purpose is merely to note that Lewis holds up for our Contemplation a world in which the fretted roof of the firmament has both importance and significance. But where is the Enjoyment? Where is the sense of participation in these 'spiritual symbols'? Como notes that Narnia invites a medieval 'mode of perception,' a 'belief-in,' not just 'belief-that'; and he gives as an example the challenge Ramandu issues to Eustace's 'belief that' a star is merely a huge ball of flaming gas:[67] 'Even in your world, my son, that is not what a star is but only what it is made of.' Eustace needs to 'believe in' the stars as well. But that is just one brief moment in one story. Where is *connaitre* on the larger scale?

Perhaps it is not there. After all, Milton—one of Lewis's poetic heroes— did not think it necessary to communicate Enjoyment in his great large-scale work. In *Paradise Lost,* according to Lewis, 'we are not invited (as Alexander would have said) to enjoy the spiritual life, but to contemplate the whole pattern within which the spiritual life arises.'[68] However, in Dante—Lewis's favourite poet—we find a different *modus operandi.* As we read *The Divine Comedy* we Enjoy 'a poetical expression of religious experience'[69]; we share in an individual's spiritual pilgrimage, looking along the same hopes and fears as the pilgrim. It is this example, I will argue, that Lewis imitates, *mutatis mutandis,* in the Narniad.

It was in large part through his love of Dante that Lewis grew to be so enchanted by the Ptolemaic universe. He rhapsodises about its portrayal in the *Paradiso,* describing the third canticle of the *Comedy* as

> like the stars—endless mathematical subtility of orb, cycle, epicycle and ecliptic, unthinkable & unpicturable, & yet at the same time the freedom and liquidity of empty space and the triumphant certainty of movement. I should describe it as feeling more *important* than any poetry I have ever read . . . its blend of complexity and beauty is very like Catholic theology—wheel within wheel, but wheels of glory, and the One radiated through the Many.[70]

I shall, as far as space permits, trace some of Lewis's debts to the *Comedy* in what follows. One debt is secrecy, for Dante thought of poetry as something 'to be 'adorned as much as possible,' to have its 'true sense' hidden beneath a rich vesture of 'rhetorical colouring.''[71] Another debt is the Christianisation of that cosmos, for Dante was the only poet, in Lewis's view, to have infused the medieval model of the heavens with 'high religious ardour.'[72] I hope to demonstrate that Dante is no longer alone in this latter respect because Lewis has joined him. It seems appropriate then that, in projecting the analysis of Lewis's imagination that will occupy us for the rest of this book (an analysis which will be more expository than evaluative), we should note his own plans for studying the great Florentine:

> The aim is to surprise the imagination of the poet in its more secret workings, to disengage that incessant orchestration which accompanies his drama and which, though it may escape notice while our attention is fixed on the stage, probably contributes in the highest degree to the total effect.[73]

THREE

Jupiter

Winter passed and guilt forgiven.
—'The Planets' (lines 89–90)

My aim in chapters 3 to 9 will be three-fold: to track each of the seven planets as it appears throughout the course of Lewis's writings, to analyse the deployment of the relevant planet's imagery in each Chronicle, and then to assess the theological messages embodied in and expressed by that deployment. I will show that the Chronicles, like all good works of art, 'are complex and carefully made objects,'[1] and that close attention to the very objects they are is both required and amply repaid. Indeed, until we realise the nature of each Chronicle as 'something made' (*poiema*), we will have little chance successfully to interpret it as 'something said' (*logos*). And we will not properly understand the *poiema* unless we first understand the planets.

Of the seven medieval planets only one is named by Lewis in the Narniad: Jupiter,[2] the planet of kingship, which, as Milward has noted, 'is evidently his favourite.' Jupiter has a long pedigree in Lewis's works: it shows strongly in his scholarship and poetry, makes a central contribution to the Ransom Trilogy, and, most important, as I will argue, animates the imaginative vision of *The Lion, the Witch and the Wardrobe*. I will contend that this first Chronicle was deliberately designed to communicate the Jovial spirit: the main events of the plot, numerous points of ornamental detail, and the manner of the portrayal of Aslan conspire to express this Jovial kappa element. The story-telling technique that is thus manifested is something that I believe to be a new phenomenon in imaginative literature. It is a subtle and sophisticated technique. I will be calling it *donegality*.

The Pre-eminence of Jupiter

Lewis's first published encomium on Jupiter appeared in 1935 in the article on alliterative metre that accompanied 'The Planets.' So far we have not examined in its entirety the introduction he gives to that poem. It is now time to see how he chooses to conclude it:

> the characters of the planets, as conceived by medieval astrology, seem to me to have a permanent value as spiritual symbols—to provide a *Phänomenologie des Geistes* which is specially worth while in our own generation. Of Saturn we know more than enough, but who does not need to be reminded of Jove?[3]

As a key to Lewis's imagination, the final sentence of this quotation is highly significant. There is permanent symbolic value in all seven planets, but the most timely value is that found in Jupiter; the least timely is in Saturn, the planet of old age, ugliness, death, and disaster. Saturn will be considered in chapter 9. This present chapter addresses what it was about the symbolic qualities of Jupiter that made Lewis think them so particularly worth while for his own generation.

Jupiter in Lewis's Scholarship

Three years before his article on alliterative metre, Lewis had for the first time given his series of Oxford lectures entitled 'Prolegomena to Medieval Poetry,' which found permanent form in *The Discarded Image*. Its fifth chapter, 'The Heavens,' summarises his thoughts about the spheres of the Ptolemaic cosmos and deals with Jupiter as follows:

> Jupiter, the King, produces in the earth, rather disappointingly, tin; this shining metal said different things to the imagination before the canning industry came in. The character he produces in men would now be very imperfectly expressed by the word 'jovial,' and is not very easy to grasp; it is no longer, like the saturnine character, one of our archetypes. We may say it is *Kingly*; but we must think of a King at peace, enthroned, taking his leisure, serene. The Jovial character is cheerful, festive, yet temperate, tranquil, magnanimous. When this planet dominates we may expect halcyon days and prosperity. In Dante wise and just princes go to his sphere when they die. He is the best planet, and is called The Greater Fortune, *Fortuna Major*.[4]

Lewis acknowledges that Jupiter is no longer archetypal for the modern imagination, and he fastens on the Jovial metal as emblematic of this loss. It is 'disappointing' that Jupiter's metal should be tin. Though seemingly a minor point, this observation flags up the very change Lewis is reporting. No medieval writer could have used *tinny* as Lewis elsewhere uses it of authors who seemed to him 'thin.'[5] The medieval mind would have made tin's 'shining' quality the focus of imaginative response, for brightness was then as attractive as bigness is to the modern mind. But since the arrival of the canning industry Jove's metal has connoted hollowness and cheapness, by association with 'tin-can' and 'tin-pot.' And as with Jove's metal, so with Jove's whole personality, Lewis avers: 'Changes in outlook . . . have almost annihilated Jupiter.' Concluding his summary of the planets in *The Discarded Image*, he comments, 'We find no difficulty in grasping the character of Saturn'; Jove, on the other hand, 'almost evaded us.'

Lewis was troubled by this modern inability to recognise Jove at a glance and by Saturn's usurpation of his throne. Jupiter was a staple figure in Western literature, not only in classical sources, but also—Christianized—in medieval and renaissance texts. In nearly four decades of teaching the Western canon at Oxford and Cambridge, Lewis came to a full awareness of Jupiter's centrality. He refers to the use made of the Jovial character by a wide range of writers, including Statius, Chaucer, Dante, Lydgate, Spenser, Shakespeare, and Milton,[6] many of whom had done so with the intent of figuring the deity of their believed religion under a pagan veil. How should students of the twentieth century properly understand the Christian themes of that literature if the Jovial archetype were allowed to be forgotten? Anxious to prevent Jupiter's complete disappearance, Lewis began a campaign on his behalf. He put himself forward as Jove's standard-bearer, telling his university audiences that he himself had been born under Jupiter;[7] he advanced Jove's cause in various poetic and fictional operations, as we shall see below; and (which is our concern in this section) he repeatedly defended Jove as a yardstick of judgement in his literary criticism.

One example occurs in *The Allegory of Love* where Lewis contends that Chaucer's 'Troilus and Criseyde' is a Jovial poem. He writes:

> The poetry which represents peace and joy, desires fulfilled and winter overgone, the poetry born under festal Jove, is of a high and difficult order: if rarity be the test of difficulty, it is the most difficult of all. In it Chaucer has few rivals and no masters.[8]

Our interest here is not in assessing the validity of Lewis's judgements; we are simply trying to penetrate his imagination and it is enough to acknowledge what he considered Jovial poetry to be: good in its moral qualities, but difficult poetically to achieve, and rare for that reason (perhaps for the moral reason too). These opinions, I suggest, are likely to have had a bearing on his own poetic practice. Lewis's moralising compass would have directed him toward Joviality for its goodness; his ambitiousness would have drawn him to its difficulty; his canniness along with his popularising instincts would have noted the implications of its rarity, for there is always a keen and widespread demand for that good which is scarce.

It is worth noting also how Lewis construes Joviality in his comments on 'Troilus and Criseyde.' He extends the meaning beyond festal and magnanimous kingship to encompass 'desires fulfilled and winter overgone.' This focus upon the aestival aspect of Jove's influence was derived, in part, from Lewis's observation of the development of the Criseyde story in post-Chaucerian English poetry. In Henryson's fifteenth-century version, 'The Testament of Cresseid,' Saturn is depicted as a condemnatory and malign Jack Frost character, cold and withering, who is outshone by his son. When Jupiter appears, 'Fra his father Saturne far different,' wintry imagery is replaced by imagery of early summer. Upon Jupiter's head is 'ane garland, wonder gay, / Of flouris fair, as it had bene May.'[9]

Another appeal to Jove is found in *Seventeenth Century Studies Presented to Sir Herbert Grierson*. Lewis's contribution, 'Donne and Love Poetry in the Seventeenth Century,' is unusual in the Lewis corpus for consisting largely of an attack on its subject. Normally, he writes to praise an accepted author or to rehabilitate an overlooked one, rarely is his motive to downgrade, and, as so often when we find literary Lewis in depreciatory mode, T. S. Eliot is at the back of it. Eliot had effectively rediscovered Donne for the twentieth century; he rated him very highly. But to Lewis, Donne was, if not our saddest poet, then at least the most uncomfortable, because—paradoxically—he exposes to us something that we find very congenial:

> It would be foolish not to recognize the growth in our criticism of something that I can only describe as literary Manichaeism—a dislike of peace and pleasure and heartsease simply as such. To be bilious is, in some circles, almost the first qualification for a place in the Temple of Fame. We distrust the pleasures of imagination, however hotly and unmerrily we preach the pleasures of the body.... We want, in fact, just what Donne can give us—something stern and tough, though not necessarily virtuous, something that does not conciliate. Born under Saturn, we do well to confess the liking complexionally forced upon us; but not to attempt that wisdom which dominates the stars is pusillanimous, and to set up our limitation as a norm—to believe, against all experience, in a Saturnocentric universe—is folly.[10]

Lewis fully admits—as a veteran of the trenches he could hardly deny—the Saturnine shadow cast over his contemporaries (that generation which was 'born under Saturn'). It is sometimes forgotten that Lewis had been a teenage officer in the Great War; he had witnessed 'horribly smashed men . . . sitting or standing corpses'[11] and as an ex-serviceman was under no illusions: he knew that Saturn was the *zeitgeist*. He turned thither for inspiration himself as he composed the grimmer poems of *Spirits in Bondage*. But he eventually tired of Saturnocentricity (see below, chapter 9) and he tired too of those poets who insisted on repeatedly serving up Saturnine gruel, poets such as Owen, Pound, Sassoon, and Eliot.

Lewis never explicitly critiques the poetry of Owen or Pound, though his defence of Horatian patriotism in *The Abolition of Man* is presumably in part a response either to Owen's 'Dulce et Decorum Est' or to Pound's 'Hugh Selwyn Mauberley' or to both. But Lewis did pass explicit comment on the poetry of Sassoon and that of Eliot (who began work at a London bank in 1917 around the time Lewis volunteered for active service in the front line). Sassoon's poetry he regarded as stuck in the phase of disillusionment; his was a case of arrested emotional development.[12] Disillusionment was not necessarily a bad thing: it could be a natural phase of maturation and needful for the attainment of deeper realism. Adopted as a fixed perspective, however, it was insufficient. Similarly, the 'penitential' quality of Eliot's poetry at its best was worthy of 'honour'[13], but to conclude that all poetry must share that quality would be a *non sequitur*. Such a settled regimen of 'prayer and fasting,' such an avoidance of cakes and ale, amounted in Lewis's eyes to a kind of rapprochement with bleakness; it painted its canvas full of unrelieved malcontentment. This was what he meant when he said he found an 'ultimate deformity' in Eliot's poetry.[14]

Stephen Medcalf has shown some significant similarities between the later Lewis and the later Eliot.[15] Of the earlier and (for Lewis) far more significant dissimilarities between the two writers we may find a convenient token in the following examples of artistic licence. Lewis was driven to Whipsnade in late September 1931, but says there were bluebells in flower at the time.[16] Eliot was driven to Little Gidding in May 1936, but when it emerged in poetic form he had turned the event into winter.[17]

Lewis would not have seen these two examples of poetic rewriting as equal and opposite options. Although his Christianity was as dualistic as he could make it,[18] he believed that, in the last resort, Jove and Saturn are not equals: Jupiter's wisdom 'dominates the stars.' Therefore he conceived it his Christian duty to be as Jovial as possible, and to give Saturn his due, but no more than his due. The way *The Pilgrim's Regress* satirises the fashionably Saturnine post-Armistice attitude through the characters of the silly Clevers, who are ever harking back to 'the mud and the flood and the blood,' is one early indication of this resolve. And in his essay on Donne he concludes by observing that Donne's influence on the poets of the seventeenth century is seen to best advantage when his successors (Carew, Lovelace, Marvell) take a Donne-like conceit and translate it into 'ordinary poetry' where beauty and cheerfulness, 'the great regal name of Jove' and an 'Olympian' mastery of Saturnine sensations, can break in.

The three scholarly works we have considered all date from the 1930s. The article on alliterative metre came first in 1935; *The Allegory of Love* followed in 1936; the Grierson festschrift appeared in 1938. Lewis seems to have recognised the dangers of over-playing a hand and we find no further explicit appeals to Joviality in his remaining works of literary criticism. But if 1938 saw his farewell to Jupiter as a public tool of literary scholarship, it also saw his emergence as a writer of fiction,[19] a department of letters where different and more relaxed rules apply. Imaginative writers are allowed—indeed, expected— to adopt symbol systems, and Lewis transported his love of Jove into this new realm with exuberance.

Jupiter in the Ransom Trilogy

The Ransom Trilogy puts into prose fiction much of what Lewis had already expressed about Jupiter in his lectures and literary criticism, and it is remarkable how little attention this astrological symbolism has attracted from students of these works. For instance, even the best study of *That Hideous Strength*, that by Myers, mentions only the manifestation of Mercurial power. Downing likewise gives a cursory treatment. Robert Houston Smith is alone in recognizing that 'Lewis seemed to imply . . . that Jupiter is the center of his fictional universe.' Since Jupiter's wisdom is the dominant power in the heavens we should expect to find a considerable focus on Jovial qualities in these inter-planetary adventures. And we do find that. Although Ransom never visits the planet Jupiter, something more important happens: over the course of the trilogy he becomes Jovial himself.

Out of the Silent Planet

At the end of *Out of the Silent Planet*, Ransom, standing on Mars, looks up at the firmament and sees 'the true king of night' threading his way through the western galaxy, 'making its lights dim by comparison with his own.' That is, he sees 'Jupiter rising beyond the Asteroids.' Ransom ruminates on what the inhabitants of Mars (the Malacandrians) say about the stars:

> They call the Asteroids the 'dancers before the threshold of the Great Worlds'. The Great Worlds are the planets. . . . Glundandra[20] (Jupiter) is the greatest of these and has some importance in Malacandrian

thought which I cannot fathom. He is 'the centre', 'great Meldilorn', 'throne' and 'feast'. They are, of course, well aware that he is un-inhabitable, at least by animals of the planetary type; and they certainly have no pagan idea of giving a local habitation to Maleldil[21]. But somebody or something of great importance is connected with Jupiter.

Those are very nearly the closing words of *Out of the Silent Planet*; they come in a letter supposedly written by Ransom to the narrator. This letter, as Lewis told one of his real-life correspondents, was meant as a way of preparing a sequel.

Perelandra

But Lewis was not at this stage clear what kind of sequel there was going to be. In the very final sentence of *Out of the Silent Planet* there is an indication that any further voyages to the planets will have to involve time-travel. This sentence was intended to cue up Tolkien, who had agreed to write a story about time-travel if Lewis would write one about space-travel. But Tolkien never came up with the goods; his abortive attempt was entitled, not inappositely, 'The Lost Road.' As a consequence, in an attempt to justify the final words of *Out of the Silent Planet*, Lewis roughed out an opening to a time-travel story of his own in that work to which Hooper has given the title *The Dark Tower*. This he eventually abandoned, though not without first salvaging the image of the tower and a little of the time-travel theme for later use in *That Hideous Strength*.[22] Then, dismissing the idea of time-travel for the immediate sequel and getting down to what really interested him, he returned to the threads which he had left dangling in the much longer and far more significant passage at the end of *Out of the Silent Planet*, namely the lines about Jupiter. This, as we shall see, links the first book to the second and both to the third.

The link between the first and second books is small but important. Almost the last words of Ransom in the first book had been, 'Somebody or something of great importance is connected with Jupiter.' The very first words spoken by Ransom in *Perelandra* are, 'By Jove, I'm glad to see you.'[23] He says this out of relief that *Lewis* (the Lewis in the story) has survived the spiritual barrage that had bombarded him as he arrived at the cottage in Ransom's absence. But it is not merely a conventional expostulation; it is a literally meant expression. *Lewis*'s survival and Ransom's gladness at it have both been brought about 'by Jove.' A recurrent feature of the Ransom Trilogy is semantics: dead metaphors are brought back to life, decayed meanings are reawoken in various words, Ransom's own name is given an alternative etymology. If we take this opening 'By Jove!' as an empty phrase, we are missing a trick.[24] Jupiter has brought about *Lewis*'s safe arrival at Ransom's cottage and now the second story can get under weigh. Having linked the end of the Martial book with the beginning of the Venereal book, Jupiter has performed that action which is to be one of his main functions in the third story when Lewis makes him into a priest-king who draws lineages together by his sovereign power and marries them by his sacerdotal authority.

A central theme of the Ransom Trilogy is sex or gender (or both). Having developed, as it were in the background, images of masculinity and femininity, respectively, in the first two books, Lewis foregrounds the theme in Ransom's own mind at the end of *Perelandra* when he tries 'a hundred times' to put into words the difference between the ousiarchs of Mars and Venus:

> He has said that Malacandra affected him like a quantitative, Per-
> elandra like an accentual metre. He thinks that the first held in his
> hand something like a spear, but the hands of the other were open with
> the palms towards him.... All this Ransom saw, as it were, with his
> own eyes.... With deep wonder he thought to himself, "My eyes have
> seen Mars and Venus. I have seen Ares and Aphrodite."[25]

The scene is now set for the third book in which these masculine and feminine principles will be united.

That Hideous Strength

'Matrimony' is the first word of *That Hideous Strength*. The story focusses upon the marriage of Mark and Jane Studdock, a relationship which turns out to be the mundane expression of mighty cosmic forces. Mark's name derives from Mars and over the course of the tale he becomes, as we shall discover in the next chapter, a Martial character. Jane becomes a Venereal character, as we shall see in chapter 8.

The priestly-kingly operations of Jove manifest themselves in two main ways in *That Hideous Strength*: at a human level in the character of Ransom and at a cosmic level in the actual descent of Jupiter in chapter 15.[26]

RANSOM

It has not before been noted by critics of *That Hideous Strength* that Ransom has by this stage in the trilogy turned into a human version of Jupiter. Although 'Ransom isn't the king of this country or trying to become king,' he is unmis-takably a king of a kind. He is likened to Solomon, Arthur, and to the King in MacDonald's *The Princess and Curdie*; he is seated in a 'throne room'; and he longs to return to the 'House of Kings' where he will join 'Melchisedec the

King.' That this 'House of Kings' is located in the 'cupshaped land of Abhalljin' (on Perelandra) reminds us that Venus, *Fortuna Minor*, has a special relationship with Jupiter, *Fortuna Major*, as we will have occasion to note several times below. And that this House is the resting-place of Melchisedec strengthens Ransom's Jovial identity. Ransom reminds Merlin that 'Melchisedec is he in whose hall the steep-stoned ring sparkles on the forefinger of the Pendragon.' Ransom is the current Pendragon and Melchisedec is a Hebrew name meaning 'My king is Jupiter.' Melchisedec appears in the Book of Genesis as a priest-king and Lewis knew that, as such, he 'resembles (in his peculiar way he is the only Old Testament character who resembles) Christ Himself,'[27] a resemblance made explicit by the author of the letter to the Hebrews (Heb. 5:5–10). Melchisedec, like Christ, is associated with bread and wine (Gen. 14:18–20; Luke 22:14–20), and Ransom now survives on that very diet.

As if this complex web of Jovial-kingly-priestly-Christological imagery were not sufficient, we are told that Ransom's name has changed so that he is now known as Mr Fisher-King. In Arthurian romance the Fisher King was a king encountered during the quest for the Holy Grail and in some versions of the story he is identified with the Wounded King Pelles. Ransom's own woundedness is mentioned numerous times, and when Jane is 'drawn into his orbit' she 'tasted the word *King* itself with all linked associations of battle, marriage, priesthood, mercy, and power.' Later, after she emerges from an audience with him she finds herself 'in the sphere of Jove, amid light and music and festal pomp, brimmed with life and radiant in health, jocund and clothed in shining garments.' Clearly, Ransom has become a personification of Jupiter, and it is no surprise in the final chapter when we see him sitting 'crowned, at the right of the hearth.'

In his priestly-kingly capacity, Ransom acts as wounded healer. His wound is in his foot (an allusion to the messianic text, Gen. 3:15) and his pontifical role emerges partly when he serves as the 'bridge' across which the planetary powers pass and partly as he bridges the growing divide in Jane's marriage to Mark, though he makes it clear to her that 'it is not a question of how you or I look on marriage but how my Masters look on it.'[28] Participating in that Jovial wisdom which governs the heavens, Ransom is able to reunite Jane and Mark with their respective governing planetary powers.

After her interview with Ransom, Jane resolves to 'give Mark much more than she had ever given him before.' Her resolution will, among other things, lead to an abandonment of contracepted sexual intercourse. The Studdocks' marriage has been emotionally sterile partly because it has been wilfully infertile at the physiological level; but spiritually Jane is learning what it means to be 'left without protection.' In chapter 14, 'Real Life is Meeting,' Jane encounters Maleldil 'with no veil or protection between' and from that point onwards, having 'become a Christian,' she can receive the virtue of Venus. Once Mark has encountered the crucified Christ and undergone a similar conversion, being freed by Martial strength from his whelpish anxieties, he can likewise obediently play his part. Thus restored to their true selves, their marriage is saved and the book ends with their conjugal reunion in the bedroom at the Lodge.

Ransom, like the reader, is left outside the bedroom door, but he knows (as we do) what is going to happen. By choosing to put themselves under the influence of Venus 'baptised,' instead of Venus 'untransformed,' Jane and Mark[29] are demonstrating their obedience to true, not demoniac, kingship.[30] Like Merlin, who is 'a true King's man,' they accept the kingly authority of Ransom, and through him, that of Jupiter, whose sovereignty works through all the heavenly bodies, not only his own. It is to the planetary Jupiter considered in his own right that we must now turn our attention.

GLUND

Ransom, of course, is only a vicegerent on behalf of Jupiter himself, who descends majestically in chapter 15, last of five planets to do so:

Suddenly a greater spirit came—one whose influence tempered and almost transformed to his own quality the skill of leaping Mercury, the clearness of Mars, the subtler vibration of Venus, and even the numbing weight of Saturn.

In the kitchen his coming was felt. No one afterwards knew how it happened but somehow the kettle was put on, the hot toddy was brewed. Arthur—the only musician among them—was bidden to get out his fiddle. The chairs were pushed back, the floor cleared. They danced. What they danced no one could remember. It was some round dance, no modern shuffling: it involved beating the floor, clapping of hands, leaping high. And no one while it lasted thought himself or his fellows ridiculous. It may, in fact, have been some village measure, not ill-suited to the tiled kitchen: the spirit in which they danced it was not so. It seemed to each that the room was filled with kings and queens, that the wildness of their dance expressed heroic energy and its quieter movements had seized the very spirit behind all noble ceremonies.

Upstairs his mighty beam turned the Blue Room into a blaze of lights. Before the other angels a man might sink: before this he might die, but if he lived at all, he would laugh. If you had caught one breath of the air that came from him, you would have felt yourself taller than before. Though you were a cripple, your walk would have become stately: though a beggar, you would have worn your rags magnanimously.

Kingship and power and festal pomp and courtesy shot from him as sparks fly from an anvil. The pealing of bells, the blowing of trumpets, the spreading out of banners, are means used on earth to make a faint symbol of his quality.[31] It was like a long sunlit wave, creamy-crested and arched with emerald, that comes on nine feet tall, with roaring and with terror and unquenchable laughter. It was like the first beginning of music in the halls of some King so high and at some festival so solemn that a tremor akin to fear runs through young hearts when they hear it. For this was the great Glund-Oyarsa, King of Kings, through whom the joy of creation principally blows across these fields of Arbol, known to men in old times as Jove and under that name, by fatal but not inexplicable misprision, confused with his Maker—so little did they dream by how many degrees the stair even of created being rises above him.

At his coming there was holiday in the Blue Room...[32]

Thus Jupiter arrives on earth and under his wisdom, 'that wisdom which dominates the stars,' the other planets are ordered aright in the operations of their influence. Mercury confuses the language of the banqueters at Belbury; Mars inflames the animals against the members of the N.I.C.E., who in turn attack one another; Saturn brings a variety of deaths to the evil characters; and Venus at St. Anne's-on-the-Hill presides over the loves of the animals and the married couples, including, of course, the Studdocks.

Mark and Jane are 'but lately married' and Jupiter is planning to work through their bodies, bringing to birth the child who is to save Logres. The final chapter title, 'Venus at St. Anne's,' should not lead us to conclude that Venus, rather than Jupiter, has suddenly become Lewis's chief object of interest. As we learn from one of Lewis's poems, 'The Small Man Orders His Wedding,' it is in 'Jove's monarchal presence bright' that 'Aphrodite's saffron light' may shine. Venus, more than any of the other planets, can properly operate only under Jupiter's sovereign and cynosural influence. (For more on this, see chapter 8.) Furthermore, the purpose of Mark and Jane's intercourse is Jovial, and that in two senses.

At one level, their physical act of love is typically Jovial by dint of being counter-Saturnine. Jane's doctoral dissertation was to have been on Donne's 'triumphant vindication of the body'; she and Mark originally preferred having a thesis to having children. Now, they together are vindicating their own bodies and 'the body' more generally considered (as against the disembodied head of the N.I.C.E.) by forgetting Jane's *imagined* vocation[33] and having 'children instead.'[34] Donne, that poet whom Lewis habitually associated with the 'saturnine' spirit,[35] is overcome as husband and wife at last embrace each other's fertility.

At another level, their act of love will make up for the missed opportunity of which Merlin speaks: 'For a hundred generations in two lines the begetting of this child was prepared; and unless God should rip up the work of time, such seed, and such an hour, in such a land, shall never be again.' Rowan Williams finds this reference 'puzzling,'[36] but it becomes explicable if Jove is kept at the centre of interpretation. Ransom disagrees with Merlin; he believes that the Studdocks' child 'may yet be born,' even though the most auspicious hour for its begetting has passed. And indeed, it will be born: it will be the next Pendragon, Ransom's successor. Ransom was the seventy-ninth Pendragon; he inherited the office from a senex in Cumberland who himself had been 'the successor of Arthur and Uther and Cassibelaun.' But Ransom is now about to hand over his mantle and 'tomorrow we shall know, or tonight, who is to be the eightieth.' The monarchal presence presiding over Mark and Jane's bed will bring to life that eightieth Pendragon. We know this from the highly important detail that Jane's maiden name was 'Tudor,' a distinction of which she tries not to be excessively proud. Although *That Hideous Strength* does not disclose the significance of 'Tudor,' we know from one of his letters what it meant to Lewis. He believed that the mythical British or Celtic line (the heritage of Logres) was the one 'that goes back through the Tudors to Cadwallader and thence to Arthur, Uther, Cassibelan, Lear, Lud, Brut,[37] Aeneas, Jupiter.'[38] Thus the Ransom Trilogy concludes with the imminent conception of the heir of Jove.

Jupiter in Lewis's Poetry

The delights of the marriage bed are celebrated in one of Lewis' most astrological poems, 'The Small Man Orders his Wedding,' to which we have already made brief reference. It is worth quoting a little more fully, partly in order to understand the effects that Lewis was aiming to achieve at the end of *That Hideous Strength*, and partly in order to introduce the next stage of our survey: Jupiter in Lewis's poetry. The final two stanzas run as follows:

> What flame before our chamber door
> Shines in on love's security?
> Fiercer than day, its piercing ray
> Pours round us unendurably.
> It's Aphrodite's saffron light,
> And Jove's monarchal presence bright
> And Genius burning through the night
> The torch of man's futurity.

For her the swords of furthest lords
Have flashed in fields ethereal;
The dynasts seven incline from heaven
With glad regard and serious,
And ponder there beyond our air
The infinite unborn, and care
For history, while the mortal pair
Lie drowned in dreaming weariness.[39]

The poem is Jovial, heavily indebted to the 'festal' *Epithalamion* of Spenser, which Lewis clearly regards, like Chaucer's 'Troilus,' as having been written under Jove: 'Those who have attempted to write poetry will know how very much easier it is to express sorrow than joy. That is what makes the *Epithalamion* matchless. Music has often reached that jocundity; poetry, seldom.'[40] Here in 'The Small Man' Lewis tries, with considerable success, to recreate Spenser's combination of 'jollity' and 'pomp' in his own blending of 'merriment' and 'trumpet blare.' Jove is both mentioned in the poem and evoked by its events and images: he is at once an actor in the drama (one of 'the dynasts seven') and the 'monarchal presence' felt throughout.

Jupiter appears, under various guises, in at least eight of Lewis's other poems.[41] We will reserve 'Quam Bene Saturno,' and *Dymer* for consideration in chapter 9. 'The Turn of the Tide' and 'The Day with a White Mark' will be touched on in later sections of this chapter. 'Le Roi S'Amuse'[42] tells how Jove created colours, vegetation, animal life, Aphrodite, Athene (Reason) and, with her, Man; the link between Jove and Reason will be mentioned further in chapter 10. A translation from a Latin poem by Milton does not require comment.[43] That leaves just two. We deal first with the Jupiter section of 'The Planets.' The following lines are the relevant portion:

Soft breathes the air
Mild, and meadowy, as we mount further
Where rippled radiance rolls about us
Moved with music—measureless the waves'
Joy and jubilee. It is JOVE's orbit,
Filled and festal, faster turning
With arc ampler. From the Isles of Tin
Tyrian traders, in trouble steering
Came with his cargoes; the Cornish treasure
That his ray ripens. Of wrath ended
And woes mended, of winter passed
And guilt forgiven, and good fortune
Jove is master; and of jocund revel,

Laughter of ladies. The lion-hearted,
The myriad-minded, men like the gods,
Helps and heroes, helms of nations
Just and gentle, are Jove's children,
Work his wonders. On his wide forehead
Calm and kingly, no care darkens
Nor wrath wrinkles: but righteous power
And leisure and largess their loose splendours
Have wrapped around him—a rich mantle
Of ease and empire.[44]

Ignoring the complex quantitative and alliterative technique, we focus on the imagery of these lines, noting some of the recurrent themes in Lewis's presentation of Jupiter: his 'kingly' aspect, his 'festal' aspect, his association with waves and with the passing of winter, 'winter passed / And guilt forgiven.' 'Jove's children' means mortals who exhibit his influence, not necessarily young people. 'Arc ampler' is a Ptolemaic detail, for the sweep of Jupiter's sphere is wider than that of Mars (the subject of the preceding lines). 'Faster turning' is also Ptolemaic (the nearer the sphere was to the Empyrean, the quicker its speed of rotation) but possibly has a post-Copernican meaning too, given that Jupiter, though the largest of the planets in the Solar System, has been found to be the quickest at turning on its own axis, performing one revolution in less than ten hours. (Lewis would have known this for he was a keen amateur astronomer and in his correspondence frequently details his observations of Jupiter in the night sky.[45]) The 'Isles of Tin' is a reference to the British Isles and, specifically, to Cornwall and the Scilly Isles, an area known to the merchantmen of Tyre as the Casseritides or 'Tin-Land,' because of its extensive natural deposits of this metal. In particular Lewis may be alluding to Himilco's voyage (c. 500 B.C.) round Spain to Great Britain, as recorded in Pliny.[46]

These Tyrian (that is, Phoenician) traders also make an appearance in the final Jovial poem which we have to consider here. It is the 'Prologue' to *Spirits in Bondage*, which opens thus:

As of old Phoenician men, to the Tin Isles sailing
Straight against the sunset and the edges of the earth,
Chaunted loud above the storm and the strange sea's wailing,
Legends of their people and the land that gave them birth—
Sang aloud to Baal-Peor, sang unto the horned maiden,
Sang how they should come again with the Brethon treasure laden,
Sang of all the pride and glory of their hardy enterprise,
How they found the outer islands, where the unknown stars arise;
And the rowers down below, rowing hard as they could row,

Toiling at the stroke and feather through the wet and weary weather,
Even they forgot their burden in the measure of a song,
And the merchants and the masters and the bondsmen all together,
Dreaming of the wondrous islands, brought the gallant ship along.[47]

The similarities between the 'Prologue' and 'The Planets' are obvious. In the one, Lewis gives us 'Tin Isles,' 'Phoenician men,' 'Brethon treasure,' 'toiling... through... weary weather'; in the other, 'Isles of Tin,' 'Tyrian traders,' 'Cornish treasure,' 'trouble steering.' Although the 'Prologue' does not explicitly mention Jupiter, it is so strikingly similar to the lines from 'The Planets' and it heads up a collection in which sidereal imagery is so prevalent, that it may justifiably be counted as one of Lewis's Jovial poems; in fact, the earliest.[48] Taken along with the Jovial treatment of the Arthurian legend in *That Hideous Strength*, these two poems show that Lewis repeatedly conceived of Jupiter as the presiding deity of Britain. He may have been consciously following the system propounded in the Ghâya, a tenth-century Arabic manual of astrology, in which each planet is said to hold sway over a certain region of the earth. Writing about the Ghâya, Seznec reports that 'Jupiter is the ruler of the Western countries, and for that reason, as the Ghâya expressly states, is the patron of the Christians.'[49] Lewis marked this sentence in his copy of Seznec that is now in the Wade Center at Wheaton.

Whether or not Lewis had encountered the Ghâya before he read Seznec (which was some time after 1953) is unknown. However, we know for certain that Lewis had reason to associate Jupiter not just with Christendom but with Christ himself well before that date. In 1948 he published *Arthurian Torso*, his study of Charles Williams's poetry. There he analyses 'Taliessin in the Rose Garden' (from *The Region of the Summer Stars*) in which Williams had written, with characteristic density, 'Pelles bleeds / below Jupiter's red-pierced planet.' About this mysterious image Lewis comments as follows:

> Williams assumes that the huge reddish spot which astronomers observe on the surface of Jupiter is a wound and the redness is that of blood. Jupiter, the planet of Kingship, thus wounded becomes, like the wounded King Pelles, another ectype of the Divine King wounded on Calvary.[50]

This interpretation of Jupiter's 'Eye', or Great Red Spot, helps shed light on the link Lewis makes in *That Hideous Strength* between Ransom (in his capacity as Fisher King) and *Fortuna Major*, and strengthens my contention that the novel is to be understood as the Jovial conclusion to the trilogy; it also helps to explain the work of fiction that followed *Arthurian Torso*. With this explicit connection between Jupiter and Christ firmly established in his mind, Lewis was readying

himself to capitalise upon all the scholarly and imaginative energy he had devoted to Jove over the years. Everything was now set for the final (and, as it
turned out, most successful) push in his campaign to express the Jovial character
and beat back the imaginative forces of Saturn. In that same year, 1948, Lewis
began to compose *The Lion, the Witch and the Wardrobe*.

Jupiter in *The Lion, the Witch and the Wardrobe*

In this first of the Narnia Chronicles, Lewis used Joviality in a new way. Jupiter
is not merely summarised, as he is in the *The Discarded Image*, nor merely
sketched, as he is in 'The Planets,' nor merely personified, as he is by Ransom
and Glund in *That Hideous Strength*. The closest precedent for what Lewis was
trying to achieve here is 'The Small Man Orders His Wedding' where Jove both
features as a named character within the poem and is evoked by the whole poem.
But in *The Lion, the Witch and the Wardrobe* Lewis attempts something more
sophisticated than in 'The Small Man' where he had done little more than paint
a Jovial tableau in the manner of Spenser's *Epithalamion*. In the first Chronicle
he goes inside Jove, as it were, and writes from within specifically Jovial imagery
so that Joviality is turned into a story. Jupiter is never named for our Contemplation, but is evoked in an Enjoyable fashion and, most significantly, Aslan
focusses and condenses (we might almost say, incarnates) that presiding spirit.
In the following analysis, we will look first at the *The Lion* as 'something made,'
then examine it in its capacity as 'something said.'

The Jovial *Poiema*

Perhaps the best way to approach the Joviality embodied in this tale is by looking
at the central turning-point in the story, the change from winter to summer. It
would be a mistake to think that this seasonal change is simply a way of depicting the advent of generic 'new life.' Of course it does depict 'new life,' but it
does more. It also conveys the peculiarly Jovial spirit, for Jupiter brings about
'winter passed' ('The Planets'), 'winter overgone' (*The Allegory of Love*); he
'overmatches' the 'freezing wastes' and 'unendurable cold' of Saturn and defeats
Frost, Wither, Winter, Stone, Steele, *et al*, producing 'torrents of melted snow'
(*That Hideous Strength*). In 'The Turn of the Tide,' a poem about the nativity at
Bethlehem, we are told that, at the birth of Christ, 'Saturn laughed and lost his
latter age's frost, / His beard, Niagara-like, unfroze.'[51] It would be inconsistent
to admit the presence of astrological imagery in all these earlier works and not
admit the distinct probability that Lewis was attempting to communicate a
similar thing in *The Lion*.

In *The Lion* the aestival influence of the Jovial Christ accounts for this key architectonic feature of the story: the overthrow of the White Witch's reign. She had made it 'always winter. Always winter and never Christmas; think of that!' (23); 'always winter in Narnia—always winter, but it never gets to Christmas' (42); 'always winter and never Christmas' (57); 'always winter and never Christmas' (98). But this Saturnocentric world is about to be brought to its end. Sumer is icumen in. To underscore the connection between Aslan's coming and the change of season, Lewis includes an 'old rhyme' which prophesies this very occurrence:

When he bares his teeth, winter meets its death,
And when he shakes his mane, we shall have spring again.

The great transition away from winter and toward summer starts in chapter 10 ('The Spell Begins to Break') and continues gradually throughout the book, culminating in the arrival at the sea in the final chapter. There is not space here to trace the full movement and all the light touches by which Lewis communicates this atmospheric change, but it is worth quoting the main section dealing with the thaw at the end of chapter 11 and the beginning of chapter 12:

Every moment the patches of green grew bigger and the patches of snow grew smaller. Every moment more and more of the trees shook off their robes of snow. Soon, wherever you looked, instead of white shapes you saw the dark green of firs or the black prickly branches of bare oaks and beeches and elms. Then the mist turned from white to gold and presently cleared away altogether. Shafts of delicious sunlight struck down on to the forest floor and overhead you could see a blue sky between the tree tops.

Soon there were more wonderful things happening. Coming suddenly round a corner into a glade of silver birch trees Edmund saw the ground covered in all directions with little yellow flowers—celandines. The noise of water grew louder. Presently they actually crossed a stream. Beyond it they found snowdrops growing.

"Mind your own business!" said the dwarf when he saw that Edmund had turned his head to look at them; and he gave the rope a vicious jerk.

But of course this didn't prevent Edmund from seeing. Only five minutes later he noticed a dozen crocuses growing round the foot of an old tree—gold and purple and white. Then came a sound even more delicious than the sound of the water. Close beside the path they were following a bird suddenly chirped from the branch of a tree. It was answered by the chuckle of another bird a little further off. And then, as if that had been a signal, there was chattering and chirruping in every direction, and then a moment of full song, and within five minutes the whole wood was ringing with birds' music, and wherever Edmund's eyes turned he saw birds alighting on branches, or sailing overhead or chasing one another or having little quarrels or tidying up their feathers with their beaks.

"Faster! Faster!" said the Witch.

There was no trace of the fog now. The sky became bluer and bluer, and now there were white clouds hurrying across it from time to time. In the wide glades there were primroses. A light breeze sprang up which scattered drops of moisture from the swaying branches and carried cool, delicious scents against the faces of the travellers. The trees began to come fully alive. The larches and birches were covered with green, the laburnums with gold. Soon the beech trees had put forth their delicate, transparent leaves. As the travellers walked under them the light also became green. A bee buzzed across their path.

"This is no thaw," said the dwarf, suddenly stopping. "This is Spring. What are we to do? Your winter has been destroyed, I tell you! This is Aslan's doing."

"If either of you mention that name again," said the Witch, "he shall instantly be killed."

While the dwarf and the White Witch were saying this, miles away the Beavers and the children were walking on hour after hour into what seemed a delicious dream. Long ago they had left the coats behind them. And by now they had even stopped saying to one another, "Look! There's a kingfisher," or "I say, bluebells!" or "What was that lovely smell?" or "Just listen to that thrush!" They walked on in silence drinking it all in, passing through patches of warm sunlight into cool, green thickets and out again into wide mossy glades where tall elms raised the leafy roof far overhead, and then into dense masses of flowering currant and among hawthorn bushes where the sweet smell was almost overpowering.

They had been just as surprised as Edmund when they saw the winter vanishing and the whole wood passing in a few hours or so from January to May. They hadn't even known for certain (as the Witch did) that this was what would happen when Aslan came to Narnia. But they all knew that it was her spells which had produced the endless winter; and therefore they all knew when this magic spring began that something had gone wrong, and badly wrong, with the Witch's schemes. And after the thaw had been going on for some time they all realized that the Witch would no longer be able to use her sledge. After that they didn't hurry so much and they allowed themselves more rests and longer ones. They were pretty tired by now of course; but not what I'd call bitterly tired—only slow and feeling very dreamy and quiet inside as one does when one is coming to the end of a long day in the open. Susan had a slight blister on one heel.

They had left the course of the big river some time ago; for one had to turn a little to the right (that meant a little to the south) to reach the place of the Stone Table. Even if this had not been their way they couldn't have kept to the river valley once the thaw began, for with all that melting snow the river was soon in flood—a wonderful, roaring, thundering yellow flood—and their path would have been under water.[52]

This passage expands to the full what Lewis had elsewhere summarised in a couple of words: 'winter passed,' 'winter overgone.' The mention of 'May' is especially notable, for he gives pride of place to May in his analysis of the theme of Jocundity in Spenser's *Mutabilitie Cantos*. It is a reminder of Henryson's Jupiter who is crowned with a garland 'Of flouris fair, as it had bene May.'

Jupiter's May crown leads us to the second major Jovial theme which we find constituting *The Lion, the Witch and the Wardrobe*: kingliness. This theme is introduced in the very first description of Aslan. The children are told that he is not a man, as they had assumed, but 'the King of the wood and the son of the great Emperor-beyond-the sea. Don't you know who is the King of the Beasts?' In case they missed it, they are told again, almost immediately, 'He's the King.' Aslan is 'the true king' who has a 'crown' and a 'standard'; he is 'royal, solemn,' 'royal and strong,' with a 'great, royal head.' Nowhere else in the Narniad is he 'royal.'[53] When the children finally encounter him, he is portrayed, as Glover has noted, like 'a medieval king in his cloth of gold pavilion and surrounded by his courtiers.' The theological messages that Lewis wishes to convey by means of this monarchical imagery will be discussed below. Our purpose here is to note that Aslan's kingship is only the most obvious form of sovereignty on display.

This is a tale in which kingliness cascades down from 'the Emperor' to 'the King of the wood' to the High King Peter, and thence to Susan, Edmund, and Lucy. Aslan shows Peter 'the castle where you are to be King' and the four thrones 'in one of which you must sit as King . . . you will be High King over all the rest.' The children's coronation will not confer a transitory or accidental attribute, but will represent a permanent and essential transformation: 'Once a king or queen in Narnia, always a king or queen' (as Aslan says in his final speech); 'Once a King in Narnia, always a King in Narnia' (as the Professor later confirms). It is Edmund's hatred of the source of true Kingship ('that awful Aslan') which drives the plot.

Edmund prefers the usurping 'Queen of Narnia and Empress of the Lone Islands' to the King of the beasts and the prospect of sharing sovereignty with his siblings. The White Witch has ensnared him with her declaration that she wants a boy 'who would be King of Narnia after I am gone'; and soon afterward she promises him, 'You are to be the Prince and—later on—the King.' Edmund is convinced this is his destiny; he thinks 'about Turkish Delight and about being a King ('And I wonder how Peter will like that?' he asked himself) and horrible ideas came into his head'; he wants 'to be Prince (and later a King) and to pay Peter out for calling him a beast'; he resolves to 'make some decent roads' when 'I'm King of Narnia' and this 'set him off thinking about being a King.' Eventually, however, he realises that he has been tricked and trapped: 'It didn't look now as if the Witch intended to make him King.' He finds himself bound to a tree and hears the sound of a knife being sharpened. The Witch hopes to confound the prophecy about her reign being over when the four thrones at Cair Paravel are filled by making sure that no more than three of them can be filled.

So we see that starkly opposing approaches to kingship are central to the storyline of this first Chronicle, and not only is Lewis interested in differentiating good kingship from bad, he is also concerned to associate good kingship with a certain set of resplendent material accoutrements. As a literary critic he was interested in images that conveyed the atmosphere of sovereignty typified by Solomon, Charlemagne, Haroun-al-Raschid, and Louis XIV, those kings who sat upon 'thrones of ivory between lanes of drawn swords and under jewelled baldachins.'[54] In *That Hideous Strength*, he had suggested this kind of grandeur, sketchily, in his depiction of Ransom's 'throne room' where he reclines in a space full of light upon a sofa placed on a dais under what seem to Jane to be 'massed hangings of blue.' In *The Lion* he goes further, supplying two descriptions of regal splendour. One is the pavilion where Aslan is first encountered in chapter 12: 'A wonderful pavilion it was—and especially now when the light of the setting sun fell upon it—with sides of what looked like yellow silk and cords of crimson and tent-pegs of ivory; and high above it on a pole a banner which bore a red rampant lion fluttering in the breeze.' The second description serves as the climax of the kingly theme, the coronation of the four children:

> In the Great Hall of Cair Paravel—that wonderful hall with the ivory roof and the west wall hung with peacock's feathers and the eastern door which looks towards the sea, in the presence of all their friends and to the sound of trumpets, Aslan solemnly crowned them and led them to the four thrones amid deafening shouts of 'Long Live King Peter! Long Live Queen Susan! Long Live King Edmund! Long Live Queen Lucy!'...So the children sat on their thrones and sceptres

were put into their hands.... And that night there was a great feast at Cair Paravel, and revelry and dancing, and gold flashed and wine flowed.[55]

In this passage Lewis is drawing on the descriptions of Solomon's court in 1 Kings 10 and 2 Chronicles 9 which are full of thrones, lions, gold, ivory, and peacocks. Jupiter is 'throne' and 'feast',' according to *Out of the Silent Planet*, and here the images of 'throne' and 'feast' (and also 'crown'), which have been recurrent terms throughout *The Lion*, show themselves to have grown to something of great constancy: in the moment of their crowning the children participate as fully as possible in the kingly spirit that bears up their world.

The two subjects which we have so far examined (kingliness and the passing of winter) are clearly fundamental to the book. They do not ornament the story: they comprise the story. But there are a good many other Jovial images that supplement these foundational ones. The question then arises: 'How far can we—indeed, should we—trace the other images in the book to Jupiter?' Although I aim to show that there are numerous tributaries (some sizeable, some mere rivulets) that supply further Joviality to *The Lion*, I do not propose to hunt them all down to the last drop, for, as Lewis himself wisely advises, 'it is the chief duty of the interpreter to begin analyses and leave them unfinished.'[56] Also, of course, the more minutely I trace the links, the more debatable certain small connecting points will inevitably become. Avoiding minutiae then, let us proceed by cross-referencing *The Lion* with the various Jupiter passages that preceded it in Lewis's oeuvre and with what is independently known of Jupiter from classical and medieval sources. By doing so we will discover that this opening Narnia tale is insolvent to the king of the gods.

If we look first at *That Hideous Strength*, we observe that it contains the prototype of both the wardrobe and the beavers. In Ransom's house is a large upstairs room 'which occupied nearly the whole top floor of one wing at the Manor, and which the Director [Ransom] called the Wardrobe.' It is in this Wardrobe that the heroes gather at the end of the story to select their various 'court dresses':

> If you had glanced in, you would have thought for one moment that they were not in a room at all but in some kind of forest—a tropical forest glowing with bright colours. A second glance and you might have thought they were in one of those delightful upper rooms at a big shop where carpets standing on end and rich stuffs hanging from the roof make a kind of woven forest of their own. In fact, they were standing amidst a collection of robes of state—dozens of robes which hung, each separate, from its little pillar of wood.[57]

This 'Wardrobe' is clearly a Jovial place: first, because it is located in Ransom's house; second, because the clothes it contains are described as 'festal garments' and 'robes of state'; and third, because the different outfits selected betoken the planets over which Jupiter holds sway. Mrs Dimble wears a flame-coloured robe with a great copper brooch to show that she is the personification of Venus (see below, chapter 8); MacPhee wears an ash-coloured, monastic-looking robe, showing that he is under the influence of Saturn (see below, chapter 9); Camilla is described as looking 'like starlight,' 'like a meteor.' These robes 'glow of themselves' as if lit with an unearthly light.

In *The Lion*, this image of the wardrobe is both simplified and developed. It is simplified because the wardrobe in the Professor's house now contains only Jovial costumes—the 'rich mantles' that the children find there, as we will note further below—and it is developed because it has now become a doorway to a Jovial world, or rather, it now contains that whole Jovial world.

Another thing that Lewis takes with him from *That Hideous Strength* into *The Lion* is the beavers. They appear in the earlier book in a striking passage where Dimble summons up a picture of how Britain used to be before it was an island, with 'wolves slinking, beavers building,' the Pre-Roman Britain of ogres and wood-wooses and 'little strongholds of unheard-of kings.' We have already noticed how Lewis habitually thought of Jupiter as the presiding deity of Britain, and it is not hard to imagine how he took this picture of the British Dark Ages, 'the dark pit of history which lies between the ancient Romans and the beginning of the English,' and simply covered it in snow to give him the setting for his first Narnia Chronicle. The Narnian beavers in their cosy dam become a little outpost of jollity in this pre-Jovial or de-Jovialised world; as does Tumnus, the faun from Roman mythology, with his red scarf and his lament for the lost days of 'jollification.' Into this sad world burst both the King of the Wood and the four great kings and queens who will reign under him at Cair Paravel, that castle which shines 'like a great star resting on the seashore.'

Turning now to the Jupiter section of 'The Planets,' we note certain other images and ideas that helped feed the creation of *The Lion, the Witch and the Wardrobe*.

First, according to the poem, Jupiter inspires the 'lion-hearted.' In the first Chronicle not only do we encounter the great lion, Aslan, but also another lion, who is very excited when he hears Aslan use the phrase 'Us Lions': 'Did you hear what he said? *Us Lions*. That means him and me. That's what I like about Aslan: no side, no stand-offishness. *Us Lions*. That means him and me.' Lewis once explained to a young correspondent that Aslan's leonine form was chosen because it 'meant the Lion of Judah'[58] (from Gen. 49:9 and Rev. 5:5). As with so much of what he wrote about the Chronicles this is true as far as it goes, but it is not the whole picture. In addition to the lion of Judah, Lewis meant the lion of Jupiter. His intention to express Joviality accounts for both Aslan and the other lion. Lewis's technique here is an echo of that iconographical ambiguity of sixteenth-century poets, of whom he wrote: 'It was not felt desirable, much less necessary, when you mentioned, say, Jove, to exclude any of his meanings; the Christian God, the Pagan god, the planet as actually seen, the planet astrologically considered, were all welcome to enrich the figure, by turns or even simultaneously.'[59] Thus here: the Jovial imagery informs both the Christological lion and the other lion at once. Significantly, 'other lions' never appear again in the other Chronicles, for the later books are written to embody and express planets other than Jupiter.[60]

Second, according to 'The Planets,' Jupiter is master of 'jocund revel, / Laughter of ladies,' an accurate description of the happy, laughing romp which Susan and Lucy (but neither of the boys) enjoy with the resurrected Aslan.

Third, according to 'The Planets,' Jupiter influences people so that they turn into 'helms of nations,' which is just what the four children have become by the end of the tale when they are hailed, crowned, sceptred and enthroned at the helm of Narnia.

Fourth, Jovial nations are 'just and gentle,' according to 'The Planets.' It is significant that Edmund is given the title 'Just,' and Susan the title 'Gentle.' Peter's title is also Jovial. He is known as 'Magnificent,' a designation which, on the face of it, has no specific link to the semantic field out of which Lewis habitually works when writing about Jupiter. On closer inspection, Lewis is deliberately perpetuating an error Spenser made ('due to some bad Latin translation') when he mistook Aristotle's *megaloprepeia* for *megalopsychia*, 'Magnificence' for 'Magnanimity.'[61] The Jovial character is 'magnanimous' according to the Jupiter passages of both *The Discarded Image* and *That Hideous Strength*. 'King Peter the Magnanimous' is the real meaning of his name. As for Lucy's title, 'Valiant,' this is perhaps derived from Giordano Bruno's presentation of virtues as cosmic potencies or constellations: 'In this view, *Fortezza* (valour) assumes the place of honour.'[62] Of the four children, Lucy is the closest to the King of the Beasts: it is therefore apt that she should be named after this sovereign moral quality, 'the palladium of every other virtue.'[63]

Fifth, according to the poem, Jupiter wears a 'rich mantle / Of ease and empire.' Both mantle and empire feature in *The Lion*, and both in good and bad modes. With regard to the clothing, the good mantles are the long fur coats that the children find in the wardrobe and that look 'more like royal robes than coats when they had put them on.' The bad equivalent is the Witch's 'mantle', and Edmund's abandonment of his robe at the Beavers' house is a clear indication of his preference for the wrong kind of kingship. With regard to 'empire,' Aslan's father is the 'Emperor' or 'Emperor-over-the-Sea,' and the usurping Witch lays claim to the title 'Imperial Majesty' and 'Empress.' As the story progresses and the Jovial influence works its effects, all names are 'restored to their proper owners.'

Sixth, according to 'The Planets,' Jupiter brings about 'wrath ended / And woes mended'; according to the book, 'Wrong will be right, when Aslan comes in sight, / At the sound of his roar, sorrows will be no more.' Compare Henryson's 'Testament of Cresseid': 'In his right hand he [Jupiter] had ane groundin speir, / Of his father [Saturn] the wraith [wrath] fra us to weir [ward off].'[64]

And finally we turn to a couple of Jove-related images, the oak and the minotaur, which may well, I suspect, have found their way into *The Lion* because of their Jovial connotations. The oak, sacred to Jupiter in classical literature, appears three times in the opening Chronicle: we read of 'bare oaks', 'sunny glades of oak', and of Aslan requiring the Witch to leave her wand behind her at 'that great oak' before the parley. The minotaur (the bull-headed man) was known in classical mythology as 'the infamy of Crete', an island especially associated with Jupiter (the Cretan Jove is mentioned in *That Hideous Strength*), and thrice we find minotaurs named among the monsters at the slaying of Aslan. It may be asked what connection there is between Jove and the non-oak trees mentioned in *The Lion* (the firs, beeches, elms, and so on), and between Jove and the non-minotaur monsters (the Efreets, Sprites, Orknies, Wooses, Ettins, and so forth). Is it not incumbent upon me to show that they too are present for a Jovial reason? But that is to press the argument further than I intend to take it. I am contending for an atmosphere or a flavour; I am not suggesting that Lewis pedantically selected every single word of this story for its unequivocal Joviality. When Lewis needed trees and monsters, almost any tree or monster might qualify for inclusion. The tree that must not be excluded, however, would be the oak, and the monster that obviously had to be enrolled would be the minotaur. Like seasoning in a dish, they supply that Jovial tincture which, I believe, Lewis knew he should not omit at these points of creative choice. As a skilful literary chef he understood both when to add salt and, just as important, when to stop adding it.

And this chapter too must conclude its identifications of Jovial imagery. As we draw to a halt we return to the start—'winter passed.' Not only does *The Lion* depict the coming of spring to the countryside, it also presents the thawing-out of the stone statues in the Witch's castle. Lewis is here partly drawing on Shakespeare's *Winter's Tale* and the revivification of the statue of Hermione, a scene which always moved him greatly.[65] The Jovial spirit manifest in *The Winter's Tale* is no doubt one of the main reasons that Lewis valued it so highly, but that aspect of the play is not so relevant for our present purpose as the structural oddities evident in the work. Lewis wrote of them:

The irregularities in *The Winter's Tale* do not impair, but embody and perfect, the inward unity of its spirit.... A supreme workman will never break by one note or one syllable or one stroke of the brush the living and inward law of the work he is producing. But he will break without scruple any number of those superficial regularities and orthodoxies which little, unimaginative critics mistake for its laws. The extent to which one can distinguish a just "license" from a mere botch or failure of unity depends on the extent to which one has grasped the real and inward significance of the work as a whole.[66]

Those comments are worth quoting because of a frequent criticism that has been levelled at *The Lion, the Witch and the Wardrobe*. Starting with Green,[67] several critics (none of them little and unimaginative) have cavilled at its inclusion of Father Christmas. Kilby calls his presence 'incongruous'; Glover says it 'strikes the wrong note'; Schakel opines: 'To be true to his fantasy world, Lewis should perhaps have created a Narnian equivalent to our Christmas instead of taking it into Narnia.'[68] All these are fair criticisms, on the face of it. But once one has grasped 'the real and inward significance of the work as a whole', its kappa element, one can see why Lewis was so adamant to retain Father Christmas, despite Green's objections. Father Christmas is, in modern culture, the Jovial character *par excellence*, loud-voiced, red-faced, and jolly. Of *The Lion*'s cast, he is the one most unmistakably born under Jupiter. In his copy of *The Golden Bough*, Lewis underlined Frazer's observation that Roman generals, celebrating a triumph, would wear the costume of Jupiter and would have their faces 'reddened with vermilion'[69] so as to imitate the rouged features of the divinity who had brought them victory. And this Jovial redness is part of the colour scheme of Lewis's palette: he uses it at many different points on the canvas and in both attractive and unattractive shades. The Witch has a 'very red mouth'; Maugrim the wolf has a 'great red mouth'; 'evil-looking red flames' rise from the torches of the Witch's accomplices. On the brighter side of the picture, honest Tumnus in his 'red muffler' has skin that is 'rather reddish' and his house is dug out of 'reddish stone'; the robin has 'such a red breast . . . you couldn't have found a robin with a redder chest'; and Peter's shield bears the emblem of 'a red lion, bright as a ripe strawberry.' Understood in this context, Father Christmas's gladdeningly red cheeks and his 'bright red robe (bright as holly-berries)' are not a botch, but entirely within the spirit of the book.

Moreover, his redness is strongly reminiscent of what George MacDonald, Lewis's 'master,'[70] once wrote about certain stories he had read in translation: 'As stories they just want the one central spot of red—the wonderful thing which, whether in a fairy story or a word or a human being, is the life and depth—whether of truth or humour or pathos—the eye to the face of it—the thing that shows the unshowable.'[71] Father Christmas standing against the snow represents just that splash of vivid red-on-white that a tale of Joviality requires. He is the eye to the face of this story, the eye of Jupiter.

The Jovial *Logos*

Having paid close attention to the *poiema* of the first Chronicle, we are now better equipped to consider the message that the story communicates, its *logos*.

And the first thing to point out is that, in one sense, as Marshall McLuhan famously said, 'the medium is the message.' The 'message' of the book is the book itself in all its fullness. To extract religious or philosophical or moral 'truths' from the story is to misread it, according to Lewis's critical principles (which, incidentally, are of considerable use in understanding his creative works). 'What it 'says' is the total, concrete experience it gives to the right reader—the πεπαι-δευμένος.'[72] Literary criticism can never replace that gestalt encounter between reader and text. However, it can provide useful markers by which the reader may navigate the next such reading, and in what follows I aim to achieve that end by comparing *The Lion* with *That Hideous Strength* and noting four main ways in which Lewis's handling of Joviality improves on the earlier work.

The first improvement has to do with simplification. *That Hideous Strength* is an overstuffed book: the Joviality on display there has to compete with so many other elements that it struggles to make an impression. In *The Lion*, Lewis homes in on his Jovial theme. Not only that: he chooses the ideal form for a Jovial story because the kingly aspect of Joviality perfectly suits the fairy-tale genre.[73] He was of the view that 'the world of fairy-tale...makes the heart and imagination royalist.'[74] No sincere fairy-tale ever began, 'Once upon a time there was a President and a First Lady,' but many have begun, 'Once upon a time there was a King and a Queen.' To pack a fairy-tale full of Jovial imagery, then, is to swim imaginatively with the current of the genre and as a result Lewis finds himself able to go much further into the imagery of kingship than he had in the Ransom book.

In *That Hideous Strength* Ransom and Glund were both kingly, but Maleldil, though also described as a king, had hardly any role to play. *The Lion*, in contrast, because it tries to do less overall, can do more with the particular theme of kingship and can extend it so that it is more fully used in the portrayal of the divine character. This again is to swim with the current, for it was Lewis's belief that 'the world of Christianity,' no less than the world of fairy-tale, 'makes the heart and imagination royalist.'[75] Lewis accepted the scriptural understanding of Christ as 'the King of kings' (Rev. 17:14; 19:16) and was of the view, with Hooker, that 'the universe itself is a constitutional monarchy.'[76] If he had lived to learn of Philip Pullman's 'republic of heaven'[77] he would not have regarded it as a satisfactory alternative to the traditional monarchical conception of the divine dwelling-place; he would have thought it an imaginative solecism because it is anthropocentric. A 'republic of heaven,' presumably with its own elected President, would be a Feuerbachian example of religion as projection, the creation of God in the citizens' own image.

Christianity makes the imagination royalist, in Lewis's view, because human kings (that is, good kings—things are defined by their perfection) are a reflection at the creaturely level of an aspect of divine nature which naturally attracts respect. 'Where men are forbidden to honour a king they honour millionaires, athletes, or film-stars instead: even famous prostitutes or gangsters. For spiritual nature, like bodily nature, will be served; deny it food and it will gobble poison.'[78] By the nature of their office, elected prime ministers and presidents could not elicit honour in the same manner as kings, Lewis thought, because their status is temporarily meritocratic, not innate or confirmed by religious sanction. However politically desirable a republic might be, it remains unable to compete imaginatively with monarchy because monarchy in principle more completely mirrors the nature of divine authority. One of the great imaginative advantages of the genre of fairy-tale or romance is to allow for the presentation of such a principle. In fairy-tale the author can leave behind the shallows of the 'realistic' novel, and is free to show the reader something better than mundane norms. What might it be like if human kings really did exhibit perfect kingship? *The Lion, the Witch and the Wardrobe* attempts an answer.

Aslan's kingly power is not self-assertive, but rests on a foundation of submissive acceptance to his Father's appointment. He will not work against 'the Emperor's magic' but demonstrates his complete devotion to it by dying to achieve Edmund's ransom. Aslan's father, the Emperor, named on six occasions, never features in the story in his own person, but nevertheless his presence is felt in this first book more than in any of the others; in fact, he is mentioned more often in this tale than in the rest of the septet put together. (He is not referred to at all in *The Silver Chair* or *The Magician's Nephew* and is mentioned only once in each of the other four stories.) The form of the 'perfect Empire' was one of the things beheld by Dante in the sphere of Jupiter, and the emphasis that Lewis places on the Emperor in this book is exactly what we should expect of one so engrossed by the *Paradiso*.

Peter's kingship, like Aslan's, is obedient to higher authority: when he first meets Aslan he apologises for the way he has treated Edmund ('I think that helped him to go wrong') and his sincerity is tested when, at Aslan's bidding, he risks his life to save Susan from the wolf. Later, Edmund learns the same lesson of willing subjection to higher authority in his private conversation with Aslan, and he acts accordingly in his apology to his siblings and in his courage on the battlefield. As Richard Harries observes, Edmund had wanted 'to make himself king, deceiving himself in the process,'[79] for accession and coronation are receptive, not proactive, rites. True human kingliness (taking its form from Christ) finds its authority in submission to the commands of the higher king and issues in service of the lower king, who in turn communicates royalty to the rank below him, and so on through all creation. This principle may have guided Lewis's choice of the name 'Cair Paravel,' a combination of 'cair' meaning *walled city* or *castle*, and 'paravail,' meaning *beneath* or *under* (a 'tenant paravail' holds property under another person who is himself a tenant). Cair Paravel thus means something like 'Castle Under Castle.'

Since Lewis believed humanity to be made in the image of God, he thought there would inevitably be a reflection of divine kingship in human nature, and it was for this reason that he was so deeply moved when he watched the coronation of Queen Elizabeth II: 'The pressing of that huge, heavy crown on that small, young head becomes a sort of symbol of the situation of *humanity* itself: humanity called by God to be His vice-gerent and high priest on earth, yet feeling so inadequate.... One has missed the whole point unless one feels that we have all been crowned and that coronation is somehow, if splendid, a tragic splendour.'[80] The paradox of 'tragic splendour' takes us back to his Jovial colour scheme and to that redness which suggests not just healthful exertion, merriment, and jollity, but also sacrificial blood (Lucy and Susan wipe away 'the blood and the foam' from Aslan's corpse as well as they can). The colour signifies both things at once; it is a powerfully ambivalent image.

This brings us to the second way in which *The Lion* improves upon *That Hideous Strength*: the priestly aspect of Joviality is more deftly managed. Unlike Ransom, Aslan brings no couple together in marriage (though his crowning of two boys and two girls together is a distant echo of this theme), but with respect to the sacrificial dimension of priestliness, Aslan's death for Edmund is a far deeper exploration of this subject than is Ransom's rather inconsequential bleeding heel. Ransom's woundedness has no particular dramatic significance in *That Hideous Strength*; it is merely a left-over from *Perelandra*. Its non-functioning aspect contributes to the impression that his Joviality is slightly theatrical. He has too many of the trappings of a role in proportion to the actions he is called upon to perform; there is a whiff of grease-paint in the Blue Room. On the one hand, he has a tremendous physical presence (strong, young, golden, bearded), but on the other hand, he is an invalid on a couch, at the mercy of his sidereal masters, and faint with longing for the Perelandrian Avalon. And it is these latter qualities which seem to linger in the minds of even quite sympathetic readers. Hence Dorothy Sayers cheerfully mocks Ransom for having become 'golden-haired and interesting,'[81] and Rowan Williams can say that Ransom is 'de-humanised,' 'disembodied.'[82] They have a point. Ransom's sacrificial aura, which he bought at a price in the caves of Perelandra, has become etiolated by the time of the third book. He has turned into a passive valetudinarian, a role which is unsuitable for a Jovial hero, however muscular his arms and shoulders remain.

But in *The Lion*, Aslan's sacrifice, which lays upon the altar the dearest and the best, is dramatically central. It is performative and effectual, not theatrical; this is kingliness in action, the tragic splendour of true goldenness, gentleness, and strength. As a consequence, the children's reactions to Aslan feel clean and honest. There is no frisson of masochism in their self-abasement before him. He has earned their deepest devotion.

However, the centrality of sacrifice in *The Lion* is a centrality in terms of plot and atmosphere, not in terms of its particular theology of atonement. The Narnian atonement is a means to an end, not an end in itself. As Kort points out: 'the children do not dwell on the sacrifice of Aslan. They know that it is grave, painful, and terribly significant, but they do not try to understand it.'[83] Kort is right. Lewis was not so much interested in *how* the atonement worked as in the fact *that* it worked.[84] 'How' questions, though useful up to a point, were, in his view, inexhaustible. We can never 'look at' the atonement from the outside, determining scientifically its means of operation, the relative quantities of human and divine action, the precise calibration of the juridical element. At some point we must simply Enjoy it as one feature of the divine life. Myers approaches the right kind of opinion when she says: 'the desired response to *The Lion, the Witch and the Wardrobe* is not to believe in the vicarious suffering of Christ but to *taste* it, as Jane tasted kingship in *That Hideous Strength*.'[85] The kingship offered to our palates in *The Lion* is a fuller-bodied kingship than that in the final Ransom book, and vicarious suffering is only one ingredient in it, but the principle Myers enunciates is correct.

This sacrificial bloodshed is not an end in itself, then; rather, it is important for what it achieves, the overthrow of all anti-festal forces as symbolised by the Saturnine winter. The third way in which *The Lion* improves upon *That Hideous Strength* is by a much fuller treatment of this important aspect of Joviality. In *That Hideous Strength* the 'sudden warmth' and the 'torrents of melted snow' are only very briefly dealt with and could in any case be considered as much the result of Venereal as of Jovial influence. Lewis might have met this objection by pointing out that he was only following Spenser, for whom 'a single emblem might have many meanings,'[86] but he might have agreed with the objection for he had doubts about the coherence of the novel.[87] His symbols are so numerous in this story that they sometimes get in the way of one another. Furthermore, the planetary gods in this third Ransom story occupy an awkward space between humanity and divinity, which leads Rowan Williams to complain, with some justification, that there is a confusion of the preternatural with the supernatural. It would be better to use the planets more clearly as symbols of the divine character and to focus on one planet in one book at a time so that its characteristics can be understood in an uncluttered context.

In *The Lion*, the aestival effect is the result of Jovial influence and no other. Edmund's heart gives 'a great leap (though he hardly knew why) when he realised that the frost was over,' for at root he recognises that the Queen is 'bad and cruel.' The Witch's defeat and the coming of summer are very explicitly said to originate with the Christ-figure: 'this is what would happen when Aslan came to Narnia.' Christ's miraculous demonstrations of power over Nature (so Lewis argued in *Miracles*) 'proclaim that He who has come is not merely a king, but *the* King, her King and ours';[88] Christ is 'the Captain, the fore-runner' who 'is already in May or June' while his followers on earth are still living 'in the frosts and east winds of Old Nature—for "spring comes slowly up this way."'[89] Here in *The Lion*, Lewis is able imaginatively to show Christ's followers catching up with their king, coming out of the 'cosmic winter' and entering into that 'cosmic summer' and the 'high mid-summer pomps' in which the Son of Man already dwells.[90]

By means of this aestival image, Lewis communicates the idea that divine kingship has practical and observable consequences: its effects are not limited to the interiors of individual souls, but are efficacious for the whole of society (releasing Narnia from dictatorship) and even for the non-human environment (trees and rivers and birds and animals all participate in this new spiritual season). The whole creation, which had been groaning in travail, is set free to share in the glorious liberty of the heirs of God. The transformation is universal.

And the universal nature of the change carries us over to the fourth and final way in which *The Lion* improves upon *That Hideous Strength*: Contemplation is exchanged for a rich mix of Contemplation and Enjoyment together. In *That Hideous Strength* Ransom and Jane and the others know that their world is being invaded by planetary powers on a mission from Maleldil. What is lacking from the book is an understanding of how Maleldil might be already present in Planet Earth before the mission is undertaken. There is no account given of divine presence in soul and spirit: only in *novitas*. But in *The Lion*, the children, and other characters are already upheld and surrounded by Jove. They may not know it at the Contemplative level, but they know it through Enjoyment. Their whole experience of the Narnian world is contained in a Jovial wardrobe where royal robes hang waiting, and the story's climax (coronation) is already implicit in its premise. Jupiter comes to the children not simply from outside, but also from inside, from their whole previous history in Narnia as it has been related in this book. The divine character is not a deistic god who has finally decided to do something for his created world; rather he is a theistic god who is always and already involved in its life.

But of course he is more than theistic, he is the Christian God. Though God is 'always everywhere' (thus the poem 'No Beauty We Could Desire'), there is an incarnation of divinity, an incarnation in *The Lion* of Joviality, which throws God's nature into relief before the conscious mind. 'The world which would not know Him as present everywhere was saved by His becoming *local,*' as Lewis writes in *Miracles*. Aslan's bodily presence is the concentration of the Jovial supra-personality in one place, one character. That kingship which cannot be seen in the transcendent Emperor (because it is beyond creaturely discernment) or in the broader Narnian cosmos (it escapes attention like a large word on a map) becomes focussed in the King of the Wood. Peter and his siblings can hear the name of this manifestation of Jupiter. Better, they can actually observe him: 'they saw what they had come to see.' Better still, they can touch him and even stroke him. As the theologian Austin Farrer puts it, the human mind is 'in the presence of God always' but remains unable to see him until God 'finds a mirror in created existence which will in some measure reflect his image.'[91] And we will find that, in each book, Aslan is the embodiment of the presiding planetary personality. His character and behaviour in each story are determined by that qualitative reality which each story embodies and expresses.

As the children come to know Aslan they find themselves living increasingly in his spirit. The presence of Joviality in the children is progressively evidenced by their fruit; it is by the children's actions that they discover of whose spirit they are. Edmund chooses the right kind of kingship; Peter accepts his destiny as the High King; Susan matures into a gracious queen whose hand is sought by 'kings of the countries beyond the sea'; Lucy learns to love and obey the King of the Beasts, and 'the princes of those parts desired her to be their Queen.' All four children grow up in the same spirit and mystically participate in its kingly life: 'So they lived in great joy and if ever they remembered their life in this world it was only as one remembers a dream.' They become saturated with Joviality: 'nothing is left over or outside the act' (which is how Lewis described the holistic nature of his own conversion).[92] Their bodies, their clothes, their pastimes, their very patterns of speech become regal as they increasingly submit themselves to Contemplation of the Jovial Aslan and to Enjoyment of the kingdom of his heaven.

Donegality

In the same way that the four children are inside this experience of spiritual growth, so readers are intended to Enjoy the Jovial influence in the book as its kappa element; it is the beam we are meant to 'look along,' not 'look at.' For Lewis to have disclosed the planetary theme would have been to destroy the very thing he was trying to achieve. (For a critic to discover it more than fifty years after the book's publication will, I hope, have no similarly destructive effect; for more on this see chapter 11.)[93] As he wrote in *The Discarded Image*, the characters of the planets 'need to be seized in an intuition rather than built up out of concepts.'[94] If we think about the atmosphere of *The Lion, the Witch and the Wardrobe* we are (assuming Lewis has been successful) intuiting the character of Jupiter.

In this first Chronicle, Aslan-as-Jupiter is responsible, so to speak, for the whole Narnian world and everything in it: royal coats in a wardrobe, melting snow, clemency, kings, lions, thrones, feasts, revels, oaks and rubicund faces. Winter does not pass simply as a convenient symbol of regeneration consequent upon the arrival of a Christ-figure: his arrival, his leonine form as the king of the beasts, his crowning of the children, and the passing of winter are all interdependent images which are selected in order to give expression to Jove, whose character is being deployed to present a theological message of considerable complexity and subtlety, within a framework of superficial simplicity.

We must not think that the Jovial elements are stuck on afterwards to a story that could otherwise exist without them. Rather we should understand that the whole enterprise is a Jovial undertaking. Because we know so well 'the Christ story' and can see it, apparently 'disguised,' at the centre of this tale, we are apt to assume that it was Lewis's starting point; and we feel supported in this belief when we hear Lewis say that he wanted to cast Christianity into an imaginary world, stripping it of its stained-glass and Sunday School associations. But in another place he said that 'Aslan came bounding into' an imaginative process that had already begun,[95] and it has been the purpose of this chapter to show that that earlier process was consciously configured under the rubric of Jove. The fundamental and governing imaginative scheme was Joviality; only secondarily was it allegory or 'supposition.' The artist took certain old familiar pictures in his head and threw them into a pot labelled 'Joviality'; and as they simmered there, marinading and reducing, they began to smell somewhat of the Gospel story. But only somewhat. The 'allegorical' elements are fragmentary and allusive, no more than that. And that is what we should expect if Lewis's basic imaginative co-ordinates (not, of course, his theological co-ordinates) were located elsewhere than the pages of the New Testament.

In *That Hideous Strength*, Jupiter is explicitly mentioned and held up for our attention, so much so that Lewis has to explain that this planetary deity has by some been 'confused with his Maker.' In *The Lion* there is no need for Lewis to have to distinguish Jovial imagery from the imagery used for the divine figure because they are kneaded into one: the whole Narnian universe is Jove's. Jovial symbolism is simply appropriated and put to work as Christian symbolism. In this respect, Lewis is ingeniously reversing the normal pattern of his medieval and renaissance sources. 'In Spenser, as in Milton and many others, Jove is often

Jehovah incognito.'[96] In *The Lion*, the divine figure is Jove incognito.[97] When we read of the 'spring air flooding into all the dark and evil places' we might assume that 'air' is being used in the typically Biblical sense to suggest the wind of the Holy Spirit. Yes, indeed, it is being used in that sense, but that is a convenient coincidence. The fundamental sense is an astrological sense: this 'spring air' is the means by which Jupiter accomplishes his peculiar *influenza*. But it is left unstated, implicit.

As we saw in chapter 1, the implicit quality or atmosphere of a romance was the artistic *ipseitas* by which Lewis set so much store throughout his life. In *The Lion* this *ipseitas* is not an atmosphere that the author discovers as he writes, but one which had an existence in his mind before he put pen to paper. He works within the images with which he is already well acquainted and moves about in that imaginal world so as to create a Jovial setting, a Jovial cast, and a Jovial story.

The images that he thus disposes are analogous to the musical notes that Holst arranged in the fourth item of his *Planets Suite*: 'Jupiter, the Bringer of Jollity.'[98] Lewis greatly admired Holst's orchestral interpretation of the planetary characters[99] and the *Suite* presumably played a part in the various sources of inspiration which led him to write the Chronicles. This presumption is made not only because of the obvious material similarity between the two works and the fact that Lewis knew and liked the piece, but also because he often drew comparisons between the composition of fairy-tale or romance and the sorts of effects that musicians were able to achieve. He thought that literary images, like musical motifs, should be richly expressive of mood, existing 'in every possible relation of contrast, mutual support, development, variation, half-echo, and the like.' He goes on:

> A story of this kind [a romance] is in a way more like a symphony than a novel. Corresponding to the themes of the musical form, the literary form has images . . . worked into the experience or the world of the characters . . . it is always the symphonic treatment of the images that counts, the combination that makes out of them a poetic whole.[100]

The Chronicles of Narnia likewise have their images 'worked into the experience or the world of the characters.' In this they do not differ from other romances (such as *The Faerie Queene*); where they do differ is that the 'poetic whole' that they are intended to evince consists of something that already existed in the author's mind and that he intended also to express by means of a Christological character who localises that 'whole.'

Since there seems to be no precise literary precedent for what Lewis was trying to achieve, it requires a new word. For the quality or atmosphere which arises out of a novel or a romance we may conveniently go on using such terms as 'quality' and 'atmosphere,' but for the deliberate encapsulation (or, at any rate, the deliberate attempt at encapsulation) of a *pre-existing* quality along with the presentation of an individual, Christological incarnation of that quality, it will be useful to have a new term. Surveying the various words which Lewis uses to denote *ipseitas*, I propose to elect 'Donegality' for this particular destiny. Biographically it is appropriate because Lewis loved Donegal all his life.[101] Semantically it is appropriate because of the imagined etymology: 'don' (as presiding intelligence) + egalité (equality), yielding a word meaning 'something equal to a presiding intelligence.' But the best reason to coin 'Donegality' in this sense has to do with Jovial imagery. Jupiter gives rise to 'the waves' joy and jubilee,' and Donegal, that Irish county whose craggy coast-line fronts the Atlantic, was the place which Lewis especially associated with the joy of waves. In *Surprised by Joy* he writes of enjoying 'glorious hours of bathing in Donegal . . . in which the waves, the monstrous, emerald, deafening waves, are always the winner, and it is at once a joke, a terror and a joy to look over your shoulder and see (too late) one breaker of such sublime proportions that you would have avoided him had you known he was coming. But they gather themselves up, pre-eminent above their fellows, as suddenly and unpredictably as a revolution.'[102]

Lewis is discreetly employing Jovial imagery here in his spiritual memoir. God is about to cause a revolution in his whole outlook, and Lewis 'would have avoided him' if he had had the chance. This God is Glund, 'like a long sunlit wave, creamy-crested and arched with emerald, that comes on nine feet tall, with roaring and with terror and unquenchable laughter.' This is 'the cloudily crested, fifty-league long, loud uplifted wave / Of a journeying angel's transit roaring over and through my heart.'[103] Lewis, 'like a surf-bather,' is 'happily overwhelmed.'[104]

'Donegality' then will serve very aptly as a technical term. By donegality we mean to denote the spiritual essence or quiddity of a work of art as intended by the artist and inhabited unconsciously by the reader. The donegality of a story is its peculiar and deliberated atmosphere or quality; its pervasive and purposed integral tone or flavour; its tutelary but tacit spirit, a spirit that the author consciously sought to conjure, but which was designed to remain implicit in the matter of the text, despite being also concentrated and consummated in a Christologically representative character, the more influentially to inform the work and so affect the reader.

'Donegality' applies especially appropriately to *The Lion, the Witch and the Wardrobe*, but will be used equally for it and for all the Chronicles of Narnia. Like the word 'angel' it denotes both the first rank and all the subsequent ranks of its kind.

The surf of Donegal—that is, the surf of Jove—makes an appearance in *The Lion, the Witch and the Wardrobe* and the passage in which it comes provides the orchestral climax of the story: musically the moment is *maestoso e appassionato*. After all the enclosed spaces (wardrobes, dams, caves) and all the tests and trials (the treachery of Edmund, the fight with the wolf, the sacrifice of Aslan, the defeat of the Witch), the children together finally gain sight of their royal home and have a first taste of the spacious days awaiting them as kings and queens in a Jovial world.

> They began marching eastward down the side of the great river. And the next day after that, at about teatime, they actually reached the mouth. The castle of Cair Paravel on its little hill towered up above them; before them were the sands, with rocks and little pools of salt water, and seaweed, and the smell of the sea and long miles of bluish-green waves breaking for ever and ever on the beach. And oh, the cry of the sea-gulls! Have you heard it? Can you remember?[105]

The two questions which the narrator asks the reader are curious: have we heard the sea-gulls' cry and can we remember it? Can we *remember* it? If we have heard it, of course we can remember it! But literal memory is not here the point. What the narrator is after is something far deeper, something beyond the limited time-frame of human life and human memory. He tells us that the waves break 'for ever and ever,' as if they belong to an eternal realm; and this is indeed what he is wanting to evoke, what the whole book has been intended to evoke: a glimpse of supernatural reality, a window onto an aspect of the divine nature. Lewis is attempting to awaken an awareness of Jupiter—kingly, magnanimous, festive, full-blooded Jupiter—in the hearts of readers born under Saturn.

FOUR

Mars

He is cold and strong, necessity's son.
—'The Planets' (lines 78–79)

A s he let his imagination range over the Ptolemaic heavens, Lewis found his strongest affinity with Jupiter, but his earliest interest was in Mars, one of Jupiter's many children. Hooper suggests that Lewis 'can't have been much more than five or six years old'[1] when he began, but did not complete, a story entitled 'To Mars and Back.' The extant fragment (reproduced in Gilbert and Kilby's *C. S. Lewis: Images of His World*) never even gets as far as Mars, so it is hardly surprising that it contains no Martial imagery: at this young age Lewis had not developed his technique of striking the keynote in the opening page or paragraph. However, other works of juvenilia, such as the poem entitled 'The Old Grey Mare,' about a knight and his steed, and his Boxonian stories, with their knightly hero, Samuel Macgoullah, point in the likely direction the imagery would have taken. The young Lewis was clearly enthralled by the chivalric ideal. At the age of seventeen he was delighted by his discovery of Chaucer's *Knight's Tale*, which he considered 'a perfect poem of chivalry.'[2] In that tale, the combat between Palamon and Arcite occurs, significantly, on a Tuesday, the day of Tyr, the Norse equivalent of Mars, and it is partly for this reason that Lewis writes, 'the character and influence of the planets are worked into the *Knight's Tale*.'[3] In this chapter we shall see how Lewis followed Chaucer's example as we trace his use of Martial imagery in poetry, scholarship, the Ransom Trilogy and in the donegality of his second Chronicle of Narnia, *Prince Caspian*.

Mars in Lewis's Poetry

At the age of eighteen Lewis volunteered for active duty and began gaining first-hand knowledge of army life, something he had hitherto only read about and imagined. He joined the Officers' Training Corps, was given a commission as a Second Lieutenant, and after a few months' training was sent to France. Arriving at the front-line trenches on his nineteenth birthday, he saw most of his action at Fampoux and Monchy before being wounded in the Battle of Arras in the spring of 1918. In *Surprised by Joy* he described this whole military experience as 'an odious necessity.'[4]

Necessity is a major feature of the symbolic value that Lewis, as a poet, located in Mars. The god of war is 'necessity's son,' as he put it in 'The Planets.' The complete Martial section runs as follows:

> But other country
> Dark with discord dins beyond him [Sol],
> With noise of nakers, neighing of horses,
> Hammering of harness. A haughty god
> MARS mercenary, makes there his camp
> And flies his flag; flaunts laughingly
> The graceless beauty; grey-eyed and keen,
> —Blond insolence—of his blithe visage
> Which is hard and happy. He hews the act,
> The indifferent deed with dint of his mallet
> And his chisel of choice; achievement comes not
> Unhelped by him;—hired gladiator
> Of evil and good. All's one to Mars,
> The wrong righted, rescued meekness,
> Or trouble in trenches, with trees splintered
> And birds banished, banks fill'd with gold
> And the liar made lord. Like handiwork
> He offers to all—earns his wages
> And whistles the while. White-feathered dread
> Mars has mastered. His metal's iron
> That was hammered through hands into holy cross,
> Cruel carpentry. He is cold and strong,
> Necessity's son.[5]

The depiction of Mars given in these lines is finely balanced. Lewis knows that Mars is a bad planet, *Infortuna Minor*, and so he readily acknowledges Martial cruelty, trouble, haughtiness, gracelessness, mercenariness, insolence, coldness. On the other hand, he knows that, above the orbit of the Moon, there is nothing bad *per se*. And so we find listed alongside many Martial vices, many Martial virtues: righting wrongs, rescuing the meek, laughter, beauty, keenness, blitheness, happiness, achievement, courage, strength. He balances these positive and negative qualities not because he thought Mars innately ambiguous, like Luna, but because Mars is indifferent to his effects: 'all's one to Mars.' When 'hired' by evil, Mars will work his violent work to evil ends. When hired by good, he will work just as hard, but for a worthy purpose. Mars is not necessarily evil; rather his is the spirit which, used aright, enables hard but necessary tasks to be accomplished. Even the crucifixion of Christ may be considered a project carried out under the influence of Mars: 'His metal's iron / That was hammered through hands into holy cross.' The poem does not specify whether Mars inspired the evil crucifiers or strengthened the innocent crucified or did both things at once.

Other poems in which Martial imagery may be traced include three early efforts: 'Exercise on an Old Theme,' which has chivalry as its subject matter, and 'To the Gods of Old Time' and 'Sonnet,' in both of which Ares makes an appearance.[6] The Norse Ares, Tyr, whose hand was bitten off by a wolf, appears in a later poem, 'A Cliché Came Out of Its Cage,' and we hear of 'the hard virtue of Mars' in 'The Adam at Night.' Two of his narrative poems, 'The Queen of Drum' and 'Launcelot,' also feature Martial symbolism. In the former we are told that it is 'In Paphos, Sir, not midst the watchful stars / Of public heaven, does Venus welcome Mars.'[7] In the latter we are given an extended celebration of the Arthurian knight, Sir Launcelot, and learn how 'saving and calamity together make / The Advent gospel, telling how the heart will break / With dread, and stars, unleaving from the rivelled sky.'

Mars in Lewis's Scholarship

Despite his interest in Launcelot and his love of chivalry in general, Lewis writes less about Mars in his scholarship than he does about any of the other planets, and the short paragraph that he devotes to Mars in *The Discarded Image* will be spliced into other portions of this chapter instead of receiving its own separate treatment here. However, it will be worth spending a little more time on the question Lewis raises of how there come to be malefical planets in the heavens beyond Luna, a part of the firmament which is supposed to be unfallen and perfect. Clarifying this issue will be of use to us in the remainder of this chapter and even more so, in a later chapter, in connection with Saturn, *Infortuna Major*. The answer Lewis finds is that

> The fault lies not in the influence but in the terrestrial nature which receives it. In a fallen Earth it is permitted by Divine justice that we and

our Earth and air respond thus disastrously to influences which are good in themselves. 'Bad' influences are those of which our corrupt world can no longer make a good use; the bad patient makes the agent bad in effect.... If all things here below were rightly disposed to the heavens, all influences... would be extremely good (*optimos*). When an evil effect follows them, this must be attributed to the ill-disposed subject.[8]

This understanding helps explain why Lewis, the amateur astronomer, was prepared to describe Mars negatively: in his correspondence he mentions 'the eye of baleful Mars—very visible these nights,'[9] using 'baleful' as short-hand for 'having an influence that is effectively baleful because of the nature of its recipient.' But essentially, Mars is no more baleful than Jupiter or any of the planets. Martial influence qualifies a person to become as murderous as Attila only when the influence is turned the wrong way. Taken aright, Mars strengthens noble warriors and gives resolve to the martyr. Dante, in fact, went so far as to make his Mars the heaven of martyrs—partly for the obvious reason that martyrs usually die a violent death, but partly, Lewis thinks, because of 'a mistaken philological connection between *martyr* and *Martem*.' This understanding of the fundamentally good nature of Mars also helps explain why, in *Out of the Silent Planet*, it is depicted as such a pleasant place. Despite his effect on some ill-disposed men, Mars is not evil in his own nature, and 'Martians may be delightful creatures.'[10]

Mars in the Ransom Trilogy

Out of the Silent Planet

In the first volume of his Ransom Trilogy, Lewis gives Mars the name Malacandra and locates most of the story there. The planet is not merely the setting for the drama, its temper is also an actor of sorts in that drama. Following Ransom's arrival on Malacandra, every incident and image is designed to communicate the Martial spirit, for 'What's the excuse for locating one's story on Mars unless "Martianity" is through and through used?... Emotionally and atmospherically *as well as* logically.'[11] The principal Martial element that *Out of the Silent Planet* does *not* contain is an active Christological character; that would come only with *Prince Caspian*.

The most striking feature of Malacandrian 'Martianity,' in terms of imagery, is verticality. Throughout the book we encounter things that are described as high, narrow, steep, pointed, elongated, 'needling.' We find soaring columns, pinnacles, pillars; the vegetation which Ransom first encounters is likened to organ-pipes and rolls of cloth standing on end. Certain unnamed creatures whom Ransom sees just after his arrival are compared to giraffes; mountains are likened to pylons. He meets *sorns*, who are creatures of giant stature, cadaver-ously lean; also *hrossa*, who are 'six or seven feet high and too thin for [their] height, like everything in Malacandra.' The third rational species is *pfifltriggi*, miners and artisans, who, being associated with the underground world, are the only group who are not tall and thin. They are the social base of Malacandra on whom the other two species rely: the hrossa live above them, higher up in the valleys (the *handramit*), and the sorns live higher still, close to the table-land (the *harandra*). Thus, built into the social topography of Mars we find again the 'theme of perpendicularity—the same rush to the sky.'

This perpendicularity is a manifestation of Mars's masculinity. Lewis, though no follower of Freud, was of course aware of the use that could be made of phallic imagery, and he is clearly deploying it here. Although each species on Malacandra is male and female, the planet as a whole is masculine,[12] just as Perelandra (Venus) is feminine, even though it has a king as well as a queen. The repeated images of height and uprightness connote the taller stature of the male vis-à-vis the female, the straight lines of the male musculature and the phallus. But once we have acknowledged the phallic aspect, we must not automatically conclude that perpendicular imagery is simply sexual. It is not simple, but complex. The complexity Lewis finds in such imagery is perhaps best expressed if we refer to *Till We Have Faces* and say that Malacandra is a 'weaponed' world, where 'weaponed' means a man who is not a eunuch.[13] A key artefact of Ma-lacandrian craft is the spear. This simultaneously serves as a token of war and of maleness. The hrossa long to kill the monstrous *hnakra* with a 'straight spear.' Ransom, enrolled in the hnakra-hunt, finds himself in a boat with a 'pile of throwing-spears between his knees.' It is this weapon which Lewis uses later on in the trilogy as the characteristic symbol of Mars. When Ransom tries to summarise the difference between Mars and Venus, 'he thinks that the first held in his hand something like a spear, but the hands of the other were open with the palms towards him.'[14] The Martial spear does not 'represent' the penis any more than it 'represents' war. It represents both in one of those primal unities that Barfield identified and that fascinated Lewis.

In addition, then, to maleness, the perpendicular imagery symbolises the warring element of the Martial spirit. War—against the *hnakra*—is an essential part of Malacandrian life. It is the danger posed by these aquatic monsters that makes the forests bright and the water warm and love sweet. Although the hrossa hate the hnakra as their enemy, they also respect him as a necessary element of their own identity.

Ransom observes 'the war-like nature' of the preparations for the hnakra-hunt and it speaks to something long-sleeping in his blood. The Martial influence—'something in the air he now breathed'—is making Ransom strengthen and become a man, a hunter. Early in the book we learn that 'the gap between boyhood's dreams and his actual experience of the [Great] War had been startling.' (Ransom had fought on the Somme, like Tolkien, on whom he may be partly based.) We are reminded of that immaturity when later we discover that he could hardly ride a trotting horse when he had been 'in the army.' He is frightened before the hunt, but the hunt 'was necessary, and the necessary was always possible.'[15] His participation in it gives him a 'new-found manhood'; and when he turns out to be the hnakra-slayer we are told that 'he had grown up.' In short, *Out of the Silent Planet* is, as Lewis elsewhere puts it, Ransom's *enfances*.[16] We have already examined the culmination of his development when he becomes kingly in *That Hideous Strength*. The mid-point of his journey, in *Perelandra*, will be looked at in chapter 8.

Before leaving *Out of the Silent Planet* we must comment upon two other important images in the book. The first is the great age of Malacandra. Ransom is told it 'is older than your own world,' that its history extends to a time before there was life on Thulcandra. Its surface (the harandra) long ago became uninhabitable and the 'old forests' there have turned to stone; now it is covered by 'the bones of ancient creatures; it was once full of life and noise. It was then these forests grew, and in and out among their stalks went a people that have vanished from the world these many thousand years.' As Lewis reminded one of his correspondents, 'Malacandra belongs to the old order.'[17] Its antiquity is part of its masculinity, a quality opposite to the youth-giving qualities of Perelandra, and intended, perhaps, to put us in mind of the Adam who lived in Eden before the creation of Eve.

The second important image, which is linked to the first, is that of the tree. The ancient woods, now petrified, on the harandra, are not the only forests on the planet. The pfifltriggi live in 'forest lowlands'; the hrossa live surrounded by forests (mentioned innumerable times throughout the story); the sorns are likened to trees; at Meldilorn Ransom comes across 'such trees as man had never seen'; and in the liturgy for the dead hrossa vegetation is a key element in the funerary rite.

At first glance it might appear that this arboreal imagery is just a variation on the theme of perpendicularity. On closer inspection it turns out to be a fundamental aspect of the planet's presiding deity and it reinforces the sense of Malacandra being an archaic world. Mars was not always or only a god of war. Originally, he was a god of vegetation and fertility, the husband of the vestal Rhea Silvia, as Lewis knew (in *Arthurian Torso* he mentions the 'twins whom Rhea Silvia bore to Mars and who were suckled by a wolf'); his functions were rustic. Under the name of *Mars Silvanus* (who later became a god in his own right), he lived in forests and mountains and looked after the well-being of cattle. Among the plants and trees that were dedicated to him were the dog-wood, the fig-tree, and the laurel; the wood-pecker, the wolf, and the horse were creatures especially associated with his name. He was the spring-time divinity (the vernal month of March became consecrated to and named after him) and *Mars Gradivus* ('to become big, to grow') was another of his titles. His warrior functions only came later, but in the end they superseded his former roles, which then became the preserve of Liber and Ceres. When he became the god of battle, Mars retained his former title of *Gradivus*, but it had changed its meaning and was now connected with the verb *gradi*, 'to march.' Lewis would have known all this from—among other sources—Cato the Elder[18] and Frazer's *The Golden Bough*.[19]

This helps to explain why Ransom's visit to Mars is not the occasion for much fighting. To be sure, we are shown the ritual hnakra-hunt and we are told that the Oyarsa of Malacandra once fought a 'war' against the Oyarsa of Thulcandra; the Oyarsa also tells Ransom to 'fight' Weston and Devine. But the specifically militaristic happenings and imagery are not the most obvious aspects of Malacandra. This is partly because we see the planet through the eyes of Ransom, who suffers alongside Hyoi (the martyr), rather than becoming murderous (Attila-like), as Weston and Devine do, and we find it odd that the Martial spirit should be as much evident in the former as in the latter. Partly, the absence of war is owing to the fact that the Malacandrian Oyarsa is one of the 'subjects of Maleldil' and therefore, despite his ability to inspire war, has an essential 'peace.' But mostly it is because Lewis is drawing on the god's origin as a vegetation deity to supplement and balance the militaristic aspects.

We leave the last word on Malacandra to Lewis's theologian friend, Austin Farrer, who, after speculating in *Saving Belief* about the existence of hypothetical races on other planets, rather idiosyncratically includes a little comic poem upon *Out of the Silent Planet*. Farrer advises his readers:

> Go aboard. I will leave you and Lewis in orbit;
> With him for your pilot, perhaps you'll
> Encounter the Martian mind, and absorb it;
> I'm backing to earth in my capsule.[20]

That Hideous Strength

Having encountered the Martian mind, absorbed it, and come back to earth, Ransom obeys the Oyarsa's command to fight his enemies. He finds himself at the head of those forces, human and planetary, who are going to do battle with 'the Bent One' on Thulcandra, and he is well equipped to lead them for he has 'learned war' in his monomachy with Weston in *Perelandra*.[21] The Martial element in *That Hideous Strength* has three main manifestations: the growing conflict between the N.I.C.E. and St. Anne's; the descent of Malacandra in chapter 15; and the individual story of Mark Studdock.

THE CONFLICT BETWEEN THE N.I.C.E. AND ST. ANNE'S

In terms of the conflict between the villains of the N.I.C.E. and the heroes of St. Anne's, Mars appears, on the face of it, to influence only the former. We hear Feverstone remarking on the need for 'a real war with real casualties,' Straik promising 'violence,' and Frost mentioning the 'sixteen major wars' which help constitute his 'plan of campaign.' Their 'army' mounts an 'invasion' of Edgestow, catching Bracton College 'in the net of necessity' and establishing 'a terror.' By the time we get to chapter 10 ('The Conquered City') Jane has been 'tortured' and Edgestow 'occupied.' The N.I.C.E. splinter Bragdon Wood with 'the rattle of iron,' '*saeva sonare verbera, tum stridor ferri tractaeque catenae.*'[22] There are machine-guns, barricades, and manufactured riots, and the whole operation seems to be going largely their own way until we reach chapter 11, 'Battle Begun.'

'Battle has started,' say Dimble and Ransom. The heroes' motley 'army' has seemed slow to engage the enemy, despite its declared willingness 'both to kill and to die.' It is not until more than half way through the book that Ransom announces, 'We're going into action at last.' Jane's dreams have finally given them something to go on and even now the plan is very roundabout. All they have in mind is the capture of Merlin, so that the N.I.C.E. are not able to press him into service first. Dimble, Denniston, and Jane, armed only with a revolver, set out to find him. But they do not fire any shots, nor indeed do they find him. He turns up at St. Anne's of his own accord, and no explanation for his arrival is given. We are to understand that the 'passion of patience,' in which their heroism largely consists, has paid off. The company at St. Anne's have, in fact, been just as Martial as their opponents, but since they are turning his influence to good effect, it makes them into martyrs: they courageously witness to truth in spite of danger, and Merlin is providentially drawn to their side.[23] He is told of the dire predicament in which Logres stands, offers his help, but confesses he is 'no longer much of a man of war.' Ransom declares: 'I have stood before Mars himself in the sphere of Mars and before Venus herself in the sphere of Venus. It is their strength, and the strength of some greater than they, which will destroy our enemies.' This brings us to the second main Martial feature of the story, the actual descent of Mars in chapter 15.

THE DESCENT OF MALACANDRA

Lewis presents the arrival of the Martial god as follows:

Down in the kitchen MacPhee sharply drew back his chair so that it grated on the tiled floor like a pencil squeaking on a slate. "Man!" he exclaimed, "it's a shame for us to be sitting here looking at the fire. If the Director hadn't got a game leg himself, I'll bet you he'd have found some other way for us to go to work." Camilla's eyes flashed towards him. "Go on!" she said, "go on!" "What do you mean MacPhee?" said Dimble. "He means fighting," said Camilla. "They'd be too many for us, I'm afraid," said Arthur Denniston. "Maybe that!" said MacPhee. "But maybe they'll be too many for us this way too. But it would be grand to have one go at them before the end. To tell you the truth I sometimes feel I don't greatly care what happens. But I wouldn't be easy in my grave if I knew they'd won and I'd never had my hands on them. I'd like to be able to say as an old sergeant said to me in the first war, about a bit of a raid we did near Monchy. Our fellows did it all with the butt end, you know. "Sir," says he, "did ever you hear anything like the way their heads cracked." "I think that's disgusting," said Mother Dimble. "That part is, I suppose," said Camilla. "But ... oh if one could have a charge in the old style. I don't mind anything once I'm on a horse." "I don't understand it," said Dimble. "I'm not like you, MacPhee. I'm not brave. But I was just thinking as you spoke that I don't feel afraid of being killed and hurt as I used to do. Not tonight." "We may be, I suppose," said Jane. "As long as we're all together," said Mother Dimble. "It might be ... no, I don't mean anything heroic ... it might be a *nice* way to die." And suddenly all their faces and voices were changed. They were laughing again, but it was a different kind of laughter. Their love for one another became intense. Each, looking on all the rest, thought, "I'm lucky to be here. I could die with these." But MacPhee was humming to himself:

King William said, Be not dismayed, for the loss of one commander.[24]

Upstairs it was, at first, much the same. Merlin saw in memory the wintry grass of Badon Hill,[25] the long banner of the Virgin fluttering above the heavy British-Roman cataphracts, the yellow-haired barbarians. He heard the snap of the bows, the *click-clack* of steel points in wooden shields, the cheers, the howling, and the ring of struck mail. He remembered also the evening, fires twinkling along the hill, frost making the gashes smart, starlight on a pool fouled with blood, eagles crowding together in the pale sky. And Ransom, it may be, remembered his long struggle in the caves of Perelandra. But all this passed. Something tonic and lusty and cheerily cold, like a sea breeze, was coming over them. There was no fear anywhere: the blood inside them flowed as if to a marching-song. They felt themselves taking their places in the ordered rhythm of the universe, side by side with punctual seasons and patterned atoms and the obeying Seraphim. Under the immense weight of their obedience their wills stood up straight and untiring like caryatids. Eased of all fickleness and all protestings they stood: gay, light, nimble, and alert. They had outlived all anxieties; care was a word without meaning. To live meant to share in this processional pomp. Ransom knew, as a man knows when he touches iron, the clear, taut splendour of that celestial spirit which now flashed between them: vigilant Malacandra, captain of a cold orb, whom men call Mars and Mavors,[26] and Tyr who put his hand in the wolf-mouth.

In this powerful passage Lewis is attempting to convey, as he put it, 'the *good* element in the martial spirit, the discipline and freedom from anxiety,' as distinct from the evil elements that he thought were present in Holst's *Planets*.[27] This aspect of Mars's influence reminds us of Ransom's march to Meldilorn in *Out of the Silent Planet*, which he performs confidently and soberly 'in the clear light of an accepted duty'; it is his 'resolution,' rather than his desire, that 'drives him up the road' with a kind of 'mechanical rhythm.' In *That Hideous Strength* we see a similar sort of calm and determined dutifulness arise out of the experience of Mark Studdock.

MARK STUDDOCK

Mark, as his name indicates, has a special connection with Mars. Although 'Mark had never seen war,' he is to be tried in his own personal battle with the N.I.C.E. Frost is determined to bring Mark to that state of subjugation where obedience is, ever after, 'a matter of psychological, or even physical necessity.' Mark, who had in childhood imagined himself as a 'hero and martyr,' realises that he is facing a 'straight fight,' and that now he will find out the truth of his childhood fancies. He finds that this prospect, 'after the long series of diplomatic failures, was tonic.' He pictures himself 'in the front-line: Jane was almost a non-combatant.'

The moment of martyrdom (that is, of witnessing to Christ despite danger) arrives when Mark is required, but refuses, to trample on a crucifix, a scene that Rowan Williams has approvingly described as 'the gospel with knobs on.'[28] Mark, 'thinking hard,' looks down at the defenceless wooden figure beneath him, at its wooden hands 'nailed and helpless,' and the object becomes for him 'a picture of what happened when the Straight met the Crooked, a picture of what the Crooked did to the Straight, what it would do to him if he remained straight. It was, in a more emphatic sense than he had yet understood, a *cross*.' He remains 'straight,' identifying his own predicament with that of Christ, and finds himself 'frightened by the very fact that his fears seemed to have momentarily vanished.' He, so to speak, accepts the imprint of the 'iron / That was hammered through hands into holy cross,' as he turns to Frost and says: 'It's all bloody nonsense, and I'm damned if I do any such thing.' Mark has passed the test and has lived up to his name. By choosing to imitate the example of Christ and to 'go down with the ship,' he makes himself patient of Mars's good effects. He becomes strong enough to accomplish the hard but necessary task.

Consequently, Mark acquires the status of a Christian knight and is therefore able to discover the true meaning of the word 'lady,' which before had only ever been 'part of his vocabulary' either as a 'pure form or else in mockery.' He now perceives that he has been a boor, that he has treated his wife with an offensively proprietorial spirit, 'as if he were native to that fenced garden and even its natural possessor.' At the end of the story, in his connubial reunion with Jane, Mark embodies 'the typically medieval theme of the proud young man (Bayard-Troilus) tamed by Venus.'[29] Botticelli's 'Mars and Venus' was a particular favourite of Lewis's, and a copy of it hung in his rooms at Magdalen College.[30] The Studdocks' conjugal embrace is his literary homage to that painting, as well as the resolution of the trilogy. In myth, Mars and Venus had a child, Harmonia: in *That Hideous Strength*, the story ends with Mark and Jane about to become parents, helping bring harmony to planet Earth in the form of that child who will be the new Pendragon.

Although he had thus brought the Ransom Trilogy to its conclusion, Lewis's imaginative involvement with all things Martial was far from satisfied. In the second Narnia Chronicle, to which we now turn, he revisits the theme he had first tackled when five or six years old, taking the four Pevensie children, as it were, 'to Mars and back.'

Mars in *Prince Caspian*

The Martial *Poiema*

Glover calls *Prince Caspian* a 'chivalric romance'[31] and Myers notes the central importance of the image of 'plant life.'[32] Between them they have identified the two main aspects of the Martial influence—militarism and silvanism—under which the second Chronicle is written.

The military theme is the stronger, for Lewis is chiefly motivated to make his readers 'look along the beam' of medieval chivalry.[33] The four Pevensie children find that they have arrived in Narnia 'in the middle of a war.' The war in question is 'the Great War of Deliverance,' as it is referred to in a later Chronicle, or simply the 'Civil War' in Lewis's 'Outline of Narnian History.'[34] It is 'a real war to drive Miraz out of Narnia' and restore the kingdom to Caspian. At the start of the story he is a mere boy, hardly aware of the Martial spirit which is already abroad. When Glenstorm tells Caspian: 'I and my sons are ready for war. When is the battle to be joined?,' Caspian replies that he had 'not been thinking of a war.' Glenstorm asks why it is, then, that he goes 'clad in mail and girt with sword'; he informs him that the omens are good: the planets foretell success. Nerved, Caspian thinks it 'quite possible that they might win a war and quite certain that they must wage one,' so he convenes a 'Council of War.' The Council authorises action and Caspian leads the skirmishing forces as they engage the usurper's army. Once the Pevensies arrive, Peter challenges Miraz to 'monomachy.' Miraz is killed, not by Peter as it turns out, but by one of his own men, Glozelle,[35] after which 'full battle' is joined.

This brief summary mentions only the more important Martial events (good and bad) in the story. There are numerous subsidiary episodes, too: the children's rediscovery of their armour, the rescue of the dwarf from the soldiers, the swordsmanship and archery test, the revelation that Caspian's father was murdered, Nikabrik's urge to kill the prince, the arrow attack on the children in the wood, the fight with the werwolf and the hag. The cast-list consists very largely of military figures: 'armies,' 'warriors,' 'messengers,' 'enemies,' 'captains,' 'sentries,' 'sentinels,' 'knights,' and 'scouts.' The properties department is filled with 'weapons,' 'mail-shirts,' 'helmets,' 'horns,' 'hauberks,' 'daggers,' 'bows,' 'shields,' and 'swords.' 'Marches,' 'combat,' 'attacks,' 'salutes,' and 'sorties' are the dramatic business in a setting of 'battlements,' 'strongholds,' 'towers,' 'castles,' and 'camps.'

It may be enquired what other language Lewis could have used to tell a war-story. The question is worth asking. Simply because the book deals largely with military events need not mean that it was deliberately crafted to convey a Martial atmosphere. We must look at the text more closely to demonstrate donegalitarian intent.

Three lists are illuminating for the item which appears first. In the list of things which the children find in the treasure chamber, the first item mentioned is the 'suits of armour.' In the list of memories that the children have of the Golden Age, the first thing they recall is 'the battles.' In the list of subjects which Caspian is taught, the first is 'sword-fighting.'

Historical references are also telling. Lucy informs Trumpkin that his account of Narnian history is 'worse than the Wars of the Roses'; Peter mentions the 'Crusaders.' We learn that Caspian's distant ancestor was 'the Conqueror,' for the Telmarines came to power in Narnia by conquest and not (as the four children did in the first book) by divine election.

These lists and references (which could easily have been different without affecting the plot) suggest that Lewis had his eye on creating a Martial atmosphere and, indeed, the very word 'martial' appears twice in *Prince Caspian*, the only one of the seven Chronicles in which it occurs at all. Reepicheep is described as a 'martial mouse' and Miraz frets over his 'martial policy.' In something of a Martial pun, 'marshals'[36] are appointed to oversee the lists.

The Martial temperament is one of 'sturdy hardiness,' according to *The Discarded Image*, and the Martial visage is 'hard and happy,' according to 'The Planets.' This 'hard virtue of Mars' (to quote 'The Adam at Night') appears frequently throughout *Prince Caspian*. Peter looks 'hard' at Lucy; the soldiers escorting Trumpkin have faces that are 'bearded and hard'; we meet three badgers called the 'Hardbiters'; when the children are lost in the woods they find that retracing their steps was 'hard work, but oddly enough everyone felt more cheerful'; Aslan tells Lucy 'it is hard for you [to wake the others] . . . it has been hard for us all'; Peter's army at the end of the battle are found 'breathing hard . . . with stern and glad faces.'

More significantly certain characters visibly become Martial as the story progresses: Caspian begins 'to harden' as he sleeps 'under the stars'; the children, 'jingling in their mail,' begin to look and feel more like Narnians and less like schoolchildren; the 'hard' ground and 'the air of Narnia' work on Edmund so that 'all his old battles came back to him'; he and Peter have become 'more like men than boys' by the time they march off to the How. The iron has entered their soul, as is to be expected, for these characters are responsive to the Martial *influenza*, to that same 'magic in the air' that has saved Susan's bowstring from perishing.

The boys do not simply harden, they become knightly. In *Prince Caspian* knightliness is one of the key, recurring images: we hear of 'knights-errant'; in the ruins of Cair Paravel we see 'rich suits of armour, like knights guarding the treasures'; Peter is 'Knight of the Most Noble Order of the Lion'; Edmund is 'Knight of the Noble Order of the Table,' a 'very dangerous knight'; Caspian is knighted and then instantly knights Trufflehunter, Trumpkin, and Reepicheep; even the chess piece discovered at the start of the story is a 'chess-knight.'[37] This War of Deliverance is a good, medieval, knightly conflict, formalised 'by the art of heraldry and the rules of chivalry';[38] hence the shining armour,[39] the banners, the ornamented shields, the elevated language of Peter's challenge.

For Peter is the model knight, able to hew the treacherous and murderous Sopespian in pieces (slashing his legs from under him and walloping off his head with the backswing of the same stroke), but gentle enough to kiss the furry head of the badger. He has physical courage (risking his body in the single combat) but also pays attention to forgotten and seemingly unimportant traditions (the Bears' hereditary right to be Marshals). He is sensitive to his army's morale (cheering up Wimbleweather by appointing him to the parley); adroit in decision-making (his handling of the bumptious Reepicheep is skilfully diplomatic); and self-effacing toward Caspian ('I haven't come to take your place, you know, but to put you into it'). He demonstrates the acme of knightliness in refusing to attack Miraz when he is down; this to the frustration of Edmund: 'Oh, bother, bother, bother. Need he be as gentlemanly as all that? I suppose he must. Comes of being a Knight *and* a High King.' This is that 'knightly behaviour, in which morality up to the highest self-sacrifice and manners down to the smallest gracefulness in etiquette were inextricably blended by the medieval ideal.'[40]

In his volume on sixteenth-century literature, Lewis quotes Sir John Bourchier: 'I know by the course of the planettes that there is a Knyght comynge.'[41] In *Prince Caspian* he dramatises that sentence. Glenstorm tells Caspian, 'The time is ripe. I watch the skies . . . Tarva and Alambil have met in the halls of high heaven.' Tarva, the Lord of Victory, 'salutes' Alambil, the Lady of Peace, in a conjunction witnessed by Caspian and his tutor, Dr Cornelius, who declares: 'Their meeting is fortunate and means some great good for the sad realm of Narnia.' It is just possible that Tarva and Alambil are intended to suggest Narnian versions of Mars and Venus, respectively, but this seems to me unlikely because we know from elsewhere that the Narnian Morning Star is called Aravir, not Alambil.[42] I suspect that that Tarva and Alambil are meant to be taken as the two sides of the Martial influence, for Mars is not only a fighting-machine: he has a more pacific, life-giving dimension, too. And this brings us to the second major Martial theme of the book.

Mars Silvanus, upon whom Lewis drew upon so extensively in *Out of the Silent Planet*, is also clearly in evidence in *Prince Caspian*. 'Dryads and Hamadryads and Silvans' come to the combat between Peter and Miraz in chapter 14, and the inclusion of 'Silvans' (who never appear elsewhere in the Chronicles) is only the most obvious manifestation of an aspect of Martial influence that, in fact, is present throughout the whole story.

When the children first arrive in Narnia they are deposited 'in a woody place—such a woody place that branches were sticking into them and there was hardly room to move.' Peter exclaims, 'I can't see a yard in all these trees' for the wood is 'thick and tangled,' forcing them to 'stoop under branches and climb over branches' and blunder through 'great masses of stuff like rhododendrons.' When they finally get through to the ruins of the castle there is a long explanation about the orchard, which mentions Pomona (goddess of fruit trees and gardens), and there they find that ivy covers the doorway to the armoury.

Trees and vegetation of all kinds are everywhere in *Prince Caspian*. Caspian and Dr Cornelius cannot clearly see the conjunction of Tarva and Alambil for the interposition of a tree; Cornelius repeatedly mentions waking the trees; Caspian comes from a race 'who cut down trees wherever they could and were at war with all living things' and 'though he himself might be unlike other Telmarines, the trees could not be expected to know this'; 'tree after tree rose up' in front of Caspian when Destrier bolts and he is finally unhorsed when a branch strikes him on the forehead; Trufflehunter laments that they cannot 'wake the spirits of these trees,' for 'once the Trees moved in anger, our enemies would go mad with fright'; Aslan's How now stands in the middle of 'the Great Woods' and there Caspian's army must flee; Lucy tries to wake the trees in chapter 9, but fails; in chapter 10 the children's progress is hampered by the fir wood, but it provides them with cover when they have to run from the arrows of Miraz's sentries; later in chapter 10 Lucy, at night-time, finds the trees awake in the presence of Aslan; in chapter 11 the trees stir at the sound of his roar and then join in the riotous procession of Bacchus and Silenus.

The theme reaches its climax when the 'Awakened Trees' plunge through the ranks of Peter's army and pursue the Telmarines, like Birnam Wood come to Dunsinane. At this moment, Mars Gradivus and Mars Silvanus unite:

> Have you ever stood at the edge of a great wood on a high ridge when a wild south-wester broke over it in full fury on an autumn evening? Imagine that sound. And then imagine that the wood, instead of being fixed to one place, was rushing *at* you; and was no longer trees but huge people; yet still like trees because their long arms waved like branches and their heads tossed and leaves fell round them in showers.[43]

At the sight of this onslaught, the Telmarines 'flung down their weapons, shrieking, "The Wood! The Wood! The end of the world!"' and are then pursued to the river where they find their escape route destroyed: sprouting ivy has pulled down the bridge. The restrictive, government-inspected school is likewise destroyed by 'a mass of shimmering green'; a child-abuser is turned into a withered tree; a sad, overdressed schoolgirl is helped out of her 'unnecessary clothing.' In the final chapter, at night, the trees come forward, throwing off spare strands and fingers, to form a great woodland bonfire, cleansing themselves, as it were, of the battle and restoring Narnia to its proper, 'divinely comfortable' state. Tarva, Lord of victory, has indeed saluted Alambil, the Lady of peace.

The burgeoning vegetation in the story reminds us that Mars was the god of March, the only one of the seven planets whose name was linked to a month of the year. In ancient Rome, the festival of Mars (the *Feriae Marti*) began on the first day of March and Bacchanalian festivities followed on the sixteenth and seventeenth, just after the Ides of March (the fifteenth) on which, famously,

Julius Caesar was assassinated. Given the Bacchanalian revelry recorded in this story (in chapters 11 and 14), given the fact that Miraz is betrayed and stabbed in the back by his own men, and given the fact that the only named Narnian month in the entire septet is 'Greenroof,' during which all the events of *Prince Caspian* take place, the connections with Mars grow ever more evident.

But we will not (indeed, are not able to) trace every last detail to Mars.[44] A few remaining, noteworthy Martial elements may be summarised briefly:

First, iron makes a brief but important appearance in the story. The treasure chests found in the armoury are 'strengthened with iron bars,' and, interestingly, the chests are made of oak, Jupiter's special wood. Oak strengthened with iron suggests kingship reinforced with knighthood; thus the second Chronicle is discreetly linked to the first. Trumpkin's helmet, significantly, is copper, not iron, indicating (as indeed his behaviour shows) that he is not yet fully in tune with Aslan's Martial spirit.

Second, the archaic aspect of Mars, which we noted in the section on *Out of the Silent Planet*, is communicated both by means of recurrent imagery and by narrative technique. Schakel has noted the story's 'pervasive sense of antiquity, of the past, of the old days, of old stories.'[45] At the end of the first chapter the children find themselves in the overgrown ruins of an ancient castle and slowly the memory of former days comes back to them. Later, Caspian wishes he 'could have lived in the Old Days'; Cornelius urges him to be like 'King Peter of old'; the 'Old Narnians' base their headquarters in a mound 'raised in very ancient times,' one that seems 'to belong to an even older Narnia' than the one Caspian has been taught about. By continually summoning up ancient history in this way, Lewis creates 'a great longing for the old days when the trees could talk in Narnia.' And stylistically he reinforces this sense of a deep, layered past by plunging the reader into a long flashback, consisting of the fourth, fifth, sixth, and seventh chapters. When he releases us from the flashback at the start of chapter 8, the narrator has to remind us which time-frame we are now in, the only occasion in the Narniad that he does this.

Third, Lewis had toyed with the idea of calling the story 'A Horn in Narnia' and it is worth noting that the blowing of Caspian's horn, 'the greatest and most sacred treasure in Narnia,' is what initiates the whole story (from the Pevensies' point of view). It resounds so that 'the whole air was full of it' and it makes a noise 'strong enough to shake the woods,' reminiscent of the 'bosteous brag' blown upon the horn of Mars in Henryson's 'Testament of Cresseid.'

Fourth, the blowing of the horn does not put Caspian at the head of a new, reinforced army. On the contrary, it subordinates him to a new commanding officer, for as soon as Peter arrives he takes charge so as to restore proper order. Part of the Martial spirit is a ranked and patterned orderliness, and this aspect of his influence is especially evident in the character of Trumpkin, who volunteers to go to Cair Paravel even though he does not believe in the magic powers of the horn. He tells Caspian, 'I know the difference between giving advice and taking orders. You've had my advice, and now it's the time for orders.' His soldierly obedience is emphasised later when the children debate whether to go with Lucy. Trumpkin regards her claim to have seen Aslan as 'bilge and beanstalks,' but adds, 'If you all go, of course I'll go with you; and if your party splits up, I'll go with the High King.' Trumpkin knows that military discipline requires following a chain of command, regardless of personal beliefs or preferences. The capricious and rebellious instincts that characterise Miraz, Glozelle, and Sopespian are the mirror image of this aspect of Mars.

Fifth, of the creatures particularly associated with Mars (the wolf, the woodpecker, and the horse), all three appear in *Prince Caspian*. The wolf, who seems to betoken only the ill-disposed use of Martial influence, makes a prominent showing in chapter 12, in the form of the verminous werwolf who bites Caspian, rather as if the Prince is a reincarnation of Tyr. Lewis wrote elsewhere that lycanthropy is always a possibility for those knights in whom the inner animal 'has, all along, lived untamed and uncorrected inside that chivalry,' like Williams's Lancelot.[46] Arrows thocking into wood sound 'like the stroke of a woodpecker.' Caspian's horse is named 'Destrier' which means *war-horse* or *charger*.

Sixth, Lewis, who had a smattering of Turkish, seems to have known that Mars is called *Mirikh* by the Turks, to whom it means 'Torch.'[47] This would help explain a small but telling detail. The children try to make sticks into 'torches' and find they cannot do it, but Edmund happens to have been recently given an electric torch for his birthday, and this comes to their aid. The last sentence of the book is: '"Bother!" said Edmund. "I've left my new torch in Narnia."' Like the Jovial robes left behind in *The Lion*, Edmund's Martial torch links the planetary influence experienced in Narnia with the children's life back in England.

The Martial *Logos*

Perhaps the most obvious message conveyed by means of the Martial *poiema* of *Prince Caspian* is what Lewis communicates explicitly in *Mere Christianity*, namely that 'the idea of the knight—the Christian in arms for the defence of a good cause—is one of the great Christian ideas.' Writing in the aftermath of a war that had threatened his country with Nazi rule, Lewis had obvious reason to champion this tradition of gallantry. In the second volume of the Narniad, he aims to acquaint (and to delight) the reader with what it feels like to live inside that chivalric tradition; his purpose is not to point out any deficiencies it might have had. Rather, it is as though he says to the reader, 'Instead of stripping the

knight of his armour you can try to put his armour on yourself.'[48] He is attempting to provide his audience with imaginative access to the discipline and
the freedom from anxiety that arise out of participation in the Martial spirit.
This is the principal *logos* conveyed by his Narnian 'War of Deliverance.'

Deliverance by means of war is, apparently, an unavoidable necessity.
Peaceful protest is not an option because Narnia has degenerated into a tyranny
under Miraz. Elsewhere, however, Lewis states that '"necessity" was always "the
tyrant's plea."'[49] He has in mind a number of tyrants, or commentators upon
tyrants, including Livy,[50] Cromwell,[51] Milton,[52] and Pitt,[53] who observed how
the claim of necessity could be used to excuse any kind of behaviour, however
brutal and cruel. Knowing this, how did Lewis hope to make out that the
'necessary' War of Narnian Deliverance might be anything other than a ty-
rannical evil itself?

Abusus non tollit usum. The claim of necessity and actual necessity are two
different things. However often tyrants falsely claim it, necessity itself remains
where it was. For Lewis, as for Augustine (whose thoughts on this matter he
quotes to a correspondent),[54] the weapons of war could sometimes be legiti-
mately wielded if real and honest need arose. But how to characterise real necessity? Lewis wishes to call it 'the Necessity of Chivalry,' as he does in an article
of that name published in the dark days of August 1940.[55] If we are to avoid
tyranny we must have chivalrous soldiers who, like Theseus in *The Knight's Tale*,
know how to make a 'vertu of necessitee.' In his article, Lewis repeatedly em-
phasizes that the knightly ideal brought together 'two things which have no
natural tendency to gravitate towards one another. It brought them together
for that very reason.' He writes: 'The knight is a man of blood and iron' but also
'a gentle, modest, unobtrusive man'; 'he is fierce to the *n*th and meek to the *n*th':
he 'combines both characters.' To Lewis the knightly ideal was not an out-
dated curio but a living reality, 'practical and vital'; he was no less admiring of it
in his adulthood than he had been as a boy before he saw active service, and
he appears to be proud of the fact that, on his mother's side, 'the blood went
back to a Norman knight whose bones lie at Battle Abbey'.[56] Some of Lewis's
contemporaries—the R.A.F. pilots 'to whom we owe our life from hour to
hour'—were modern equivalents of the medieval knight; and their successors
must be bred up if men are to escape from a world 'divided between wolves who
do not understand, and sheep who cannot defend, the things which make life
desirable.'

Martial hardness, then, is not to be confused with heartlessness or the
gratification of lust for physical power. Rather, properly understood, it is that
strength which, on the one hand, gives backbone to the milksop and, on the
other hand, reins in *machismo*. Within these two extremes, war service, if it is
necessary, may be entered into with 'a kind of gaiety and wholeheartedness.'[57]

It is this unashamed wholeheartedness that may explain why Hollindale and Sutherland think they have found in Narnia a 'glorification of conflict and retribution' and a 'legitimizing of cruelty.'[58] Lewis would, I suspect, have agreed with the first part of their diagnosis (glorification) if it means no more than an unapologetic acceptance of and proper respect for heroism in the service of duly retributive justice.[59] He was unabashed in his belief that there was such a thing as a just war and, indeed, he once even went on the offensive, taking the fight to his opponents, addressing a pacifist society in Oxford in 1940 under the title 'Why I Am Not A Pacifist.'[60] The brave knight who risks life and limb for the sake of the oppressed richly deserves to be honoured, and if this honour happens to be easily corrupted by propagandizing politicians, no matter. Again, abuse does not abolish use.

However, Lewis would have rebutted the allegation of cruelty with vigour. Chivalry imposes restraints on the practice of war so as to avoid unnecessary (that is, cruel) violence; and *Prince Caspian* memorably depicts (by means of the hag and the werwolf) the kind of unrestrained warring spirit that Lewis regarded as unacceptable. Further attempts to avoid a jingoistic tone are made by an acknowledgment of the fearfulness attendant upon physical risk (during the single combat), by Peter's averting his eyes from the corpses of his enemies, and by his determination to honour even the traitor Nikabrik with appropriate burial.

Lewis divided poets of war into the 'Enchanted' (Sidney, Macaulay, Chesterton, Brooke), the 'Disenchanted' (Sassoon), and the 'Re-enchanted' (Homer, the *Maldon* poet), and he obviously intends to include himself among the Re-enchanted: 'One is not in the least deceived: we remember the trenches too well. We know how much of the reality the romantic view left out. But we also know that heroism is a real thing.'[61] He aimed to strike a balance between propaganda on the one hand and protest on the other. No doubt chivalry is a failure, but it is not such a failure as pacifism. Wars (even just wars) inevitably involve evil, but not so much evil as is involved in passively allowing aggressors to have their way. In his *magnum opus* he summed up these views by stating: 'We have discovered that the scheme of "outlawing war" has made war more like an outlaw without making it less frequent and that to banish the knight does not alleviate the suffering of the peasant.'[62]

The plight of the suffering peasantry (the Old Narnians who live in hiding) is not left unalleviated. Aslan's great thundering war-cry in chapter 11 ('The Lion Roars') signals that the Narnian lord of hosts is on the march:

> Aslan, who seemed larger than before, lifted his head, shook his mane, and roared.
>
> The sound, deep and throbbing at first like an organ beginning on a low note, rose and became louder, and then far louder again, till the

earth and air were shaking with it. It rose up from that hill and floated across all Narnia. Down in Miraz's camp men woke, stared palely in one another's faces, and grasped their weapons. Down below that in the Great River, now at its coldest hour, the heads and shoulders of the nymphs, and the great weedy-bearded head of the river-god, rose from the water. Beyond it, in every field and wood, the alert ears of rabbits rose from their holes, the sleepy heads of birds came out from under wings, owls hooted, vixens barked, hedgehogs grunted, the trees stirred. In towns and villages mothers pressed babies close to their breasts, staring with wild eyes, dogs whimpered, and men leaped up groping for lights. Far away on the northern frontier the mountain giants peered from the dark gateways of their castles.[63]

This is the most militaristic moment in Aslan's role in the story. Although he is clearly the commander-in-chief, who requires Lucy's absolute obedience, takes the boys' salute, and instructs Peter to knight Caspian, he is otherwise not directly involved with the war. He holds back from the battle and does not 'come roaring in and frighten all the enemies away—like last time.' There are two good donegalitarian reasons for this.

First, Mars is different from Jupiter: knightliness is not the same as kingliness. The king must be 'first in every desperate attack and last in every desperate retreat;'[64] therefore, *quâ* Jupiter in the first book, Aslan tackles the Witch directly. The knight, on the other hand, is a soldier among soldiers, and in the military chain of command, discipline is everything; every man must do his duty and the General is, in this sense, no more important than the Private: each must stick to his post. Hence we see Aslan and his underlings equally 'taking their places in the ordered rhythm of the universe.' *Quâ* Mars, Aslan commands: that is his obedience to the military order. He marshals and inspires his troops, but does not, on this occasion, enter the front line.

Second, knightliness is evident as much in gentleness as in hardness. When Peter chooses not to exploit his advantage after Miraz trips during the single combat, Edmund concedes, 'I suppose it is what Aslan would like.' The Christ-figure is thus cleverly brought into the combat, even in his absence. And he is absent, of course, because he is busy expressing and participating in that very aspect of Martianity which Martial hardness exists to protect—blitheness, keenness, and happiness as symbolised by the Bacchanalian romp. Lewis is attempting to show that, even as Aslan braces his troops for war, he restrains violence from turning into cruelty because he is working toward the pleasures of peace. Peter's forbearance in the monomachy shows that he comes from, and is going back to, a world in which fertility and fun, dancing and drinking are ends in themselves, and to which war is a means.

Thus we see that the growing vines and the swaying trees—the Mars Silvanus images—are present to balance and orientate the Mars Gradivus theme. Knights win their spurs and do their bloody, necessary work to the greater glory of God and in service of their fellow creatures—and to that extent war is its own justification regardless of its outcome. But in the larger picture Mars Gradivus is only a hired hand; his work is undertaken in order to preserve or regain a state in which all creatures, not only knights in the lists, may give honour to the Divine Being:

> Pale birch-girls were tossing their heads, willow-women pushed back their hair from their brooding faces to gaze on Aslan, the queenly beeches stood still and adored him, shaggy oak-men, lean and melancholy elms, shock-headed hollies (dark themselves, but their wives all bright with berries) and gay rowans, all bowed and rose again, shouting, 'Aslan, Aslan!' in their various husky or creaking or wave-like voices.[65]

But there is another, more profound, reason that Mars Gradivus has a limited range of influence. Although the knightly ideal is a high one, it is not the highest aspect of the Martial character. 'To the perfected Christian the ideal of honour is simply a temptation. His courage has a better root, and, being learned in Gethsemane, may have no honour about it. But to the man coming up from below, the ideal of knighthood may prove a schoolmaster to the ideal of martyrdom. Galahad is the *son* of Lancelot.'[66] It is for this reason that Reepicheep, the 'martial mouse' and epitome of the chivalric spirit, is gently mocked by Aslan: 'I have sometimes wondered, friend, whether you do not think too much about your honour.' Martyrdom, not knighthood, is the summit of Martial achievement and contains no worldly dignity or honour, only crucifixion-like shame that must be 'despised' (Heb. 12:2). In *Prince Caspian* Lewis gives us three martyrs, that is, three characters who witness to the truth and suffer for it: Caspian's Nurse, Dr Cornelius, and Lucy Pevensie.

Lucy's story is the most developed. Twice she tries and fails to receive the Martial spirit—once when she misses what the trees are saying in chapter 9, and once, later in the same chapter, when she allows her vision of Aslan to be overruled. In chapter 10, however, she has a full encounter with Aslan. He says, 'It is hard for you, little one.... It has been hard for us all in Narnia before now,'—a reference to his death in the previous book. Lewis cannot depict Aslan's own martyrdom in *Prince Caspian* because it has already been dealt with, under the impress of Jupiter, the priest-king, in *The Lion, the Witch and the Wardrobe*, and 'things never happen the same way twice.'[67] But the key word in his comforting of Lucy—'hard'—indicates that, for the purposes of the present story, we are to understand that earlier sacrifice as a Martial as well as a Jovial event. The focus then shifts to Lucy and to her own adoption of his Martial spirit:

> Lucy buried her face in his mane to hide from his face. But there must have been magic in his mane. She could feel lion-strength going into her. Quite suddenly she sat up.
> 'I'm sorry, Aslan,' she said. 'I'm ready now.'
> 'Now you are a lioness,' said Aslan. 'And now all Narnia will be renewed.'[68]

Lucy wakes the others:

> It is a terrible thing to have to wake four people, all older than yourself and all very tired, for the purpose of telling them something they probably won't believe and making them do something they certainly won't like. 'I mustn't think about it, I must just do it,' thought Lucy.[69]

This is the turning-point in the story. Lucy does her duty, witnesses to what she has seen, and turns the company about so that, eventually, even Susan, the most anaemic of the children, can receive the Martial spirit. At first, Susan had resisted; then she had followed reluctantly, having been told (by Trumpkin) to 'Obey.' Her reluctance slowly evaporates as she does just that, taking Mars's 'weight of obedience'[70] upon her shoulders, accepting his discipline and the consequent freedom from anxiety:

> 'You have listened to fears, child,' said Aslan. 'Come, let me breathe on you. Forget them. Are you brave again?'
> 'A little, Aslan,' said Susan.[71]

Thus Lewis gives us, by means of the Martial donegality, a version of that image used by the Greek Fathers (St. Basil among them) of the iron in the fire gaining fiery properties as man acquires the spiritual qualities of the Holy Spirit by living in Him. Like the dwarves at their smithy forging armour out of 'red-hot metal' for Caspian, Aslan tempers the children with his own Martial quality, that combination of strength and gentleness, that capacity both to hew down and to build up, that ability, above all, to enjoy a kind of unshakeable gaiety that comes from finding and faithfully defending one's proper place in the ranks.

The *miles christianus* has as his great weapon 'the shield of faith' (Eph. 6:16), by which he may 'turn to flight the armies of the aliens' (Heb. 11: 34). Lewis refers to these scriptural sources in his discussion of Spenser's 'knight of faith,'[72] and they help explain why he so emphasises Peter's shield in the single combat with Miraz. Faithful obedience is the chief virtue that Aslan imparts to his followers under the aegis of Mars. It is a virtue of which MacDonald had written (in a passage Lewis anthologised):

Do you ask, "What is faith in Him?" I answer, the leaving of your own way, your objects, your self, and the taking of His and Him...*and doing as He tells you*. I can find no words strong enough to serve the weight of this necessity—this obedience.[73]

Discipline—obedience—faithfulness—strength—growth. It is this spectrum of qualities that becomes available to the well-disposed characters. They steadily and increasingly Enjoy the Martial influence that Aslan, incarnate and discarnate, spreads abroad in this tale. Mars, the 'unknown god' of *Prince Caspian*, surrounds and upholds Lucy and the others, forging them into warriors or woodlanders or witnesses or a mixture of all three. As the apostle Paul had once stood on the Areopagus and proclaimed to the men of Athens the person of Jesus Christ 'in whom we live and move and have our being,'[74] so, in the second Chronicle of Narnia, Lewis does something similar from his own Mars Hill.

FIVE

Sol

Broadening eastward, clear and cloudless.
—'The Planets' (lines 46–47)

To the modern mind, raised on a belief in the Solar System, it seems odd that the medieval Sun should have featured as merely one among seven planets. It seems odder still that, of the four superlunary planets that were considered beneficent in their influence, Sol should not even have ranked as *Fortuna Minor*, let alone *Fortuna Major*. Has not the Sun always been known to be the most dominant of the heavenly bodies? How could it not accordingly have had the dominant role in the myth of the planets? Lewis acknowledges this oddity in *The Discarded Image*:

> Sol is the point at which the concordat between the mythical and the astrological nearly breaks down. Mythically, Jupiter is the King, but Sol produces the noblest metal, gold, and is the eye and mind of the whole universe.[1]

It is one of those peculiarities of human imagination that the Sun, worshipped by Egyptians, Japanese, and Native Americans alike, treated throughout world literature as an archetype of the good, the beautiful, and the true, and proposed as the astronomical centre-point 1,800 years before Copernicus,[2] should have a status in the European myth of the heavens below that of Jupiter and even that of Venus.[3]

Sol's confused status does not restrict Lewis's imaginative practice. As we saw in the previous chapter, Lewis is prepared to use Mars *(Infortuna Minor)* to image certain things about the divine nature, and as we shall see in chapter 9, he is prepared to use even Saturn *(Infortuna Major)* for the same purpose. That being so, Sol need present no problem. And, in any case, although Sol may not rank as one of the two *fortunas*, still 'the Sun is an image of the Good for Plato and therefore of God for Spenser.'[4] Indeed, long before Plato, the psalmist had found it natural, in Lewis's favourite psalm (the nineteenth), to pass from Solar imagery into a eulogy on the law of the Lord, and the equation of God/Christ with the sun or the sun's illuminating power is a scriptural commonplace.[5] The primitive Church found it easy to Christianise sun gods, such as Apollo in Greek mythology and Sol Invictus in Roman, and there is a third-century mosaic of Christ as a solar deity in a mausoleum under St. Peter's Basilica in Rome. So Lewis had good precedents for heliotic theological imaginings, and was in any case of the view that the very shape of the human mind dictated such a response to the Sun and its influence. He thought that 'God is, or is like, light . . . for every devotional, philosophical, and theological purpose imaginable within a Christian, or indeed a monotheistic, frame of reference.'[6] Similarly, he believed that Solar gold, of itself, could never be a symbol of evil 'to any human poet.'[7]

Lewis's own imaginative engagement with the Sun seems to have been fired early in life when he he came across the words:

I heard a voice that cried,
Balder the beautiful
Is dead, is dead . . .[8]

Instantly, Lewis records, he was transported into a realm of desire so strong that its intensity was almost sickening. What he does not mention is that Balder is the Norse counterpart of Helios (the Greek forerunner of Sol); he was the god of light, son of Odin and Frigg, as Helios was the son of Hyperion and Theia. Lewis's youthful passion for 'Balder and the sunward-sailing cranes' sparked an interest in Solar deities that endured throughout his life.[9] He claimed that he 'loved Balder before Christ,'[10] and although eventually he came to believe that 'Christ is more than Balder,'[11] he was still ready to argue, as late as 1961, that Balder's similarity to Christ worked in the latter's favour.[12] And for a while Lewis was also interested in using Balder poetically. He appears, for instance, in the final stanza of *Dymer*, alongside Saturn (see below, chapter 9), but thereafter morphs into Sol in Lewis's poetry, part of the general drift in Lewis's imagination toward an acceptance of the seven Ptolemaic planets as his controlling symbol-system. This chapter traces that growing responsiveness to Sol in scholarship, poetry, and fiction and shows how a Solar donegality irradiates the third book in the Narniad, *The Voyage of the 'Dawn Treader.'*

Sol in Lewis's Scholarship

In his *Discarded Image* summary of Solar qualities, Lewis points out, as we have already seen, that 'Sol produces the noblest metal, gold, and is the eye and mind of the whole universe.' He goes on to complete his summary as follows:

> [Sol] makes men wise and liberal and his sphere is the Heaven of theologians and philosophers. Though he is no more metallurgical than any other planet his metallurgical operations are more often mentioned than theirs. We read in Donne's *Allophanes and Idios* how soils which the Sun could make into gold may lie too far from the surface for his beams to take effect... Spenser's Mammon brings his hoard out to 'sun' it. If it were already gold, he would have no motive for doing this. It is still hore (grey); he suns it that it may become gold. Sol produces fortunate events.[13]

Of the seven sentences in that summary, five deal with Sol's aurifying influence. Whether or not Lewis was right so to emphasise this metallurgical faculty is not our concern; we are interested in his theological imagination, rather than his historical-critical judgements. But we certainly find that his own poetic practice is in accordance with those judgements. When we examine the use to which Lewis put Solar symbolism in his poetry, it is the Midas-touch or the philosopher's stone effect that almost invariably takes pre-eminence.

Sol in Lewis's Poetry

Sol finds his way into several of Lewis's poems, but we shall concentrate our attention upon those four where his metallurgical influence is on display,[14] the first of which is 'The Planets':

> Far beyond her [Venus]
> The heaven's highway hums and trembles,
> Drums and dindles, to the driv'n thunder
> Of SOL's chariot, whose sword of light
> Hurts and humbles; beheld only
> Of eagle's eye. When his arrow glances
> Through mortal mind, mists are parted
> And mild as morning the mellow wisdom
> Breathes o'er the breast, broadening eastward
> Clear and cloudless. In a clos'd garden

(Unbound her burden) his beams foster
Soul in secret, where the spoil puts forth
Paradisal palm,[15] and pure fountains
Turn and re-temper, touching coolly
The uncomely common to cordial gold;
Whose ore also, in earth's matrix,
Is print and pressure of his proud signet
On the wax of the world. He is the worshipp'd male,
The earth's husband,[16] all-beholding,
Arch-chemic eye.[17]

The non-metallurgical imagery of these lines must be noted as well as the metallurgical; it may be usefully paralleled by the *Discarded Image* summary, as follows: Sol engenders 'mellow wisdom' ('he makes men wise'); unbinds burdens ('he makes men . . . liberal'); gives rise to the 'paradisal' ('his sphere is the Heaven of theologians'); clears mists from the mind ('his sphere is the Heaven of . . . philosophers'). The metallurgical imagery itself is given the best part of six lines: Sol turns the 'uncomely common to cordial gold'; his 'ore' is the 'print and pressure of his proud signet / On the wax of the world'; his eye is 'arch-chemic.' These Solar images symbolise Spirit in its psychological and rational senses, glancing only briefly at its *novitas* sense; but Solar imagery is taken and applied for more obviously theological ends in the second poem we have to consider, 'A Pageant Played in Vain':

Watching the thought that moves
Within my conscient brain,
I learn how often that appearance proves
A pageant played in vain.

Holding what seems the helm,
I make a show to steer,
But winds, for worse and better, overwhelm
My purpose, and I veer.

Thus, if thy guidance reach
Only my head, then all
Hardest attempt of mine serves but to teach
How oddly the dice fall.

To limbs, and loins, and heart,
Search with thy chemic beam,
Strike where the self I know not lives apart,
Beneath the surface dream.

Break, Sun, my crusted earth,
Pierce, razor-edged, within,
Where blind, immortal metals have their birth,
And crystals clear begin.

Thy spirit in secret flows
About our lives. In gloom,
The mother helping not nor hindering, grows
The child within the womb.

The Sun here is a deity ('*thy* chemic beam,' '*thy* spirit') and the poem, though not displaying Lewis's talents at their best, is interesting on several counts. First, for its sailing imagery in stanza 2: we shall see below how Lewis chooses a sea voyage as a major element in his Solar donegality. Second, for the use of the word 'strike' in the fourth stanza, a verb with astrological significance.[18] Third, for the unknown 'self' in the same stanza and the 'secret spirit' in the final stanza. Here Lewis touches on the matter that is a main theme of this book: the way spiritual life exceeds conscious human awareness. And its fourth interesting feature is the one that most concerns us at the moment, its metallurgical imagery: the searching 'chemic beam,' the penetrative Sun bringing 'blind, immortal metals' to birth. It is noteworthy that Lewis writes 'metals' not 'metal.' This perhaps suggests that Sol is being given a proprietorial power, able to command not just gold, but the metals of all the different planets. Such a role is certainly ascribed to him in 'Noon's Intensity':

Till your alchemic beams turn all to gold
There must be many metals.[19] From the night
You will not yet withdraw her silver light,
And often with Saturnian tints the cold
Atlantic swells at morning shall enfold
The Cornish cliffs burnished with copper bright;
Till trained by slow degrees we have such sight
As dares the pure projection to behold.
Even when Sol comes ascendant, it may be
More perfectly in him our eyes shall see
All baser virtues; thus shall hear you talking
And yet not die. Till then, you have left free,
Unscorched by your own noon's intensity
One cool and evening hour for garden walking.[20]

In the first eight lines the poet is waiting for Sol to transmute all metals into the noblest, gold. He mentions Luna's silver, Venus's copper, and 'Saturnian tints' (that is, streaks of lead) as subjects fit for aurification. Then in lines 9–11 the poet wonders whether Sol's ascendancy might not in fact metamorphose those 'baser' metals into gold, but rather perfect them without transmuting them. This is that theme which Lewis elsewhere calls 'Transposition': the flooding of a lower medium and the raising of it to a new significance by incorporation into a higher medium.[21] However, the poem gives no clear signal as to whether Sol will transmute or transpose, and it ends on an equally ambivalent note. The 'cool and evening hour for garden walking,' which is 'free' and 'unscorched,' presents an attractive image of restfulness and temperance. On the other hand, it connotes God's 'walking in the garden in the cool of the day' and Adam and Eve's hiding in shame (Gen. 3:8); in this sense it is an image of fearfulness and resistance. The ambivalence is a Herbert-like note, recognising human inertia alongside pious desire.

'Noon's Intensity' remained unpublished during Lewis's life and it is not known when it was written, but it looks as though it might be a revisitation of subjects dealt with in two of the poems in *The Pilgrim's Regress*, namely 'Caught' (where the poet's reaction to 'noon's long-drawn Astonishment' is even more reluctant) and the final poem of metallurgical significance that we have to consider, 'Scazons':

> Walking to-day by a cottage I shed tears
> When I remembered how once I had walked there
> With my friends who are mortal and dead. Years
> Little had healed the wound that was laid bare.
>
> Out little spear that stabs! I, fool, believed
> I had outgrown the local, unique sting,
> I had transmuted wholly (I was deceived)
> Into Love universal the lov'd thing.
>
> But Thou, Lord, surely knewest thine own plan
> When the angelic indifferencies with no bar
> Universally loved, but Thou gav'st man
> The tether and pang of the particular,
>
> Which, like a chemic drop, infinitesimal,
> Plashed into pure water, changing the whole,
> Embodies and embitters and turns all
> Spirit's sweet water into astringent soul,
>
> That we, though small, might quiver with fire's same
> Substantial form as Thou—not reflect merely
> Like lunar angels back to Thee cold flame.
> Gods are we, Thou hast said; and we pay dearly.[22]

As in 'Noon's Intensity,' the poet touches on how Sol might or might not 'transmute' loved things into 'Love universal.' He concludes that an aspect of being human is to place value in particulars, and suggests that that very understanding of particularity is a gift from Sol (a 'chemic drop'), which works its magic, turning the waters of the 'Spirit' (the discarnate spirituality that angelic life consists in) into human 'soul' (a quibble on 'Sol,' repeating the quibble of 'his beams foster / Soul in secret' in 'The Planets').[23] Thus God transposes man's local loves without annihilating them in the process. This particularity in universality is what differentiates men from angels. Angels, according to the penultimate line, are 'lunar,' reflecting God's light straight back to him with disembodied and purely rational immediacy. But the poet's love does not merely reflect back, like a moon; it reflects internally also, like (as Lewis puts it elsewhere) 'a dewdrop.'[24] The purpose of knowing the divine nature is to 'quiver with fire's same substantial form.' The idea of sunlight shining inside 'sweet water' would become a memorable dramatic episode in *The Voyage of the 'Dawn Treader'*. Here it is dealt with in a matter of a few brief words.

Sol in *That Hideous Strength*

And Sol's appearances in *That Hideous Strength* are also remarkably brief; he receives far less attention than any of the other six planets. Sol does not descend upon St. Anne's in chapter 15, and in this he is no different from Luna; but, unlike Luna, Sol (or Arbol, as Lewis calls him here) makes only a very minor contribution to the imagery in the rest of the story. One explanation of this near-absence is that Lewis has deliberately incorporated Sol into Jupiter, reflecting the near-breakdown in the medieval concordat between the mythical and the astrological. (That certainly seems to be the case with the depiction of Ransom, as we shall see presently.) Another possible explanation is that the virtual omission of Sol is a structural flaw in the work, one of the reasons that Lewis came close to despairing of it.[25]

All the appearances of Solar influence in Lewis's poetry are positive depictions. In *That Hideous Strength*, however, Solar imagery—like so much in that book—polarises into the morally good and the morally bad.

Ransom has a few flecks of Sol augmenting his general depiction as a Jovial character. We are told that he has 'gold hair' and a 'gold beard.' Jane likens him to Solomon, and 'the bright solar blend of king and lover and magician which hangs about that name' steals back upon her mind. His 'voice also seemed to be like sunlight and gold. Like gold not only as gold is beautiful but as it is heavy.'

The deployment of Solar imagery for negative purposes is also brief, but more significant. At Bracton College we are shown into 'the Soler, the long upper room on the south of Lady Alice [Quadrangle].' It 'is very hot in the Soler on a sunny afternoon' and it is there, as the Bursar drones on hypnotically about 'money matters,' that the Fellows' stipends take on a quality antithetical to Bragdon Wood. The implication is that the Fellows' greed is turning Solar influence to ill effect. Their love of money is the root of all the evil that follows in the book as they think more and more of the luciferous, and less and less of the luciferous, end to which Bragdon Wood may be put. These terms for the alternative motives that may characterise scientific enquiry (the mercenary and the enlightening motives) were coined by Francis Bacon, whose *Novum Organum* established him as the chief trumpeter of the era of applied science, and this short scene in the Soler initiates one of the larger themes of *That Hideous Strength*, the abuse of Nature through scientific manipulation. It is the same theme that Lewis addressed in *The Abolition of Man* (the philosophical counterpart to *That Hideous Strength*), where he notes that Bacon sought knowledge not for its own sake but for its 'fruit': like Marlowe's Faustus, 'It is not truth he wants . . . but gold and guns and girls.' The truly liberal (that is, Solar) motive was lacking from his thought, as the novel indicates in its mention of Bacon alongside Agrippa and Paracelsus. The only reason Bacon, that would-be alchemist, did not line up with these magicians was because their experiments 'attained not to greatness and certainty of works.'[26]

Lewis argues that magic and science were consanguineous: 'One was sickly and died, the other was healthy and throve. But they were twins. They were born of the same impulse.' He denies that he is attacking science: 'No doubt those who really founded modern science were usually those whose love of truth exceeded their love of power.'[27] But he is struck by the 'unhealthy neighbourhood' and the 'inauspicious hour' in which modern science appeared. It is a theme he returns to in *English Literature in the Sixteenth Century*, where he opines, in a long passage on astrology and the scientific revolution, that 'Bacon and the magicians have the closest possible affinity.'[28] And as with Bacon, so with his successors, such as Boyle and Newton, who were both alchemists.[29] Although Lewis nowhere develops this line of thought in considered detail, it evidently drummed a beat in the background of his mind as he pondered the progress of the scientific enterprise from the sixteenth century up to the modern day, including Darwin *en route*. In his essay 'The World's Last Night' he wonders whether the origins of the Darwinian myth of progress may be traced 'to the German idealists and thence (as I have heard suggested) through Boehme back to Alchemy. Is the whole dialectical view of history possibly a gigantic projection of the old dream that we can make gold?'[30] We do not have space to explore these ideas in their own right, but it is worth noting their existence in Lewis's thinking. The connection in his imagination between Solar influence (improperly received) and the will to power helps explain certain aspects of his mature treatment of this planet's character in the third of the Narnia Chronicles.

Sol in *The Voyage of the 'Dawn Treader'*

The Solar *Poiema*

In contrast to his somewhat elliptical treatment of Sol in *That Hideous Strength*, Lewis's Narnian treatment of 'the eye and mind of the whole universe' is obvious, indeed the most obvious of the seven Narnian donegalities.[31] In *The Voyage of the 'Dawn Treader,'* the Solar influence governing the story could be divined from the title alone, for this is a tale about a journey toward the rising Sun. As is the case in most of the other books, the prevailing planetary spirit becomes progressively more intense as the story proceeds, but only in this story is the planet actually located and identified as the destination of the plot: 'the very eastern end of the world,' 'the utter East.' Reepicheep, whose literal orientation helps motivate the quest, swears he will 'sink with his nose to the sunrise' if it is the last thing he does, which indeed it turns out to be, as Sol in one of his guises—that of Apollo Smintheus, 'Apollo the Mouse-catcher'— plays his part.

In constructing this picaresque romance, Lewis had many sea-voyage stories to draw upon, such as Homer's *Odyssey*, the Irish tradition of *immram*, the Anglo-Saxon poem *The Seafarer*, the voyage of St. Brendan, and Mandeville's *Voiage and Travaile*. Of sun-voyage stories there are fewer sources, but it seems likely that one model was *Paradise Lost*. In his Preface Lewis notes:

> Towards the end of Book III Milton takes Satan to visit the sun. To keep on harping on heat and brightness would be no use; it would end only in that bog of superlatives which is the destination of many bad poets. But Milton makes the next hundred lines as Solar as they could possibly be.[32]

Lewis points out how Milton proceeds from gentle warmth, to penetrating virtue, to a pun on Galileo's sun-spots, to alchemy and 'archchemic properties,' to shadowlessness, to the world's eye, and God's own singular eye. He then observes: 'This is not, of course, the sun of modern science; but almost everything which the sun had meant to man up till Milton's day has been gathered together and the whole passage in his own phrase, 'runs potable gold.'

In Lewis's own attempt to deploy images 'as Solar as they could possibly be,' he gives us 'drinkable light'—the sweet water of the Eastern sea—as his version of 'potable gold,' and follows the Miltonic example by not harping on heat and brightness.

He hardly mentions heat at all because it would necessarily involve images of sweat and melting that would be out of place and might also call to mind Icarus, an unhelpful example. There are only one or two references: the air becomes 'warmer day by day'; the nights are 'very warm'; the Sun is 'not too hot.'

Brightness is adroitly handled, chiefly by the device of contrasting the increasing light with occasional plunges into darkness. The storm in chapter 5, the night-time salvation of Eustace in chapter 7, the Dark Island in chapter 12, and the overnight vigil in chapter 13 punctuate the growing brilliance so that the final three chapters of uninterrupted light do not feel *de trop*, but rather the deserved reward of dedicated seekers after luminosity. Sol, who is 'banischer of nicht,'[33] exerts his influence climactically in the magnificent sunrise on Ramandu's island when he expels the last vestiges of 'greyness' and 'grey clouds' once and for all: 'And as Edmund said afterwards, "Though lots of things happened on that trip which *sound* more exciting, that moment was really the most exciting".' Thereafter, there is only light. As the voyage continues we read: 'every morning when the sun rose out of the sea the curved prow of the *Dawn Treader* stood up right across the middle of the sun. Some thought that the sun looked larger than it looked from Narnia, but others disagreed.' Later, 'there was no mistaking it.' And later still, 'the sun when it came up each morning was twice, if not three times, its usual size.' Ultimately, Sol is 'beheld only / Of eagle's eye,' as 'The Planets' has it: 'if their eyes had not by now grown as strong as eagles' the sun on all that whiteness—especially at early morning when the sun was hugest—would have been unbearable.'

Just as Milton and his medieval forebears emphasized Sol's metallurgical power, so does Lewis. It is only Sol, among all his planetary donegalities, whose metal-making power is actually shown in operation. The subject is given a whole episode to itself in chapter 8, when the royal party discovers on an island a pool that turns things to gold. Significantly, this hill-top pool is the source of the 'eastern' stream where Drinian had wanted to water the ship. But he is over-ruled and instead anchors the ship off the 'western' stream and 'it was a good thing he did' ('Sol produces fortunate events'). In other words, the western stream (the one opposite the place of sunrise) has no such dangerous metal-lurgical powers.

At the bottom of the pool lies a life-size figure of a man:

> It lay face downwards with its arms stretched out above its head. And it so happened that as they looked at it, the clouds parted and the sun shone out. The golden shape was lit up from end to end.[34]

The adventurers wonder whether they can dive for it and drag it out, though Edmund reckons that if it is of solid gold it will be too weighty to salvage. He lowers a spear into the water to test its depth and the spear becomes so heavy that he has to drop it; the others observe that it has turned the same colour as the statue. Edmund then notices that the tips of his boots have turned to gold and he shouts out sharply, 'Get back! Back from the water. All of you. At once!' He explains: 'That water turns things into gold. It turned the spear into gold, that's why it got so heavy. And it was just lapping against my feet (it's a good thing I wasn't barefoot) and it turned the toe-caps into gold. And that poor fellow on the bottom - well, you see.' The golden statue is the dead body of one of the lost lords, Restimar, killed by aurification. Caspian tests the alchemical properties of the water by dipping a spray of heather into the pool. 'It was heather that he dipped; what he drew out was a perfect model of heather made of the purest gold, heavy and soft as lead.'

The heather's leadenness is not just a metallic simile. To be sure, the golden spray is like lead in its weight and malleability, but, at the astrological level, there is a darker meaning. Lead is the metal of Saturn, *Infortuna Major*, who brings about calamity and death. As soon as we have heard that the golden heather is like lead (and that Edmund's boots have similarly turned leaden), we know that this pool is a dangerous place:

> 'The King who owned this island,' said Caspian slowly, and his face flushed as he spoke, 'would soon be the richest of all the Kings of the world. I claim this land for ever as a Narnian possession. It shall be called Goldwater Island. And I bind you all to secrecy. No one must know of this. Not even Drinian—on pain of death, do you hear?'
>
> 'Who are you talking to?' said Edmund. 'I'm no subject of yours. If anything it's the other way round. I am one of the four ancient sovereigns of Narnia and you are under allegiance to the High King my brother.'
>
> 'So it has come to that, King Edmund, has it?' said Caspian, laying his hand on his sword-hilt.
>
> 'Oh, stop it, both of you,' said Lucy. 'That's the worst of doing anything with boys. You're all such swaggering, bullying idiots—oooh!—' Her voice died away into a gasp. And everyone else saw what she had seen.
>
> Across the grey hillside above them—grey, for the heather was not in bloom—without noise, and without looking at them, and shining as if he were in bright sunlight though the sun had in fact gone in, passed with slow pace the hugest lion that human eyes have ever seen. In describing the scene Lucy said afterwards, 'He was the size of an

elephant,' though at another time she only said, 'The size of a cart-horse.' But it was not the size that mattered. Nobody dared to ask what it was. They knew it was Aslan.[35]

The imagery of colour in that last paragraph is variously suggestive. In one way, the greyness of the hillside suggests leadenness again, and therefore a *genius loci* that turns Solar influence to ill effect ('there is a curse on this place,' says Reepicheep, and he renames it Deathwater Island). In a second way, the greyness is reminiscent of the hoard of Spenser's Mammon: 'it is still hore (grey); he suns it that it may become gold.' From another point of view the heather is grey because, botanically, it is not in bloom: it will only bloom if the sun continues to shine on it. However, Lewis's primary concern is not with the literal sun: 'the sun had in fact gone in.' He is concerned with the one of whom the Sun is an image, the golden lion. 'Nobody dared to ask what it was. They knew it was Aslan'—an echo of John 21:12 ('None of the disciples dared ask him, 'Who are you?' They knew it was the Lord'). This episode is an example of Lewis's skill in blending romance, medieval astrology, literary and Biblical allusion, and his own 'suppositional' allegory. The powers of co-ordination and translation required to achieve such a sophisticated imaginative mix without overwhelming the narrative—indeed without making the narrative seem anything other than entirely natural and consistent—should not be under-estimated.

Before we leave the subject of metallurgy we must note that it is not confined to chapter 8; the engolding influence of Sol is evident in other places, too. The ship's flag bears the picture of a 'golden lion' and inside the stern cabin there is a 'flat gold image of Aslan.' In the other Chronicles, Aslan's image—on shields and banners—is usually Jovial red;[36] but in this story the special power of Solar alchemy means it is only ever gold.

And Sol's metallurgical operations have clearly been having their effect on the ship itself: she is largely covered in gold leaf: 'Her prow was gilded. . . . The sides of the ship—what you could see of them where the gilded wings of the dragon ended—were green'; 'The look-out man [stood] on a little shelf inside the gilded dragon's neck'; '[Behind the tiller] the dragon's tail rose up, covered with gilding.' The ship itself could not be made of solid gold or it would sink; but its gilding suggests that the sun's influence has been at work. And with that, we leave the subject of Solar transmutation and turn to the Sun's other qualities.

Sol is 'the sphere of philosophers,' and of all medieval philosophers Boethius was one of the most prominent. His *De Consolatione Philosphiae* was, in Lewis's opinion, among the most influential books ever written in Latin; he thought that to acquire a taste for it was almost to become naturalised in the Middle Ages. Boethius's treatment of Fortuna, which has its greatest legacy in

Dante's *Inferno* (VII, 73 ff), is 'Stoical and Christian alike, in full harmony with the Book of Job and with certain Dominical sayings,'[37] and it is upon this tradition that Reepicheep is drawing when he offers comfort to the endragoned Eustace in chapter 7:

> He would explain that what had happened . . . was a striking illustration of the turn of Fortune's wheel, and that if he had Eustace at his own house in Narnia . . . he could show him more than a hundred examples of emperors, kings, dukes, knights, poets, lovers, astronomers, philosophers, and magicians, who had fallen from prosperity into the most distressing circumstances, and of whom many had recovered and lived happily ever afterwards.[38]

Both with his mention of 'philosophers' (not a word which reappears in the Narniad) and in his Boethian philosophy, Reepicheep shows himself to be a lover of wisdom. Since Sol 'makes men wise' this is no more than we should expect. We find the desire for wisdom occurring also in Coriakin's hope that one day the monopods may by 'governed by wisdom instead of this rough magic' (an allusion to the 'rough magic' of Shakespeare's Prospero, himself an alchemist),[39] for the monopods are 'duffers,' foolish or unwise people, and the chief duffer's daughter is aptly named Clipsie, from *clipsi*, 'under eclipse, dark.' More generally, we find clarity of mind being symbolised in the advance toward the sunrise. 'The Planets' speaks of a 'broadening eastward / Clear and cloudless' and in *The 'Dawn Treader'* the 'unclouded' skies, the 'clear' and 'clearer' waters, the powerful sense of a kind of spacious intensity which the travellers encounter as they journey further east—these things become objective correlatives of a growing spiritual wisdom and a truly liberal philosophy.

Sol 'makes men liberal,' and liberality is a theme played in various keys throughout the book. By 'liberal' Lewis means a great many things; it is a word whose history he had studied minutely. A comparison of his academic discussion of the term in *Studies in Words* with his imaginative treatment of the same thing in *The 'Dawn Treader'* is highly instructive.

At one level, 'liberality' means generosity. Caspian, that 'golden-headed boy' (a glance, perhaps, at Apollo Chrysocomes, 'Apollo of the golden locks'), is conspicuously generous: he provides ale for the old salts, rum for the ship's company after the fight with the Sea Serpent, 'grog all round' following their escape from the Dark Island, and he promises 'gold or land enough' to make the sailors rich if they will accompany him to the utter East. More significantly, he helps bring about the release of Pug's slaves on the Lone Islands by offering a cask of wine to the slovenly guards at Narrowhaven, forgiving Gumpas his debt, and reimbursing both Lord Bern and the Calormene traders. Thus generosity is put in the service of 'fredom,' for, as he writes in *Studies in Words*, '*Liberales* are the sort of people who ransom prisoners,'[40] and he quotes Lord Berners (whose name presumably suggested that of Lord Bern): 'He and all his companye shal depart frank and free at their pleasure.'

At another level, liberality appears in the sense of 'liberal study,' the pursuit of knowledge that (as Newman wrote) 'stands on its own pretensions, which is independent of sequel . . . refuses to be informed (as it is called) by any end.'[41] Lewis, as a staunch defender of liberal education, was keen to keep alive the idea that 'free study seeks nothing beyond itself and desires the activity of knowing for that activity's own sake. That is what the man of radically servile character . . . will never understand. He will ask, "But what *use* is it?" '[42]

> 'Use?' replied Reepicheep. 'Use, Captain? If by use you mean filling our bellies or our purses, I confess it will be no use at all. So far as I know we did not set sail to look for things useful but to seek honour and adventure.'[43]

Thus Drinian is rebuked for asking 'what manner of use' it would be to plough into the amorphous blackness of the Dark Island; his question betrays an illiberal, utilitarian trait in his character.

And at a third level, liberality is associated in Lewis's mind with the meaning '*gratis*, not to be paid for,' that which opposes or frustrates cupidity. We have already touched on two episodes in the story where this kind of liberality is held before us, as Pug the slaver (in chapter 4) and the whole royal party (in chapter 8) learn something of what it means. There are four other places where this theme is played out and they are all presented by means of dragons and the defeat thereof. And here it is of utmost importance to note that Sol's forerunner, the Greek sun-god, Apollo, was famously a killer of dragons. He was known as 'Apollo Sauroctonus', Apollo the Lizard-slayer. 'Saura' is the Greek word for lizard or serpent or worm or dragon (a 'dinosaur' is a monstrous lizard); it gave Tolkien the name of his chief villain, Sauron, in *The Lord of the Rings*. Lewis is clearly enrolling Sol in his capacity as Apollo Sauroctonus in the defeats of the four dragons encountered during the course of this story.

The first of these defeats occurs in chapter 6 when we see the death of an old lugubrious dragon. This episode is powerfully redolent of the killing of the dragon Python in the Homeric *Hymn to Apollo*. There we learn that the sun-god sent arrows into the monster so that it lay 'rent with bitter pangs, drawing great gasps for breath and rolling about that place. An awful noise swelled up unspeakable as she writhed continually this way and that amid the wood; and so she left her life, breathing it forth in blood. Then Phoebus Apollo boasted over her.'[44] In *The 'Dawn Treader'* we read that there came from the dragon 'a great croaking or clanging cry and after a few twitches and convulsions it rolled round on its side. . . . A little dark blood gushed from its wide-opened mouth.' Lewis frames the account of this death by telling us, first, 'the sun beat down' and then, straight afterward, 'the sun disappeared.' However, here it is not Apollo Sauroctonus who boasts over the dragon's corpse but Eustace, who 'began to feel as if he had fought and killed the dragon instead of merely seeing it die.' His presumptuous claim to Solar power is shortly to be upended when he is turned into a dragon himself.

Eustace, whose metamorphosis occurs after he falls asleep on the dead dragon's hoard 'with greedy, dragonish thoughts in his heart,' finds that he is unable to free himself of 'the giant lizard' or 'serpent with legs' that he has become; for that to happen he has to submit to Aslan, the true Sol (that is, the true God, figured as Sol). We will look at Aslan's undragoning of Eustace below in the 'Solar *Logos*' section. All we need note at this point is that Eustace is indeed released from his cupidity by Aslan for, as soon as he is restored to human form, he slips the bracelet (which he had planned to steal) off his arm and announces, 'Anyone can have it as far as I'm concerned.' This same spirit of liberation from greed is communicated to the whole ship's company: no one feels any desire to go back to the first dragon's valley to search for its treasure.

Receptiveness to Solar influence among the ship's company is tested in the very next chapter as they have to defeat the third dragon of the story, the great Sea Serpent which tries to crush the ship, but which only succeeds in breaking off the *Dawn Treader*'s carved stern.

That carved stern is shaped, we must remember, like a dragon's tail, just as its bowsprit is like a dragon's head and its sides like dragon wings. The ship itself is the fourth dragon in the story, and here Lewis modulates the theme of liberality into a more theological or religious key. The ship may be taken as the expression of Caspian's own avariciousness: he is her maker (she is the first ship he has built, we are told) and his own cabin is decorated, ominously, with 'crimson dragons.' Despite all his nobility and heroism, Caspian is not immune from the worst kind of illiberal motivation. 'All dragons collect gold,' says Edmund, in connection with the dragon-that-is-Eustace, and the *Dawn Treader*'s dragon-shape tells us something about her builder and king. In the final chapter we suddenly discover that Caspian harbours a self-serving ambition to abdicate and seize Aslan's country by his own will. His urgent wish to go beyond the eastern edge of the world is another manifestation of dragonish greed, a kind of simony, a rapacious desire to grasp religious enlightenment— even at the price of his own life. It is akin to what Austin Farrer perceptively calls, in connection with Lewis's suspicions about the origins of *sehnsucht*, 'the ultimate refinement of covetousness.'[45] Caspian is restrained from this course of action first by the near-mutiny of the ship's company, then by a painful encounter with Aslan: 'it was terrible—his eyes'. This religious crisis brings the Sauroctonus theme to an intense and unexpected, but entirely appropriate, climax. Aslan-as-Sol burns away the dross in Caspian's motives. He makes the dragonish king and his dragonish ship subject to the spirit of gratuity, symbolized now in three main ways: by the freshening of the sea so that it can be drunk in deep enriching draughts; by the mysterious current that carries them across windless seas; and by the sublime 'fate' that directs the last moments of the voyage. Borne forward by this generous-hearted Solar deity, the voyagers finally tread the dawn:

> Up came the sun. . . . They could look at the rising sun and see it clearly and see things beyond it. What they saw—eastward, beyond the sun— was a range of mountains. . . . No one in that boat doubted that they were seeing beyond the End of the World into Aslan's country.[46]

Lewis is here borrowing Charles Williams's Sarras, the land of the Trinity, seen 'on a sea-site / in a light that shone from behind the sun.'[47] The glimpse is only fleeting: 'As the sun rose the sight of those mountains outside the world faded away.' But the vision is not the end of the voyage, for there is something even better to experience, the kiss of a golden lion on the children's foreheads. Then the backdrop rends and they find themselves in that other (and far less appealing) eastern place, 'the back bedroom in Aunt Alberta's home in Cambridge.'

Aunt Alberta thinks Eustace has become commonplace and tiresome and that (in the very last words of the book) 'it must have been the influence of those Pevensie children.' Lewis is here having a private joke at the expense of Mrs Scrubb, who clearly does not know the true metaphorical import of the word 'influence.'

> If *influence* occurs in an explicitly astrological passage we shall not go wrong; but unless we have our whole imagination so impregnated with the old point of view that reference to it has become habitual, we shall almost certainly fail to respond to the metaphorical uses of *influence* (say, in Milton). In our own language the metaphorical use of this word is the only one, and the metaphor is thoroughly dead. In the older writers is it glitteringly alive.[48]

The change in Eustace has been brought about not by the influence of his cousins, but by the *influenza* of Sol.

The Solar *Logos*

In analysing the Solar *poiema* we have already touched on elements of the Solar *logos*, Lewis's 'message.' This is inevitable, since the distinction between *poiema* and *logos* is far from absolute and, in the case of Sol, whose sphere is the heaven of theologians and philosophers, the boundary is even more indistinct than usual. Indeed, *The Voyage of the 'Dawn Treader'* is so full of *logos* that I cannot here attempt a comprehensive treatment. I shall confine the discussion to two things: the appearances of Aslan and Lucy's reading of the magician's book.

Aslan appears seven times in the course of the story. Each time he becomes a little more Solar.

His first appearance is to the endragoned Eustace. Lewis distances the episode by presenting it in retrospect: Eustace tells Edmund about his encounter with the lion after the event, and Aslan's words are given in reported speech. The meeting has occurred at night and therefore there is no sunlight, except at one remove, via the moon: 'there was no moon last night, but there was moonlight where the lion was,' 'there was always this moonlight over and round the lion wherever we went.' This emphasis on moonlight is appropriate for a Solar Christophany that is presented in indirect speech, for moonlight is 'sunlight at second hand.'[49] Sol, who 'hurts and humbles' according to 'The Planets,' has both these effects upon Eustace as he is undragoned: 'It hurt worse than anything I've ever felt'; 'it hurts like billy-oh'; 'and by the way, I'd like to apologize.' As Eustace is relating all this to Edmund, the last bright star fades and dawn arrives: 'though they could not see the sunrise because of the mountains on their right, they knew it was going on because the sky above them and the bay before them turned the colour of roses.' Here Lewis alludes to Homer's rosy-fingered Eos, the goddess of the dawn, who opened the gates of heaven so that Helios could ride his chariot across the sky. Aslan's Solar nature is introduced very subtly and skilfully in this scene.

In Aslan's second appearance, on Deathwater Island (which we have already looked at above), he is slightly more Solar. Though the sun has gone in, he shines 'as if he were in bright sunlight.' He says nothing as he passes majestically by, and the royal party look at one another 'like people waking from sleep' (another gentle touch of dawn imagery).

His third and fourth appearances occur on the Island of the Duffers. Lucy, who is searching Coriakin's book of spells,[50] sees a picture of Aslan in the book which 'was painted such a bright gold that it seemed to be coming towards her out of the page.' His face is stern and she hastily decides against uttering a spell to make herself beautiful 'beyond the lot of mortals.' Aslan's face fades and she continues turning over the pages until she finally reaches the spell she is looking for, the spell 'to make hidden things visible.' She utters it, not expecting the spell to have any effect except on the monopods and so she is surprised suddenly to find Aslan with her in the room, this time in bodily, not just pictorial, form; she buries her face in his 'shining mane' and says it was kind of him to come: 'I have been here all the time,' said he, 'but you have just made me visible.' Since

Aslan is figured in this book under the mask of Sol, the god of light, the effect Lucy has unwittingly wrought is similar to that which Robin had wished for in 'The Man Born Blind': the seeing of light itself, rather than simply the seeing of other things by means of it. She Contemplates what she was previously only Enjoying.

Aslan's fifth appearance is a further variation on the Alexander technique. When the 'Dawn Treader' is trapped in pitch blackness, lost in that 'Dark Country'[51] that Mandeville situates *en route* to Paradise, Lucy—who is standing aloft on the fighting-top—prays a desperate prayer for help. A 'tiny speck of light' becomes visible and 'a broad beam of light fell from it upon the ship.' We then read:

> Lucy looked along the beam and presently saw something in it. At first it looked like a cross, then it looked like an aeroplane, then it looked like a kite, and at last with a whirring of wings it was right overhead and was an albatross. It circled three times round the mast and then perched for an instant on the crest of the gilded dragon at the prow. It called out in a strong sweet voice what seemed to be words though no one understood them. After that it spread its wings, rose, and began to fly slowly ahead, bearing a little to starboard. Drinian steered after it not doubting that it offered good guidance. But no one except Lucy knew that as it circled the mast it had whispered to her, 'Courage, dear heart,' and the voice, she felt sure, was Aslan's, and with the voice a delicious smell breathed in her face.
>
> In a few moments the darkness turned into a greyness ahead, and then, almost before they dared to begin hoping, they had shot out into the sunlight and were in the warm, blue world again.[52]

Lucy looks 'along the beam'; she practises Enjoyment. There is no part of her left over or outside the act. And in that act of seeing, her eyes gradually see more and more. The two-dimensional cross develops motive power as an aeroplane; it then turns from a mere machine into a kite borne aloft on the wind, before becoming something organic, Coleridge's image of Christ, an albatross, the bird with the widest wing-span, which soars the longest and can fly by night. The suggestiveness of these images cannot be adequately addressed here. The most important element, theologically, is that Aslan is found in a shaft of sunlight: his status as a Solar deity is becoming clearer and clearer.

His sixth appearance is relatively minor, a lull before the full dawn. He comes alive before Caspian in 'the flat gold image' inside his cabin and we only hear about it briefly afterward. As with his effect on Eustace, Aslan 'hurts and humbles' Caspian, leaving him white-faced and tearful. It is through moments such as these that Lewis prevents his Christ-figure from degenerating into a cute little sunbeam. Sol, he reminds us, is terrible as well as life-giving; blinding and absolute as well as warming and enlightening.

And it is this divinely paradoxical nature that is evident in Aslan's seventh and final appearance, at the Very End of the World. The sun is now so proximate that it is ceasing to be golden and is becoming albescent. Lewis introduces this new colour scheme in connection with a mysterious sight that turns out to be miles and leagues of lilies: 'whiteness, shot with faintest colour of gold, spread round them on every side.' Later, the children see 'something so white on the grass that even with their eagles' eyes, they could hardly look at it.' But, in the words of 'Noon's Intensity,' they have been 'trained by slow degrees [to] have such sight / As dares the pure projection to behold.' They behold a Lamb. With 'a sweet milky voice' he invites the children to 'come and have breakfast,' another allusion to John 21:12. As the Lamb speaks, 'his snowy white flushed into tawny gold and his size changed and he was Aslan himself, towering above them and scattering light from his mane.' This is the final metallurgical operation of the book, the transformation of the white-gold Lamb into the scintillating Lion. His Solar character could hardly be more explicitly conveyed. Sol 'comes ascendant,' and in him more perfectly the reader sees all 'baser virtues,' including less precious metal (namely the silver of 'The Silver Sea') and less completely Solar images of Aslan (cross, aeroplane, kite, albatross, lamb). The search for that thing 'more gold than gold,'[53] has been accomplished.

It might be asked why Lucy's vision of the cross in the sunbeam is not the ultimate goal. What theological rationale is governing Lewis's use of Solar imagery so as to relegate the cross to such a minor position several chapters before the finale? Do Lewis's 'solar ethics'—to borrow a term from Don Cupitt—have sufficient regard for the categories of the incarnation and the passion of the Christ-figure?

A similar question could be asked with respect to Lucy's reading of Coriakin's book and the spell she utters for the 'refreshment of the spirit.' This spell is more like a story than a spell. It is the loveliest story that Lucy has ever read, and she forgets that she is even reading it—she seems to be living it: it is the story of a cup and a sword and a tree and a green hill. She asks Aslan, 'Shall I ever be able to read that story again . . . ? Will you tell it to me, Aslan? Oh do, do, do.' The answer she hears is: 'Indeed, yes, I will tell it to you for years and years.' Since this story is clearly the Gospel (good spell) story, one might ask why it comes in chapter 10 and not at the climax of the book. The 'loveliest story'— about the eucharistic cup, the sword that pierces Mary's heart, the tree of salvation, and Calvary's 'green hill far away without a city wall'—would appear to have been downgraded, rather like the cross in the beam of light. Why is Lewis so chary of foregrounding the Christ-event?

One reason, of course, is that he has already foregrounded it in *The Lion, the Witch and the Wardrobe*. Another, more pertinent, reason is that he is deliberately attempting to ballast his Solar imagery with scriptural particularities before he cuts it free in the closing chapters of the story. One of the dangers of Solar theological imagery is that it tends toward a kind of docetism, the heretical view that Christ only *appeared* to be human, and Lewis naturally, as a self-consciously mainstream, orthodox writer, wanted to avoid giving a docetic presentation of Christ. In order to understand his thoughts on this matter, it will be worth looking at what he says elsewhere about Akhenaten's *Hymn to the Sun* (1400 B.C.).

The Solar monotheism of the *Hymn to the Sun* seems better, in one way, Lewis argues, than the primitive Judaism we find in the early books of the Old Testament, but it does not follow that 'Akhenatenism' would have been a better first step in the history of divine revelation. Akhenaten was astonishingly advanced; he did not identify God with the Sun in a strictly heliolatrous way but understood the visible disc as a divine manifestation. This early Egyptian religion, 'a simple, enlightened, reasonable Monotheism,' looks much more like developed Christianity, from one perspective, than those first documents of Judaism in which Yahweh appears to be little more than a peculiar tribal deity. However, Lewis concludes:

> If Man is finally to know the bodiless, timeless, transcendent Ground of the whole universe not as a mere philosophical abstraction but as the Lord who, despite his transcendence, is "not far from any one of us", as an utterly concrete Being (far more concrete than we) whom Man can fear, love, address, and "taste", he must begin far more humbly and far nearer home, with the local altar, the traditional feast. . . . It is possible that a certain sort of enlightenment can come too soon and too easily. At that early stage it may not be fruitful to typify God by anything so remote, so neutral, so international and (as it were) so interdenominational, so featureless, as the solar disc. Since in the end we are to come to baptism and the Eucharist, to the stable at Bethlehem, the hill of Calvary, and the emptied rock-tomb, perhaps it is better to begin with circumcision, the Passover, the Ark, and the Temple. For "the highest does not stand without the lowest". Does not stand, does not stay; rises, rather, and expands, and finally loses itself in endless space. For the entrance is low: we must stoop till we are no taller than children in order to get in.[54]

It is Lewis's intention in *The Voyage of the 'Dawn Treader'* to typify the divine figure by means of the Solar disc, to emphasize his transcendence and universality. Aslan here is very different from the furry beast who romps and battles cheek-by-jowl with the children in the first two books. He floats in and out of this story in intense moments of conversion, prayer, reproof, spiritual illumination, and mystical ecstasy; he has a rarefied, exalted existence, which is constantly at risk of being lost in endless space like 'the ultimate refinement of Golden poetry, Gold 'to ayery thinnesse beate,' without weight, ready to leave the earth.'[55] But this is a risk that Lewis has to take in order to fulfil his donegalitarian purpose. The tether and pang of the concrete particularities mentioned in the magician's book (cup, sword, tree, hill), just like the metamorphosing objects seen in the beam of light (cross, plane, kite, bird), provide a needed counterweight to Lewis's aureate intention. These very solid and mundane things appear in advance of the finale not because Lewis is wanting to get them out of the way so as to conclude with a docetic message, but precisely because he recognises the Christological dangers inherent in Solar imagery: it needs to be pegged and freighted and prevented from soaring aloft prematurely. Although 'a certain sort of enlightenment can come too soon,' it is, in this case, the sort of enlightenment that the story is deliberately designed to communicate—a poetic, Johannine presentation of Christ. Just as in the New Testament canon John's Gospel is preceded and, as it were, offset by the less artful and more simply historiographical perspective of the three synoptic gospels, so Lewis contrives something of a synoptic-like ballast earlier in the story, allowing him to move steadily, deliberately, and orthodoxly to his Johannine climax.

The two allusions to John 21:12 are not the only Johannine elements in the book. Very near the end of the story, Edmund asks Aslan, 'Are you there [in our world] too, Sir?,' to which Aslan replies, 'I am.' By putting these words in Aslan's mouth, Lewis evokes the divine title that was first revealed to Moses and that John the Evangelist redeploys throughout his Gospel in the various 'I am' sayings of Christ. In particular, given the context, he evokes John 8:12: 'I am the light of the world; he who follows me will not walk in darkness, but will have the light of life.' Lewis does not spell out for us his Christ-figure's Solar characteristics, any more than he spells out the other elements of the story's Solar theme. His intention was to make us 'look along' those beams and, by definition, one cannot see what one looks along. This chapter, if its argument is correct, has just made those hidden things visible, but they have been there all the time.

SIX

Luna

A drizzling glamour enchants us.
—'The Planets' (lines 4–5)

Lewis adopted a protective stance toward Luna's literary reputation, rebuking writers who treated her badly and approving writers who treated her well. He thought so highly of Lodge's line—'Daughter of Jove and sister to the Sunne'—that he would repeat it to himself 'for sheer pleasure.'[1] But he was outraged when his friend Katharine Farrer described the Moon 'like the white face of an idiot lost in a wood' and told her that she was denigrating 'the high creatures of God'; he suggested she learn Psalm 136 by heart as a penance and added, 'Not safe, either, to be rude to goddesses.'[2] Sometimes he found that the same author could both honour and dishonour Luna. He analyses two passages by Lyly, one that he calls 'really suitable to the tale of a man who loved the moon' and one he thinks 'frigid.'[3] It is Lyly's former example which Lewis tried to imitate in his scholarship, in *That Hideous Strength*, in his poetry, and in *The Silver Chair*.

Luna in Lewis's Scholarship

Luna provides Lewis's imagination with a potent symbol of ambiguity. Her association with this quality comes from her astronomical position on the borders of the realm of mutability, which Lewis summarises as follows in *The Discarded Image:*

At Luna we cross...the great frontier...from aether to air, from 'heaven' to 'nature,' from the realm of gods (or angels) to that of daemons, from the realm of necessity to that of contingence, from the incorruptible to the corruptible. Unless this 'great divide' is firmly fixed in our minds, every passage in Donne or Drayton or whom you will that mentions 'translunary' or 'sublunary' will lose its intended force. We shall take 'under the moon' as a vague synonym, like our 'under the sun,' for 'everywhere,' when in reality it is used with precision. When Gower says

> We that dwelle under the Mone
> Stand in this world upon a weer

...he means exactly what he says. If we lived above the Moon we should not suffer *weer* (doubt, uncertainty). When Chaucer's Nature says

> Ech thing in my cure is
> Under the Moone that mai wane and waxe

...she is distinguishing her mutable realm from the translunary world where nothing grows or decreases.[4]

Given the Moon's position between these two realms she can become a symbol of either, and so we find Lewis treating her now as a thing of beauty,[5] now as a thing of ridicule ('moonshine' is a common Lewisian term for idle nonsense).[6] Her surface is solid and bone dry and yet she is the watery planet, insubstantial and inconstant.[7] Her association with such contradictory qualities arises not just from her position at the Ptolemaic boundary of aether and air, but also from her own behaviour: she can be the brightest object in the night sky but can sometimes disappear altogether; when visible she wanders rapidly, changing shape and size and colour.

As a result of this unstable behaviour, Luna has another influence, closely related to uncertainty:

> In men she produces wandering, and that in two senses. She may make them travellers so that, as Gower says, the man born under Luna will 'seche manye londes strange'... But she may also produce 'wandering' of the wits, especially that periodical insanity which was first meant by the word *lunacy*[8]... These are the 'dangerous, unsafe lunes' of the *Winter's Tale* (II, ii, 30); whence (and on other grounds) *lunes* in *Hamlet* (III, iii, 7) is an almost certain emendation for...Folio's unmetrical *lunacies*. Dante assigns the Moon's sphere to those who have entered the conventual life and abandoned it for some good or pardonable reason.[9]

Lewis's summary of Luna in *The Discarded Image* is about three times longer than any of his other planetary summaries, but this imbalance is not reflected in his scholarship in general. Indeed, there is only one other notable appearance of the Moon in his academic writings, and that in connection with Luna's metal, which is silver. Lewis takes Derek Traversi to task for incorrectly identifying Spenser's Diana as Britomart, when, if there had been any realistic alternative, it ought to have been Belphoebe. In choosing between Diana and Belphoebe, Traversi could have got his identification right simply by looking at the material of the buskins worn by the characters in question: 'Silver is a Lunar metal, and therefore appropriate for Diana. Belphoebe, on the other hand, is a daughter of the sun, and accordingly wears golden buskins.'[10] Lewis's point illustrates the importance he attached as a critic to iconographical attention. I hope this book is demonstrating that the same sort of attention serves to unlock his own practice as a poet and writer of fiction. It is to his longest work of fiction that we now turn.

Luna in *That Hideous Strength*

Luna, like Sol, does not participate in the descent of the gods in *That Hideous Strength*. However, unlike Sol, Luna has a large role to play elsewhere in the novel despite this absence. The two main Lunar characteristics that Lewis draws on are boundary status and maddening influence.

The boundary position of Luna is central to the plan of the N.I.C.E., who are under the impression that 'nothing from outside could pass the Moon's orbit.' Wither's dark Masters (the Macrobes) have assured him of the existence of 'a barrier which made it impossible that powers from Deep Heaven should reach the surface of the Earth.' But these Masters, it transpires, have been 'completely out in their calculations,' and the descent of the gods takes them and their human pawns by surprise.

Merlin is equally surprised, for although he was once conversant with the planets, it was only with their earthly wraiths, not their heavenly originals.[11] In conversation with Ransom, he refers to 'the Seventh Law,' which decrees that Maleldil 'will not send down the Powers to mend or mar in this Earth until the end of all things.' He wonders, therefore, whether the last days are now coming to pass.[12] Ransom says he does not know, adding: 'Maleldil may have made it a law not to send down the Powers. But if men by enginry and natural philosophy learn to fly into the Heavens, and come, in the flesh, among the heavenly powers and trouble them, He has not forbidden the Powers to react. For all this is within the natural order.' And because Weston has indeed learnt to fly beyond the Moon, the whole enterprise of the N.I.C.E. turns out to be self-defeating. 'The wicked man had brought about, even as Judas brought about, the thing he least intended. . . . Our enemies had taken away from themselves the protection of the Seventh Law. They had broken by natural philosophy the barrier which God of His own power would not break.'

From these remarks one might suppose that Lewis was opposed to universal exploration and the progress of science, a charge that was levelled at him by the biologist and biochemist, Professor J.B.S. Haldane.[13] Lewis did indeed have a reluctance to see man conquering space, for he considered it an historical fact that conquest invariably brought suffering to the conquered peoples and places.[14] However, this attitude is not the sum total of his thoughts on the matter. He has Ransom speak thus, from a different perspective:

> 'Sulva is she whom mortals call the Moon. She walks in the lowest sphere. The rim of the world that was wasted goes through her. Half of her orb is turned towards us and shares our curse. Her other half looks to Deep Heaven; happy would he be who could cross that frontier and see the fields on her further side.'[15]

With these words Ransom (and, we may suppose, Lewis) acknowledges a proper place for translunary exploration. By being kidnapped and taken to Mars in *Out of the Silent Planet* and then deployed to Venus in *Perelandra*, Ransom has in any case quite innocently traversed the Lunar divide and, as a result, has been enabled to draw down the powers of Heaven to Earth and thus save Thulcandra from danger: 'For now there was one man in the world—even myself—who was known to the Oyéresu and spoke their tongue.' Ransom becomes a 'bridge' across which the saving influences of the translunary realm may pass.

When considering Luna, the members of the N.I.C.E. have no interest in 'crossing the frontier' to her further side. They are concerned only with her accursed face, the bloodless, sterile side of her character which dominates chapter 8, 'Moonlight at Belbury.' Filostrato flings back the curtains to show Mark the Moon:

> 'There is a world for you, no?' said Filostrato. 'There is cleanness, purity. Thousands of square miles of polished rock with not one blade of grass, not one fibre of lichen, not one grain of dust. Not even air. Have you thought what it would be like, my friend, if you could walk on that land? No crumbling, no erosion. The peaks of those mountains are real peaks: sharp as needles, they would go through your hand. Cliffs as high as Everest and as straight as the wall of a house. And cast by those cliffs, acres of shadow black as ebony, and in the shadow

hundreds of degrees of frost. And then, one step beyond the shadow, light that would pierce your eyeballs like steel and rock that would burn your feet. The temperature is at boiling point. You would die, no? But even then you would not become filth. In a few moments you are a little heap of ash; clean, white powder.'[16]

Rowan Williams calls this passage 'brilliant' and describes the whole depiction of the anti-natural, anti-organic phenomenology of evil in *That Hideous Strength* as one of the book's great virtues, 'enormously good.'[17] We hear more of the disembodying effect of the earthward-face of the Moon when Ransom tells Merlin how 'on this side [of Sulva], the womb is barren and the marriages cold. There dwell an accursed people, full of pride and lust. There when a young man takes a maiden in marriage, they do not lie together, but each lies with a cunningly fashioned image of the other, made to move and to be warm by devilish arts, for real flesh will not please them, they are so dainty (*delicati*) in their dreams of lust.'

This, at any rate, is Ransom's perspective. Filostrato has a different view about which side of the Moon is the dark side. He tells Mark:

'Her surface is not all as you see. There are still surface-dwellers—savages. One great dirty patch on the far side of her where there is still water and air and forests—yes, and germs and death. [The inorganic race] are slowly spreading their hygiene over the whole globe. Disinfecting her. The savages fight against them. There are frontiers, and fierce wars, in the caves and galleries down below. But the great race presses on. If you could see the other side you would see year by year the clean rock—like this side of the Moon—encroaching: the organic stain, all the green and blue and mist, growing smaller.'[18]

The N.I.C.E. have wrenched away one aspect of Natural Law—the desire for physical purity—and swollen it to madness in isolation from the rest. For though, as Ransom acknowledges, virginity is a good thing, it is not the only thing. There is also the body, which has been honoured by its Christological assumption when Maleldil became a man, and which must not be deprecated. Filostrato scorns the fertile side of the Moon as nothing more than 'tarnished silver.' He and his fellow members of the N.I.C.E. are interested only in her near side, what the narrator calls 'not the voluptuous Moon of a thousand southern love-songs, but the huntress, the untameable virgin, the spear-head of madness.' Therefore they are given their hearts' desire and become truly mad. Grace Ironwood predicts that their overemphasis on the head will produce 'lunacy,' and when Frost and Wither genuflect before the tramp near the end of the story the narrator tells us it was a moment of 'pure lunacy.'

On the other hand, the company of St. Anne's come under Sulva's voluptuous influence, that of 'a thousand southern love-songs.' It is a note no sooner struck than it is taken up by Luna's sister, Venus, who 'comes more near the Earth than she was wont to—to make Earth sane.' With these words Ransom contradicts Dimble's earlier quotation from *Othello*:[19] it is not madness, but purest sanity which the heroes and heroines enjoy as they make love at the end of the story. For Luna marks not only the boundary between sanity and madness, but also the boundary between two different kinds of goodness, the virginal and the voluptuous. The symbolism here is admittedly somewhat blurry—eliding one aspect of the Lunar influence into the Venereal—but it just about succeeds in keeping its head.

Luna in Lewis's Poetry

Luna appears in at least six of Lewis's poems.[20] She never dominates a whole poem, but is merely added in as one symbolic ingredient among many. Nor does Lewis seem to favour one aspect of her influence over the others; he selects from the wide range on offer as occasion requires. In 'French Nocturne,' her earliest appearance in his poetry, she is a 'False, mocking fancy,' where 'fancy' is a specifically Lunar trait.[21] In 'To G. M.' and 'Two Kinds of Memory' it is the dry, mineral aspect of her nature which the poet draws upon; in 'The Turn of the Tide,' her inconstancy.

The two most extensive poetic treatments of Luna are found in 'The Queen of Drum' and 'The Planets.'

In the former we find a long Lunar episode (V, 121–220) in which the Queen is 'filled all through with virtue of the moon.'[22] The passage features the Lunar metal ('silvery lakes,' 'silver haze,' 'elven silver,' 'silver rush'); Lunar water ('rivers,' 'lakes,' 'smooth like liquid,' 'like the moon herself, / Lapped in a motion which is also rest'); Lunar ambiguity ('The queen whose shafts destroy and bless'); a range of Lunar goddesses (Hecate, Titania, Artemis, Diana 'the pure Huntress riding low'); and Lunar deception (the 'thornbush, milky white' that is mistaken for 'a giant's head'). As with much of Lewis's early poetry, the range of reference is impressively wide, but the atmospheric unity is weak.

In 'The Planets,' where Lewis relies less on the scatter-gun approach, we are given the following description:

Lady LUNA, in light canoe,[23]
By friths and shallows of fretted cloudland
Cruises monthly; with chrism of dews
And drench of dream, a drizzling glamour,

1. Pauline Baynes' original cover art for *The Lion, the Witch and the Wardrobe* (1950).

> Of wrath ended
>
> And woes mended, of winter passed
>
> And guilt forgiven, and good fortune
>
> Jove is master; and of jocund revel,
>
> Laughter of ladies. The lion-hearted,
>
> The myriad-minded, men like the gods,
>
> Helps and heroes, helms of nations
>
> Just and gentle, are Jove's children.
>
> —'The Planets' (1935)

2. Jupiter and his children. One of a series of woodcuts by Hans Sebald Beham (1500–1550), depicting all seven planetary gods (Photo: Warburg Institute). Jupiter, enthroned in the heavens, inspires hunting (background), judgement (mid left), and coronation (foreground).

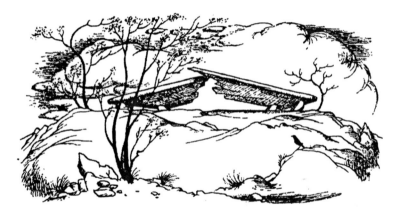

3. Hunting the White Stag: King Peter the Magnificent, Queen Susan the Gentle, King Edmund the Just, and Queen Lucy the Valiant. *The Lion, the Witch and the Wardrobe* (Illustration: Pauline Baynes).

4. The Stone Table, place of judgement. *The Lion, the Witch and the Wardrobe* (Illustration: Pauline Baynes).

5. The castle of Cair Paravel, its Great Hall roofed with ivory and hung with peacock's feathers, where the four children are hailed, enthroned, crowned and sceptred. *The Lion, the Witch and the Wardrobe* (Illustration: Pauline Baynes).

6. Mars in his capacities as god of war (Mars Gradivus) and god of woods (Mars Silvanus). Mural in the Casa di Venere, Pompeii.

7. 'Martial policy': Miraz in single combat with the 'great warrior' Peter, overseen by Dryads, Hamadryads and Silvans. *Prince Caspian* (Illustration: Pauline Baynes).

8. Apollo Sauroctonus, the lizard-slayer. Copy of a bronze statue by Praxiteles, fourth century B.C., in the Vatican Museum, Rome (Photo: Warburg Institute).

9. Eustace Clarence Scrubb, transformed 'like a giant lizard,' despairs of undragoning himself. *The Voyage of the 'Dawn Treader'* (Illustration: Pauline Baynes).

10. Caspian and his eastward-bound party discover the metallurgical properties of the pool on Goldwater Island. *The Voyage of the 'Dawn Treader'* (Illustration: Pauline Baynes).

11. Luna drives her horse-drawn chariot across the heavens.
Bas relief in the Malatestian Temple, Rimini, c.1470
(Photo: Warburg Institute).

12. The 'wanderers' escape Underland astride Coalblack and Snowflake. *The Silver Chair* (Illustration: Pauline Baynes).

13. Cartouche showing the boundary between Moon and Sun. *The Silver Chair* (Illustration: Pauline Baynes).

14. Mercury, messenger of the gods. Copy of a statue by Giovanni da Bologna (c.1524–1608), erected in Tom Quad, Christ Church, Oxford, 1928 (Photo: Michael Ward).

15. 'Run, run: always run': Shasta hastens toward Archenland with his message. *The Horse and His Boy* (Illustration: Pauline Baynes).

16. 'Meeting selves, same but sundered': identical twins, Cor and Corin, reunited. *The Horse and His Boy* (Illustration: Pauline Baynes).

17. Venus holding an apple. Oil painting by Bartholomeus van der Helst (1613–1670) in the Musée des Beaux-Arts, Lille.

18. Digory gives to his Mother the Apple of Life from the Western Garden.
The Magician's Nephew (Illustration: Pauline Baynes).

19. Aslan commands the newly created pairs of animals to awaken and to love. *The Magician's Nephew*
(Illustration: Pauline Baynes).

20. Saturn eating one of his children. Panel painting above the stage in Shakespeare's Globe Theatre, London (Photo: Richard Kalina).

His mouth shut like a box when he had said this, and in the great silence of that cave the children felt that they would not dare to speak again. The bare feet of the gnomes, padding on the deep moss, made no sound. There was no wind, there were no birds, there was no sound of water. There was no sound of breathing from the strange beasts.

When they had walked for several miles, they came to a wall of rock, and in it a low archway leading into another cavern. It was not, however, so bad as the last entrance and Jill could go through it without bending her head. It brought them into a smaller cave, long and narrow, about the shape and size of a cathedral. And here, filling almost the whole length of it, lay an enormous man fast asleep. He was far bigger than any of the giants, and his face was not like a giant's, but noble and beautiful. His breast rose and fell gently under the snowy beard which covered him to the waist. A pure, silver light (no-one saw where it came from) rested upon him.

"Who's that?" asked Puddleglum. And it was so long since anyone had spoken, that Jill wondered how he had the nerve.

"That is the god Saturn, who once was a King in Over-land," said the Warden. "And now he has sunk down into the Deep Realm and lies dreaming of all the things that are done in the Upper world. Many sink down and few return to the sunlit lands. They say he will wake at the end of the world."

21. Page 121 of the typescript of *The Silver Chair*, the only surviving typescript from the Narniad (Bodleian Library, Oxford). For the published version, Lewis amended 'That is the god Saturn' to 'That is old Father Time.' In *The Last Battle,* the Saturnine Chronicle, Father Time stirs from sleep and brings Narnia to its end.

22. 'Narnia is no more': Cair Paravel filled with dead Narnians, and Roonwit the Centaur lying dead with an arrow in his side. *The Last Battle* (Illustration: Pauline Baynes).

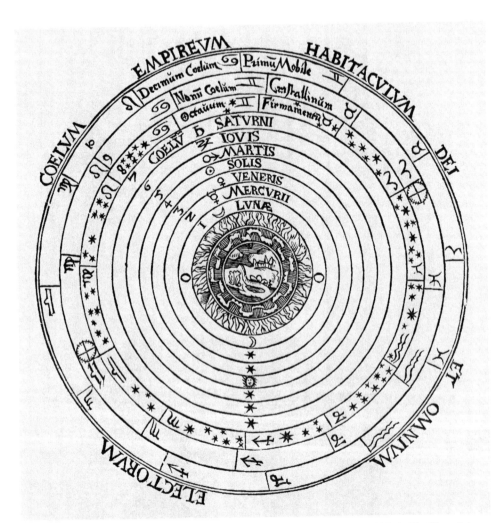

23. A diagram of the pre-Copernican universe from Peter Apian's *Cosmographia* (c. 1585). In *The Discarded Image* Lewis, following Dante in *The Divine Comedy*, mentions only one sphere between that of Saturn and the Primum Mobile: the Stellatum, heaven of the fixed stars.

Enchants us—the cheat! changing sometime
A mind to madness, melancholy pale,
Bleached with gazing on her blank count'nance
Orb'd and ageless. In earth's bosom
The shower of her rays, sharp-feathered light
Reaching downward, ripens silver,
Forming and fashioning female brightness,
—Metal maidenlike. Her moist circle
Is nearest earth.[24]

Here there is obviously a key-note: wateriness. In just thirteen lines we are presented with the substantive images of *canoe*, *friths*, *shallows*, *chrism*, *dews*, *shower*, and *moisture*, and active images of *cruising*, *drenching*, and *drizzling*. And it is this watery aspect which is at the forefront in his Narnian expression of Lunar qualities in *The Silver Chair*.

Luna in *The Silver Chair*

The Lunar *Poiema*

Lewis has the Moon's drenching, drizzling, dewy effects in mind throughout *The Silver Chair*. It is a theme introduced on the very first page of the first chapter where we meet a girl called Jill Pole,[25] who is crying on a 'damp little path.' She is joined by Eustace (whom we know from the previous book), who sits down on 'grass that was soaking wet.' We also read of drops that 'dripped off the laurel trees,' that 'drip off the leaves,' and of 'drops of water on the grass.' Nothing of significance to the plot comes of these images, but they are beginning to create a definite atmosphere.[26]

In the second chapter, water has a more obvious role to play, in connection with Jill's tears and the stream from which she is desperate to drink. After Jill has slaked her thirst, Aslan blows her down into Narnia, and in his breath she can move as freely 'as you can in water (if you've learned to float really well)'; she is blown into the 'wet fogginess' of a cloud[27] and emerges from it with 'her clothes wet'; she is then splashed by a wave of the sea 'drenching her nearly to the waist'; the chapter ends with her exclamation, 'How wet I am!'

It would be tedious to detail every other reference to water and wetness in the book, but it is worth noting Jill's baths in chapters 3 and 8, her 'wet pillow,' the frequent 'rain' (mentioned at least six times), Caspian's 'watery' eyes, the fountain where Rilian's mother met her death, the marshes in chapter 5 with their 'muddy water,' their 'countless channels of water'; and, above all, the suggestively named marsh-wiggle, Puddleglum.[28]

Puddleglum belongs to a race who do 'watery' work and he himself is thrice described as a 'wet blanket.' A 'flood' features among the disasters he imagines have struck the land; he says his firewood 'may be wet'; his pipe-smoke trickles out of his bowl like 'mist'; he mentions the river Shribble and its lack of bridges; predicts 'damp bowstrings'; snores like a waterfall; wonders if rain is on its way. His drunkenness in chapter 7 is a further manifestation of Luna, both because it causes confusion and because it comes from liquidity.

Once Puddleglum has joined Jill and Eustace on their quest, they ford the Shribble (which makes Jill wet to the knees), pass 'countless streams' on Ettinsmoor, and are 'never short of water'; they see a river 'full of rapids and waterfalls' and become 'sick of wind and rain.' On their way to Harfang they endure 'nasty wet business' and everyone 'got wet,' 'too wet by now to bother about being a bit wetter.' They are rowed by the gnomes of Bism in a boat on an underground sea; the enchanted Rilian's words are 'like cold water down the back,' but later they are glad to find real 'water for washing.' Eventually a 'flood' does indeed strike the land, but it is the witch's kingdom, not Narnia, which is inundated. When we see the last of Puddleglum he is still pointing out that bright mornings bring on 'wet afternoons.'

From the instability of water we move to the spatial and mental instability that derive from Lunar influence. The three adventurers' search for Prince Rilian, a search that is fitful and hapless, suggests both kinds of wandering.[29] In Rilian himself these effects are even more clearly depicted. We hear of the 'wanderings' he underwent when seeking his mother's murderer and we see the same impulse when he dallies with the possibility of exploring Bism. And with regard to wandering of the wits, we are told that he is 'like a man out of his wits' and that there comes an hour each night 'when my mind is most horribly changed' by a 'fury,' a 'frenzy,' 'ravings.' During that hour he turns into 'a lunatic' and his horrifying fantasy about being 'buried alive' and 'dragged down under the earth' is a repeat performance of the 'lunacy'[30] evinced by Weston in *Perelandra*, who also fears being 'buried alive'[31] and sucked down into the earth's core away from God, who remains 'outside, like a moon.'[32] Once Rilian has been disenchanted he describes himself and his rescuers as 'we four wanderers.'

Luna inspires men to 'seche manye londes strange,' and in *The Silver Chair* there are a total of five different lands, more than in any other Chronicle.[33] England, Aslan's Country, Narnia, the Underworld, and Bism. But more significant than their number is the geographical arrangement of the four sub-created worlds: they comprise a quadruple-decker universe. Here we see how Lewis has built Luna's boundary status into the architectonics of his story.[34] The difference between Aslan's country and Narnia is clearly modelled on the Lunary divide; it is Lewis's version of Deguileville's earlier Christian dramatization of the same thing.[35] Robert Houston Smith writes: 'The contrast between the purity of the atmosphere in Aslan's country and the thickened, miasmic vapors of Narnia is particularly redolent of the [medieval] Model.'[36] He does not pursue this lead and reflect upon the further divide between Narnia and the witch's kingdom (where the air is even thicker), nor the *third* such divide, between the Underworld and the land of Bism. This succession of divisions, and the reversal back through them, means that the story is constructed like the letter V.

Chapters 1 & 2		Chapter 16
(England and		(England and
Aslan's Country)		Aslan's Country)

	Chapters 2–9	Chapters 15–16	
	(Narnia)	(Narnia)	

Chapters 9–14
(Underland, with
a glimpse down
to Bism)

We are told of 'the freshness of the air' in Aslan's country, which makes Jill think 'they must be on the top of a very high mountain,' even though 'there is not a breath of wind.' Looking down, Jill and Eustace see distant white things beneath them that at first could be taken for sheep, but are actually clouds. The 'real bottom' is further below those clouds than the children are above them.

Aslan gives Jill the signs and warns her about her coming adventures: 'Here on the mountain the air is clear and your mind is clear; as you drop down into Narnia, the air will thicken. Take great care that it does not confuse your mind. And the signs which you have learned here will not look at all as you expect them to look, when you meet them there.' This turns out to be the case: Eustace does not realise that the old man he has seen departing on a ship is the same Caspian whom he had once known as a young king; the adventurers do not perceive that the trenches they fall into are really huge letters carved in the rock. Ignorance, forgetfulness, rain, wind, and snow all play their part in befuddling their minds, and Jill gives up repeating the signs to herself. Confusion leads to confusion until in chapter 10 ('Travels without the Sun') they fall down into Underland, having built a 'barrier' between themselves and Narnia. Jill feels she is being 'smothered'; the place is 'suffocating'; they begin to wonder whether 'sun and blue skies and wind and birds had not been only a dream.' As they are repeatedly told, 'Many fall down, and few return to the sunlit lands.' Under the enchanting music and scent and warmth engineered by the witch they begin to lose all remembrance of the Overworld, until Puddleglum, 'talking like a man who hasn't enough air,' recalls the stars and the sun but, intriguingly, not the Moon.

The Moon—that is, the Narnian Moon—does not feature as frequently in the story as one might at first expect. This is because, in the central section of the book, Lewis is wanting to remove all sense of height and space: continually to be taking our mind's eye to the heavens would frustrate this purpose.[37] In chapter 4, Glimfeather carries Jill by moonlight to the Parliament of Owls,[38] but by the time the meeting is over 'the moon had disappeared' and it does not properly reappear for eleven chapters. As the heroes approach Harfang, they see lights which, significantly, are 'not moonlight,' and it is in Jill's dream, rather than waking reality, that 'the moon shone bright.' Only after the adventurers have escaped from Underland are they again allowed to see 'moonlight,' a 'moonlit night.' And when Jill and Eustace clamber 'out from the blackness into the moonlight' and see 'the moon and the huge stars overhead,' they find that they can't 'quite believe' any longer in the existence of Underland, that sub-sublunary world.

Although the Moon itself does not appear between chapters 4 and 15, from chapter 9 onward (that is, from the descent into the witch's realm) the Lunar influence already at work in the story is intensified in one very obvious respect. We have already read of pale hills, pale sunlight, and of Puddleglum's face 'so pale that you could see the paleness under the natural muddiness of his complexion.' Now, almost everything becomes 'melancholy pale,' as 'The Planets' has it. Melancholia is most evident in the faces of the witch's slaves: 'every face in the whole hundred was as sad as a face could be . . . so sad that . . . Jill almost forgot to be afraid of them'; even the famously pessimistic Puddleglum is impressed by their dolefulness. And the adjective 'pale,' which is how Lewis glosses Henryson's 'haw,'[39] is found attached to almost every available noun: pale Earthmen, pale sand, pale lanterns, pale beaches, pale lamps, pale light, Eustace's face is 'pale and dirty,' Rilian's face is 'as pale as putty'; a Lord 'with a pale face' welcomes Caspian home who is himself 'very pale'; Aslan touches the 'pale faces' of Jill and Eustace. Lewis was of the view that the recurrence of a single word can be an 'undoubtedly necessary'[40] element in establishing the tone of a passage. This is an example of an occasion where he overdoes it.

Lewis's use of 'silver' is more evenly spaced throughout the book. It appears first in the title; as with *The Voyage of the 'Dawn Treader'* and *The Last Battle*, the identity of this story's presiding planet could be divined from the title alone. Once past the cover, we find 'a row of shields, bright as silver' at Cair Paravel; a 'silver mail shirt' for Caspian; a 'silver ear-trumpet' for Trumpkin; a lamp in Jill's castle room that hangs by 'a silver chain.' During her night-time flight on Glimfeather Jill sees a patch of 'watery silver'; the Porter at the Giants' Castle complains that 'the silver [cutlery, salt cellars, etc.] *will* keep on getting over here'; in the Underworld they see 'a pure silver light'; the witch has 'soft silver laughs'; Bism has 'real silver,' different from the 'dead silver' of the superficial mines; Rilian's black shield turns 'bright as silver' upon his disenchantment and he re-clothes himself in 'silver mail'; the dying Caspian is welcomed home by 'a flourish of silver trumpets.' Chief of all the silvers, of course, is the eponymous 'silver chair,' that 'vile engine of sorcery,' whose origin John Cox traces to Spenser's 'siluer seat' or 'siluer stoole' upon which Proserpina (Persephone) sits in the *Faerie Queene*.[41] 'Persephone' probably means 'destroyer of light'; she was originally known as Kore, and under that name was abducted while out gathering flowers at the fountain of Arethusa and taken to the underworld by Hades, rather as Rilian's mother is killed while 'maying' near a fountain and is replaced in his affections by the serpentine Queen of Underland.

Spenser's *Faerie Queene* may also have supplied Lewis with the idea for the two horses which appear in the book. The Mutability Cantos mention Cynthia's (that is, Luna's) 'two steeds, th'one black, the other white' (VII, vi, 9) that pull her chariot across the heavens. Lewis calls them Coalblack and Snowflake, names he may have derived from Lyly's moonstruck fish which 'at the waxinge of the Moone is as white as the driuen snowe, and at the wayning as black as burnt coale,' a passage he critiques at some length in his sixteenth-century volume.[42]

There are many more detailed points of Lunar influence which might be analysed, such as Jill's huntedness[43] and the fact that the witch is dressed in green, connoting the 'vestal livery . . . sick and green' worn by 'the envious moon' in *Romeo and Juliet*.[44] But there is not space here to complete a full survey. Before we move into exegesis of these images, it is worth observing one final aspect of Lunacy that helps explain an episode in the book which Goldthwaite and Holbrook have condemned: the corporal punishment administered at the end of the story to the bullies of Experiment House.[45] This episode, too, has its efficient cause in the Moon. In the Dantean scheme which linked the seven planets with the seven medieval arts, the Moon was associated with grammar. Lewis records in *The Discarded Image* how grammar, in the form of *grammary*, came to mean magic, and from *grammary*, by a familiar sound-change, came *glamour*; hence the 'drizzling glamour' mentioned in 'The Planets.' As a pedagogue and disciplinarian, Grammar did not spare her charges the rod, and Lewis daily saw a statue of her, 'with her birch,' looking down on the cloisters of Magdalen.[46] When Jill plies her crop, and Eustace and Caspian the flat of their swords, on the little hitlers of Experiment House, Luna is exerting her influence most palpably. Since this is a school where bullies are deemed 'interesting psychological cases' and the cane is frowned upon, it is no surprise that, as a consequence of her school's brush with Grammar, the Headmistress should be found 'behaving like a lunatic,' nor that she then resigns to take up a job as a school-inspector, and finally becomes a Member of Parliament.

The Lunar *Logos*

Luna presents Lewis with a peculiar problem apropos the communication of a theological message. Luna is different from the other six planets in that she borders the realm of mutability and to some extent shares its imperfections: 'the rim of the world that was wasted goes through her. Half of her orb is turned towards us and shares our curse.' This is a different problem from the one presented by the two *infortunas*, Mars and Saturn. Here, with Luna, Lewis has to express something 'about Christ' using a symbol that is not good *per se* (as all six translunary planets are), but partially corrupt. How can Aslan be depicted as the incarnation of such a spiritual symbol?

The answer is by having him assume the good, upper half of Luna's qualities, and the opposite of the bad, lower half. We will address his assumption of the good, upper half later in this section; his assumption of the opposite of the lower half will be addressed straightaway. Rather than Aslan taking on Lunar doubt and insanity and so on, he is shown to be literally above all that, and to be opposed to it. As Como notes, 'Only in Aslan's country—where all harms are healed—are the highest claims, especially that of certainty, affirmed.'[47] The lower half of the Luna world is not one that he can embody or in which he can appear in very truth, for the whole point of the lunary divide is that, below that line, very truth is not to be had. The only way Aslan can manifest himself in this realm of uncertainty is through the four Signs, delivered before certainty has been left behind, and in the brief revelatory dream that Jill has in chapter 8.

It might be contended that Aslan does appear in Narnia *in propria persona*, for in chapter 16 he suddenly turns up behind Jill, 'so bright and real and strong that everything else began at once to look pale and shadowy.' However, when we examine the passage carefully, we find that his arrival is not quite so simple. Jill has apparently summoned Aslan by saying, 'I wish I was at home,' and instantly a deep voice from behind her says, 'I have come.' 'I have come' is not, on the face of it, a granting of Jill's wish, but we are meant to understand that Jill is now 'at home' because she is in the presence of Aslan. And where is the location of this 'home'? Jill, not perceiving what has happened, repeats her wish, asking, 'May we go home now?' Aslan replies: 'Yes. I have come to bring you Home.' The capital 'H' and the verb 'bring,' rather than the expected 'take,' help make Lewis's point that home can be no other place than where the Christ-figure is. Aslan does not descend from his lofty Mountain and arrive at his destination in Narnia like a traveller moving through space; rather he brings his whole

Mountain-home with him. To make doubly sure that we realise it is Jill's location that has changed, not Aslan's, Lewis provides the following clarification:

> Then he opened his mouth wide and blew. But this time they had no sense of flying through the air: instead it seemed that they remained still, and the wild breath of Aslan blew away the ship and the dead King and the castle and the snow and the winter sky. For all these things floated off into the air like wreaths of smoke.[48]

Jill and Eustace find that the lowly realm of inspissated air is replaced by the higher realm of heavenly aether; the 'smoke and stir'[49] of Narnia evaporate under the 'great brightness of midsummer sunshine' on the Mountain of Aslan. As soon as Aslan arrives, so does his lunary (or, rather, upper lunary) country.

Christologically, then, it would seem that *The Silver Chair* is a thin story. Aslan never incarnates himself in Narnia, nor does anyone express a hope that he might become present or remember a time when he was. The children only encounter him before they enter Narnia and after they leave it. In this respect, the Lunar donegality appears to be incompletely Christian and indeed, at one point Lewis does seem deliberately to be echoing an Old Testament, pre-incarnation understanding of the awareness of God. When Aslan tells Jill, 'remember, remember, remember the signs. Say them to yourself when you wake in the morning and when you lie down at night, and when you wake in the middle of the night. And whatever strange things may happen to you, let nothing turn your mind from following the signs,' the attentive reader cannot fail to hear the Judaic Shema in the background: 'And these words which I command you this day shall be upon your heart; and you shall teach them diligently to your children, and shall talk of them when you sit in your house, and when you walk by the way, and when you lie down, and when you rise.'[50]

How, then, is *The Silver Chair* 'about Christ'? Why does Lewis make no apparent attempt to overcome Lessing's ugly ditch, bridging the eternal verities to the world of historical contingency? Is this tale an example of Lewis's alleged 'neo-Platonism,'[51] his tendency to revert to an idealist kind of philosophy and to overlook, as Farrer suggests he was apt to do, 'the full involvement of the reasonable soul in a random and perishable system'?[52] Is the Creed on display here no more than Vaughan's proto-Romantic hope: 'My soul, there is a country, far beyond the stars'?[53] We know that Lewis 'would be at Jerusalem.'[54] We know that he believed this world to have 'some refreshing inns' but that 'Our Father . . . will not encourage us to mistake them for home.'[55] Is the theology of this Chronicle not rather Manichaean and escapist than fully Christian? Where is the serious doctrine of good creation and of redemption through incarnation?

These questions approach *The Silver Chair* from the wrong angle. If we allow the *poiema* of the story to set the agenda, rather than trying to fit the story to a grid of doctrinal categories that we presume to be relevant, we will see that this story is connected to Lewis's thinking about first and second things. 'First and Second Things,' an essay he published in 1942, is a popularisation of ideas about hierarchy and equality derived from Milton, Shakespeare, and 'nearly all literature before the revolutionary period'[56], a set of ideas which Lewis discusses at some length in chapter 11 of his Preface to 'Paradise Lost'. According to these ideas, if first things are put first, second things will naturally follow: if second things are put first, then not only will the first things be lost but also, eventually, the second things for whose sake they were sacrificed.

Understood in this light, the theological issue at stake in The Silver Chair is not how to 'bring Christ down,' but how to imitate Christ's filial submission to the Father, how to accept second billing. For though Aslan does not descend, Jill and Eustace do; they are, as it were, 'incarnated' into Narnia: their task is to remain anchored to the Mountain of Aslan and not to 'go native' down where the air is thick. Lessing's ditch is seen, importantly, from the upper side, with the story beginning and ending in the place of certitude and truth, beyond the pale; all the vicissitudes through which the heroes pass in the middle act are to be seen from that perspective. Will the *missio dei* be fulfilled or not?

In some respects, it is not. After the descent into Narnia, the Lunar imagery allows Lewis to present the clouding effects of 'weer' on the imaginations of the three adventurers, for example when the witch paints for them a picture of warm baths and square meals at Harfang. The repeated entertaining of this picture in their minds' eyes leads them into danger. It is a nod toward the blinding effects of 'false imagination' in the sphere of Dante's Moon.[57]

This pattern is repeated in the second 'incarnation' of the story, when the adventurers descend even further, to the Underworld. Will they hold true to Narnia (and the Country above Narnia) or will their heads be turned by the witch's magic? Rilian is a sad case of a man who has already been enchanted, who sees the world upside down as in a 'little pool' (another glance at Dante's Lunar heaven and its pool-enamoured swain).[58] As Myers correctly notes: 'That [Rilian] is dressed like Hamlet symbolizes his doubt and uncertainty.'[59] Hamlet, for Lewis, was the archetypal lunatic, a man 'with his mind on the frontier of two worlds . . . unable quite to reject or quite to admit the supernatural.'[60]

Like Feuerbach or Freud or Marx, the witch argues that the supposed supernatural realities—what she calls 'fancies'—are merely extrapolations of particular Underworld images (sun from lamp, lion from cat) and that the higher world of Narnia does not really exist: 'you can put nothing into your make-believe without copying it from the real world, this world of mine, which is the only world.' Rilian wins provisional freedom for himself by recalling 'the bright skies of Overland . . . the great Lion . . . Aslan himself '; then his rescuers undergo a similar test. Battling against the sweet smell from the fire, the soft thrumming of the music, and the lulling words of the witch, Eustace manages to recall 'the sky and the sun and the stars.' But he is overpowered, admitting there 'never was such a world.' Then Puddleglum remembers the heavens again: 'I've seen the sun coming up out of the sea of a morning and sinking behind the mountains at night. And I've seen him up in the midday sky when I couldn't look at him for brightness.' 'What is this *sun* that you all speak of?' asks the Queen, 'There never was a *sun*.' 'No. There never was a sun,' said the Prince, and the Marsh-wiggle, and the children.' The Moonwitch will acknowledge no Solar supremacy: her light must be uncreaturely, self-sustaining, not derived or dependent.[61]

This diabolical egocentricity reminds us of 'the usages of Sulva' in *That Hideous Strength*, Merlin's term for Jane and Mark's refusal to meet each other wholeheartedly, their wilful ignorance of each other's full femininity and masculinity; also of Ransom's statement that 'On this side [of the Moon], the womb is barren and the marriages cold.' In other words, the earthward face of Luna represents a rejection of alterity, a determination to decline the gift of another locus of reality in all its independent integrity. By clinging on to their memory of the Sun, the heroes show themselves to be unwilling to make that turn to the self; they belong spiritually to 'the upper half' of the Moon's sphere and its openness to the radiant heavens where 'day never shuts his eye.'[62] Ransom explains that '[Sulva's] other half looks to Deep Heaven; happy would he be who could cross that frontier.' Aslan's country, that land with its 'blaze of sunshine' like 'the light of a June day [pouring] into a garage when you open the door,' is to be understood as located on the other side of that frontier.

This helps explain why Aslan's image on the flag at Cair Paravel is 'golden', also why Aslan himself is three times described as 'golden': he has a golden voice, a golden back, and looks to Jill at one point like a 'speck of bright gold.' Lewis has not forgotten the donegality of the book and suddenly decided to depict him under the rubric of Sol; rather, under the rubric of Luna, he is saying something important about Christ's submission to the Father, which was one of his favourite Christological themes.[63] Lewis accepted the Nicene and Athanasian Creeds with their insistence on the co-eternity of the Son with the Father, but believed that the essential equality of divine being among the Persons of the Trinity was not incompatible with an ordering, even a kind of hierarchy, therein. Obviously, Christ was subject to the Father as man; but Lewis also thought he was subject to the Father as God.[64] This position is distinguishable from the heresy of subordinationism; its *locus classicus* is 1 Cor. 15:27–28. Within the Godhead, the Father has a primacy, He is the First Person of the Trinity. The Father is (so to speak) golden, as the Son, the Second Person, is silver. Lewis thought that 'we do not disparage silver by distinguishing it from gold'[65] and that, in any case, 'comparative evaluations of essentially different excellences are ... senseless.'[66] (This is not to imply that Lewis thought the Son and the

Father were not of the same divine essense; it is to imply that the begetting Father, quâ begetter, enacts divinity in a manner essentially opposite from and reciprocal to that of the begotten Son.) Nevertheless, because the Son is *perfectly* silver he is also, within the mystery of the Trinity, perfectly golden because he is utterly receptive to that higher (but no more divine) light coming forth from the First Person, 'the Father "with rayes direct" shining full on the Son,' as Lewis quotes Milton in his *Preface*.[67] The Son, unlike the witch, does not deny what is above him, but accepts it fully, with eternal filial submissiveness.

Aslan's goldenness in this book is a different kind of goldenness from the one we find in *The Voyage of the 'Dawn Treader.'* There it was Solar; here it is, paradoxically, Lunar—the good upper half of the Lunar nature. If the scriptural justification for *The 'Dawn Treader'* was 'I am the light of the world,' the scriptural justfication for *The Silver Chair* is 'The Father is greater than I' (John 14: 28) *and yet* 'He who has seen me has seen the Father' (John 14:9). The task for the heroes is to demonstrate that kind of Son-like humility and to beat down the temptation to believe that there is nothing higher than themselves.

Alister McGrath observes how, in *The Silver Chair*, Lewis 'plants a series of powerful images in our imaginations, and leaves them there, to bear their theological fruit.' He suggests that 'the reader is left with a faint sense of smug-ness' as the witch's sophistry is deflated.[68] It is true that there is a strain of Socratic irony running throughout chapter 12 that might, if focussed on, provoke a sense of superiority. But then, it is partly Lewis's point that the perspective of the Overlanders *is* superior. The Overlanders know both the higher and the lower realm; the witch knows (or pretends) that there is only the lower realm.[69]

However, Lewis's message is not simply that the witch is wrong and the rescuers right: it also has to do with how right belief can be maintained in a hostile environment. The narrator is not present in chapter 12 to remind the reader of 'the truth.' Rather, the reader is left seeing the scene through the eyes of Rilian, Jill, Eustace, and Puddleglum, all of whom are—temporarily at least—persuaded of the witch's point of view. Empathising with these char-acters, the reader is left not so much with a faint sense of smugness as with a strong sense of fear: there seems to be a real chance that they may be over-whelmed by the witch's 'false, mocking fancy' (to recall a telling phrase from an early poem[70]) and end up as lunatics. It is not through their superior insight that the heroes win the day, but through *corage*, through sacrifice. Philosophising and rhetoric cannot settle this dispute (though Puddleglum's speech, a dra-matised version of the Ontological Proof, is undeniably stirring[71]) because the witch's logic is impeccable, as far as it goes. Only action is sufficient to counter it. Active sacrifice (stamping on the fire) turns out to be the solution to uncertainty, and physical risk (facing up to the serpent)[72] the path to freedom.

It is through reaching for the stars by means of an excruciating act of self-denial that the heroic Marsh-wiggle brings home to himself an awareness of the true order of his universe. When Puddleglum insists on the objective reality of the sun, in the face of Lunacentric demands, he is fulfilling his duty to give 'first things' priority. As a result, the adventurers get to enjoy both first things and second things. Not only do they return to Overland, they take possession of Underland, too: 'The opening in the hillside was left open, and often in hot summer days the Narnians go in there with ships and lanterns and down to the water and sail to and fro, singing, on the cool, dark underground sea.' Lewis ends *The Silver Chair* by inviting his readers, if ever they visit Narnia, 'to have a look at those caves.' Now that they are defumigated of 'weer' they are good and worthwhile places for everyone to see. Despite the fact that Jill and Eustace can't 'quite believe' any longer in the existence of the Underworld, it still exists and its continued existence is to be acknowledged and utilised. It is an objective correlative of the Wellsian myth of the Cave-Man, which Lewis rejected but which he found to be imaginatively valuable, in its place: 'I shall always enjoy it as I enjoy other myths. I shall keep my Cave-Man where I keep Balder and Helen and the Argonauts: and there often revisit him.'[73] For when the true God arrives, then, and only then, 'the half-gods can remain.'[74] It is a case of 'Seek ye first the kingdom of God and all these things shall be added unto you.'[75] Half-gods, recognised as such, have their own proper excellence. We do not have 'to throw away our silver to make room for the gold.'[76] 'It is lawful to rest our eyes in moonlight—especially now that we know where it comes from, that it is only sunlight at second hand.'[77]

Just as the Underworld can be retained if Narnia is put first, so, *mutatis mutandis*, Narnia can be retained if the Mountain of Aslan is put first. Puddleglum goes on living in Narnia. Jill and Eustace are whisked up to the Mountain, a comparatively golden place. But only comparatively, not absolutely. We must remember that Aslan's Country in this book is conceptualised in Lunar, not Solar, terms. Although there is no silver here, because of the Country's perfect receptivity to the metallurgical 'eye and mind of the whole universe,' nevertheless there are other Lunar qualities—good Lunar qualities—most notably water.

Aslan's first words in the book are said to the tearful Jill, 'If you're thirsty, you may drink.' He says this over 'the delicious rippling noise' of a stream that is driving Jill 'nearly frantic' with thirst. The scene between them recalls the meeting of Christ and the woman at the well (John 4:4–30) in which he offers her 'living water . . . whoever drinks of the water that I shall give will never thirst.' Aslan gives Jill no assurance that he will not eat her up if she stoops down to drink, but she conquers her uncertainty and does so: 'It was the coldest, most refreshing water she had ever tasted. You didn't need to drink much of it, for it quenched your thirst at once.'

In the final chapter of the book, this stream is again the focus of the action. Here it has become a baptismal Lethe, a 'fair fresh stream' in which the dead king Caspian rests upon a bed of 'golden gravel . . . with the water flowing over him.' Jill's eyes again fill with tears, because Aslan has become 'so beautiful' and the funeral music 'so despairing'; Aslan and Eustace weep, too, as they look down at the dead body of the King. Eustace is told to go into a thicket and pluck the thorn that he will find there; he must then drive the thorn into Aslan's paw so that Caspian may be resurrected by a drop of his blood. Paul Fiddes comments: 'Many biblical echoes of salvation are awoken by this incident— among them the pierced hands of Christ, the ram caught 'in a thicket,' the waters of death and the waters of baptism—but a new myth is being created which has a power of its own.'[78]

However, although there is an appropriately Lunar emphasis on 'waters' in the depiction of Aslan's country, has Lewis not undercut his own insistence on the lunary divide? How can despairing music be heard above the 'rim of the wasted world'? How can Christ's blood stream in the firmament? Sacrifice is a response to sin, is it not? But according to the Ptolemaic system, there is no sin or evil *per se* above the orbit of the Moon. How is it, then, that death can be present on the sunward side of Luna?

In Lewis's Christology, sacrifice is not only a response to sin, but also, and more importantly, a filial response to the love of the Father. Christ, as Lewis puts it,

> gives Himself in sacrifice; and that not only on Calvary. For when He was crucified He "did that in the wild weather of His outlying prov-inces which He had done at home in glory and gladness". From before the foundation of the world He surrenders begotten Deity back to begetting Deity in obedience. . . . From the highest to the lowest, self exists to be abdicated and, by that abdication, becomes the more truly self, to be thereupon yet the more abdicated, and so forever.[79]

Death of a kind and rebirth of a kind are to be found in the immanent Trinity, not just in the economic Trinity, and therefore Aslan can bleed and resurrect even on the far side of his Lunar Mountain. His self-giving for the life of Caspian is not just a soteriological function, conditioned by the needs of the realm of mutability, but also (and more importantly) part of the eternal and perfect essence of his life as the Emperor's Son. His translunary submissiveness is the ideal form of sacrifice in which Jill and Eustace and Puddleglum have fitfully participated during their sublunary quest.

In this Lunar deity there is a 'sure and certain hope of the resurrection to eternal life' because the Son is eternally surrendering to and being exalted by His Father. Patient receptivity is the role of every rank below the Father, first within the uncreated Trinity of co-equal Persons,[80] second within creation itself. Every level in the cosmic hierarchy is required to become bright like 'a mirror filled with light,'[81] or like 'a body ever more completely uncovered to the meridian blaze of the spiritual sun.'[82] The Moon, as Lewis put it in an early poem, is 'a stone that catches the sun's beam,'[83] and that is the correct way of understanding things according to the divinely ordained great chain of being.

In Lewis's view, perhaps 'the greatest statement of the Hierarchical conception' comes in the speech about 'Degree' by Ulysses in Shakespeare's *Troilus and Cressida*. It contains the following lines:

> The heavens themselves, the planets, and this centre
> Observe degree, priority, and place,
> Insisture, course, proportion, season, form,
> Office, and custom, in all line of order.
> And therefore is the glorious planet Sol
> In noble eminence enthron'd and spher'd
> Amidst the other; whose med'cinable eye
> Corrects the influence of evil planets.[84]

The Narnian Moonwitch with her chthonic silver chair will not allow Sol any such primacy. She suffers from what Ulysses goes on to describe as 'an envious fever / Of pale and bloodless emulation.'[85] She will not rest content with creaturely, reflective status, but desires instead to invert the hierarchy, rebelling against higher ranks by tyrannising lower ranks, for she cannot achieve her objective of ruling Narnia except by enslaving the inhabitants of Bism, the country beneath Underland. Such anti-hierarchical action, though temporarily successful, 'cannot succeed' in the long run; 'it has made the very nature of things its enemy.'[86] The very nature of things means the divine nature of things: God's own being is hierarchical, constituted by a co-eternal, asymmetrical reciprocity of paternal and filial love in the Holy Spirit; and the Son does not count equality with the Father a thing to be grasped.[87]

According to Lewis, the special importance of the *Troilus* speech lies in its clear statement of the alternative to Hierarchy:

> If you take 'Degree' away 'each thing meets in mere oppugnancy,' 'strength' will be lord, everything will 'include itself in power.' In other words, the modern idea that we can choose between Hierarchy and equality is, for Shakespeare's Ulysses, mere moonshine.'[88]

For Lewis, too.

SEVEN

Mercury

Meeting selves, same but sundered.
—'The Planets' (lines 17–18)

I t was pointed out in chapter 3 that Lewis liked to regard Jupiter as his personal presiding deity, but Mercury would have been almost as apt a choice, for Lewis had been extraordinarily favoured by that Intelligence whom, in 'The Planets,' he calls the 'Lord of language'; both as a speaker[1] and as a writer[2] Lewis was uncommonly fluent. However, despite these talents, despite the fact that he saw Mercurial as well as Jovial strains in his paternity,[3] and despite his opinion that Mercury shared with Jupiter a special need of rehabilitation,[4] Lewis claimed no special relationship with the planet of the second sphere. In fact, he confesses that the Mercurial essence is almost beyond his grasp:

> It is difficult to see the unity of all [Mercury's] characteristics. 'Skilled eagerness' or 'bright alacrity' is the best I can do. But it is better just to take some real mercury in a saucer and play with it for a few minutes. *That* is what 'Mercurial' means.[5]

It is a nice irony that Mercury, the god of clerks, should elude Lewis's clerkly attempts to communicate his nature. Not that he abandoned his efforts to do so. In his scholarship, fiction, and poetry we see Lewis chasing those characteristics that constitute Mercury's personality until he captured a donegalitarian account in *The Horse and His Boy*.

Mercury in Lewis's Scholarship

Mercury runs throughout Lewis's works of scholarship, but we do not have space to address every appearance. We begin with *The Discarded Image*, where Lewis writes:

> Mercury produces quicksilver. Dante gives his sphere to beneficent men of action. Isidore, on the other hand, says this planet is called Mercurius because he is the patron of profit *(mercibus praeest)*. Gower says that the man born under Mercury will be 'studious' and 'in writinge curious'... The Wife of Bath associates him especially with clerks. In Martianus Capella's *De Nuptiis* he is the bridegroom of Philologia—who is Learning or even Literature rather than what we call 'philology.' And I am pretty sure that 'the Words of Mercury' contrasted with 'the Songs of Apollo' at the end of *Love's Labour's Lost*[6] are 'picked,' or rhetorical prose.[7]

Of all these characteristics, the one which appealed best to Lewis is that first mentioned: quicksilver. He considered the Mercurial metal to be a most instructive and significant image, as we will see if we look at the earliest reference to Mercury in Lewis's published writings, which comes in his essay 'The Personal Heresy in Criticism.' Here he provides a detailed account of Mercury's influence in action. Taking a passage from Keats's 'Hyperion,' which includes the lines

> Those green rob'd senators of mighty woods,
> Tall oaks, branch-charmed by the earnest stars...

he proceeds to give the following analysis:

> In the... line ('green-rob'd senators') the whole idea of republican Rome... is called up, in order that these senators may bring the sudden flavour of their silence and grandeur out of Plutarch and Livy, and that this, set for a moment beside the trees, may make them a little different.... With 'branch-charmed by the earnest stars' the sources are more complex. 'Charmed' brings in the idea of magic. There, again, we... have dipped... into the storehouse of public history. But this is instantly modified by the word 'branch'. Here we are thrown back on sense. We have seen the trees with branches stretched up in intense stillness towards the stars. We have imagined or been told of people compelled by magical charms to stand as still as trees. Lay the two side by side and add the word 'earnest'—which is exactly the point where the sensible image and the idea of insensible 'magic' merge

beyond hope of distinction—and the whole, like meeting drops of quicksilver, becomes a single perception.[8]

Our interest in this passage has nothing to do with Lewis's actual reading of Keats or with his case against 'the Personal Heresy.' Our focus is on his use of a metaphor drawn from Mercury as a tool for analysing Keats's *poiema*. For Lewis, there was life in the old god yet. Mercury was not a dried up mythological cliché to be swept aside in order to make room for that new-forged armoury of scientific-sounding terminology—'plurisignation,' 'steno-language,' 'iconology,' 'intentionality'—which language theorists were developing at this time. Rather, the god of quicksilver remained a current and vibrant metaphor for the poetic synthesis of disparate materials. Under the living and active image of Mercury, Lewis praises Keats 'because the poet has found the proper scraps of ordinary seeing which, when put together, will unite into a new and extraordinary seeing.'[9]

Not that such unities are stable or permanent. The fusing action of Mercury is only temporary and is just one half of an influence which is continually joining and parting. Lewis found in Mercury what Albertus found in Phantasy, the faculty of '*componendo et dividendo*, separating and uniting.'[10] This may explain why Mercury is 'the god of theft'[11] (those littered under Mercury are snappers up of unconsidered trifles)[12] because stolen property leaves its owner and is united to the thief and then is typically divided up, fenced, and resold, before—sometimes—being regained by its original possessor. *Componendo et dividendo* is also applicable to the linguistic side of Mercurial action. Under Mercury, the meanings and spellings of words bifurcate and ramify but equally intertwine and overlap. *Studies in Words*, that semantic tracery of matrices and interstices, demonstrates Lewis's concentrated scholarly interest in these phenomena. His work as a whole manifests a general interest in the same things. He was an arch-definer whose oeuvre is strewn with the written equivalent of '*Distinguo!*' (his habitual cry in conversation and debate), but he had also a fascination for particular strains or families of words and for the miscellaneous conjugation represented by homophones, homonyms, synonyms, and onomatopoeias.[13]

It is worth noting how, when Lewis invoked Mercury in 'The Personal Heresy,' his stylistic form expressed the content of his sentence; this is another dimension to Mercury's melding power. Lewis's final sentence runs: 'Lay the two side by side and add the word "earnest"—which is exactly the point where the sensible image and the idea of insensible "magic" merge beyond hope of distinction—and the whole, like meeting drops of quicksilver, becomes a single perception.' This is a deliberately fugal sentence, in which the idea of two things becoming one is formally conveyed three times:

1. 'side . . . side . . . add'
2. 'sensible . . . insensible . . . merge'
3. phrastically in the culmination of (1) and (2) in 'the whole . . . like meeting drops . . . becomes'

This desire to unite form and content into 'a single perception' is found throughout Lewis's corpus,[14] and when he describes Shelley's *Witch of Atlas* as a 'mercurial poem'[15] it would appear that he had just this kind of splicing in mind. Shelley's poem has a formal 'lightness and liquidity,' it is 'Mozartian,' 'playful.' But its matter, too, is Mercurial, featuring both a winged hermaphrodite (blessed with 'the soul of swiftness') and its eponymous witch who is herself a great match-maker:

> Friends who, by practice of some envious skill,
> Were torn apart—a wide wound, mind from mind!—
> She did unite again with visions clear
> Of deep affection and of truth sincere.[16]

The witch of Atlas and *The Witch of Atlas* separately and together evince Mercurial power. In *That Hideous Strength*, to which we now turn, Lewis attempted, among other things, to portray the abuse of this power in the speech of the villains, where ultimately neither form nor content retains Mercury's presence.

Mercury in *That Hideous Strength*

Although it has been argued above that Jupiter is the most important planetary influence present in *That Hideous Strength*, it must be recognised that Mercury also plays a major part. Mercury is the most obviously agential planet at work in this third volume of the trilogy; it is his articulacy that overcomes the dumbness oppressing Thulcandra, 'the silent planet.' Silence and the abuse of language that leads to silence are among the chief presenting symptoms of the N.I.C.E's 'devilry,' and the centrality of this theme is expressed by the title of the book, which is taken (as was noted in chapter 2) from David Lyndsay, describing the shadow of the Tower of Babel.[17] When Busby remarks that 'we all have our different languages,' he is saying more than he realises, and when he adds 'we all really mean the same thing' he says the opposite of what the novel shows to be the case. One of Lewis's purposes is to indicate how words which are formally identical may yet have diametrically opposed meanings, depending on the spiritual state of the speaker. Compare, for instance, the various uses throughout the novel of the terms 'head,' 'damn,' 'we,' and 'obedience.'

The first time we discover that Mercury will be involved in addressing this difference is when Dimble prepares what he is going to say to Merlin. As he utters 'the Great Tongue' it seems as though

> the words spoke themselves through him from some strong place at a distance—or as if they were not words at all but present operations of God, the planets, and the Pendragon. For this was the language spoken before the Fall and beyond the Moon and the meanings were not given to the syllables by chance, or skill, or long tradition, but truly inherent in them as the shape of the great Sun is inherent in the little waterdrop. This was Language herself, as she first sprang at Maleldil's bidding out of the molten quicksilver of the star called Mercury on Earth, but Viritrilbia[18] in Deep Heaven.[19]

Mercury supplies 'truly inherent' meaning, meaning united to the warp and woof of the words which convey it. The company of St. Anne's are open to having their tongues quickened by this Mercurial spirit, this creature of Maleldil: the members of the N.I.C.E. are not. The latter see language merely as an instrument. Wither wields it to avoid committing himself to any definite proposition. After several pages of his euphemisms, hesitations, obfuscations, and circumlocutions it comes as a relief to hear, in answer to Jane's question, Camilla's blunt 'Yes.' And this dichotomy between the two approaches to language continues throughout the book.

'There is no such thing as Man—it is a word. There are only men,' says Filostrato. His nominalism is philosophically twin with that logical positivism which is one of Lewis's least disguised spittoons in the book. Filostrato can only conceive of words as labels for empirically perceptible units of experience. He has no time for deductive thinking or for unseen realities from which specifics derive and in which they participate. Lewis appears to be particularly interested in tracing this line of thought to the great renaissance thinker, Francis Bacon, whom he believed had introduced a 'contempt for all knowledge that is not utilitarian' (a subject we touched upon in chapter 5).[20] Not that Bacon was a strict nominalist or materialist; he had inherited, in a Christianized form, Platonic dualism. But his interest in the sublunary realm, Lewis thought, was mechanistic and instrumental; he helped formulate the idea of 'laws of nature' by analogy with jurisprudence, and it may be for this reason that Bracton College has a 'Bacon Professor' who still studies Law. Bacon sought knowledge 'for the sake of power'[21] and, in this respect, had 'the closest possible affinity' with the magicians of his day: hence Lewis's mention of Bacon in the same breath as Paracelsus and Agrippa in chapter 9. One of the means by which Bacon tried to achieve this power was by reducing nature to her mathematical elements; another was by regulating language so as to remove errors resulting from linguistic confusions (*idola fori*). In *The Advancement of Learning* (1605), Bacon noted the Chinese system of 'real characters' which he regarded as capable of giving precise expression to fundamental '*Things* or *Notions.*'[22] Bacon's intellectual descendants in this respect, such as C. K. Ogden and I. A. Richards, Lewis's contemporaries, are the implicit target throughout *That Hideous Strength*. And not entirely implicit: Lewis cannot resist a swipe at Richards's 'Basic English,' ridiculing it through the mouth of Fairy Hardcastle.[23]

Myers has argued convincingly that Lewis in large part intended *That Hideous Strength* as a counter-blast to the trends in language theory represented by Ogden and Richards.[24] His fiction is being deployed here to dramatise the point that Barfield (himself mentioned in chapter 12) made repeatedly in his writings, that those who try 'to cut away and expose all metaphorical usage' do not thereby 'escape the curse of Babel.'[25] In fact, they invite a redoubling of that curse. Metaphor rests on the 'psycho-physical parallelism (or more)'[26] that characterises the universe, and therefore to deny or to restrict metaphor (the 'carrying over' of meaning from physical units to metaphysical entities) is a mental move similar to a denial of the relationship between material creation and immaterial Creator. To say 'There is no such thing as Man, there are only men' is to resist the imagination's power of seeing beyond sensory data; it is to stultify that faculty which operates also in the realm of faith.

Lewis argued in 'Bluspels and Flalansferes' that it was practically impossible to deny metaphor, since all but the most elementary human thinking depends upon it. Nevertheless, fools and villains might still attempt to make that denial, and in the process the despised and suppressed faculty of metaphor would not be idle; it would become frustrated and twisted, ready to burst out at inopportune moments and exact revenge. Lewis dramatises the effects of the theoretical denial of metaphor near the end of the book when the members of the N.I.C.E. lose all control over their language during the banquet at Belbury. To Frost's great embarrassment, Wither mentions how anachronistic it would be to trust to Calvary for salvation in modern warfare. He means *Cavalry*. The next moment, Wither is demanding that the madrigore of verjuice be talthibianised. Panic ensues. The 'curse of Babel' descends. Mercury, riding in the saddle of Merlin's soul, inspires him to cry, above the riot of nonsense: *Qui Verbum Dei contempserunt, eis auferetur etiam verbum hominis* ('They that have despised the word of God, from them shall the word of man also be taken away').

The role that Mercury plays in that dénouement must now be examined in more detail. Ransom and Merlin have already met, 'like two drops of quicksilver.' In chapter 15, the quicksilver god descends to meet them *in propria persona*:

> Up till now they [all those downstairs at St. Anne's] had instinctively
> been talking in subdued voices, as children talk in a room where their

elders are busied about some august incomprehensible matter, a funeral, or the reading of a will. Now of a sudden they all began talking
loudly at once, each, not contentiously but delightedly, interrupting
the others. A stranger coming into the kitchen would have thought
they were drunk, not soddenly but gaily drunk: would have seen heads
bent close together, eyes dancing, an excited wealth of gesture. What
they said, none of the party could ever afterwards remember. Dimble
maintained that they had been chiefly engaged in making puns.
MacPhee denied that he had ever, even that night, made a pun, but all
agreed that they had been extraordinarily witty. If not plays upon
words, yet certainly plays upon thoughts, paradoxes, fancies, anec-
dotes, theories laughingly advanced yet (on consideration) well worth
taking seriously, had flowed from them and over them with dazzling
prodigality. Even Ivy forgot her great sorrow. Mother Dimble always
remembered Denniston and her husband as they had stood, one on
each side of the fireplace, in a gay intellectual duel, each capping the
other, each rising above the other, up and up, like birds or aeroplanes
in combat. If only one could have remembered what they said! For
never in her life had she heard such talk—such eloquence, such melody
(song could have added nothing to it), such toppling structures of
double meaning, such sky-rockets of metaphor and allusion.

A moment after that and they were all silent. Calm fell, as suddenly as when one goes out of the wind behind a wall. They sat staring
upon one another, tired and a little self-conscious.

Upstairs this first change had a different operation. There came an
instant at which both men braced themselves. Ransom gripped the
side of his sofa; Merlin grasped his own knees and set his teeth. A rod
of coloured light, whose colour no man can name or picture, darted
between them: no more to see than that, but seeing was the least part
of their experience. Quick agitation seized them: a kind of boiling and
bubbling in mind and heart which shook their bodies also. It went to a
rhythm of such fierce speed that they feared their sanity must be
shaken into a thousand fragments. And then it seemed that this
had actually happened. But it did not matter: for all the fragments—
needle-pointed desires, brisk merriments, lynx-eyed thoughts—went
rolling to and fro like glittering drops and reunited themselves. It was
well that both men had some knowledge of poetry. The doubling,
splitting, and recombining of thoughts which now went on in them
would have been unendurable for one whom that art had not already
instructed in the counterpoint of the mind, the mastery of double and
treble vision. For Ransom, whose study had been for many years in the

realm of words, it was heavenly pleasure. He found himself sitting within the very heart of language, in the white-hot furnace of essential speech. All fact was broken, splashed into cataracts, caught, turned inside out, kneaded, slain, and reborn as meaning. For the lord of Meaning himself, the herald, the messenger, the slayer of Argus, was with them: the angel that spins nearest the sun: Viritrilbia, whom men call Mercury and Thoth.[27]

These paragraphs deserve more analysis than we can accord them here. The central element of this thrilling parousia, however, would appear to be Mercury's gift of polysemy: downstairs, punning; upstairs, 'double and treble vision.' The members of the N.I.C.E., in contrast, have no awareness of the multivalent dimensions of language, but since it is still human language that they are speaking, it is necessarily metaphorical and capable of double meaning. When Feverstone exclaims 'By Jove,' we know that it is, for him, merely a dead metaphor; he has no knowledge of the gods and would not be interested in them if he did. Similarly, when Frost tells Mark, 'Pray be quick' and 'Pray make haste,' he has no inkling of the aptness of his words. The villains' imperceptiveness is never overtly commented upon by the author; observing it, the reader feels tacitly complimented for having penetrated the insulating context. The summit of irony is reached when Feverstone, after witnessing the massacre at the banquet, laconically lights his cigarette and says to himself, with imperturbable urbanity, 'Well, I'm damned!' He, like his colleagues, can talk, but without intelligence. The two, as MacPhee points out in chapter 9, are not the same thing.

The sense of superiority that this device may breed in the reader is objected to by some critics. Carpenter dismisses it as Lewis 'working out his schoolboy resentment of bullies.'[28] Even Barfield (who was at one with Lewis on the importance, indeed the religious significance, of metaphor) finds a 'psychic or spiritual immaturity'[29] in 'the opera-bouffe climax' to *That Hideous Strength*. There is some force in these judgements, especially if we regard the Ransom Trilogy as a set of ordinary realistic novels. But of course, they are not realistic, or at least, not simply realistic: they are also fantastic and satiric. *That Hideous Strength*, in particular, is deliberately shaped as a 'fairy-tale for grown-ups,' in which a realistic opening leads to a fantasy ending. It may be that the transition is fumbled or over-hasty, but in intent at least Lewis was attempting to imitate a well-tried literary form. Read from this perspective, there is no need to sympathise with the plight of Feverstone, Frost, Wither *et al*. To do so would be to show literary tone-deafness, not moral maturity, for in a fairy-tale 'evil characters' may be thoroughly distinguished from 'good characters,' and in satire the butts of the author's humour deserve no pity as they would in real life. This story was intended as 'holiday'[30] fiction, not in the sense of being unserious, but

in the sense of being a holiday from a po-faced kind of excessive moral seriousness. And Mercury is relevant, as well as generic considerations, to this line
of interpretation. Mercury is a playful deity, and the reader must be willing to
be tickled. His comedy lets out the bottled-up tensions behind normal cour-
tesies and etiquettes, and refusal to be amused here springs from frigidity rather
than gravity. Chesterton once remarked: 'I am almost certain that many
moderns suffer from what may be called the disease of the suppressed pun.'[31]
Lewis, catching medieval Mercury in his butterfly-net and exhibiting his jizz to
the over-solemn twentieth century, agreed: the medievals knew 'better than
some know now, that human life is not simple. They were able to think of two
things at once.'[32]

And this 'counterpoint of the mind' is still practised among the company at
St. Anne's where words are continually regathering older or fuller senses. The
terms 'king,' 'awful,' 'decent,' and 'lady' are examples of words made fresh in this
way. This newly-acquired semantic depth of vision is attributable to Viritrilbia
and, through him, to his creator, Maleldil.

Christopher argues that 'Maleldil' means 'Lord of the Sign,'[33] which, if
correct, would be apt, for Lewis's Christian God is multi-significant. In the incarnation Christ manifested σημεῖα (signs) which witness to his own person[34]
and was himself the κaραχτήρ (character or representation) of the Father;[35]
and in creation Christ's making and sustaining Word issued in multiform,
revelatory ways,[36] including in the inspiration of scriptural authors so that their
words acquired significance at many different levels, for example in the Psalms,
where 'double or treble vision is part of the pleasure . . . part of the profit, too.'[37]

Thus it could be said that God knows 'plurisignation' from within His own
Triune, enfleshed, and creative nature; there is a divine mandate for double and
treble vision in the three-fold nature of God, the two natures of Christ, and in
the various significations of His creation itself. Monotheism, in Lewis's view,
must be construed carefully so as to preserve this understanding of complex
divinity. The monotheism of Islam, for instance, falls short in this respect, he
thought, because it so affirms 'unity' that 'union is breached.'[38] Although Lewis
considered it a matter for rejoicing that Islam had overcome the dualism of
ancient Persia, he seems to have regarded the conquest as an overcorrection: the
'living, paradoxical, vibrant, mysterious truths' of Christianity are defeated by
it. Christians who effectively practise mere 'Jesus worship'[39] adopt a similarly
simplistic and reductionist position.

Deity is not simple, Lewis believed. Rather, there is a multivalence in the
nature of the one God, both in the immanent Trinity and in the economic.
Underlying Lewis's presentation of Mercury in *That Hideous Strength* is a profound theological disposition, a disposition which—it is worth pointing out—

is absent from the treatment of a very similar theme in another great work of 1940s dystopia, George Orwell's *Nineteen Eighty-Four*. In Newspeak, Orwell also satirises linguistic reductionism: 'Every concept that can ever be needed will be expressed by exactly *one* word, with its meaning rigidly defined, and all its subsidiary meanings rubbed out and forgotten.'[40] This simplism is seen in *Nineteen Eighty-Four* as only a philosophical, rather than as also a spiritual, failure, and, as such, is significantly different from the N.I.C.E's version of the same thing. Nevertheless, it is possible that Lewis's work was an influence on Orwell,[41] and it is remarkable how Orwell, though writing without an undergirding theology, was yet aware of an atheistical bent in anti-metaphorical thinking.[42]

It could fairly be said of Orwell, as Patrick says of Lewis, that he understood words as things 'to be listened to because they are doorways to reality, not despised as ineffective instruments because they refuse to yield their substance exhaustively to philosophic propositions.'[43] Both writers, in their different ways, stood against those positivist and neo-nominalist movements in early twentieth-century thought which, they felt, were attempting to clip Mercury's wings. Orwell saw the danger coming through political bureaucracies and scientific planners from bad philosophy. Lewis saw the danger coming through bureaucrats, planners, and philosophers alike, from a far deeper and darker source.[44]

Mercury in Lewis's Poetry

'Devils are unmaking language,' Lewis declares in his sonnet 'Re-Adjustment.' The title of the poem is a reference to Richards's theory of the purpose of poetry, that it produce an 'adjustment' in its readers.[45] Lewis reflects in this poem that he himself will have to adjust to the sad situation with which he is confronted by Richards and those of his ilk, a situation in which he finds himself part of the last generation of men 'who could understand a story.'[46] By 'understanding a story,' Lewis means not just being able to comprehend a linear chain of events, but having the ability to discern a story's hidden meaning, 'something that has no sequence in it.'[47]

In 'Re-Adjustment,' as also in 'The Country of the Blind,' we find Lewis addressing the subject of language in dismayed, even cataclysmic, mode. However, Lewis was willing to engage with his opponents' views as well as lament their ascendancy. He was not oblivious to the seriousness of the problems which philosophers of language were raising, and he acknowledges the reality of many of the difficulties addressed by Richards. In his poetry the place where he does this most fully is 'The Birth of Language':

How near his sire's[48] careering fires
Must Mercury the planet run;
What wave of heat must lave and beat
That shining suburb of the Sun.

Whose burning flings supernal things
Like spindrift from his stormy crown;
He throws and shakes in rosy flakes
Intelligible virtues down,

And landing there, the candent air
A transformation on them brings,
Makes each a god of speech with rod
Enwreathed[49] and sandals fledged with wings.

Due west (the Sun's behest so runs)
They seek the wood where flames are trees;
In crimson shade their limbs are laid
Beside the pure quicksilver seas,

Where thick with notes of liquid throats
The forest melody leaps and runs
Till night lets robe the lightless globe
With darkness and with distant suns.

Awake they spring and shake the wing:
And on the trees whose trunks are flames
They find like fruit (with rind and root
And fronds of fire) their proper names.

They taste. They burn with haste. They churn
With upright plumes the sky's abyss;
Far, far below, the arbours glow
Where once they felt Mercurial bliss.

They ache and freeze through vacant seas
Of night. Their nimbleness and youth
Turns lean and frore, their meaning more,
Their being less. Fact shrinks to truth.

They reach this Earth. There each has birth
Miraculous, a word made breath,
Lucid and small for use in all
Man's daily needs; but dry like death.

So dim below these symbols show,
Bony and abstract every one.
Yet if true verse but left the curse,
They feel in dreams their native Sun.[50]

According to the mythic story of this poem, human language operates at two removes from its source: language originates in the Sun, is then transformed on Mercury, and is finally born on Earth after suffering a substantial diminution. Although the Babel myth does not feature explicitly, it is alluded to in the penultimate line with its mention of 'the curse.' The words available for human use are 'dry,' 'dim,' 'bony,' 'abstract.'

The poem thus presents the bifocal vision of Lewis's understanding of language. From one perspective, he has the highest possible view: language is a metaphysical reality with a transcendent origin. From another point of view, he sees that it is, in this sublunary world, subject to severe constraints. As he writes to a correspondent in 1949:

> In a sense, one can hardly put anything into words: only the simplest colours have names, and hardly any of the smells. The simple physical pains and (still more) the pleasures can't be expressed in language. I labour the point lest the devil shd. hereafter try to make you believe that what was wordless was therefore vague and nebulous. But in reality it is just the clearest, the most concrete, and most indubitable realities which escape language: not because *they* are vague but because language is.... Poetry I take to be the continual effort to bring language back to the actual.[51]

Language, then, in Lewis's view, can give access (albeit limited) to 'the actual,' to concrete but wordless realities. Before we turn to his attempt at a wordless depiction of that spiritual reality symbolised by Mercury, in the donegality of the fifth Narnia Chronicle, we must take a look at his earlier, and very wordy, depiction of the same character, in 'The Planets.'

Next beyond her [Luna]
MERCURY marches; —madcap rover,
Patron of pilf'rers. Pert quicksilver
His gaze begets, goblin mineral,
Merry multitude of meeting selves,
Same but sundered. From the soul's darkness,
With wreathèd wand, words he marshals,
Guides and gathers them—gay bellwether
Of flocking fancies. His flint has struck

The spark of speech from spirit's tinder,
Lord of language! He leads forever
The spangle and splendour, sport that mingles
Sound with senses, in subtle pattern,
Words in wedlock, and wedding also
Of thing with thought.[52]

Here we see a compact expression of Mercurial qualities: his metal ('pert quicksilver'); his kleptic influence ('patron of pilf'rers'); and his spirit of *componendo et dividendo* ('Same but sundered'). This last attribute is also suggested by various plural nouns (*pilferers, selves, words, fancies, senses, words* again) alongside synonyms of joining (*meeting, marshalling, gathering, flocking, mingling, wedding*).

To use words to describe the god of words might be thought of as a kind of narcissism. But how to capture the Lord of language except through language? A poet has no other medium. However, through the technique of donegality a poet can deploy that medium in a way which approaches wordlessness. He can marry 'thing with thought,' not by frontal assault on his readers' conscious minds, but by embracing their whole reading experience with the thing he means to make them think. He can communicate his theme through participatory cognition, Enjoyment consciousness. By this method, his readers may, so to speak, 'feel in dreams' the essence of Mercury, much as words themselves might feel their true origin 'if true verse but left the curse.' Lewis attempts this ambitious task in *The Horse and His Boy*.

Mercury in *The Horse and His Boy*

'We planned a story of a trip to Mercury—but couldn't get very far with it.' So wrote Green of an evening's conversation he had with Lewis in November 1950.[53] Their inability to get far with the story is intriguing. Lewis's fertile imagination did not usually fail him in conversation, and upon a subject such as this—cosmic romance—he would have been better equipped than most to expatiate till the small hours. One assumes that he was anxious not to pursue the theme because it would have involved constant avoidance of his own recent attempt to write a story which had the Mercurial character as its hidden inner meaning. Indeed, of all people, Green was the one whom he had most reason to steer away from such a topic. Less than four months previously, in July 1950, Green had been discussing with Lewis the proofs of *The Horse and His Boy*.

The Mercurial *Poiema*

The *componendo et dividendo* theme is the place to start in analysing the Mercurial donegality of the fifth Chronicle. The reunion of the twins, Shasta (Cor) and Corin, is an example of what 'The Planets' calls 'meeting selves, / Same but sundered,' for these brothers are not only identical, but were separated shortly after birth, and their coming back together is the main event of the plot; they reunite rather as Ransom and Merlin met in *That Hideous Strength*, 'like two drops of quicksilver.' Because Shasta's identity is at first a mystery, his similarity to Corin is repeatedly remarked upon: he is Corin's 'double'; they are 'as like as two peas,' 'almost exactly like'; 'as like as two twins'; 'two peas'; 'two boys'; 'two brothers.'

There are other pairs of brothers—Dar and Darrin, Cole and Colin ('brothers' names run like that in Archenland')—and one suspects (though we are not told) that they, too, are twins. The reason for so suspecting is that the main pair of brothers, Cor and Corin, are not just twins, but reflections of *the* Twins: Gemini. This constellation is relevant to Lewis's theme because, in astrology, Gemini is ruled by Mercury.[54] Gemini consists of the stellated brothers, Castor and Pollux, who are the models for Shasta and Corin.

Remarkably, critics have not previously noticed this debt. Homer (whom the young Lewis 'worshipped')[55] described Castor as a great breaker of horses and Pollux as a renowned boxer.[56] Shasta, it is true, does not break Bree in the literal sense of taming him: he is already a great war-horse. Nonetheless, Shasta is a 'horse-boy,' who acquires 'a true horseman's seat' and who breaks Bree's pride and self-conceit: 'At least [Shasta] ran in the right direction: ran *back*. And that is what shames me most of all. I, who called myself a war-horse and boasted of a hundred fights, to be beaten by a little human boy—a child, a mere foal.' And just as Shasta is based on Castor, so Corin is based on Pollux, for Corin is a great fighter: he floors a boy who insults Queen Susan, then floors the boy's brother, then the first boy again; he threatens to knock down Thornbut before the Battle of Anvard; he demands to be allowed to 'box' Rabadash; no one 'could ever equal Corin as a boxer'; and after he has 'boxed' the Lapsed Bear of Stormness 'without a time-keeper for thirty-three rounds' he gains the nickname 'Corin Thunder-Fist.' According to Greek mythology, Hermes (the Attic equivalent of the Roman Mercury) invented boxing; and it is not just Corin who demonstrates the pugilistic spirit: both Arsheesh and the Calormene soldier also 'box' Shasta. The unfortunate Shasta is 'used to hard knocks,' and this is just as well, because all his fights with his brother 'ended (if they didn't begin) with Cor getting knocked down.' Their fights are not simply brotherly tussles, but further manifestations of Gemini: 'the Twins tear each other,' as Lewis wrote in *Arthurian Torso*.[57] He chuckled over Barfield's pun on 'Castor and Bollux'[58] and it seems likely that he chose the name Shasta (Cor) as a piece of his own wordplay: Cor/Shasta suggesting the portmanteau, Castor.

The twinning of brothers is only the most notable of the many pairs in the story: 'two armies'; 'two girls'; 'two hands'; 'two horses'; 'two humans'; 'two human children'; 'two peaks'; 'two rivers'; 'two slaves'; 'two lumps of sugar'; a 'two-headed giant.' Lewis frequently opts for the two-fold image where he could just as easily have chosen the single. Thus we see Corin seizing 'both [Cor's] hands'; Susan's 'hands' on Cor's 'shoulders'; 'a forehead and a pair of eyes' where we might have had just 'the upper half of a face'; 'four pairs of eyes' where the word 'all' would have served. And then there are images of symmetrical doubles: six soldiers on either side of the city gate; two cypresses on each side of the doorway; Aravis looking between the heels of the slave; Cor and Corin straddling the window-sill, facing each other; King Lune and King Edmund shaking hands across the battering ram at the gate of the castle; 'the huge real moon overhead and the huge reflected moon.'

From the static images we turn to the dynamic ones, for the spirit of *componendo et dividendo* is woven into the movement of the story. Shasta is united with Bree; Aravis is united with Hwin; these pairs are then driven close to each other by roaring lions; at one point Bree veers off to the right just as Hwin veers off to the left, but they are then forced back together 'neck to neck and knee to knee,' 'side by side.' In Tashbaan (that 'devilish city') they separate (Shasta with the Narnians, Aravis with Lasaraleen, the horses with the stable-hand) but are reunited at the Tombs and journey together across the desert. At the hermit's house, Shasta runs on ahead, alone, but returns there later.

And it is not just the four protagonists who act like mercury rolling round a dish. The river 'divided itself into two streams' at Tashbaan and reunites on the other side so that the city is built on an eyot. On the far side of the desert, the protagonists come to 'the water's-meet of the two rivers.' At one moment in the Battle of Anvard the Hermit relates how 'Rabadash and Edmund almost met then, but the press has separated them.' After the battle the heroes' breathless and excited conversation suddenly 'all united and swelled into a great roar of laughter.' The destination of the journey is not just Narnia but 'Narnia and Archenland both,' and we read of 'plenty of comings and goings between Narnia and Archenland.' The separating and uniting imagery is consummated in the action of Shasta and Aravis, who become 'so used to quarrelling and making it up again that they got married so as to go on doing it more conveniently.'

Closely related to this motif of division and reunification is that of bifurcation. Mercury was the god of the crossroads, and in ancient Greece columnar pedestals carrying busts of Hermes (known as 'herms') were set up as boundary-markers or signposts at important junctions. This helps explain why, inside

Tashbaan, 'everyone seemed to be going either to the left or right'; why Aravis and Lasaraleen have to go 'either left or right'; and why Shasta, in the mountain-pass, finds that 'the road divided into two' and realises that 'if I stay at the cross-roads I'm *sure* to be caught.'

To hesitate is to be lost in this story, for speed is of the essence of Mercury. There is a great sense of urgency throughout the tale, with repeated cries of 'Narnia and the North!' Bree gallops for sheer joy, then for sheer terror. Aravis says, 'There's not a moment to lose' after overhearing Rabadash's plans. Aslan chases them to the Hermit's dwelling, causing Bree to discover that he has 'not really been going as fast—not quite as fast—as he could.' Aravis mentions 'swift horses', Edmund a 'swift galley', Rabadash the 'swiftest of the galleys'; the Tisroc urges his son to 'be swift'; a river is 'far too swift' for swimming; Aslan is 'swift of foot'; Chervy has 'speed'; there was a 'wonderful chase' of Lord Bar in the back-story; the *Splendour Hyaline* will be 'running for home'; Shasta is told to 'run now, without a moment's rest . . . run, run: always run'; he sees a slope of grass and 'a little heather running up before him . . . he had only to run.' When chapter 9 ends with the word 'slowly' we feel (as we are meant to feel) that something is going dangerously wrong.

Of course, Mercury was swift not for the sake of swiftness but because he was the messenger of the gods. Shasta, as the fleet-footed messenger to the King of Archenland, is reminiscent of a traditional picture of Mercury, which has him with wings on his heels. Interestingly, a Narnian lord wears a steel or silver cap 'with little wings on each side of it,' a nod toward the '*Petasus*, or Mercurial hat.'[59] Aravis effects her escape from forced marriage with the as-sistance of 'the Chief of the Messengers . . . O dispatcher of messages'; later, she sees a trumpeted 'Herald.' After reading and writing, the first thing Shasta will be taught is 'heraldry.'

Shasta's forthcoming education is itself another aspect of Mercurial in-fluence, for Mercury inspires the studious and clerkly. Shasta, who 'had read no books at all,' discovers that 'Education and all sorts of horrible things' are going to happen to him; he laments that he is 'going to be *educated*.' The way that the learned Lewis here pokes fun at the prospect of learning is itself a nice example of the playful Mercurial temperament. Sammons suggests that Shasta's name is based on the Hindu word *Shastri*, 'one who is learned, who teaches.'[60] Unaware of the Mercurial donegality, she does not see that this choice of name (assuming her guess to be correct) would have been an apt one for Lewis to make. She has nevertheless made a suggestion which I am happy to purloin.

Mercury is the patron of pilferers, and accordingly, Shasta several times goes 'raiding.' He is troubled that this might be considered theft, but Bree assures him that what he takes is 'booty' or 'spoil.' He steals money, food and wine, sacks, rope and clothes, oranges, melons, figs, and pomegranates; Aravis and Hwin 'steal' themselves away. In addition there are recurrent discussions of 'horse-stealing,' although Bree points out that they might as well say that he stole Shasta as that Shasta stole him. (Lewis had considered entitling the book *The Horse Stole the Boy*.) In order to show that Mercury promotes not just dishonest gain, but honest profit too, Lewis throws in a couple of references to 'water-sellers,' 'sweetmeat sellers,' and 'wine merchants.'

But the chief characteristic of Mercury has yet to be mentioned: it is skill in speech. A central theme of *The Horse and His Boy* is language, that faculty of which Mercury is 'Lord.' On the very first page of the book we learn that the Calormenes liked 'talking to one another very slowly about things that sounded dull.' We are told of the 'loquacity' and 'idle words' of the Calormenes. We hear their vain repetitions about the Tisroc ('may he live for ever') and are informed by Bree that this is 'slaves' and fools' talk,' 'Southern jargon.' We are given numerous examples of their prolix and vapid proverbial utterances: 'Application to the root of business is the root of prosperity, but those who ask questions that do not concern them are steering the ship of folly toward the rock of indigence'; 'For as a costly jewel retains its value even if hidden in a dung-hill, so old age and discretion are to be respected even in the vile persons of our subjects'; 'For nothing is more suitable to persons of gravity and decorum than to endure minor inconveniences with constancy.' In contrast, Narnian proverbs are brief, pithy, and witty: 'Easily in but not easily out, as the lobster said in the lobster pot!'; 'Maybe Apes will grow honest'; 'Come live with me and you'll know me'; 'Nests before eggs.'

Calormene and Narnian poetry are also contrasted. Ahoshta says that Narnian poetry 'is not, like ours, full of choice apophthegms and useful maxims, but is full of love and war.' He observes, 'How well it was said by a gifted [Calormene] poet . . . that deep draughts from the fountain of reason are desirable to extinguish the fire of youthful love.' When Shasta and Aravis attend the grand feast at Anvard they prepare to be bored as the bard with his fiddlers steps forward, 'for the only poetry they knew was the Calormene kind, and you know now what that was like. But at the very first scrape of the fiddles a rocket seemed to go up inside their heads.' The word 'rocket' refers us back to the 'sky-rockets of metaphor and allusion' in the Mercury passage from *That Hideous Strength*. It also refers us forward to Lewis's study of the literature of the sixteenth century, where a similar contrast between dull and dancing poetry is described. There Lewis coins the term 'Drab' for the doggerel which he thought afflicted the earlier part of the period. The Drab, Hudibrastic versifier, Whetstone, a 'very lugubrious and sententious poet', the title of one of whose pieces (*Fiftie apples of admonicioun late growing on the tree of good government*) Lewis mocks, is reminiscent of the Calormene poet appealed to by Ahosta.[61] However, change occurred in the sixteenth century, as it does in *The Horse and*

His Boy. With William Harrison (1534–1593) the century turns the corner away from Drab—'Mercury has succeeded Saturn'[62]—ushering in Sir Philip Sidney, whose work 'rises out of the contemporary Drab almost as a rocket rises.'[63] The rocket which goes off in the heads of Aravis and Shasta is likewise shooting for (or from) Mercury.

The theme of language also works itself out with respect to the two horses, both of whom have had to pretend, while living in Calormen, not to be talking beasts. Early on, Shasta says to Bree, 'I wish *you* could talk, old fellow.' Bree reveals that he can indeed speak but that, ever since he was taken captive by the Calormenes, he has been pretending to be 'dumb and witless,' like their horses. Set alongside the drab qualities of 'Calormene talk' and the 'maxims and verses' of Calormene poetry, the assumed muteness of the horses helps present a very un-Mercurial picture of life in this Southern land, which is necessary if we are to feel the growing influence of Mercurial power as the story progresses and moves to the poetic North.

Rabadash moves, as it were, further South, as the story continues. His refusal of the Mercurial Aslan's mercy means that he is turned, temporarily, into a donkey. The centrality of language in Lewis's understanding of human nature is indicated during the transformation scene: '[Rabadash's] human speech lasted just a moment longer than his human shape.' However, true to form, Lewis is prepared to find an exception to the prevailing Calormene abuses of language. Aravis's story-telling style—'the grand Calormene manner'—is praised by the author.[64] It is clearly directed against what Lewis elsewhere calls 'the Words-worthian heresy,'[65] by which he means the theory, as outlined in the Preface to *Lyrical Ballads*, that heightened or artificial diction prevents the communication of deep feeling. Lewis was of the view that the organization of a response was not the same as the pretence of a response and that there were certain things that could only be said in a high style. That Aravis's story-telling is oral is also significant, for Lewis had a high view of the pre-scribal tradition. However, one suspects that Lewis praises Aravis here largely to show how much more praiseworthy is the bard's singing of the lay at the end of the story. It is his own version of the 'Eloquence versus poetry' debate from *Love's Labour's Lost*. Re-jigging Shakespeare, Lewis intends to demonstrate that the songs of Mercury are more glorious than even his very best prose.

Our final ichneutic task is to observe how Mercury's metal makes its way into the story, for although the word 'mercury' never appears, quicksilver itself does. We may be helped to see where if we cross-refer, oddly enough, to the long Lunar passage in 'The Queen of Drum.' Here, in a context dominated by the Moon, we read of 'rivers of mercury.'[66] It is perplexing that mercury should intrude among images of the silvery goddess until we recall that mercury is itself a kind of silver. It is listed in the Periodic Table as 'Hg,' that is, *hydrargyrum*, water + silver; it is a 'double' metal, both solid and liquid. Turning back to the ninth chapter of *The Horse and His Boy*, 'Across the Desert,' we read: 'Under the moonlight the sand, in every direction and as far as they could see, gleamed as if it were smooth water or a great silver tray.' Of course, Lewis cannot tilt this silver tray of water, as he suggests tilting a saucer of quicksilver, in order to make its contents divide into glittering drops. However, he does show us the effects upon it of a swift sunrise when the sand is lit up in an instant, 'strewn with diamonds.' *That* is what 'Mercurial' means!

The Mercurial *Logos*

When we turn to the theological messages conveyed under the auspices of Mercury, the most obvious thing to consider is the depiction of Aslan. His encounter with Shasta in the mountain-pass in chapter 11 is one of the high-points in the Narniad, and, indeed, in the entire Lewisian corpus. When Shasta asks his unwelcome fellow traveller, 'Don't you think it was bad luck to meet so many lions?,' Aslan replies, 'There was only one lion.' Shasta is confused: 'What on earth do you mean? I've just told you there were at least two the first night, and—' He is interrupted: 'There was only one; but he was swift of foot.' 'How do you know?' asks Shasta.

> 'I was the lion.' And as Shasta gaped with open mouth and said nothing, the Voice continued. 'I was the lion who forced you to join with Aravis. I was the cat who comforted you among the houses of the dead. I was the lion who drove the jackals from you while you slept. I was the lion who gave the Horses the new strength of fear for the last mile so that you should reach King Lune in time. And I was the lion you do not remember who pushed the boat in which you lay, a child near death, so that it came to shore where a man sat, wakeful at midnight, to receive you.'[67]

As the incarnation of Mercury, Aslan is 'swift of foot,' the living and active principle of *componendo et dividendo*. Shasta has apprehended him hitherto only in division. Here in this paragraph, Aslan reveals that all those many 'lions' were but components of a single Lion: the anaphora is a stylistic embodiment of the very thing being expressed.

And then, to show that Mercury does not only combine multiplicity in singularity, but also singularity in multiplicity, Lewis presents the most ex-plicitly Trinitarian moment in the entire Narniad:

'Who are you?' asked Shasta.

'Myself,' said the Voice, very deep and low so that the earth shook: and again 'Myself,' loud and clear and gay: and then the third time 'Myself,' whispered so softly you could hardly hear it, and yet it seemed to come from all round you as if the leaves rustled with it.[68]

In this passage, Lewis neatly deploys his Mercurial imagery to present 'One Lion in a threefold Myself,' one God in three Persons, a Christianised Hermes Trismegistus (Thrice-Great Hermes). It is the obvious theological message to communicate via Mercury. But because the theological message is so familiar it would be easy to conclude that it was Lewis's starting-point, as if he sat down one day and decided to insert an episode which would be the romance equivalent of the Athanasian Creed. In reality, I would argue, the images associated with Mercury were Lewis's imaginative data; he then inhabited those images and, so to speak, moved about in that image world, before coming to realise that the symbols of Mercury naturally disposed themselves in a Trinitarian orientation. Imaginative composition was, for Lewis, the process of 're-combining elements made by [God] and already containing *His* meanings.'[69] The task of the poet was to discover those meanings. Finding the Holy Trinity in Mercury is perhaps the clearest example of Lewis's heuristic imagination at work.

But there is a good deal more *logos* in this Mercurial *poiema* than a brief presentation of the Trinity. As Aslan 'guides and gathers' the children and the horses, leading these pious *animae* to the happy dwellings,[70] he also teaches them to speak in a new way, a way that encompasses silence.

It is interesting to note that the Lion is not named 'Aslan' during his encounter with Shasta in the mountain-pass; he is described first as 'the Thing (or Person),' then as 'the Large Voice,' and finally as just 'the Voice.' Shasta, in contrast, has virtually no voice: "Who are you?' he said, scarcely above a whisper.' Aslan's reply—his first recorded utterance in the story—is significant: 'One who has waited long for you to speak.' As 'Lord of language,' Aslan has come both to speak and to be spoken to.

McGrath is of the opinion that 'one of the many merits of the writings of C. S. Lewis is that they take seriously the way in which words can *generate* and *transform* experience.'[71] This is an important observation, and most relevant to this passage in *The Horse and His Boy*, but we must be clear what kind of experience is being generated. It is not, principally, an experience containable by more mere words. Shasta does not suddenly start talking. On the contrary, he 'gaped with open mouth and said nothing'; then, 'after one glance at the Lion's face he slipped out of the saddle and fell at its feet. He couldn't say anything but then he didn't want to say anything, and he knew he needn't say anything.'

A similar silence falls on Aravis and the horses after their encounter with Aslan in chapter 14: 'Strange to say, they felt no inclination to talk to one another about him after he had gone. They all moved slowly away to different parts of the quiet grass and there paced to and fro, each alone, thinking.'

When the Mercurial Aslan meets his astrological children they do not all start chattering excitedly, as do the characters in the kitchen during the descent of Viritrilbia in *That Hideous Strength*. Rather, they are moved to silence. This silence is not, however, simply an absence of words; it is an eloquent silence, an articulacy of a spiritual kind. It is like what happens to Ransom and Merlin who find themselves sitting without saying anything in 'the white-hot furnace of essential speech'; the 'shining whiteness' by which Shasta finds himself enveloped in the mountain-pass may be a reworking of that image. Silence is not the same as wordlessness, for there is a kind of thinking which occurs without language, a faculty which linguists call 'mentalese.' Given what Lewis wrote elsewhere about language at the interface between divinity and humanity, one suspects that it is some special sort of mentalese, a hesychastic experience, which he intends to depict in the transformation of Shasta and Aravis, Bree and Hwin.

Lewis held the view that 'prayer without words is best'; one should try 'not to verbalise the mental acts.'[72] He believed that prayer could not be identical with normal human language because no form of words would be fully adequate to the task of addressing its ineffable subject. Hence the poem John utters in *The Pilgrim's Regress* in which he concedes that, 'Taken at their word, all prayers blaspheme'; literal sense needs to be translated into God's 'great, / Unbroken speech' if we are to avoid being 'idolaters, crying unheard / To a deaf idol.'[73] And even the mental acts needed to be relativised: 'From all my thoughts, even from my thoughts of Thee, / O Thou fair silence, fall and set me free,' Lewis prays, in another of his poems.[74] God is the supreme example of those concrete realities which are too definite for language: 'The ultimate Peace is silent through very density of life. Saying is swallowed up in being.'[75] Thus the divine Word descends upon the children and the horses, or elevates them into itself. They are not rendered 'dumb and witless' by the encounter; rather they find themselves speaking at the highest pitch of articulacy, through an irradiation of their whole selves with significance and relation, and by means of physical acts, such as Shasta's prostration, a response which is not merely verbal, but actual. It imitates that language which is 'a language more adequate'[76] than any other, namely the historical, 'lived' language of the incarnation, crucifixion, and resurrection. It is the Word *sans paroles*.

After all, what are words without the Divine Mercury? Only so much hot air, like the long-winded jargon of the Calormenes or the 'many words' of the Gentiles.[77] Orual comes to a similar conclusion in *Till We Have Faces* when she realises that language spoken in the absence of the god's face is 'only words, words; to be led out to battle against other words.' Orual's great triumph is to discover 'the speech which has lain at the centre of [her] soul'; it is 'dug out' of her. She gives birth, as it were, to articulacy, which is entirely appropriate for one also known as Maia, who in mythology was the mother of Mercury, as Jupiter was his father.

Since God Himself is the Word, no other utterance can suffice. The Christian is but 'one articulation' of that Word[78] and it is not from merely human resources but 'by the Spirit that we cry *Abba*.'[79] Therefore, in true prayer, 'God speaks to God.'[80] The task of the pray-er is to become the increasingly willing participant in that divine speech, not by means of 'psychological gymnastics,'[81] but by 'the union of wills [ours and God's] which, under Grace, is reached by a life of sanctity.'[82]

In coming to this understanding of wordless prayer, Lewis has, in a sense, made that 'total leap out of language' which, according to Steiner in *After Babel*, is death.[83] Or rather he has gone 'behind the scenes'[84] of language; he has plunged down into language and up again into its ur-form. It is there that one can pray from so essential a part of oneself that one scarcely has need to verbalise the mental acts: God lets down the bucket deep inside the pray-er so that such small and inflexible things as words are buoyed up by meaning, rather than forming the receptacle of it.

Interestingly, the very grass over which Aravis and Bree and Hwin walk, following their encounter with Aslan, is described as 'quiet.' Its vegetable soul knows, in a way which is more difficult for the human soul to know, how to participate in the divine *Actus purus*: it is like 'the voice of the garden, heard in / Our hearts'[85] in one of Lewis's poems. That Mercury should remove the inclination to talk (or rustle) is ironic—doubly so in the case of the horses, who had earlier been told, whatever they did in Tashbaan, not to 'start *talking*,' and triply so in the case of Bree, who had been so ashamed of his behaviour in fleeing the Lion that Hwin was unable to 'get a word out of him.' But the silence of the lawn and of those walking over it is only temporary: it is a kind of baptismal silence, eloquent of God's glory,[86] which lasts for 'about half an hour.'[87]

Bree, whose name is pleasingly polysemous,[88] has a further lesson to learn about language. Bree is a monophysite or Eutychian heretic: he believes in the Narnian version of Aslan's 'divinity,' but not his full 'humanity' (as it were).[89] He keeps swearing 'Thanks be to the Lion' and 'By the Lion's Mane,' but he does not acknowledge the reality of Aslan's lionhood. When Aravis asks, 'If he isn't a lion why do you call him a lion?,' Bree replies, 'He's as strong as a lion or (to our enemies, of course) as fierce as a lion.' He has emptied his language of literal reference and employs it as a dead metaphor. His monoscopy may be attributable to his Calormene master, whose name is Anradin; Sammons points out that 'anrad' means 'with a single aim or purpose.'[90] Bree's lack of double and treble vision is an offence against Mercury which the Mercurial Aslan cures with one touch of his whiskers. Monophysitism presumably arrived in Lewis's mind from Dante's depiction of Justinian in the sphere of Mercury, who confesses, 'I deemed one nature and no more was in / Christ's person, and I thought that creed enough.'[91]

Lewis himself has been accused of a theological inadequacy which is reminiscent of Eutychianism. Andrew Walker argues, partly by reference to Aslan, that, in Lewis's account of the incarnation, God does not become 'sufficiently earthed as the particular human being, Jesus Christ of Nazareth. He is not so much the God-man, who is flesh of our flesh, as the temporarily earth-visiting God.'[92] On the other hand, Mary Warnock has accused Lewis of a tendency which is reminiscent of an equal and opposite error, the sort of error which issues in a kind of Arianism. She is of the view that Lewis 'would not allow himself to take seriously... that the life of Christ itself as recorded in the Gospels is a symbol, a universal-in-particular standing for something, we cannot say exactly what, but speaking to us of infinity, eternity and the triumph over time'; his response to the Gospels was one of 'literalism.'[93]

Walker and Warnock are both perceptive critics. Each sees something which is present in Lewis's work, but they come to such divergent conclusions as a consequence of looking through only one eye. Lewis's work needs to be read with the same stereoscopic vision with which it was written. As Lyle H. Smith maintains, Lewis understood 'the necessity of keeping both the metaphorical and the literal meanings of the terms of a metaphor in view simultaneously.'[94] Part of the tremendous power of chapter 11 of *The Horse and His Boy* springs from the skilful marrying of the metaphorical with the literal:

> The mist was turning from black to grey and from grey to white. This must have begun to happen some time ago, but while he had been talking to the Thing he had not been noticing anything else. Now, the whiteness around him became a shining whiteness; his eyes began to blink. Somewhere ahead he could hear birds singing. He knew the night was over at last. He could see the mane and ears and head of his horse quite easily now. A golden light fell on them from the left. He thought it was the sun.[95]

There are metaphorical meanings running under all these apparently literal statements. We do not have space to analyse the passage in depth, but the most obvious one is 'He knew the night was over at last': Shasta's dark night of the soul, his estrangement from Aslan, has come to its end. Lewis had used the same metaphor to the same intended effect in *That Hideous Strength*,[96] but without the same success: the more realistic and literalistic qualities of that novel stifle its more metaphorical potential. Admittedly, *That Hideous Strength* is described by its author as a 'fairy-tale,' but it reads more like a novel than a romance. In the Narniad, which unmistakably belongs to the romance genre, the writing has a numinous quality; one has the sense of literal and meta-phorical in consubstantial connection. Of course, the effect may not necessarily work well in excerpted quotation, for here, as in much poetry, 'the poet's battles are won in advance,'[97] and one cannot quote all ten preceding chapters. In context, however, Lewis has succeeded in running his literal and metaphorical meanings so close together that they appear, as it were, now like a centaur, now like a mounted knight. The double vision is an apposite embodiment of the geist animating the story, and it is also a liberation for some of Lewis's favourite mental habits, for, as Rossi notes, Lewis was 'delighted by the equivocal,'[98] and as Edwards remarks, his first concern was always 'to discover the invisible not behind but within the visible.'[99] In this connection Lewis himself quotes Sir Thomas Browne approvingly: '[It is] "the philosophy of Hermes that this visible world is but a picture of the invisible, wherein, as in a portrait, things are not truly but in equivocal shapes, as they counterfeit some real substance in that invisible fabrick.'[100]

In a sense, 'the night was over at last' is a pun, but a pun with a Christo-logical significance, pointing, as it does, not just to the approach of daylight but also to the effect of Aslan upon Shasta. For that matter, all good puns have Christological significance: first, because Christ himself was a punster;[101] sec-ond because there was divine wit at work (as Augustine recognised) when the Word became speechless *(infans)* in the infant Jesus;[102] and third because of the essentially polysemic import of the God-man. The incarnation of Christ, the enfleshment of the spiritual, is the tap-root of Lewis's belief in meanings beyond the literal. It is the incarnation which sanctions and underwrites both his use of word-play, one of the lowest forms of wit, and his faith in the highest double meanings of all, which he calls symbols or sacraments. The highest does not stand without the lowest,[103] and Lewis's understanding of God is that He is both 'unspeakably immanent' and 'unspeakably transcendent.'[104] To attempt to combine these theological perspectives without cancelling out their polarity was a bold endeavour and full of risk. *The Horse and His Boy* succeeds as well as it does because a river of Mercury runs through it.

EIGHT ✦

Venus

O f the seven planetary deities, Venus was the most ubiquitous in medieval poetry. To a renaissance poet such as George Herbert her omnipresence was questionable: why, he asks, should a Christian poet be required to wear 'Venus' livery'?[1] May he not plainly say 'My God, My King'?[2] To Lewis, however, who was ever aiming to undermine the long reaction against medieval conventions, Herbert's question itself needed to be interrogated: 'Why should poets not figure their believed religion under the veil of paganism?' The Olympian gods—as his friend Farrer noted—were all but dead and buried by the middle of the twentieth century; Aphrodite, for example, was 'no longer anything but the passion of love itself.'[3] An emergency operation was needed if they were to have a continuing life in the modern imagination. Lewis therefore had no hesitation in donning her livery and entering her service, becoming, like Chaucer, Venus's 'disciple.'[4]

'"Sweeter than all it is when one bed holds twain that love, and the queen of Cypris is praised of both." Queen of Cypris, you know, is Aphrodite.' Thus Lewis wrote to Arthur Greeves, in 1917, quoting Asclepiades;[5] it is the first manifestation of his literary interest in the foam-born goddess.[6] A year later he recalls to Greeves's mind 'the night when we first broached the "nameless secrets of Aphrodite."' These nameless secrets, otherwise embarrassing or shameful to the young Lewis, became thinkable and discussable under the rubric of Aphrodite/Venus and the imagery associated with her, and it was around this time that he began to develop his enduring interest in her qualities. He hung her picture in his college rooms,[7] wrote poem after poem about her,[8] stared at her in the night sky,[9] and became steadily more learned in her literary manifestations.[10]

Since this is a literary and theological, not a psychological, study, we shall not be able to mine the vein of Venus-related thought, so potent to Jung and so fascinating to Lewis, which marks the psychic descent to 'the Mothers.'[11] But in the back of our minds we may remain alert to the fact that Lewis became, as he termed himself in *Surprised by Joy*, an 'orphan' following the death of his mother in 1908 and that he experienced fairly unusual relationships with the two principal women in his adult life. His imaginative interest in the occupant of the third heaven had a personal resonance which he himself acknowledged in his later years, for he once explicitly compared Joy Lewis to Venus, quoting Shelley's translation of a Platonic epitaph:

> Thou wert my morning star among the living,
> Ere thy fair light had fled;
> Now, having died, thou art as Hesperus giving
> New splendour to the dead.[12]

While it is never safe to attribute a writer's imaginations too directly to his experience we may with a certain impunity commit the Personal Heresy and suggest that Lewis also connected Venus to his mother; there may well be auto-biographical elements at work in *The Magician's Nephew*, in which a young boy hopes to save his mother's life with an apple taken from an Hesperides-like garden.[13] Interestingly, although *The Magician's Nephew* was published sixth, it was the last of the Chronicles to be completed, having been the second one to be started.[14] Lewis had uncharacteristic difficulty in finding the right shape for the story; perhaps the personal resonances made it a painful book to write. In any case, he seems to have felt that there was unfinished business in his understanding of Venus: she continues to make a strong showing in his writings even after the conclusion of the Narniad, most obviously in *Till We Have Faces*.[15]

Venus in Lewis's Scholarship

There were academic as well as psychological reasons for his continuing interest because Venus is the most complex of the planets from the point of view of literary scholarship. For reasons of space we cannot here give a full overview of her appearances in Lewis's professional academic writings. However, a brief survey will be attempted, and the place to start is the summary given in *The Discarded Image:*

In beneficence Venus stands second only to Jupiter; she is *Fortuna Minor*. Her metal is copper. The connection is not clear till we observe that Cyprus was once famed for its copper mines; that copper is *cyprium*, the Cyprian metal; and that Venus, or Aphrodite, especially worshipped in that island, was κύπρις, the Lady of Cyprus. In mortals she produces beauty and amorousness; in history, fortunate events. Dante makes her sphere the Heaven not, as we might expect from a more obvious poet, of the charitable, but of those, now penitent, who in this life loved greatly and lawlessly.[16]

But this summary barely scratches the surface of the topic; the Venereal character is, in fact, considerably more complex. There are various 'metaphysical' Venuses distinguishable—but not fully divisible—from the strictly astrological one. To gain a full understanding of how Lewis construed Venereal influence we need to understand these satellite variants as they supplement and react upon the mother planet.

At the highest level, Venus is also a name for God, according to Cusanus,[17] and Usk can equate her with 'Divine Love.'[18] At a slightly lower level, Ficino distinguishes two kinds of *Veneres:* the first is the Angelic Mind (*Venus coelistis*) considered in its contemplation of Divine Beauty; the second is the generative power in the *Anima Mundi*—a being inferior to the angels—known as *Venus vulgaris* or *Venus naturalis*.[19] (This second power, the 'generative force in nature,'[20] is the same as that which Lewis finds in the *Romance of the Rose*, and also in Lucretius.[21]) Chapman in 'Hero and Leander' has a form-giving 'archetypal Uranian Venus,' and this shows him, in Lewis's view, to be 'taking his Venus more seriously than Marlowe would have done,' despite the fact that 'Venus dominates Marlowe's narrative and Saturn that of Chapman.'[22] But even Marlowe's Venus is better than Shakespeare's. Lewis considered the Venus of 'Venus and Adonis' to be very ill-conceived. He protested, 'This flushed, panting, perspiring, suffocating, loquacious creature is supposed to be the goddess of love herself, the golden Aphrodite. It will not do.'[23]

Spenser rather than Shakespeare provided Lewis with the richest source of Venereal imagery. He distinguishes the following kinds of Spenserian Venuses: a 'Venus-on-earth'[24] (who resembles the second of Ficino's types); a 'Venus-as-Paradigma'[25] (who comes from Plato's *Timaeus*); a 'Venus-as-planetary-deity'[26] (who is the astrological Intelligence *simpliciter*); a 'bad Venus'[27] (who is Spenser's own picture of diseased sexuality); and a 'veiled Venus'[28] (who is to be regarded as one of Spenser's 'symbols of God'). This last and divine Venus is 'constructed of elements drawn both from Christian revelation and from the intimations of poetic theology.' It would give Lewis a good precedent for his own Christological use of Venereal imagery in poetry and fiction.

Venus in Lewis's Poetry

In Lewis's poetry Venereal qualities are used only once for Christological purposes. We will examine that occurrence below, but first we must look at the earliest appearances of Venus in Lewis's published verse where her qualities serve predominantly as symbols of God's dwelling-place in paradise, rather than of God (or Christ) Himself.

When he wrote *Spirits in Bondage* Lewis was not quite sure whether he believed in God or not, but he believed in (or at any rate longed for) a state which, theologically speaking, he would have been hard pressed to differentiate from the heaven of theistic traditions. The volume contains several poems in which Venereal imagery is used to depict an ideal world beyond death. The most noteworthy are 'The Philosopher,' 'Death in Battle,' and 'Hesperus.'

In 'The Philosopher' the poet enquires:

Who shall cross over for us the bridge of fears
And pass in to the country where the ancient Mothers dwell?[29]

And the answer is: not the old man, watery-eyed and full of leaden years, but the young man, 'fresh and beautiful of show.' It is he who shall 'cross at last the shadowy bar / To where the ever-living are.' And it would appear to be this same young man who finally makes that crossing in 'Death in Battle':

Open the gates for me,
Open the gates of the peaceful castle, rosy in the West,
In the sweet dim Isle of Apples over the wide seas breast,
Open the gates for me![30]

Since stars are 'isles' in the poem 'Song,' this 'Isle of Apples' is presumably the same Hesperus that has already appeared in the poem of that name. There Lewis presents the same set of images: a western garden beyond the ocean and beyond fear, containing a sacred tree. 'Hesperus' does not actually mention that this is an apple-tree, but it is undoubtedly so, for this is an early manifestation of Lewis's 'Avalon-Hesperides-Western business.'[31] Nearly thirty years later it was still featuring in his poetry. 'The Landing'[32] tells of the poet's arrival at the garden of the Hesperides—with its 'green hill,' its 'apple-gold' headlands, its 'gum-sweet wood'—and of his dismayed discovery that it is only an imitation: the real Hesperides lies even further to the west.

In his poetic search for the country of the ancient Mothers, Lewis was repeatedly misled by a false trail, that laid by the 'bad Venus' whom he had found in Spenser. Lewis calls her 'Venus infernal' and she makes three appearances in his poetry, first in 'Wormwood' ('Venus infernal starving in the strength of fire'), second in 'Infatuation' ('Venus infernal taught such voice and eyes / To bear themselves abroad for merchandise'), and third in 'Lilith,' a poem about Adam's first wife.[33] Under her spell Lewis found that 'it was quite easy to think that one desired...the garden of Hesperus for the sake of his daughters.'[34] But eventually he learnt, by means of 'discreditable' experience, that this was not the case. In other words, he discovered that *sehnsucht* was not a disguise of sexual desire. And this was true of the proper expressions of sexual desire as much as the improper ones.[35] Nothing on earth, no appetite of flesh and blood, could satisfy the longing for the beauty symbolised by Venus.

This unsatisfiable, inexpressible aspect of Venus is communicated in 'The Planets':

> In the third region
> VENUS voyages...but my voice falters;
> Rude rime-making wrongs her beauty,
> Whose breasts and brow, and her breath's sweetness
> Bewitch the worlds. Wide-spread the reign
> Of her secret sceptre,[36] in the sea's caverns,
> In grass growing, and grain bursting,
> Flower unfolding, and flesh longing,
> And shower falling sharp in April.
> The metal copper in the mine reddens
> With muffled brightness, like muted gold,
> By her fingers form'd.[37]

The poet's 'voice falters' for 'rime-making wrongs her beauty.' If we digress from Lewis's poetry for a moment, we may find a similar expression of Venus's inexpressible beauty in his sermon, 'The Weight of Glory,' where Lewis discusses scriptural portrayals of heaven:

> [W]e are to be given the Morning Star.[38]...In one way, of course, God has given us the Morning Star already: you can go and enjoy the gift on many fine mornings if you get up early enough. What more, you may ask, do we want? Ah, but we want so much more....We do not want merely to *see* beauty, though, God knows, even that is bounty enough. We want something else which can hardly be put into words—to be united with the beauty we see, to pass into it, to receive it into ourselves, to bathe in it, to become part of it....That is why the poets tell us such lovely falsehoods. They talk as if the west wind could really sweep into a human soul;[39] but it can't....Or not yet. For if we take the imagery of Scripture seriously, if we believe that God will one day *give* us the Morning Star...then we may surmise that

both the ancient myths and the modern poetry, so false as history, may be very near the truth as prophecy.[40]

It is highly significant that Lewis should symbolise the human longing for heaven by means of the Morning Star, for the Morning Star (another of Venus's names) is a Biblical title for Christ (2 Pet. 1:19; Rev. 22:16). The fact that Lewis does not mention this in 'The Weight of Glory' is itself an aspect of the inexpressibility which he is trying to express, part of the 'shyness' which is the theme of that sermon. It is a silence which is audible again in 'Five Sonnets,' where he writes:

> Pitch your demands heaven-high and they'll be met.
> Ask for the Morning Star and take (thrown in)
> Your earthly love.[41]

'Five Sonnets' makes no attempt to flesh out what it means Christologically to 'ask for the Morning Star,' and that is to be expected for, if 'rime-making' wrongs Venus, it will certainly be insufficient to speak adequately of Christ. Prose, too, is barely sufficient, for this is a subject that 'can hardly be put into words.' However, Lewis's imagination tended to find prose a more effective vehicle than poetry and that is certainly the case with his understanding of Venus. His Ransom Trilogy is our next area of investigation.

Venus in the Ransom Trilogy

Perelandra

In the second volume of the cosmic trilogy, Ransom, like St. Paul, is 'taken up to the third heaven,'[42] which Lewis renames 'Perelandra.' There Ransom 'lived and walked on the oceans of the Morning Star,' bathing in it, receiving it into himself, becoming part of it. Indeed, he does more than unite himself to Venus, he saves the whole planet from a Fall and is given a final resting-place there.[43] Perelandra becomes for Ransom (as we are told in the final chapter) 'the Morning Star which He promised to those who conquer.'

As well as being a Christological image, the Morning Star is a Biblical term for Babylon and, by traditional extension, for Satan: 'How you have fallen from heaven, O morning star, son of the dawn!' (Isa. 14:12a). Lewis taps into this tradition in the portrayal of his own Lucifer, Weston, the great physicist who, after inviting demonic power into himself, becomes 'the Un-man.' This Un-man has 'been with Maleldil in Deep Heaven' and 'heard eternal councils.' His advent into Perelandra in his space-ship suggests an ejection from the angelic ranks: 'like a shooting star something seemed to have streaked across the sky.'

The Un-man's temptation of the Green Lady is an outing for the 'Venus Infernal' theme. He keeps attempting to poison her imagination (the first step in undermining her will) by telling her tales of tragic heroines who had been 'oppressed by fathers, cast off by husbands, deserted by lovers,' female martyrs who, if men had had their way, would have been kept down 'to mere child-bearing.' The picture he paints is 'always very nearly true.' But not quite. In fact, in ordinary terrestrial speech, these heroines were 'witches or perverts,' more reminiscent of 'Agrippina and of Lady Macbeth' than noble pioneers.

Having failed to corrupt Tinidril's imagination by means of words, the Un-man attempts the same thing by means of visual images. In parody of the ancient mythological image of Aphrodite's looking-glass, he produces a small 'English pocket mirror that might have cost three-and-six.' This, he promises, enables one 'to walk alongside oneself as if one were a second person and to delight in one's own beauty. Mirrors were made to teach this art.' As it turns out, Tinidril is only frightened, not corrupted, by the sight of her own face, and Ransom eventually perceives that the Un-man's strategy is to awaken in her mind not vanity concerning her physical beauty, but egoism concerning her beautiful soul. Not that consciousness of one's own beauty is portrayed by Lewis as an evil. On the contrary, Maleldil has already provided for Tinidril a way of seeing herself in the reflection from the sky, a phenomenon observable 'three days out of five in the planet of love. The queen of those seas views herself continually in a celestial mirror.'

However, the Un-man fails to infect Perelandra with the spirit of Venus Infernal, and the abiding impression of the book is not these temptations, but the almost overwhelming sensuous richness of the planet itself. Perelandra, Ransom recognises, is the real 'garden of the Hesperides,' the home of all sweetness and laughter and copper and warm wetness.[44] Although Eve and her apple are several times mentioned or alluded to, the story is the reverse of the Genesis myth: it is Eden without the Fall. This paradise is the 'apple-laden land' of Euripides[45] in which a 'Fixed Land,' rather than a forbidden fruit, represents the divine command, and apples have no prohibitory significance. They feature most obviously under the guise of the 'gourds' and the 'bubble trees' which Ransom both freely enjoys and freely abstains from; also, at one remove, as breasts. Apples, as Lewis wrote elsewhere, 'often symbolize the female breasts':[46] here, in a profound remythologising of the Eden apple, Ransom is 'breast-fed by the planet Venus herself.'

Thus Ransom, though 'orphaned' from 'the great Mother of his own race,' is united with a 'warm, maternal, delicately gorgeous world.' Maternal imagery and terminology abound. The Un-man, for instance, existed 'before the mothers of the mothers of [Ransom's] mother were conceived.' Ransom's own name was planned to yield a new meaning 'before his Mother had borne him, before his ancestors had been called Ransoms.' He warns the Green Lady about 'mothers wearing themselves to a ravelling.' She, he learns, has no human mother because 'I *am* the Mother.' Above her, however, is the planetary Mother, the Oyarsa of Venus, the Intelligence which guides Perelandra. Her enfolding, womb-like identity is readable in her eyes, which 'opened, as it were, inward, as if they were the curtained gateway to a world of waves and murmurings and wandering airs, of life that rocked in winds and splashed on mossy-stones and descended as the dew and arose sunward in thin-spun delicacy of mist.'

And who is the Mother of the Oyarsa? The operatic finale of the book consists of Ransom's vision of the cosmic Great Dance and the accompanying paeans of praise to Maleldil: 'Blessed be He!' Maleldil could have been depicted as a 'She,' as an even greater kind of Venus; Spenser had done something similar, as we will see below. But Lewis chooses not to take that step. Perelandra apparently has no mother any more than Malacandra had. Maleldil and 'His Father and the Third One' are conceived in masculine terms.

That Hideous Strength

In the closing volume of the trilogy, Lewis dips a toe in the water of feminine theological imagery. The descent of the gods in chapter 15 includes the descent of Venus. These gods have not suddenly become equated with Maleldil in this third book, but, as has been argued above (chapter 2), their descent is, in a certain sense, parallel to the coming of the Holy Spirit at Pentecost. By including the feminine Venus among those deities, Lewis inches toward the position he would adopt in *The Magician's Nephew*, when he presents Aslan as the incarnation of the presiding Venereal Intelligence.

But Venus has a lot more to do than merely descend in chapter 15. She is responsible for bringing about those conditions in which the heir of Jove will be conceived. The very first word of *That Hideous Strength* is 'matrimony,' which denotes not just marriage (of the Martial and Venereal principles illustrated in the first two books), but, literally, 'mother making.' Mark and Jane must come together so as to make of her the mother of the new Pendragon. There are three main Venereal strands to Lewis's depiction of this destiny: the terrestrial Venus; Mother Dimble; and the coming of Perelandra herself.

THE TERRESTRIAL VENUS

The first strand is conveyed by means of planet Earth's residual spirit of Venus whom Jane sees in a waking vision in chapter 14 and Mark likewise in chapter 17. As Ransom tells Jane, 'there is a terrestrial as well as a celestial Venus— Perelandra's wraith as well as Perelandra.' This 'earth Venus' is portrayed as a huge, half-naked, beautiful woman in a flame-coloured robe; she has darkish, honey-coloured, 'Southern' skin, large breasts, red cheeks, wet lips, black eyes, and an enigmatic expression. She sets things alight with a torch in her hand which gives off black smoke and a sticky, resinous smell; vegetation, rather than flame, springs up from whatever she touches. She is attended by several dwarf-ish, gnome-like men 'quite insufferably familiar, frivolous, and irrepressible,' who are versions of Risus, Jocus, and Petulantia, 'the natural attendants of Venus.'[47]

MOTHER DIMBLE

The second Venereal strand concerns the character of Mrs Margery Dimble. In the very first chapter we learn that 'one tended to call her Mother Dimble.' She is, in fact, 'childless'; indeed, 'barren.' However, she, unlike Jane and Mark, is open to the influence of Venus. Together with her husband, Cecil, she makes her home into a 'noisy *salon*' for all his pupils, of both sexes. She 'has not re-jected' the terrestrial Venus, as have Mark and Jane through their contracepted intercourse; rather she has 'baptised' it, according to Ransom, transforming it from its 'raw,' 'demoniac' self. She can do this because she has accepted, as Jane has not, 'all that has happened to [the terrestrial Venus] since Maleldil came to Earth.' This explains why, to Jane, the terrestrial Venus looks like 'Mother Dimble's face with something left out.' In the final chapter Mrs Dimble is dressed in a robe of that 'tyrannous flame colour which Jane had seen in her vision [of the earth Venus]' and a 'great copper brooch.' She takes on the ap-pearance of 'a kind of priestess or sybil, the servant of some pre-historic god-dess of fertility—an old tribal matriarch, mother of mothers.' Her maternal role vis-à-vis Jane is most evident when she helps to prepare the bedroom in the Lodge which will be the location of Jane's reunion with Mark.

THE DESCENT OF PERELANDRA

And the third Venereal strand of *That Hideous Strength* is the actual descent of the celestial Venus in chapter 15:

Down in the kitchen drowsiness stole over them after the orgy of [Mercurial] speaking had come to an end. Jane, having nearly fallen asleep, was startled by her book falling from her hand, and looked about her. How warm it was . . . how comfortable and familiar. She had always liked wood fires but tonight the smell of the logs seemed more than ordinarily sweet. She began to think it was sweeter than could possibly be, that a smell of burning cedar or of incense pervaded the room. It thickened. Fragrant names hovered in her mind—nard and cassia's balmy smells and all Arabia breathing from a box; even something more subtly sweet, perhaps maddening—why not forbidden?—but she knew it was commanded. She was too drowsy to think deeply how this could be. The Dimbles were talking together but in so low a voice that others could not hear. Their faces appeared to her transfigured. She could no longer see that they were old—only mature, like ripe fields in August, serene and golden with the tranquillity of fulfilled desire. On her other side, Arthur said something in Camilla's ear. There too...but as the warmth and sweetness of that rich air now fully mastered her brain, she could hardly bear to look on them: not through envy (that thought was far away), but because a sort of brightness flowed from them that dazzled her, as if the god and goddess in them burned through their bodies and through their clothes and shone before her in a young double-natured nakedness of rose-red spirit that overcame her. And all about them danced (as she half saw), not the gross and ridiculous dwarfs which she had seen that afternoon, but grave and ardent spirits, bright winged, their boyish shapes smooth and slender like ivory rods.

In the Blue Room also Ransom and Merlin felt about this time that the temperature had risen. The windows, they did not see how or when, had swung open; at their opening the temperature did not drop, for it was from without that the warmth came. Through the bare branches, across the ground which was once more stiffening with frost, a summer breeze was blowing into the room, but the breeze of such a summer as England never has. Laden like heavy barges that glide nearly gunwale under, laden so heavily you would have thought it could not move, laden with ponderous fragrance of night-scented flowers, sticky gums, groves that drop odours, and with cool savour of midnight fruit, it stirred the curtains, it lifted a letter that lay on the table, it lifted the hair which had a moment before been plastered on Merlin's forehead. The room was rocking. They were afloat. A soft tingling and shivering as of foam and breaking bubbles ran over their flesh. Tears ran down Ransom's cheeks. He alone knew from what seas and what islands that breeze blew. Merlin did not; but in him also the inconsolable wound with which man is born waked and ached at this touching. Low syllables of pre-historic Celtic self-pity murmured from his lips. These yearnings and fondlings were however only the fore-runners of the goddess. As the whole of her virtue seized, focussed, and held that spot of the rolling Earth in her long beam, something harder, shriller, more perilously ecstatic, came out of the centre of all the softness. Both the humans trembled—Merlin because he did not know what was coming, Ransom because he knew. And now it came. It was fiery, sharp, bright and ruthless, ready to kill, ready to die, outspeeding light: it was Charity, not as mortals imagine it, not even as it has been humanised for them since the Incarnation of the Word, but the translunary virtue, fallen upon them direct from the Third Heaven, unmitigated. They were blinded, scorched, deafened. They thought it should burn their bones. They could not bear that it should continue. They could not bear that it should cease. So Perelandra, triumphant among planets, whom men call Venus, came and was with them in the room.[48]

The orgasmic intensity of this passage is a kind of literary foreplay, preparing the reader for the final chapter of the book, entitled 'Venus at St. Anne's.'[49] For Venus lingers on earth, unlike the other four descended Intelligences. She does so partly in order to transport Ransom back to Perelandra, for which he has been home-sick, and partly to illustrate the 'triumphant vindication of the body.' In the latter capacity, she offers carnal delights of both stomach[50] and loins to all the beasts at St. Anne's (bears, jackdaws, horses, pigs, bats, hedgehogs, mice, and elephants) and also, of course, to the human couples (the Dennistons, the Dimbles, the Maggses, and the Studdocks). Satisfaction of every fleshly appetite is available amid an all-encompassing 'warmth and wetness.' In particular, Venus lingers to preside over Mark and Jane's bed. It is a 'rich bed' and the only bed in the Lodge, one which they must share all night, unlike the separate beds they have at home. They go to it fully cognizant at last of their own animality, for although they are more than the beasts, they are not less than them. Jane will have no more dreams; she will 'have children instead.'

But although Venus has so much to do in this book, she does not operate to the exclusion of either Maleldil or Jupiter. With respect to Maleldil, Venus works to redeem that flesh which Maleldil assumed (so we are twice reminded) at the Incarnation, and her influence should not be understood as if it were an element ultimately separable from Maleldil's presence. Myers' usual insight fails her on this score when she complains of the unfortunate juxtaposition of two kinds of nonordinary experience in *That Hideous Strength*, 'the encounter with the allegorical literary figure of Venus and the encounter with the deity of the believed religion.'[51] On the contrary, the juxtaposition is appropriate because the 'believed religion' is so mythologised in the tale that Christ and Venus are equally at home in it as Maleldil and Perelandra, respectively. To Jane, the terrestrial Venus is not an allegorical figure, but a literal manifestation of angelic power, no more and no less 'believed' than Maleldil. One of the deeper messages of the book is that one cannot be put right before God without being put right with oneself and one's fellows. For human beings are equally 'cut off from Earth their mother and from the Father in Heaven.'

Maleldil does not feature *in propria persona*; his being is represented at the creaturely level through the Jovial Oyarsa and, in turn, through that Oyarsa's own human representative, Ransom. Interestingly, it is after her audience with Ransom that Jane both finds herself 'in the sphere of Jove' and, consequently, for the first time becomes Venereally self-aware. Her meeting with the representative of kingly Jupiter means she becomes conscious of her own queen-like beauty: 'she had the sensation . . . that it was growing and expanding like a magic flower' (an echo of the 'flower unfolding' in 'The Planets'). She looks at herself in the mirror: 'Certainly she was looking well: she was looking unusually well . . . there was little vanity in this. For beauty was made for others. Her beauty belonged to the Director. It belonged to him so completely that he could even decide not to keep it for himself but to order that it be given to another.' With this realisation, Jane begins to desire the enjoying of her own beauty, which 'is the obedience of Eve'; she no longer desires the desiring of her beauty, which is 'the vanity of Lilith.'

A likely source for Lewis's idea about beauty belonging to someone so completely that he can 'order it to be given to another' is Charles Williams, on whom the portrait of Ransom in *That Hideous Strength* may be partly based.[52] His understanding of Venus was influential on Lewis and requires a section to itself.

Venus in Charles Williams

Between *That Hideous Strength* and *The Magician's Nephew* Lewis published *Arthurian Torso* which consists of Williams's unfinished poem, 'The Figure of Arthur,' and Lewis's commentary thereon. An important image in 'The Figure of Arthur' is 'the Wood of Broceliande,' which Lewis takes to be identifiable with 'what the Greeks called the *Apeiron*—the unlimited, the formless origin of forms.'[53] This wood has 'no horizon,' and the image of the horizon (what Lewis calls 'a hard straight line which at once unites and separates heaven and earth') is also an important element in the poem.

The sovereign mistress of Broceliande is named 'Nimue' by Williams. She, Lewis explains, is 'the 'mother of making'; she is 'that energy which reproduces on earth a pattern derived from 'the third heaven,' that is, from the sphere of Venus, the sphere of Divine Love.' What resides in the third heaven is 'the feeling intellect'[54] which

exists as a permanent reality in the spiritual world and by response to that archtype Nimue brings the whole process of nature into being.

Williams is here . . . reproducing the doctrine of the Renaissance Pla-
tonists that Venus—celestial love and beauty—was the pattern or
model after which God created the material universe.[55] . . .

Nimue, in obedience to her lord the Third Heaven, brings the
potentialities of Earth to perfection; just as she also brings 'to a flash
of seeing' . . . the ultimate femininity of the created universe. In the
soft fertile earth of the ploughed fields, in the waters of sea and
river . . . in all that receives, responds, brings forth and is enformed, but
most of all in the beautiful and wise woman discerned in a flash of
Beatrician seeing, Nature sets before us for our delight the unfathomable feminine principle which would otherwise lie invisible at the
very roots of Broceliande, 'the world's base.'[56]

Broceliande, though horizonless, is not the Absolute; it is rather that mysterious place, full of immense dangers and immense possibilities, which lies outside
our ordinary mode of consciousness. Within our ordinary mode of consciousness, it is possible to see a horizon, that is, to distinguish earth from heaven (for
Williams was no pantheist). In Heaven there is permanence, command, 'the
lord'; in Earth there is response, obedience, 'the mother of making.' Complete
and balanced humanity arises out of the union of the two, the Empire and
Broceliande, Divine Order and formless chaos, *Peras* and *Apeiron*, the city and
the wood. One moment of such union is portrayed by Williams in what Lewis
calls 'an image of startling beauty.' The Earth's shadow, that cone of darkness
stretching out into the heavens, touches the sphere of Venus, thus linking
Nimue's agents on earth with Nimue's archetype in the Third Heaven. 'Continuity is established between the natural order, the manifold and unstable
ectype, and its 'climax tranquil in Venus' where the 'unriven truths' dwell . . .
We are, in fact, watching the impregnation of Nimue by her Pattern.'

In part, Williams's scheme is simply that of Spenser, with which Lewis was
already familiar. In the image of the Wood, however, he introduces something
of his own, which Lewis in turn appropriated in *The Magician's Nephew*, as we
will suggest below. For now though, as we leave Williams's works, we must pass
one last comment upon the horizonlessness of his woods, for it is an image that
Lewis interestingly redeploys when characterizing the modern view of the
universe. In contrast to the builded and ordered quality of the Ptolemaic cosmos, Lewis argues that the post-Copernican universe is like a wasteland:
'[T]o look out on the night sky with modern eyes is like looking out over a sea
that fades away into mist, or looking about one in a trackless forest—trees
forever and no horizon.'[57] In that sense, he seems to be suggesting, the post-
Copernican world has returned to *Apeiron* or chaos, helped on the way latterly
by poets such as T. S. Eliot. Eliot, in Lewis's view, attacks πέρας by writing

chaotic poems, such as 'The Waste Land,' that infect people with, rather than fortifying them against, chaos.[58]

A chaotic cosmos is no cosmos, by definition. The chaos of original matter as reported in Genesis and certain pagan myths (for example, the first book of Ovid's *Metamorphoses*) was ordered and worked up into a *kosmos* (*kosmein*, to arrange, organise, embellish, whence also *cosmetics*). We do not have space here to analyse Lewis's philological assessment of the developments in meaning of *kosmos*, *world*, *mundus*, *phusis*, and *nature*, to which he gives two whole chapters in his 1960 work, *Studies in Words*. But it is amusing to note Lewis glancing in the mirror as he does so. In tracing the fine shades and shifts in the semantic histories of these words, he refers to another 1960-dated publication; it is entitled *Il Nipote del Mago* and nicely illustrates a meaning of the word *world*.[59] He gives the author as one 'G. Vivante' [sic]. In fact, Giorgina Vivanti was not the author but the translator, and the work in question was Lewis's own *Magician's Nephew*.[60] It is the only time the Narniad is ever mentioned in his works of scholarship.

Venus in *The Magician's Nephew*

The Venereal *Poiema*

If Lewis chuckled as he smuggled this Narnian reference into *Studies in Words* it would have been entirely appropriate, for Venus is 'partly a comic spirit,'[61] she is the 'laughter-loving goddess.'[62] Her donegalitarian presence in *The Magician's Nephew* explains why it is (as Myers has noted) 'lighter and more humorous than the other Chronicles.'[63]

This lightness of tone is achieved partly through authorial comment, for example, on the toughness of aunts, on how certain houses always smell of mutton, on how 'everyone' had lots of servants in those days (including, presumably, the servants). It is partly achieved through the simple device of putting plenty of laughter in the action of the story: 'roars of laughter' greet Jadis in London; the sun 'laughed for joy' at Narnia's original dawn; and a perky jackdaw makes 'the First Joke,' upon which

> all the other animals began making various queer noises which are their way of laughing and which, of course, no one has ever heard in our world. They tried at first to repress it, but Aslan said: 'Laugh and fear not, creatures. Now that you are no longer dumb and witless, you need not always be grave. For jokes as well as justice come in with speech.' So they all let themselves go. And there was such merriment

that the Jackdaw himself plucked up courage again and perched on the cab-horse's head, between its ears, clapping its wings, and said: 'Aslan! Aslan! Have I made the first joke? Will everybody always be told how I made the first joke?' 'No, little friend,' said the Lion. 'You have not *made* the first joke; you have only *been* the first joke.' Then every-one laughed more than ever; but the Jackdaw didn't mind and laughed just as loud.[64]

And finally, the spirit of levity is conjured by juxtaposing the decorum and etiquette of Edwardian England with the ferocious amorality of the Boudicca-like Jadis. Her cataclysmic destruction of the people of Charn becomes, in Digory's upper-middle class vocabulary, 'rather hard luck on them'; her ego-tistical fantasies are adjudged 'absolute bosh from beginning to end' by the no-nonsense Polly; and her evil incantations are dismissed by Aunt Letty as the 'strong language' of a drunken hussy from the circus. In addition, Uncle An-drew's genteel circumlocutions ('Madam—my dear young lady—for heaven's sake—compose yourself') and fussy appurtenances (frock coat, tall hat, eye-glass) contrast comically with Jadis's imperious curtness and disturbingly bare arms. In this context, her felling of policemen is much more comedy than tragedy.[65]

Jadis's character is derived from two main sources. First, from the warrior goddess Ishtar, the Babylonian Venus, who was especially worshipped by the Ninevites; hence her reference to Charn as 'that great city,' an echo of Jonah's description of Nineveh (Jon. 1:2; 3:2). Second, she is a representation of Venus Infernal.[66] She is descended from Lilith and her intoxicating beauty is con-stantly emphasised: 'She was beautiful. . . . Years afterwards when he was an old man, Digory said he had never in all his life known a woman so beautiful'; she has 'a white, beautiful hand'; she is 'seven foot tall and dazzlingly beautiful'; 'her height was nothing compared with her beauty.' In addition, she is stunningly vain: she speaks proudly of 'my beauty and my Magic' and when she hears the children mention Uncle Andrew she assumes that he must have seen her face 'in some magic mirror' and 'for the love of my beauty he . . . sent you across the vast gulf between world and world to ask my favour and to bring me to him.' Her error is understandable for, as 'The Planets' has it, '[Venus's] breasts and brow, and her breath's sweetness / Bewitch the worlds.' Jadis, as the Infernal shadow of Venereal influence, is able to 'bewitch' in actual fact.

When Uncle Andrew eventually meets Jadis, he, like his nephew, is deeply won over by her physical attractions. He thinks 'more and more of her won-derful beauty' and keeps on saying to himself, 'A dem fine woman, sir, a dem fine woman. A superb creature.' He imagines that 'the Witch would fall in love with him,' and even at the end of the book, when he is a sadder and wiser man, he is still obsessed by her appearance and ready to regale any visitor with an account of this 'dem fine woman,'—the very last words of the book.[67]

Jadis, of course, has no time for Uncle Andrew; her solitary self-sufficiency is part of what makes her Venus Infernal. In contrast, the celestial Venus, who in beneficence stands 'second only to Jupiter,' rejoices in that secondary status; she is naturally orientated alongside, and finds fulfilment in company with, the king of the gods. It is for this reason that we find an explicit reference to Jupiter in *The Magician's Nephew*. As Digory and Polly are being whirled between worlds in chapter 3, we are told that 'there were bright lights moving about in a black sky: Digory always thinks these were stars and even swears that he saw Jupiter quite close—close enough to see its moons.' Lewis's brief glance at Jupiter within his Venereal donegality is typical of how he sees their relations. As we noted in chapter 3, Aphrodite's saffron light burns in Jove's monarchal presence; and as we discussed earlier in this present chapter, Jane Studdock's Venereal beauty comes alive 'in the sphere of Jove.' In their capacity as the two *fortunas*, Jupiter and Venus have much in common and so it is perhaps not surprising that Lewis should have tried to write *The Magician's Nephew* immediately after *The Lion*.[68] However, he experienced difficulties in finding the right form for the story and took a long time to complete it. We suggested at the head of this chapter that these difficulties may have been related to the autobiographical elements in the story, but it is at least as possible that Lewis felt stymied at the prospect of having to express something about sexuality in a book designed for children.

Uncle Andrew's fixation with Jadis is a manifestation of Venus's influence over the carnal instinct. Its comedic portrayal expresses Lewis's view that it is never wise to be 'totally serious about Venus.'[69] But ought there not to be a serious treatment of sexual desire and sexual activity given the chosen donegality? Lewis did not dissent from the view that sex '*is* serious,' theologically, naturally, morally, and emotionally; and given that he habitually used 'Venus' as a term for the act of sexual intercourse, he clearly thought it was central to her influence.[70] However, he seems to have felt that writing for an audience which included pre-pubescents necessarily 'excluded erotic love';[71] and he had a personal reluctance to depict anything like a quasi love-affair between children.[72] Nevertheless, in *The Magician's Nephew* he still manages to communicate a sense of 'flesh longing,' as 'The Planets' puts it. He does this in two ways.

First, in the way that human and animal characters are paired off preparatory to copulation and procreation. King Frank[73] and Queen Helen[74] are told that they will 'bring up . . . children and grandchildren,' that they and their 'children and grandchildren shall be blessed,' that they will be 'father and mother of many kings.' Thus their projected future suggests something of the hymeneal aspect of Venus. There is also a nod towards it in the conjugating of the beasts: '[Aslan] was going to and fro among the animals. And every now and then he would go up to two of them (always two at a time) and touch their noses with his. He would touch two beavers among all the beavers, two leopards among all the leopards, one stag and one deer among all the deer.' Venus is 'double-natured' (according to *That Hideous Strength*) and the coupling up of these characters suggests that the Genesis command to 'be fruitful and multiply' will be heeded before long.

But there is no need directly to depict coital relations between human or animal characters because Venus's fertility has already been portrayed at a higher level in the animation of the whole Narnian universe. This is the second and fuller way in which Lewis treats 'the act of Venus.' Charles Huttar has noted how, 'at this moment, one of the climactic scenes in the whole Chronicles of Narnia, the stars burst forth again into song.'[75] It is worth comparing the descent of Perelandra in *That Hideous Strength* with this 'climactic' scene in order to observe the skilful way in which Lewis builds the Narnian creation upon Venereal imagery. When Perelandra is readying herself to come down upon earth, the temperature rises:

> It was from without that the warmth came . . . a summer breeze was blowing into the room. . . . The room was rocking. . . . A soft tingling and shivering as of foam and breaking bubbles ran over [Ransom's and Merlin's] flesh. . . . As the whole of [Perelandra's] virtue seized, focussed, and held that spot of the rolling Earth in her long beam, something harder, shriller, more perilously ecstatic, came out of the centre of all the softness. . . . And now it came. It was fiery, sharp, bright and ruthless . . . the translunary virtue, fallen upon them direct from the Third Heaven, unmitigated. They were blinded, scorched, deafened. They thought it should burn their bones.[76]

Compare that passage with the following from *The Magician's Nephew*:

> The Lion opened his mouth, but no sound came from it; he was breathing out, a long, warm breath; it seemed to sway all the beasts as the wind sways a line of trees. Far overhead from beyond the veil of blue sky which hid them the stars sang again: a pure, cold, difficult music. Then there came a swift flash of fire (but it burnt nobody) either from the sky or from the Lion itself, and every drop of blood tingled in the children's bodies, and the deepest, wildest voice they had ever heard was saying: 'Narnia, Narnia, Narnia, awake. Love.'[77]

The two passages are constructed upon a remarkably similar semantic field: 'warmth' / 'warm'; 'breeze' / 'breath'; 'rocking' / 'sway'; 'tingling' / 'tingled'; 'fiery' / 'fire'; 'burn' / 'burnt.' The image of a painless burning is particularly Venereal[78] and, interestingly, the 'swift flash of fire' (reminiscent of Williams's 'flash of seeing') comes 'either from the sky or from the Lion.' Lewis is content to allow some doubt about the matter: does the awakening of Narnia result from astrological ignition or the inspiration of Aslan? We shall examine this question in more detail below. Our present task is simply to recognise the Venereal imagery within which the story consists, and it is enough to note that the animation of Narnia is conceived and presented in terms which, in *That Hideous Strength*, are deliberately suggestive of a kind of sexual congress. Lewis need not trouble his young readers by depicting a full-blown adult romance between Uncle Andrew and Jadis, nor embarrass himself by depicting a quasi love-affair between Polly and Digory; he has infused an erotic charge into the creation of Narnia itself.

As well as this specifically orgasmic moment, there is a general theme of the fruitful and the organic throughout the story, 'a warm, good smell of sun-baked earth and grass and flowers.' Schakel has noticed the recurrent emphasis on 'country' matters,[79] as distinct from city life, and he correctly notes how this sense of 'newness, vitality, and fecundity' is the dominant quality of the book. It has two other principal manifestations: in the Wood between the Worlds and in chapters 8 and 9, where Narnia is brought to birth.

The Wood between the Worlds, where 'you could almost feel the trees growing' is an attempt to symbolise the secret springs of life which Venus oversees. The debts to the Wood of Broceliande are evident, for just as Williams's Wood is 'the world's base' without a horizon, so Lewis's Wood is the worlds' base where Digory cannot even get a 'glimpse of the sky.' It is 'very much alive' and 'rich and warm,' 'rich as plum-cake,' but quiet and dreamy and peaceful. Interestingly, Jadis hates the place; it saps all her strength, and she cannot remember it once she has left. This reinforces her status as a kind of anti-Venus. Venus, as we are informed in *Perelandra*, has eyes that open 'inward, as if they were the curtained gateway to a world of waves and murmurings and wandering airs.' Jadis has no such inscape, no secret depths or tender self-awareness. She is averse to the Wood because it is teeming with fertility at a fundamental level. It has countless pools, each giving access to a whole new creation, and this reminds us that 'moisture is the prerequisite of generation,' for only from such formlessness 'can Venus arise in her beauty';[80] the way various characters repeatedly rise up out of these pools is suggestive of Aphrodite Anadyomene. Moreover, the Wood's earth is a 'rich reddish brown,' suggesting the presence of copper ('There is even copper in the soil,' as Ransom says in *That Hideous Strength*).

With respect to the creation of Narnia, the whole creating process should be seen as a Venereal accomplishment, but it will be useful to focus on specific images which Lewis commonly used in his depictions of Venus. Just as in his

1935 poem he had written of 'grass growing, and grain bursting, / Flower unfolding,' so, at the birth of Narnia, all these features receive a mention, directly or indirectly. 'Grain bursting' is alluded to in the hymn which the Cabby sings in the darkness, 'all about crops being "safely gathered in"': the hymn is Henry Alford's 'Come, Ye Thankful People, Come' and contains a prayer that worshippers will be 'wholesome grain and pure.' The 'grass growing' is referenced more explicitly than the grain: we are told that 'the valley grew green with grass. It ran up the sides of the little hills like a wave. In a few minutes it was creeping up the lower slopes of the distant mountains, making that young world every moment softer. The light wind could now be heard ruffling the grass. Soon there were other things besides grass.' In contrast, Strawberry remembers London as a place with 'no grass. All hard stones.' And as for the 'flower unfolding,' we see the new grasslands 'sprinkled with daisies and buttercups' and Polly notices 'primroses suddenly appearing in every direction.' In the new-founded Narnia, everything is 'bursting with life and growth.'

And not only does Venus spawn life, she counteracts its opposite: 'Her union with matter—the fertility of nature—is a continual conquest of death.'[81] This brings us to the main plot-line of the story: the healing of Digory's mother, or rather, Digory's 'Mother,' for the word, which appears nearly forty times (though she herself appears in only one chapter), is almost invariably capitalised. Early in the first chapter Digory tells Polly that his 'Mother was ill and was going to—going to—die.'[82] Her fatal illness is a plot device that allows Lewis doubly to involve Venereal imagery. Not only can a life be saved through Venus (for 'while we ourselves can do nothing about mortality, Venus can'),[83] but the life in question is that of a mother, and mothers, as we have already seen, signify in Lewis's imagination just that combination of femininity and fertility which he associated with Venus.

Mrs Kirke's healing comes about indirectly. Digory and Polly, whose names are both carefully chosen,[84] set out astride Fledge, whose wings are 'chestnut colour and copper colour,' for the garden in 'the West' where Digory has to pluck an apple. But who is to be the recipient of this apple? Resting for the night 'as the bright young stars of that new world came out they talked over everything: how Digory had hoped to get something for his Mother and how, instead of that he had been sent on this message.' The mission on which they have been sent has a different purpose from that of healing Mrs Kirke: Digory's task is to take the apple to Aslan for the healing of Narnia. From its seed will spring a 'Tree of Protection' that will guard Narnia against the witch whom Digory had brought there on the day of its birth.

Venus is 'the Bringer home of all good things,'[85] and Digory, having plucked the apple, completes Aslan's commission to 'bring it back to me.' He successfully resists the blandishments of Jadis, helped in part by the bird in the tree, whose slit-eyed watchfulness may well be based on Milton's dragon with 'uninchanted eye' watching 'the fair Hesperian Tree . . . to save her blossoms, and defend her fruit / From the rash hand of bold incontinence.'[86] Once the apple is planted, the Tree of Protection grows up in an instant. From this tree Digory is quite unexpectedly given a second apple; this one for the healing of his Mother.

As a result of eating the apple, Digory's Mother is able to enjoy 'sweet natural sleep.' Sweetness is a key word in Lewis's Venereal lexicon. 'The Planets' speaks of Venus's 'breath's sweetness'; Ransom on Perelandra smells a fragrance 'warm and sweet, and every moment sweeter and purer'; Orual, as she descends into Westwind's valley in *Till We Have Faces*, finds that 'the air came up to us warmer and sweeter every minute.' Digory and Polly, as they near the Western garden, find just the same thing: 'The air came up warmer and sweeter each moment, so sweet that it almost brought tears to your eyes.' In addition, the story tells of 'sweet hope'; sugar 'sweeter than grass'; Helen arriving as 'sweetly as a bird flies to its nest'; 'sweet country'; Jadis speaking 'more sweetly' than would seem possible for one with so fierce a face.

Alongside sweetness another key Venereal term is 'gum.' We recall the 'gum-sweet wood' in 'The Landing' and Milton's Paradise which 'contained "all the right things"—odorous gums, golden fruit, thornless roses.'[87] One of Venus's properties is to produce 'night-scented flowers, sticky gums,' according to *That Hideous Strength*; and on Perelandra 'much that [Ransom's] fingers touched was gummy.' In *The Magician's Nephew* Digory repeatedly exclaims, 'By gum!,' and this is no verbal accident. Like Peter's favourite expostulation, 'By Jove!,' it has a double meaning. Lewis used the expression himself to suggest divine power: 'By gum (blessed be he)!' he exclaims, in a letter to Charles Williams.[88] Swearing by gum is swearing by Venus, and swearing by Venus is swearing by God, for God 'is the reality behind . . . Venus; no woman ever conceived a child, no mare a foal, without Him.'[89]

The Venereal *Logos*

But why 'blessed be he' and not 'blessed be she'? Since Venus is a goddess, 'the unfathomable feminine principle,' the Mother of mothers, why is Lewis not prepared to feminise the depiction of Aslan in *The Magician's Nephew*? He is willing to turn Aslan into an albatross, a lamb, and a cat in certain other Chronicles: what is stopping him from making Aslan a lioness in this book?

The answer is: imagination. Lewis was of the belief that major imaginative difficulties arose when one attempted to depict God in feminine terms. One place where he discusses the issue is 'Neoplatonism in Spenser's Poetry' where he writes:

There remains the problem of [Spenser's] Venus . . . [I]s it tolerable that, in defiance of all tradition, Form should be embodied in the feminine image and Matter in the masculine, and even called 'the Father of all formes'?

It is hardly tolerable, yet I believe we must tolerate it. [I think] that the Sapience of the fourth Hymn must be identified with the Second Person of the Christian Trinity, the Word . . . I do not say that this image, if rightly understood, is theologically shocking; it is imaginatively shocking. The intellect can accept it; but on the level of the imagination the masculinity of the Word is almost impregnably entrenched by the sixfold character of Son, Bridegroom, King, Priest, Judge, and Shepherd. Yet all these, apparently, Spenser was prepared to break through. After that, the transference of the sexes between Form and Matter sinks into insignificance.[90]

Another place where he addresses the subject is his article 'Priestesses in the Church?' where he imagines common sense asking the question:

'Why not? Since God is in fact not a biological being and has no sex, what can it matter whether we say *He* or *She*, *Father* or *Mother*, *Son* or *Daughter*?'

But Christians think that God Himself has taught us how to speak of Him. To say that it does not matter is to say either that all the masculine imagery [in the Bible] is not inspired, is merely human in origin, or else that, though inspired, it is quite arbitrary and unessential. And this is surely . . . based on a shallow view of imagery. Without drawing upon religion, we know from our poetical experience that image and apprehension cleave closer together than common sense is here prepared to admit; that a child who had been taught to pray to a Mother in Heaven would have a religious life radically different from that of a Christian child . . . [I]mage and apprehension are in an organic unity.[91]

We see in these two passages that Lewis was ready and willing to accept feminine imagery for the divine at the level of the intellect. However, at the level of imagination, his respect for scriptural precedent and his understanding of the relationship between image and apprehension prevent him from entertaining such images. The overwhelming majority of images of deity in the Bible are masculine, and for Lewis they were not allegories, but symbols or pupillary metaphors. In his view, we cannot get behind the images to some sort of imageless truth. Although rationally we have good grounds for saying that God is 'sexless,' it does not follow that masculine imagery is therefore dispensable and interchangeable with feminine imagery.

Lewis suggests two rules for exegetics. First, 'never take the images literally.' Second, 'when the *purport* of the images—what they say to our fear and hope and will and affections—seems to conflict with the theological abstractions, trust the purport of the images every time.'[92] Abstractions model spiritual reality by means of legal or chemical or mechanical metaphors, and these tend to be less adequate than 'the sensuous, organic, and personal images of scripture—light and darkness, river and well, seed and harvest, master and servant, hen and chickens, father and child.' We know, Lewis says, 'that God forgives much better than we know what "impassible" means.' Likewise, he would argue that we know that God is a Father much better than we know what 'sexless' means. To prefer abstractions is not to be more rational; it is simply to be less fully human. De-mythologisers, like Bultmann, are really only re-mythologisers; and the new mythology is poorer than the old one. A 'sexless God' is the theological equivalent of rewriting *The Romance of the Rose* as *The Romance of the Onion:* the rich and redolent image has been unwisely substituted by a less profound and less suggestive one. Of the old image (Father) it may be difficult to say in cold prose exactly what it meant, and theologians may be able to say about the new image all sorts of things which could not have been said about the old one. Like Arnom's new image of Ungit (the barbarian Aphrodite) in *Till We Have Faces*, a 'sexless God' is much cleaner and simpler than the traditional image, but it contains 'no comfort'[93] because it is a merely rational construction; its relationship with the organ of meaning has grown tenuous. Imagination's role in theological understanding must not be belittled in this way, for the result is that reason ends up trying to make bricks out of strawy abstractions. Lewis's dependence here on imagination arises from his belief that 'it is rational not to reason, or not to limit oneself to reason, in the wrong place.'[94]

All this serves to explain Lewis's thinking behind his retention of the masculinity of Aslan. However, the chosen donegality requires Lewis to portray Aslan as the incarnation of Venus. How can this be done if Aslan is not to be feminised?

The answer we suggest is that Aslan *is* feminised, but not to the complete exclusion of the masculine. And this is a fair representation of Venus, for Venus may be properly understood as containing a masculine element alongside her feminine ones. It is only because there is a permanent masculine element in Venus that her fertility, her motherliness, exists in the first place.

Lewis is following his sources. For example, to Spenser, Venus is a couple:[95]

she hath both kinds in one,
Both male and female, both under one name:
She syre and mother is her selfe alone,
Begets and eke conceives, ne needeth other none.[96]

And as well as Spenser, Lewis had authority for this understanding of Venus in Nicolas of Cusa: 'Venus, says Cusanus, was also a name for God. The universal means of generation is sexual so that "Hermes [Trismegistus]... argued, in consequence, that the Cause of All, God, comprised in Himself the masculine and feminine sexes."'[97] Lewis quotes Apuleius to a similar effect: 'You, Heavenly Venus, who, after the creation of Love, brought together the separate sexes at the very beginning of the world.'[98]

From this perspective, we can see what Lewis is attempting in *The Magician's Nephew*. He is not willing to convert all of Aslan's masculine characteristics into the feminine gender, because that would effectively be to assume that the divine being is sexless, which is an abstraction, which he regards as imaginatively un-nourishing. Hermaphroditism or androgyny, however, is different from sexlessness. Venus, though feminine, is also masculine because she is, so to speak, permanently inseminated. She is the act of coitus itself, the 'one flesh' that emerges when a man and a woman make the beast with two backs, that 'young, double-natured nakedness' which Perelandra inspires. Lewis's use of the term 'Venus' to denote sexual intercourse in *The Four Loves* suggests this very confusion or combination of sexual identities, and it is interesting to note how, at one point, he had planned to hint at the 'coupled' nature of this Chronicle's presiding planetary power by entitling it *Digory and Polly*. It is as he works out of this understanding of Venus that Lewis gives Aslan typically feminine characteristics within or alongside typically masculine ones.

Aslan brings Narnia to birth like Venus, from whom, according to Spenser, 'all the world derives the glorious features of beautie,' 'all the world by thee at first was made.'[99] 'With an unspeakable thrill, [Polly] felt quite certain that all the things were coming (as she said) 'out of the Lion's head.' When you listened to his song you heard the things he was making up: when you looked round you, you saw them.'

Aslan is 'beautiful' and Digory finds Aslan's voice 'beyond comparison, the most beautiful noise he had ever heard. It was so beautiful he could hardly bear it.' In addition, he is the source of sweetness. At the end of the story Digory and Polly look up in Aslan's face and 'such a sweetness and power rolled about them and over them and entered into them that they felt they had never really been happy or wise or good, or even alive and awake, before.' He speaks of 'my sweet country of Narnia.'

As well as being creative, beautiful, and sweet, Aslan commands that an apple be brought from the Western garden, brings health to a mother, pairs off male and female characters, and encourages the gift of laughter. He is evidently Venus incarnate. The lion form and the male pronouns should not be seen as a negation of his Venereal character, but as an essential feature of it, the masculine element without which Venus cannot be fully fertile. Although in some respects it might have been more satisfactory to depict Aslan-as-Venus in the form of a lioness with feminine pronouns, that would have been to stretch the imagination further than Lewis considered useful. And that he struggled with how to manage the Venereal theme is indicated by the lengthy composition history of this Chronicle.

It was not only Lewis's beliefs about feminine divine imagery which made composing this story difficult, but also the general complexity of Venus's literary history, for Lewis wanted to depict more than just 'Venus-as-God' in *The Magician's Nephew*. He also seems to have had in mind Ficino's two *Veneres*, the Angelic Mind *(Venus coelistis)* considered in its contemplation of Divine Beauty, and *Venus naturalis*, the generative power in the *Anima Mundi*.

Here we return to the point made above about the role apparently accorded to the stars in the creation of Narnia. At the climax of the creation of Narnia there is a to-ing and fro-ing between Aslan and the heavens. Aslan opens his mouth, but it is the firmament that sings; a flash comes from one or the other (it is not specified which); and then a voice issues a fiat, but we are not told definitely that it is Aslan speaking (the 'tingling' in the children's bodies leaves open the possibility that the stars are speaking in their very flesh).[100]

In addition to his medieval and renaissance sources, Lewis is of course drawing on the Book of Job: 'Where wast thou when I laid the foundations of the earth . . . when the morning stars sang together, and all the sons of God shouted for joy?'[101] But rather than just depicting the stars as onlookers, Lewis gives them a role in the animation of Narnia itself. The creator is shown honouring the creature by allowing it to participate in further acts of creativity. The vivification of Narnia is brought about not simply and solely because of a single creative act by the Venereal Lion. Rather, Aslan-as-Venus achieves its creation in consort with *Venus coelistis* and *Venus naturalis;* it comes forth between them, together, at once. Again we see Lewis's interest in portraying 'creaturely participation in the Divine attributes.'[102] His cosmogony is more than simply the Genesis account rehashed in fairy tale form: it is a creation narrative deliberately angled to present Venereal qualities.

The very first command given to this newly awakened Venereal country is 'Love!' Given that Venus is 'the planet of love,' we should expect the *logos* of *The Magician's Nephew* to be largely concerned with love, and in Digory's love for his Mother we find that very thing. The principal theological thrust of the story, akin to that argued in *The Four Loves*, is that human love is inordinate if entertained without reference to love of the divine. Digory has to learn that his filial affection for his mother, though felt to be of absolute importance, is actually only relative to his love for Aslan.

The very first time we see Digory in chapter 1 we are told that he has been in tears because his Mother is dying. We do not see his Mother until the end of the book (chapter 15), but Digory's concern for her is repeatedly held up for our attention (in every chapter but the fourth, fifth, and eighth) so that we do not forget that his relationship with her is the mainspring of the story. His mixture of love and fearfulness at the prospect of losing that love provides the unspoken emotional dynamic at the centre of the story.

According to Philip Pullman, who also lost a parent at a young age,[103] this is an example of Lewis 'cheating' as a writer, 'exploiting' the sympathy of his readers and failing to justify it as an integral part of the story. Pullman understands *The Magician's Nephew* as follows: 'Digory is told that if his mother were to eat one of the apples she would get better, but he mustn't steal one, because, if he did, she would get better but she wouldn't enjoy getting better, she'd be unhappy. So, as a good boy, he doesn't do this, and as a reward for being a good boy he's given the magic apple and he comes back to the real world and gives the apple to his mother and she gets better and everything's happy.'[104] Pullman goes on, 'Think what the passage is saying! It says that, if your mother is dying, it depends on you whether she gets better or not. If you're a good boy, she'll get better and if you're not a good boy, she won't get better.' He alleges that this is 'cruel,' 'utterly wicked,' 'so wicked as to be beyond the reach of literary criticism and deserve stern and forthright moral condemnation.'

However, Pullman has misread the story. Digory is not told by Aslan that a stolen apple will lead to his Mother's unhappy recovery; he is told by the witch that it will lead to her happy recovery. Only after the event is Digory told by Aslan that an unhappy recovery is 'what *would* have happened' if he had stolen the fruit rather than keeping it for the purpose he had promised to put it to. What the temptation scene is saying is therefore the reverse of Pullman's reading. If Digory is 'a good boy' (Pullman's sardonic term) and keeps his promise to Aslan, his Mother *won't* get better, which is what she herself would approve because she believes promises should be kept. Digory therefore has to choose between his love for Aslan (as betokened by the promise) and his love for his Mother (his desire that she should not die). This is an excruciating choice, and Lewis does not pretend that it is not painful: 'Digory never spoke on the way back, and the others were shy of speaking to him. He was very sad and he wasn't even sure all the time that he had done the right thing: but whenever he remembered the shining tears in Aslan's eyes he became sure.' Digory does not know, or even suspect, that keeping his promise will lead to his being given a second apple, from a different tree, which will, after all, bring healing to his Mother. There is therefore no bribery or coercion involved in his original decision. It is a morally untainted and deeply moving moment.

Lewis's reflections on the rival claims of natural and supernatural loves appear in much of his work. In addition to *The Magician's Nephew* and *The Four Loves*, this theme is also strongly present in *The Great Divorce*, *Till We Have Faces*, *A Grief Observed*, and 'Five Sonnets' ('Ask for the Morning Star and take (thrown in) / Your earthly love'). The prominence of the theme may be traced to two biographical sources: his loss of his own mother when he was nine, and his long relationship with Janie Moore, who, by all accounts, was never reconciled to the loss of her son in the Great War. Here in *The Magician's Nephew*, the theme of love and loss is treated with sensitivity and blooms out of the Venereal donegality with a naturalness and inevitability. Digory realises that 'there might be things more terrible even than losing someone you love by death'; that is, he acknowledges the possibility of denying his love of Aslan for the sake of clinging on to his Mother. Instead of preferring a reflection of divine Charity in a subsidiary, creaturely relationship, he allows himself to be embraced by 'the translunary virtue, fallen direct from the Third Heaven, unmitigated.' Perfect love casts out his fear of being orphaned because he knows that, ultimately, he cannot be orphaned in a world held within the arms of Venus.

NINE

Saturn

The last planet, old and ugly.
—'The Planets' (lines 114–115)

The last planet gave Lewis the subject for his first published poem, 'Quam Bene Saturno.' The Saturnine qualities on display in this poem are diametrically opposed to almost everything Lewis wrote about Saturn thereafter. Our first task in this chapter therefore will be to account for this *volte face*. We will then examine Lewis's mature presentation of Saturnine imagery in scholarship, poetry, and *That Hideous Strength*, before turning to see how it provides the donegality of *The Last Battle*. We will discover that, although Lewis did not believe in a Saturnocentric universe, he was fully prepared to give Saturn his due. Indeed, essential to Lewis's theodicy is this recognition, that only by acknowledging the true weight of Saturn's influence could one arrive at the real centre of the spiritual cosmos.

Saturn in Lewis's Poetry

'Quam Bene Saturno' appeared in Lewis's school magazine in 1913. He took the title from one of the Elegies of Tibullus, the Roman poet who lived 55?–19 B.C. Tibullus had written, 'Quam bene Saturno vivebant rege' ('How well they lived when Saturn was king'), and Lewis's poem was probably a school exercise in translation; it renders sixteen lines of Tibullus into twenty-eight lines of his own iambic tetrameter. The poem praises the reign of Saturn and laments the Jovial era which has succeeded it:

Alas! What happy days were those
When Saturn ruled a peaceful race,
Or yet the foolish mortals chose
With roads to track the world's broad face

Five stanzas follow in which Saturn's reign is celebrated, before the poem concludes:

But now... With Jove our haughty lord
No peace we know but many a wound:
And famine, slaughter, fire and sword
With grim array our path surround.[1]

The Saturn depicted here is the same divinity whom we find in Virgil's *Aeneid*, Horace's *Jubilee Hymn*, and repeatedly throughout Augustan poetry in general, where he stands for the mythical Golden Age which many believed or hoped was about to return. The most famous paean to this glorious Saturnalia occurs in Virgil's Fourth Eclogue, lines that Lewis translates as follows:

The great procession of the ages begins anew.
Now the Virgin returns, the reign of Saturn returns,
and the new child is sent down from high heaven.[2]

These lines were understood in the Middle Ages as a pagan prophecy of the birth of Christ; Dante viewed them as such in his *Purgatorio* (XXII: 64–73). The adult Lewis apparently made the Fourth Eclogue a regular part of his Christmas reading[3] even though, by that stage of his life, he typically understood Saturn as *Infortuna Major*, rather than as the god of the Golden Age.

The young Lewis may not have had a free choice about which lines of Tibullus to translate and so we should not attach much importance to this early appearance of the Golden Age Saturn in his corpus. However, the schoolroom exercise did perhaps establish in his poetic mind a contrast between a pacific, paradisal Saturn and a brutal, domineering Jove. Such a Jove appears again (under his Norse name) in another of the poems Lewis wrote in his early teens, 'Loki Bound' (1914). It was a piece of juvenilia significant enough for Lewis to recall it when writing *Surprised by Joy* over forty years later. He explains that 'Loki Bound' presented 'the brutal orthodoxy of Thor... Thor was the real villain, Thor with his hammer and his threats... Thor was, in fact, the symbol of the Bloods.' (The Bloods were the aristocracy of athletic older boys whom Lewis so detested at Malvern College.) Reading back from 'Loki Bound' to 'Quam Bene Saturno' we may reasonably wonder whether the Jove of the earlier poem served a function somewhat similar to that of the Thor in the later work; not, of course, that the 1913 Jove could have represented the Bloods (Lewis had not at that stage encountered them), but possibly he stood in the young teenager's mind as a symbol of the sadistic headmaster of Wynyard School, Robert Capron, a 'haughty lord' inflicting 'many a wound,' whose ungentle oversight he had only recently escaped. This is admittedly speculation, but it is worth trying to understand why, in his youth, Lewis found Jove useful for negative depictions, but preferred to deploy Saturn for such purposes in his adulthood. It would appear that evil was perceived as merciless power in his younger days; as weakness, sorrow, and death in his later years.

The change takes place gradually, and the 1926 poem, *Dymer*, is an interesting milestone in the process. *Dymer* ends with the following stanza:

> And from the distant corner of day's birth
> He [Dymer] heard clear trumpets blowing and bells ring,
> A noise of great good coming into earth
> And such a music as the dumb would sing
> If Balder had led back the blameless spring
> With victory, with the voice of charging spears,
> And in white lands long-lost Saturnian years.[4]

It is difficult to know how to take these lines. Is the reference to 'Saturnian years' positive or negative? At first sight one would say 'positive,' since these long-lost years are being brought back in triumph. On closer inspection, the matter is more complicated. Line 2 ('He heard clear trumpets blowing and bells ring') could be intended as a reference to Jove understood as *Fortuna Major*. As Lewis would later write in *That Hideous Strength*: 'The pealing of bells, the blowing of trumpets . . . are means used on earth to make a faint symbol of [Jupiter's] quality.' And in 'The Philosopher,' a poem pre-dating *Dymer*, Lewis had written, 'scarcely can he dream of laughter and love, / They lie so many leaden years behind,' a line which (because of the metal mentioned) could well be a reference to Saturn as *Infortuna Major* and, thus taken, an indicator that the Saturn in *Dymer* should be understood in the same way. If the imagery in this final stanza is meant negatively, the 'years' in the concluding phrase would be the years lost to the grim and sour Saturn (not the Golden Age Saturn), years which have now been retrieved from his numbing influence by jocund Jove.

One thing can be stated with certainty: if Saturn in *Dymer* was intended positively it was its last such appearance in Lewis's imaginative writings. Thereafter he only ever uses the imagery of the last planet in a neutral sense or in a sense that assumes he is *Infortuna Major*. There are five such appearances in his poetry. One is in the negligible 'Lines to Mr. Compton Mackenzie.'[5] Another is in 'The Turn of the Tide' ('Saturn laughed and lost his latter age's frost, / His beard, Niagara-like, unfroze'). The third and fourth are in 'Pindar Sang' and 'On W. T. Kirkpatrick,' which we shall mention in subsequent sections of this chapter. The fifth is in 'The Planets':

> Up far beyond [Jupiter]
> Goes SATURN silent in the seventh region,
> The skirts of the sky. Scant grows the light,
> Sickly, uncertain (the Sun's finger
> Daunted with darkness). Distance hurts us,
> And the vault severe of vast silence;
> Where fancy fails us, and fair language,
> And love leaves us, and light fails us
> And Mars fails us, and the mirth of Jove
> Is as tin tinkling. In tattered garment,
> Weak with winters, he walks forever
> A weary way, wide round the heaven,
> Stoop'd and stumbling, with staff groping,
> The lord of lead. He is the last planet
> Old and ugly. His eye fathers
> Pale pestilence, pain of envy,
> Remorse and murder. Melancholy drink
> (For bane or blessing) of bitter wisdom
> He pours for his people, a perilous draught
> That the lip loves not. We leave all things
> To reach the rim of the round welkin,
> Heaven's hermitage, high and lonely.[6]

Note the recapitulation of the previous six heavens in lines 7–10 of this excerpt: 'fancy,' 'fair language,' 'love,' and 'light' are, respectively, summary descriptions of Lunar, Mercurial, Venereal, and Solar influence; Mars and Jupiter are then named directly. Also noteworthy is the image of Saturn's 'perilous draught' which may be drunk either 'for bane or blessing.' In other words, his influence is bad, not *per se*, but only (and then only potentially) in relation to its recipients in the sublunary realm. The translunary realm (as discussed above in chapter 4) was considered to be unfallen and therefore unable to contain anything that was essentially malefical. But beneath the circle of the Moon a patient could make the astrological agent bad in effect by turning its influence the wrong way. 'Born under Saturn, you are qualified to become either a mope and a malcontent or a great contemplative.'[7] With this remark we have emerged from Lewis's poetry into his literary scholarship.

Saturn in Lewis's Scholarship

The Discarded Image contains the following summary of Saturnine qualities:

> In the earth his influence produces lead; in men, the melancholy complexion; in history, disastrous events. In Dante his sphere is the Heaven of contemplatives. He is connected with sickness and old age. Our traditional picture of Father Time with the scythe is derived from earlier pictures of Saturn. A good account of his activities in promoting fatal accidents, pestilence, treacheries, and ill luck in general, occurs in *The Knight's Tale* ... He is the most terrible of the seven and is sometimes called The Greater Infortune, *Infortuna Major*.[8]

In Lewis's literary criticism we find him adverting frequently to this Saturnine category. In a paper read to the British Academy he declared: 'If we feel young while we read the first two sestiads [of 'Hero and Leander'] and feel in the remaining four that youth has died away, our experience is very like Hero's. If Venus dominates Marlowe's narrative and Saturn that of Chapman, the same may be said of the events which each narrates.'[9] He later mentions the 'passages of saturnine realism' in Chapman which strengthen and thicken the poem, including the description of the women talking at a funeral in the tale of Teras.

Marlowe's and Chapman's overt deployment of the planetary gods meant that it was natural for Lewis to comment on their work by extrapolating from its planetary characters to the Venereal and Saturnine qualities of the poem's events. But sometimes Lewis brings planetary influences into his literary criticism even when there is no immediate textual reason for him to do so. For instance, in his essay, 'Variation in Shakespeare and Others,' he imagines how an Elizabethan poet would have rendered Wordsworth's couplet about 'blind Authority beating with his staff / The child that might have led him.' Lewis suggests the Elizabethan would have begun with a flourish about authority in the abstract, 'old and sour as Saturn.' And in his essay on Donne he suggests that Donne gives us a 'saturnocentric universe,' even though none of Donne's poems under discussion mentions Saturn or, indeed, any of the seven medieval planets by name. By 'saturnocentric' Lewis means astringent, stern, tough, unmerry, uncomfortable, unconciliatory, and serious, though not necessarily profound or virtuous. Elsewhere he describes Donne's love songs as 'saturnine,'[10] again without any proximate planetary reason for doing so.

Lewis had been 'intoxicated' by Donne as an undergraduate,[11] and the residue of that intoxication lingers in his mature work, for instance when he recalls Donne's dubious claim that Christ never laughed[12] and his hangman's question, 'What if this present were the world's last night?'[13] Not that the

Saturnine facets of Donne's corpus were sufficient for the young Lewis; he had a taste for even bleaker poetry. He read Paul Verlaine's *Poémes Saturniens*;[14] he sympathised with what he called the 'Heroic Pessimism' of Shelley, Swinburne, and Hardy (whose suicidal boy, 'Old Father Time,' in *Jude the Obscure*, is a particularly memorable outing for the Saturnine spirit); and Housman's line 'Whatever brute and blackguard made the world' found an echo in his bosom.[15] The tone of many of the poems of *Spirits in Bondage* shows that the young Lewis had a pessimistic daemon which was able to ferret in dark corners. However, in his early to mid thirties, he turned his back on such writers and such a disposition: Saturn's charms were overthrown as Lewis began to focus more and more intently on the qualities of Jupiter.

Saturn in *That Hideous Strength*

Lewis once wrote: 'The key to my books is Donne's maxim, "The heresies that men leave are hated most." The things I assert most vigorously are those that I resisted long and accepted late.'[16] The maxim is actually Shakespeare's,[17] not Donne's, but the misattribution is significant. Donne seems to have become for Lewis an emblem—at the literary level—of that which, theologically and psychologically, he had once entertained but had now rejected. And as he had turned away from the Saturnine spirit of Donne, so, in *That Hideous Strength*, he has Jane Studdock do something similar; as we noted above in chapter 3, her projected doctoral thesis on Donne is abandoned following her encounter with the Jovial Ransom, who reveals to her the true nature of her vocation.

However, Saturn's influence need not be rejected *tout court* for it is not always and only evil in its sublunary effects. There is also a good use to be made of his spirit, and this helps to explain why Saturn is one among the five gods who descend upon St. Anne's.[18] Saturn is not just a tool by means of which Maleldil punishes sinners; he is also a servant who comes to provoke needful qualities in the saints: in Denniston, belief; in MacPhee, potential belief; and in Ransom and Merlin, godly sorrow:

> 'Stir the fire, Denniston, for any sake. That's a cold night,' said MacPhee. 'It must be cold outside,' said Dimble. All thought of that: of stiff grass, hen-roosts, dark places in the middle of woods, graves. Then of the sun's dying, the Earth gripped, suffocated, in airless cold, the black sky lit only with stars. And then, not even stars: the heat-death of the universe, utter and final blackness of nonentity from which Nature knows no return. Another life? 'Possibly,' thought MacPhee. 'I believe,' thought Denniston. But the old life gone, all

its times, all its hours and days, gone. Can even Omnipotence *bring back?* Where do years go, and why? Man never would understand it. The misgiving deepened. Perhaps there was nothing to be understood.

Saturn, whose name in the heavens is Lurga, stood in the Blue Room. His spirit lay upon the house, or even on the whole Earth, with a cold pressure such as might flatten the very orb of Tellus to a wafer. Matched against the lead-like burden of his antiquity the other gods themselves perhaps felt young and ephemeral. It was a mountain of centuries sloping up from the highest antiquity we can conceive, up and up like a mountain whose summit never comes into sight, not to eternity where the thought can rest, but into more and still more time, into freezing wastes and silence of unnameable numbers. It was also strong like a mountain; its age was no mere morass of time where imagination can sink in reverie, but a living, self-remembering duration which repelled lighter intelligences from its structure as granite flings back waves, itself unwithered and undecayed but able to wither any who approach it unadvised. Ransom and Merlin suffered a sensation of unendurable cold; and all that was strength in Lurga became sorrow as it entered them.[19]

This sorrow deserves to be called 'godly' in the Pauline sense (2 Cor. 7:8–11) because of what it leads to. It leads to joy, as symbolised by the advent of Jupiter. He is the final god to descend, even though he comes from the sixth sphere and Saturn from the seventh: 'Lurga in that room was overmatched. Suddenly a greater spirit came—one whose influence tempered and almost transformed to his own quality . . . even the numbing weight of Saturn.' Saturnine sorrow is not central in Lewis's myth of the heavens, but it is necessary to produce the conditions under which that centre can be arrived at. We see the same process at work in the conversion of Jane Studdock in chapter 14:

For one moment she had a ridiculous and scorching vision of a world in which God Himself would never understand, never take her with full seriousness. Then, at one particular corner of the gooseberry patch, the change came.

What awaited her there was serious to the degree of sorrow and beyond. There was no form nor sound. The mould under the bushes, the moss on the path, and the little brick border, were not visibly changed. But they were changed. A boundary had been crossed. She had come into a world, or into a Person, or into the presence of a Person.[20]

Jane realises that Maleldil will not treat her with 'full seriousness'; nevertheless, her encounter with Him is 'serious to the degree of sorrow and beyond.' Very subtly Lewis has presented here the same experience at the personal level as is manifest at the astrological level. Sorrow comes, but it is not total, not 'full,' there is something 'beyond'; Saturn does not have the last word. Jane and the residents of St. Anne's, as true contemplatives, pass into an experience on the other side of Saturn, so to speak. In this they are unlike the members of the N.I.C.E., who fall under the influence of Saturn's 'ungodly sorrow,' the mal-contentment that leads to death. Fairy Hardcastle shoots Jules, then herself; Steele is trampled, Filostrato beheaded, Straik stabbed, Wither mauled, Frost burnt, Feverstone buried alive. Where Ransom's household have a life to look forward to beyond the grave—in their own resurrection as well as in the life of the heir of Jove who is about to be conceived—the villains (with the comic exception of Curry) are brought to nothing.

There are two other aspects of the passage describing Saturn's descent which are especially deserving of comment. The first is the emphasis on 'the heat-death of the universe.' This is a very common theme in Lewis's non-fictional writings. Time and again, whether it be in his literary criticism,[21] his apologetics,[22] or his journalism,[23] he emphasises the brute fact of the mortal-ity of the universe. Sometimes he does this to contextualise political idealism, sometimes to relativise temporal theological concerns, sometimes to undercut certain pseudo-scientific assumptions. This continual recurrence to the transi-toriness not just of human life, but of cosmic life as a whole, may rightly be taken as evidence of Lewis's own very serious reckoning with Saturn. Although he prefers to focus on the Jovial side of life, because Jove's wisdom 'dominates the stars', he cannot be accused of ignoring less pleasant realities. Indeed, in one place he even out-Donnes Donne, stating, with a grimness unparalleled in his work, 'Death does not die.'[24]

The other aspect of Saturn's descent in *That Hideous Strength* which we must examine is its effect on Mr Andrew MacPhee, a character who is based on Lewis's old tutor, William Kirkpatrick, with whom he lived and studied from September 1914 to March 1917. In an autobiographical poetic fragment, 'On W. T. Kirkpatrick,'[25] written in the early 1920s, he likens Kirkpatrick to 'Father Time himself,' the first indication that Kirkpatrick was to take the role of Saturn in Lewis's mythology of his own life. However, the imagery is a little inconsistent: Kirkpatrick's mind is likened to an 'iron coast,' when, of course, the metal ought to be lead for a thorough-going Saturnine character. But it is interesting to note how it was against this 'iron coast' that the young Lewis, 'with noise of yeasty waves,' flung 'the young / Spring-swellings of my uncor-rected mind.' That image is reworked in the later description of Saturn in *That*

Hideous Strength as one who 'repelled lighter intelligences from its structure as granite flings back waves.'

By the time Lewis came to publish *Surprised by Joy* (1955) he had firmly settled on Saturn as Kirkpatrick's presiding genius, with no admixture from Mars:

> [His] was a saturnine humour. Indeed he was very like Saturn—not the dispossessed King of Italian legend, but grim old Cronos,[26] Father Time himself with scythe and hour-glass. The bitterest, and also funniest,[27] things came out when he had risen abruptly from table (always before the rest of us) and stood ferreting in a villainous old tobacco jar on the mantelpiece for the dottles of former pipes which it was his frugal habit to use again. My debt to him is very great, my reverence to this day undiminished.[28]

Standing between 'On W. T. Kirkpatrick' and *Surprised by Joy* is *That Hideous Strength*, where MacPhee appears to be the one naturally Saturnine character in Ransom's household. After the descent of Lurga he is dressed by his companions, contrary to his judgement, in an 'ash-coloured and slightly monastic-looking robe.' The last we see of him he is studiously ignoring the carnal foreplay going on all round him, preparing instead to cast some accounts and reminiscing about his uncle who was Moderator of the General Assembly of the Church of Scotland. It is an affectionately mocking portrait, consonant with Lewis's opinion that 'full seriousness' is more than Saturn deserves and that one must learn, in the words of his poem 'Pindar Sang,' to tread 'the road that leads beyond the tower of Kronos.'

Saturn in *The Last Battle*

The Saturnine *Poiema*

Although Saturn may not deserve full and final seriousness, his spirit is nonetheless to be deeply respected as far as it goes. And in Lewis's view, it goes a long way: indeed, to the uttermost degree of sorrow. Lewis was impatient with clerical bromides about death being a small thing,[29] and in *The Last Battle* he takes his readers down to the very bottom rung of the ladder of sadness as he orchestrates a story of apocalyptic terror.[30] He dares to do something hardly associated with so-called 'children's literature': he kills off every single character with whom the story opens.

Rossi comments that 'the striking thing about this particular volume in the series is its bleakness of tone,' perceptively noting that one technical device which helps brings about this tone is the delayed appearance of the narrator.[31]

A second unsettling aspect of the book, as Schakel observes, is its heavy reliance on irony: 'From its opening scene, the story requires readers to discern the discrepancy between reality and appearance.'[32] A third unusual thing about this Chronicle is that it contains no quest: the protagonists are put into the passive role of continually responding to events, rather than being given a purpose and commissioned to search proactively for someone or something. And a fourth device that helps subtly to subvert the reader's expectations of a reassuring atmosphere lies in making the main character an adult. Admittedly, Tirian is far from the seventh age of man: we are told that he is younger than twenty-five. Nevertheless, he is clearly not a child—'his shoulders were already broad and strong and his limbs were full of hard muscle, but his beard was still scanty'— and in this respect he plays a unique role in the septet, requiring the reader to identify with a significantly older protagonist than usual. The young children from England (Jill and Eustace) help him: he is not there (as Puddleglum is in *The Silver Chair*) to help them. Thus the reader is put into a maturer, less protected, frame of reference than is the case in the previous six books.

And this contributes to what Myers has called 'the emotional tone of old age'[33] in the story. Saturn, so 'The Planets' has it, is 'the last planet / Old and ugly,' and accordingly Lewis ploughs a semantic field which will help establish a feeling of senectitude. Each of the three adjectives which appear in that phrase from 'The Planets' occurs repeatedly in the seventh Chronicle.

The book's title itself alerts us to the theme of finality, as does its very first sentence which starts: 'In the last days of Narnia . . .' The second chapter opens with the words, 'About three weeks later the last of the Kings of Narnia . . .' Tirian is described again as 'the last King' in chapters 4 and 13. In chapter 12 we hear of his 'last friends' shortly after the keynote sentence of the whole story: 'And then the last battle of the last King of Narnia began.'

As for 'old' and 'ugly,' Shift the Ape is both: 'He was so old that no one could remember when he had first come to live in these parts, and he was the cleverest, ugliest, most wrinkled Ape you can imagine.' When Shift reappears in chapter 3 he is 'ten times uglier' than before. He tells the bewildered Narnians: 'I'm so very old: hundreds and hundreds of years old. And it's because I'm so old that I'm so wise.'

Shift's claim to great age reflects the imprint of Saturn, whose home is that 'mountain of centuries' presented in *That Hideous Strength*: 'more and still more time.' This aspect of the planetary influence allows Lewis to usher on stage that one character who is 'common to Spenser's age and ours,' Father Time: 'his name was once Saturn.'[34] The great giant who had been glimpsed dormant in the underworld of *The Silver Chair* is roused toward the close of this final book: 'Jill and Eustace remembered . . . that his name was Father Time, and that he would wake on the day the world ended.' If there remains any doubt that Lewis means Father Time as a representation of Saturn, two things should dispel it. First, we should recall that he is described in *The Silver Chair* as having a 'snowy beard' and we should compare Saturn's beard that 'unfroze' in 'The Turn of the Tide'; both are borrowed from Lydgate's 'saturne with his frosty berd.'[35] Second, we should be aware of a tell-tale reference in the typescript of *The Silver Chair* (figure 21 in the photo gallery). According to this early draft, the Earthman in the Underworld tells Jill and Eustace, when they see the figure of the sleeping giant: 'That is the god Saturn, who once was a King in Over-land. . . . They say he will wake at the end of the world.'[36] The typescript has not been amended on the page, but evidently, before *The Silver Chair* came to be published, Lewis altered 'Saturn' to 'Father Time,' so as to keep his planetary theme more carefully hidden, and naturally he retained the change when he came to write the Chronicle in which Father Time finally awakes.

When Saturn is roused in *The Last Battle*, he extinguishes the sun by squeezing it in his hand like an orange ('the sun's finger / Daunted with darkness'). This mighty and terrifying giant is that embodiment of Time whom Lewis had read of in Hawes, who comes to 'dystroye bothe se and lande, / The sonne and mone and the sterres alle.'[37] His destruction of the stars shows that he is, as *The Discarded Image* has it, the cause of 'disastrous events', for Lewis knew his etymologies and here in the last Chronicle allows Father Time free rein to wreak literal 'dis-aster': his depredations give rise to a 'dreary and disastrous dawn.' And this study is not the first to have noticed a connection in this regard to Saturn. Patterson has observed that Father Time brings about 'that "utter and final blackness of nonentity" which Lewis first evoked [at Lurga's descent] in *That Hideous Strength*.'[38] There we were shown a 'black sky lit only with stars. And then, not even stars: the heat-death of the universe, utter and final blackness.' In the final Chronicle we are shown

> another dark shape against the sky as well as the giant's. It was in a different place, right overhead, up in the very roof of the sky as you might call it. 'Perhaps it is a cloud,' thought Edmund. At any rate, there were no stars there: just blackness. But all around, the downpour of stars went on. And then the starless patch began to grow, spreading further and further out from the centre of the sky. And presently a quarter of the whole sky was black, and then a half, and at last the rain of shooting stars was going on only low down near the horizon.
>
> With a thrill of wonder (and there was some terror in it too) they all suddenly realized what was happening. The spreading blackness was not a cloud at all: it was simply emptiness. The black part of the sky was the part in which there were no stars left. All the stars were falling: Aslan had called them home.[39]

The elision of Father Time into Aslan is clear evidence that Aslan is taking on the role of Saturn; waves splash about his forefeet just as they had splashed against, and been repelled by, Saturnine granite in *That Hideous Strength*. We shall explore his full role in the story further below. Our task at present is to note that it is not just in the heavens that disaster strikes: the world of Narnia and all the characters in it are beset by disastrous events from the very beginning of the story—indeed, from before its beginning, for we are told that Shift's discovery of the lionskin merely set in train a plan which had been laid deeper and longer ago than anyone had suspected.

Lewis conveys the atmosphere of gathering misfortune in a variety of ways. He has one disaster tread hard on the heels of another (the centaur has hardly finished telling of the ill omens before the dryad is seen dying). He suggests that events might have gone differently if only certain small things had not happened (if Tirian had been allowed to speak all might have been well, but he is struck in the mouth just too soon). He allows moments of respite and relief, after which he piles on new and unrelated agony (Poggin's defection from the group of treacherous dwarfs heartens the heroes but almost instantly they receive the new shock of Tash's arrival; they refresh themselves with happy memories of Narnia just before Farsight tells them terrible news). The author repeatedly frustrates the plans of his heroes (they send Roonwit to warn Cair Paravel, but he never reaches his destination; their decision to parade Puzzle is rendered fruitless by the unexpected cynicism of the dwarfs). He complicates already difficult and dangerous situations (Jill goes missing just as drum-beats are heard in the distance, meaning that there are now 'so many different things to worry about that they didn't know what to do'; the dwarfs become actively hostile, so that the heroes suddenly have both more enemies and fewer allies). He introduces plain ignorance (for example, about the fate of the Lamb; and about who the enemy's leader is: the Ape, the Cat, the Captain, or Tash?). Perhaps worst of all, he portrays the fulfilment of dire prophecy when Ginger reverts to being a dumb and witless beast. As 'The Planets' puts it: 'fair language leaves us.'

Lewis sometimes remarked that the worst has not come while we can still say, 'This is the worst,' and Ginger's loss of speech shows that the worst moment has finally arrived: doom is fulfilled as death descends in actual fact. Under that planet who is responsible for 'fatal accidents,' everyone who is alive at the beginning of this story is dead by the end of it. Having admitted fewer than a dozen deaths in all the preceding tales,[40] Lewis here in this last tale lets Saturn deal out death in abundance, 'bearing all his sons away.'[41] The note is struck proleptically in the first chapter when Shift cunningly predicts he 'shall probably die' if he tries to retrieve the lionskin from Caldron Pool; Puzzle retrieves it instead and is 'almost tired to death' by the time he gets it out. In the next chapter the first actual death occurs when the dryad is cut down; then Tirian and Jewel in their wrath kill two Calormenes. But to enumerate all the instances of death and deathly imagery would be almost to retell the whole tale, for the subject is pervasive. Tirian remarks, 'If we had died before today we should have been happy'; he asks, 'Would it not be better to be dead than to have this horrible fear?'; the Mice say, 'It would have been better if we'd died before all this began'; dwarfs are taken 'to die in the salt-pits of Pugrahan'; Cair Paravel is 'filled with dead Narnians.' The verbs to die, to kill, and to murder (and cognate nouns and adjectives) are numerous: the toll is over 60 in fewer than 160 pages of text.

References to coldness are another means by which Lewis communicates a deadly atmosphere. It is a feature of Saturn that Lewis particularly emphasises during Lurga's descent in *That Hideous Strength* ('cold night... airless cold... unendurable cold') and it is found frequently throughout *The Last Battle*. Puzzle becomes 'numb with cold' while fetching the lionskin from the Pool. Tirian and Jewel ford a river but are so angry 'they hardly noticed the cold of the water.' Tirian becomes 'cold,' then 'colder,' when tied to the tree. The rescue of Jewel takes place on a 'cold night,' an occasion when Tirian holds a 'cold' blade against the sentry's neck. Poggin the Dwarf joins the Narnian side during 'the coldest hour of the night.' At the appearance of Tash, Puzzle complains, 'It's so cold.' The next night 'grew cold' and Jill suffers a 'cold shock' when she realises that the Calormene army is being reinforced. 'Shivering' appears ten times. And, of course, it is not just the characters who turn as cold as any stone, it is the whole world of Narnia. 'Ice-cold air' blows through the Doorway when the sun is put out and Narnian history comes to an end ('all her glories and joys were over'), as the heavens had predicted.

It is appropriate that there should be more explicit talk of astronomy in this tale than in any of the others, for Dante associates star-lore with Saturn in the *Convivio*. Accordingly, Roonwit declares: 'Never in all my days have I seen such terrible things written in the skies as there have been nightly since this year began.... I know by my art that there have not been such disastrous conjunctions of the planets for five hundred years.... The stars never lie.... If Aslan were really coming to Narnia the sky would have foretold it.' Later, when we hear of this same 'Roonwit the Centaur lying dead with a Calormene arrow in his side' we know that the doom he voiced has struck and 'Narnia is no more,' and we know it for astrological reasons. As the entire Narnian cosmos disintegrates, Father Time blows a crowing threnody on his horn with a note 'high and terrible.' It is doubtless a goat's horn, for the tragedy (literally, 'goat song') of Narnia's destruction has been wrought by the astrological Goat of Capricorn, the zodiacal house over which Saturn presides.[42] This is his hour. Saturn overthrows Jupiter, the sign of whose house, Sagittarius, is a live centaur aiming a bow and arrow. Roonwit's death and the manner of it indicate that the kingdom first trumpeted six books earlier in Jovial triumph has finally collapsed into Saturnine ruin.

The Saturnine *Logos*

We now consider the theological messages which Lewis conveys by means of the Saturnine imagery in *The Last Battle*. At first sight, Lewis might seem to have got himself in a bind by attempting to communicate anything 'about Christ' through the symbolism of *Infortuna Major*. Generally speaking, he emphasises the extreme good fortune that springs from knowing the Christian God and insists on the absolute purity of His moral nature. Lewis would not entertain 'dark' theologies[43] or flirt with the idea of an ambiguous deity who either created or was beyond both good and evil.[44] How then could he deploy Saturn (father of disaster, coldness, ugliness, decrepitude, terror, treachery, and death) for Christological purposes? How could Aslan be shown to embody that Saturnine spirit? Indeed, where is Aslan? He seemingly makes no appearance in the story until all the characters are dead.

Worse still, doubts are introduced about Aslan's very nature. He is said to have changed so that he is now in favour of felling the Talking Trees and putting the Talking Beasts under the yoke. He now apparently approves of hard labour, not revelry, and his name can be mixed with that of Tash to form the new syncretistic portmanteau: 'Tashlan.' He is said to be very angry with all the Narnian creatures, choosing to communicate with them only via the Ape and to appear in person only at night. Tirian looks at the silent, four-legged beast which, lit by a bonfire, slouches out of the Stable, and 'horrible thoughts went through his mind.'

But these desperate thoughts soon clear: Tirian 'remembered the nonsense about Tash and Aslan being the same and knew that the whole thing must be a cheat.' His reaction reminds us that Saturn's influence is not malign *per se*, but only if it is turned to bad effect by its patient. Death is the great weapon both of Satan and of God,[45] in Lewis's view, and, by definition, no evil can be wholly evil, because existence itself is a good, and even Hell has form and limit.[46] As his kingdom is brought to its appointed end by Aslan, Tirian makes good use of Saturnine constellation by penetrating surface realities with a wise spiritual insight, exchanging his 'horrible thoughts' for a determination to be faithful despite his apparent forsakenness. Dante had made Saturn's sphere the home of contemplatives: *The Last Battle* does the same. Far from presenting Lewis with a problem, Saturn's character enables him to meditate upon that Christological attribute which he wrote about more than any other: divine presence in human loneliness and suffering.

Of all Biblical passages, the one which occurs most frequently in Lewis's writings is Christ's cry from the cross: 'My God, my God, why hast thou forsaken me?' (Matt. 27:46 and Mark 15:34, a quotation of Ps. 22:1a). Not only are its appearances in Lewis's work very numerous, they are also spread across the whole range of his corpus. In one form or another, the cry of dereliction appears in his diary, poetry, fiction, apologetics, journalism, literary criticism, correspondence, autobiography, and in his MacDonald anthology.[47] No other scriptural verse comes close to receiving a treatment in so many and various of Lewis's works; and, interestingly, two of these nineteen mentions occur even before his theistic conversion.

The cry of dereliction, although not directly quoted in *The Last Battle*, may be heard echoing in Tirian's cry from the tree, where he stands bound and bleeding:

> And he called out, 'Aslan! Aslan! Aslan! Come and help us now.'
> But the darkness and the cold and the quietness went on just the same.[48]

In spite of such desolation, Tirian persists with his prayer:

> 'Let *me* be killed,' cried the King. 'I ask nothing for myself. But come and save all Narnia.'
> And still there was no change in the night or the wood, but there began to be a kind of change inside Tirian. Without knowing why, he began to feel a faint hope. And he felt somehow stronger.

We observe here a felt abandonment, followed by self-abnegation, followed by the awakening of the contemplative faculty, the perception of spiritual presence despite unchanging external circumstances. It is admittedly vague. Tirian experiences a 'kind of change,' but it involves no 'knowing why,' it comes about 'somehow.' But it is not nothing; it is something. As with Jane's experience of sorrow, things are not visibly changed, but they are changed. Aslan does not 'come and help' in the way Tirian wants, but ultimately the King is stronger for calling on him. Aslan evidently becomes present to him in the role of Luther's 'hidden God,' the *deus absconditus*, who can only be discerned with what Lewis calls 'the seeing eye.'[49] Tirian conceives this gift of insight; Aslan appears to him, as it were, like a transparent silhouette: nothing substantial, but at least the outline of a shape. In that gap is the thing that Lewis is trying to communicate, 'the conviction of things not seen' (Heb. 11:1). Tirian demonstrates what Lewis (following MacDonald) called 'The highest condition of the Human Will... when, not seeing God, not seeming itself to grasp Him at all, it yet holds Him fast.'[50] He exercises 'obstinacy in belief,'[51] finding Aslan perceptible despite his invisibility: 'I give myself up to the justice of Aslan,' he says; 'In the name of Aslan let us go forward'; 'I serve the real Aslan.' He is resolved to take 'the adventure that Aslan would send,' for 'we are all between the paws of the true Aslan': 'Aslan to our aid!' Jewel likewise sustains faith in the face of failure, trusting that the Stable 'may be the door to Aslan's country and we shall sup at his table tonight.' In all this we are to discern a parallel with Christ's faithful contemplation of his Father, for even in his cry of dereliction he addressed the One by whom he felt abandoned: 'He could not see, could not feel Him near; and yet it is 'My God' that He cries.'[52]

Tirian, Jewel, and the others see Aslan with the eyes of their heart, thus sharing in his own resignation when, bound and shorn on the Stone Table, he had looked up at the sky and had endured its blank response in quietness and sadness. Lewis argued in *The Problem of Pain* that 'only God can mortify,' that is, put sin to death. Tirian accepts the calamities that befall him as necessary tribulations, understood from within by Aslan, that furnish him with an occasion for utter submission to the holy and perfecting purpose of the divine surgeon. As a result, after death, he receives the divine accolade: 'Well done, last of the kings of Narnia, who held firm in the darkest hour.'

Emeth, the Calormene soldier, is another example of a faithful contemplative, undeflected by the superficial appearances of his world. That he is a true child of Saturn is indicated both by his name (a Hebrew word meaning 'fidelity, truth, permanence')[53] and by the fact that he is a 'seventh son.' (Tirian similarly is said to be 'seventh in descent' from King Rilian.) As Saturn, the seventh planet, exerts his influence, Emeth wins through to the heavenly Narnia despite the disastrous disadvantage under which he has laboured all his life, namely his ignorance of Aslan. Having endured the fatal darkness of Calormene paganism with a noble heart, he is credited with worshipping Aslan all along, even though he did not know that that was what he was doing. Readers, too, must be content at first to find Aslan in the story despite his apparent absence; we are to Enjoy contemplativeness.[54]

Tirian's contemplativeness is not unremittingly hardy but issues in an ability to apprehend divine aid under representative forms: 'Oh Aslan, Aslan,' he whispered. 'If you will not come yourself, at least send me the helpers from beyond the world.' When Eustace and Jill arrive in Narnia Tirian accepts them as, in effect, manifestations of Aslan, for 'the supreme Mind, though it delegates, is not absent, and works itself in its lower agents: "such privilege hath omnipresence." '[55] The centaur with his eschatological portents, the Lamb with its innocent wisdom and, more especially, the water from the white rock,[56] should be understood as further divine agents perceptible by the contemplative spirit. In these respects Aslan is, as it were, materially (and not just 'spiritually') present in the story even though he does not appear in *propria persona* until after the end has come for Tirian and the others.

That end is skilfully depicted. 'For a moment or two Tirian did not know where he was or even who he was. Then he steadied himself, blinked, and looked around. It was not dark inside the stable, as he had expected. He was in strong light: that was why he was blinking.' Perhaps the most direct theological message of *The Last Battle* is that death is not the worst thing that can happen; rather, 'noble death is a treasure that no one is too poor to buy.' Inasmuch as the heroes learn this lesson, we witness another of the good effects of Saturn, a peculiar possibility offered by his influence. 'All fortune is good,' as Boethius said;[57] it is up to the patient to choose whether to turn it to 'bane or blessing.' Tirian and his company learn that it is sweet and fitting to die for their country.

Others in the story regard '*dulce et decorum est*' as no more than an irrational sentiment;[58] they treat nobility, patriotic feeling, and self-sacrifice with cynicism. For there are mopes and malcontents in *The Last Battle* as well as contemplatives. They are the dwarfs, to whom everything is a sensory wilderness: a rich feast of pies and tongues and trifles and ices is received by their palates as hay and turnips and raw cabbage; fine wine is ditchwater; violets are stable-litter. The dwarfs are probably modelled on the young, highly educated men, 'angry and restless,' full of 'distrust' and 'contempt,' whom Lewis identified as the inhabitants of the modern Saturnocentric universe, which he felt that Eliot (guided by his poetic forebear, Donne) was helping imaginatively to construct.[59] That generation of cynics were the ones whom 'The Wasteland' had infected with, rather than fortified against, chaos.[60] For, to Lewis's mind, 'a heap of broken images'[61] was itself an image and one that needed breaking. Such an image exacted its own price from the human imagination which continually entertained it; consequently also from the reason and the will which permitted that entertaining. Part of Lewis's *raison d'être* as a writer was to break it.

The Lewisian cosmos, therefore, although it has room for Saturn, is not Saturnocentric. We will look at the real centre below. Before we do so we must take note that Lewis's emotional relationship with Saturn was far from Stoical.[62] Although Jill refuses to wet her bowstring with her tears, and although Tirian does not show that he has given up hope as the odds turn against him, there is space for the expression of grief. The last fragments and leavings of their lives are not reflected upon stony-faced; rather, the heroes weep freely at their losses and Lucy insists that Aslan would not wish to stop them from lamenting Narnia's death. Their sorrow is described by Tirian as a 'virtue'; its omission would be a 'discourtesy.' But it is a beatitudinal mourning, not a desperate moping, a recognition (as Lewis wrote in other places) that, although 'it is somehow good to die,'[63] nevertheless, 'it is a real brook'[64] that has to be crossed: 'something is being ended.'

The end is made all the more affecting by the recapitulation of Narnian history in chapter 8. Jewel reminds Jill of the 'hundreds and thousands of years' in Narnia's past when peaceful king followed peaceful king 'till you could hardly remember their names'; he tells of Moonwood the Hare, and Swanwhite the Queen, and how King Gale obtained the Lone Islands for the Narnian kingdom. 'And as he went on, the picture of all those happy years, all the thousands of them, piled up in Jill's mind till it was rather like looking down from a high hill on to a rich lovely plain full of woods and waters and cornfields, which spread away and away till it got thin and misty from distance.' By these means Lewis suggests not only Saturn's 'mountain of centuries' and the diuturnity of the world which is now moving to its close, but also readiness for death. The image of a rich cornfield connotes harvest-time and the approach of the natural and desirable consummation of such beauty.

In a letter to a friend, Lewis reflectively comments that the times he most desires death are not when life is harshest: 'On the contrary, it is just when there seems to be most of Heaven already here that I come nearest to longing for the *patria*. It is the bright frontispiece [which] whets one to read the story itself.'[65] This metaphor of the frontispiece recurs in the final paragraph of *The Last Battle* when we are told that the children's life in this world and all their adventures in Narnia 'had only been the cover and the title page.' Now 'they were beginning Chapter One of the Great Story which no one on earth has read: which goes on forever: in which every chapter is better than the one before.' It is a paradoxical image with which to finish a story, but a paradox which nicely expresses the good fortune that *Infortuna Major* may bring to those who respond positively to his influence, finding their beginning in their end.

The Eccentricity of Saturn

But once the imagery has moved from ends to beginnings Saturn is no longer the sole presiding planet. The donegality shifts. Saturn helps focus the imagination upon the beginning which is to be found in the end of life; like the prospect of being hanged, he wonderfully concentrates the mind. However, his dominance is over as soon as new life is conceived. Saturn's sphere is not Lewis's imaginative resting-place. Rather he goes beyond Saturn, in the words of 'The Planets', 'To reach the rim of the round welkin / Heaven's hermitage.'

Heaven is the centre of Lewis's spiritual cosmos and heaven is Jovial, not Saturnine. The spirit of the sixth sphere is also the spirit which dominates the universe beyond the seventh, the resurrection home of Aslan, the Empyrean itself.[66] Repeatedly in Lewis's works Saturn yields to his kingly son. In *That Hideous Strength* Saturn is 'overmatched' by Jupiter. In 'The Turn of the Tide' Saturn is defrosted by the Jovial birth of Christ at Bethlehem. And in *English Literature in the Sixteenth Century* Lewis notes how the poet, Gavin Douglas, depicts a similar defeat of Saturn in his Twelfth Prologue. It deals with the coming of spring and the passing of night; and Lewis particularly admired 'the shining figures which Douglas makes move across his sky':

> Saturn draws off into the dim distances *behind the circulat warld of Jupiter*—Aurora opens the windows of her hall—crystalline gates are unfolded—the great assault is ready and marches forward with banners spread,
>
> > Persand the sabill barmkyn nocturnall
> > [piercing the black rampart of night]
>
> This is not simply a better or worse way of describing what we *see*. It is a way of making us see for always what we have sometimes felt, a vision of natural law in its angelic grandeur, a reminder of . . . the pomp and majesty mingled even in the sweetest and most gracious of Nature's workings. It is a true spiritualization (true, at least, to our experience) of the visible object.[67]

Douglas's Saturn is displaced by the combined forces of Jupiter and Aurora (who, as a Solar character, is another example of that mythological-astrological confusion discussed above, chapter 5). This displacement, Lewis avers, is a 'true spiritualization' of the vision one may sometimes get on earth of a spring morning: winter is passed; night is passed; Saturn withdraws.

In the last quarter (approximately) of *The Last Battle* Lewis attempts to symbolise the same sort of thing. The book is about 175 pages long; the first 125 take us up to Tirian's death. In the closing section, Saturn begins to fade and Jupiter starts to take over. Digory and Polly become 'unstiffened' and no longer feel old; Edmund's sore knee is healed; Erlian's grey-haired head regains its youthful colour; Caldron Pool, once 'bitingly cold,' now turns to a 'delicious foamy coolness'; we hear tell of 'the summer sea'; the 'air' gently blowing on the heroes' faces 'was that of a day in early summer.'

And there are certain, even more obvious, indications that Saturn has conceded centre stage. Father Time throws down his horn and is given a new, unspecified name; and Jove is mentioned directly:

> 'Isn't it wonderful?' said Lucy. 'Have you noticed one can't feel afraid, even if one wants to? Try it.'
> 'By Jove, neither one can,' said Eustace, after he had tried.[68]

This is the first mention in *The Last Battle* of *Fortuna Major* and we are back, in a sense, to where the Narniad started in *The Lion, the Witch and the Wardrobe*, six books earlier. But only in a sense. This second coming of Jove is just that, a second coming, not merely a return to the first advent. We do not find ourselves back in the Narnia of the four thrones, but have to advance to the 'Narnia within Narnia.' That this journey passes through and beyond Saturn means that the new Joviality is even more joyful than before, more meaningful and poignant, more completely diffused with 'tragic splendour.'

A sceptical account of this imaginative journey would configure it quite differently. Lewis's recidivist Joviality would be taken rather as evidence of a refusal to learn from experience, an inability to grow up and to accept the incorrigible harshness of the world. His 'boyish greatness,'[69] of which Kathleen Raine affectionately wrote, might have been a charming quality, but would it not have been more appropriate for a man to have had a 'manly greatness'? Jonathan Franzen, in his novel, *The Corrections*, mocks naive Narnian 'dearness,'[70] and Humphrey Carpenter, in *The Inklings*, suggests that the boyishness evident in the Chronicles was only the superficially attractive flip-side of prejudices against modernism, liberalism, and anything that stood opposed to the old-fashioned, conservative world in which Lewis was brought up.[71] Philip Pullman goes further and contends that there is a 'life-hating ideology'[72] at work in Lewis's willingness to massacre his cast at the end of the Narniad. Pullman thinks Lewis should have allowed Peter to 'go on and be a father.'[73] He thinks Lewis was afraid of maturation.

These criticisms serve as useful correctives to readings of the Narniad which find in it only sweetness and light and not also traces of psychological needs being met on the part of its author.[74] But such objections could equally well be made against any work of art, because every product of the human imagination comes 'tainted' with the subjective weaknesses of the artists involved and is conditioned by the peculiarities and foibles of their psychology. The extraordinary thing about Lewis, in Rowan Williams's opinion, is the degree to which he successfully manages 'to relativise his own prejudices.'[75] Lewis, though temperamentally of a sanguine humour, was not content to be merely bluff and jolly as an artist. The happy ending to *The Last Battle* is not won at anything less than the ultimate price.

More substantially, the premises upon which Lewis is arraigned by Pullman, Carpenter, and Franzen are themselves open to challenge, for their allegations about 'immaturity' assume that the more bleak an outlook, the more adult (that is, wise) it must necessarily be. This is a large question which we cannot tackle at a detailed level, but, in an attempt to find a balance, it will be worth recording the subtleties of Lewis's attitude to youth and age,[76] the arguments he mounted against those who accused him of 'Peter Pantheism,'[77] his asperity toward poets who never got 'beyond the pageant of [their] bleeding heart,'[78] the seriousness with which he regarded mortality and loss, and the donegalitarian requirements of writing a Saturnine story in which death could no more be omitted than war could have been left out of *Prince Caspian*.

Furthermore, we should note that Lewis thought that art *ought* to meet psychological needs. That, in his view, was one of its justifications. Art (good art) very properly served to awaken or maintain or strengthen those parts of the human constitution which needed such ancillary support. As we have seen, he considered his own contemporaries to be in particular need of the spiritual nourishment that could be derived from imaginatively inhabiting the sphere of Jove. Too easily, in his view, the writers of his generation assumed that brains splattered upon a wall represented what life was 'really like' and that the consolations of religion were 'really' only a trick of the nerves, never reflecting on their equivocal use of the word 'really.'[79]

Lewis wanted to know why the former 'reality' was privileged above the latter and concluded that the Jovial perspective had been selectively aborted. Of all the terrible losses inflicted by the Saturnine Great War, perhaps the most terrible—from the imaginative point of view—was this loss of belief in the kingship of Jupiter and the usurpation of his throne by Saturn.

If Saturn was not king, what was he? Lewis, like Charles Williams, believed that 'the acceptance of loss . . . combines in itself the two 'Ways,' the Romantic and the Ascetic, the Affirmation and the Rejection of images.'[80] Though his temperamental preference was for the Romantic affirmation of images, he did not rule out the Ascetic rejection of the same. He thought asceticism and mortification had their place. He was even prepared to admit that Eliot's best work had valuable 'penitential qualities.'[81] But asceticism—that sanctity which rebukes the world from above—must have a positive purpose behind its negations or else it makes common cause with the barbarism which hates the world from below. Born under Saturn, the generation that grew up between 1914 and 1918, who felt that they had been sold a false prospectus about the glory of battle and the sweetness of dying in service of their country, had an understandable cause for saying, with Graves, 'Goodbye to all that.' Lewis, however, like Tolkien (another veteran of the trenches), wished to know exactly what was meant in that catchphrase by the word 'all.'[82]

In other words, he thought that asceticism needed to have an account of the light by which it sees the darkness under reproach.[83] Failure to recognise the uncondemnable wisdom inherent in the act of condemnation is itself a condemnation of philosophies that are wholly nihilistic. Such failure constitutes what Lewis—as early as 1924—called 'The Promethean Fallacy in Ethics,' a fallacy he found in Thackeray, in Russell, and in every 'good atheist.'[84] The criticism or defiance that such a person hurls at an apparently ruthless and idiotic cosmos is really an unconscious homage to something in or behind that cosmos which he recognizes as infinitely valuable and authoritative: for if mercy and justice were really only private whims of his own with no objective and impersonal roots, and if he realised this, he could not go on being indignant. The fact that he arraigns heaven itself for disregarding them means that at some level of his mind he knows they are enthroned in a higher heaven still.[85]

Lewis thought that the Book of Job showed the legitimacy of such complaint, and his own angry lament for his wife's death, *A Grief Observed*, is an example of the same thing. He fully recognised the human need to shout and shake one's fists at God: but, equally, he recognised that, once the breast-beating was over and the passion was spent, there was something else to say.

Lewis's belief in the less than kingly status of Saturn is founded upon plain logic. Despair or outrage at crookedness only makes sense if one has a notion of the straight, and that notion could not have arisen if everything were bent, or even if everything were dualistically good and bad, for dualism is a truncated metaphysic which cannot account for the natural human preference for happiness over sorrow. Saturn with his plagues and pestilences therefore cannot be sovereign. Indeed, it is only by virtue of his deferral to Jove that Saturn can exert his true influence, making his patients into contemplatives who see beyond sorrow. Saturn, like Luna, Mercury, Venus, Sol, and Mars, is a servant of Jupiter.

Thus Lewis's model of the universe has standing room for bleakness, but no throne. In this respect, as in so many others, he differed from the modernist mainstream. As he looked about him, he pondered the causes of the twentieth century's poetical taste for nihilism and angst, such as he found in Roy Fuller's line, 'Anyone happy in this age and place / Is daft or corrupt.' He traced its origins not to the obvious source (the Great War), but much further back, suggesting that it had its beginning in Keats's praise of 'those to whom the miseries of the world / Are misery, and will not let them rest,' a line spoken by Moneta, guardian of Saturn's desolate temple in 'The Fall of Hyperion'.[86] He thought that this taste sprang from the optimistic-revolutionary illusion that the woes of the world can be rapidly and decisively cured. Contrariwise, his own belief was that the world's woes were chronic but not absolute, because the resurrection of Christ had relativised them. One must do all one can to alleviate such sufferings, but need not be overcome by their non-disappearance in this life: 'one's own cheerfulness, even gaiety, must be encouraged,' as must 'the importance of *not* being earnest.'

Hence Lewis's glad acceptance of the 'middle things' of 'merry middle earth' and his pleasure in the 'eagles and trumpets of epic poetry.'[87] Hence also his pleasure in the eagles and trumpets of Jupiter, for 'of Saturn we know more than enough, but who does not need to be reminded of Jove?'[88] Since the mind is never wholly passive in apprehension, but is always a factor in the world-view being constructed, there is no necessary reason for disillusion or inanition. Pressure and pain may be actively received, as well as suffered, so that they transpose from torture into labour and issue in a 'rebirth of images,' to use Farrer's phrase. In *The Last Battle* Lewis subjects his subcreation to full Saturnian dominance, only for it to yield new Joviality. His work manifests 'the almost crushed (but for that very reason arch-active) imagination.'[89]

Once Jupiter has regained his happy seat we may see, in retrospect, how he was present in a sense from the very beginning. For 'in a certain juncture of the planets each may play the other's part'[90] and there are certain gentle touches of Jupiter even in the opening Saturnine sections of *The Last Battle*. The Eagle, Farsight, suggests something of Jove, for eagles were sacred to Jupiter. Tirian is introduced sitting under a 'great oak,' Jove's tree. His name also is carefully chosen: it summons up those 'Tyrian traders, in trouble steering' who came with precious cargo from the Isles of Tin in the Jupiter section of 'The Planets.'

That poem—as this and the previous six chapters have implicitly argued—may be properly understood as an early draft of the atmospheric qualities communicated by the Narniad. Both works admit us to those spiritual symbols which Lewis thought were of 'permanent value'; both make full use of that '*Phänomenologie des Geistes*' which he deemed specially worth while in the calamitous twentieth century. And his use of Hegel's term is particularly relevant in connection with Saturn, for in Hegel's view:

> The life of the Spirit is not the life that shrinks from death and keeps itself untouched by devastation, but rather the life that endures it and maintains itself in it. It wins truth only when, in utter dismemberment, it finds itself.[91]

The truth of Joviality springs out of the chaotic remnants of Saturnised Narnia. It is at this point that we discover that Lewis's fictional universe (like the one he believed himself to be living in) is not Saturnocentric, nor even interminably eucratic, but has a fifth act and a finale 'in which the good characters 'live happily ever after' and the bad ones are cast out.'[92] It is true that some characters, such as Susan, are left alone to make up their mind at a later stage.[93] However, the rest have to decide which they prefer: Aslan's shadow or his welcome. The Dwarfs are irremediably Saturnocentric, carrying their prison with them: they are that 'Fraternity of Vacabonds' whose toleration of misery rests on the claim that they have in the past been so 'often deceived.'[94] They are so afraid of being taken in by unreal happiness, that they cannot be taken out of their real unhappiness. Lewis admits in his 'Meditation in a Toolshed' that 'we are often deceived by things from the inside [and] having been so often deceived by looking along, are we not well advised to trust only to looking at?'[95] *The Last Battle*, like so much of his oeuvre, gives his answer to that question: 'Often deceived, yet open once again your heart.'[96] At the end of the Narniad his aim is to make us 'look along' that spirit of open-heartedness as he orchestrates a great cosmic eucatastrophe. Wave-like, Jove-like, it overwhelms those who keep the faith: for them, everything sad becomes untrue.

'Further in and higher up!' cried Roonwit...and though they did not understand him, the words somehow set them tingling all over.' The effect of the centaur's cry indicates that the consummation of adventures has at last been attained; the 'tingling' is now complete and it is time for every 'friend of Narnia' to enter into joy. Following Dante, whose pilgrim, on the brink of Paradise, turned and looked back at the planetary realms through which he had passed, Lewis directs his readers' gaze across all the heavens traversed in the earlier Chronicles, as he summons onto the page Tumnus from Jupiter, Reepicheep from Mars, the hopping Monopods from Sol, Puddleglum from Luna, Cor and Corin from Mercury, Frank and Helen from Venus. In the final pages of his septet Lewis presents imaginatively what he had analysed critically in the *Divine Comedy*, namely 'the gathering of the Church Triumphant in Heaven [which] is the final cause of the whole historical process and may thus be called the fruit of Time, or of the Spheres.'[97]

TEN

Primum Mobile

Apologetics is controversy. You cannot conduct a controversy in those poetical expressions which alone convey the concrete.
—'The Language of Religion'

So far in this book our attention has been focussed on what I have called 'the problem of composition.' I have argued that the Chronicles were composed with a much greater degree of imaginative co-ordination, both as individual texts and as a series, than critics have previously acknowledged, and that their 'controversial' elements (militarism, corporal punishment, death) become much more explicable once we recognise the planetary basis of each book. We now turn to the problem of occasion. What was it that first moved Lewis to write in this way? Why should a childless academic in his fifties, without any previous experience of writing so-called 'children's literature,' have taken this turn?

The Problem of Occasion

Lewis himself once wrote, 'I am not quite sure what made me, in a particular year of my life, feel that not only a fairy tale, but a fairy tale addressed to children, was exactly what I must write—or burst.'[1] If Lewis was 'not quite sure' what it was that gave rise to the sudden composition of *The Lion*, is it at all probable that a convincing account should be offered here?

In response I would concede that the argument I am about to mount about the occasioning of the Chronicles is advanced more tentatively than the argument relating to the problem of composition. The donegalitarian interpretation seems to me to account for so many things that I would even dare to suggest that the burden of proof now rests with those who would dispute it. But with respect to the following contentions about a possible 'cause' of the series, I wish to throttle down a little and make my case in a slightly less bold way. I do this not because I think my argument is not plausible (on the contrary, I think it has considerable explanatory power), but simply because I am here dealing, not with texts, but with a person's actions. I am trying to show not just *that* something is the case; I am trying to show *why* something is the case. Explaining why Lewis acted as he did is a more adventurous project than demonstrating inter-textual dependencies that reveal a hidden theme.

However, his comment about not being 'quite sure' what motivated him to write *The Lion, the Witch and the Wardrobe* need not mean he was entirely unsure; a lack of complete certainty is different from a complete lack of certainty. Likewise with the argument I am about to make. Since Lewis was fond of pointing out that human life exceeds Contemplative awareness (it is something of a theme in his work, as it is of this current study), we should not be surprised that he does not claim total understanding of his own creative processes.[2] I propose that the debate at the Socratic Club about the self-contradictoriness of naturalism explains the conception of the series well. The mental pictures that Lewis had entertained since he was sixteen (a faun in a wood, a queen on a sledge, a magnificent lion) comprised the first Chronicle's ovum: the debate fertilised it.

The Debate at the Socratic Club

Lewis began writing *The Lion, the Witch and the Wardrobe* in earnest in 1948, the year after he had published *Miracles, A Preliminary Study*, his most serious work of apologetics, which a young philosopher, Elizabeth Anscombe, famously criticised at a meeting of the Oxford Socratic Club, the discussion and debating society of which Lewis was president.[3] Carpenter asks, 'What kind of mind was it that could switch from rigorous theological argument to children's fantasy?'[4] Wilson suggests an answer by arguing that '*The Lion, the Witch and the Wardrobe* grew out of Lewis's experience of being stung back into childhood by his defeat at the hands of Anscombe.'[5] He thinks that Lewis was so shaken by the debate that 'he became a child, a little boy who was being degraded and shaken by a figure who, in his imagination, took on witch-like dimensions.'

I agree with Carpenter that Lewis's sudden turn to fable invites explanation; and I agree with Wilson that the Socratic debate was intimately connected with the occasioning of the Narniad, but I would wish to contend that, far from

Lewis being 'stung back into childhood,' his composition of *The Lion*—with its innovative donegalitarian technique—was his imaginative engagement with and response to, rather than retreat from, Anscombe's critique of *Miracles*.

Wilson seems to think that Lewis could not have turned to the fairy-tale genre without it betokening some kind of psychological regression on his part. This is to beg a big question of the literary merits and psychological and social importance of fairy-tale. As I suggested in the opening paragraph of this book with the quotation from Plato, stories that are readable by children have a good claim to being the most important kind of imaginative literature that there is— and that is assuming that they are read only by children. But of course they are not read only by children, nor are they (usually) intended to be. The popular modern view that the fairy-tale genre is suitable only for juveniles is a temporary historical accident; the genre began to be associated with the nursery only when it became unfashionable in literary circles.[6] Lewis maintained in 'Sometimes Fairy Stories May Say Best What's to Be Said' that he designed the Narnia books for children only in the sense that he excluded things he thought they would not like or understand, not in the sense of writing about things he considered to be beneath adult attention. To conclude, as Wilson does, that Lewis's choice of a universally accessible genre represented a withdrawal from engagement with Anscombe's philosophical challenges is a *non sequitur* on several levels.

Which is not to say that there was nothing therapeutic for Lewis in the composing of the Narniad. 'Writing had always been Lewis's way of coping with life,' according to Carpenter. Sayer agrees: 'The way to freedom for him was through writing.' They are right. Several examples present themselves. After his bereavement he wrote *A Grief Observed*: 'By writing it all down . . . I believe I get a little outside it.'[7] In his twenties Lewis confided to his diary: 'I hoped the "King of Drum" might write itself so as to clear things up—the way "Dymer" cleared up the Christina Dream business.'[8] As early as 1916, he advised his friend, Greeves: 'whenever you are fed up with life, start writing: ink is the great cure for all human ills.'[9]

In addition to this 'self-liberating' motive for some of his writing projects, Lewis sometimes indicated that there were religious motives. For instance, he admitted in *The Problem of Pain* that 'when I undertook to write this book I hoped that the will to obey what might be a 'leading' had at least some place in my motives';[10] and in connection with his first attempt at a book on prayer, he told a correspondent that 'I find many difficulties nor do I definitely know whether God wishes me to complete this task or not.'[11]

When he came to write *The Lion, the Witch and the Wardrobe* it would seem likely that both these sorts of motives played a part, because both would seem likely responses to the bruising encounter with Anscombe. It is important not to overstate, as Wilson does, the emotional depletion which Lewis felt after the Socratic debate. Anscombe herself remembered the occasion as 'sober' and dismissed as 'projection' those accounts from observers who described it as 'a horrible and shocking experience which upset him very much.'[12] Sayer records Lewis's own reaction as unhappy and reflective, but not traumatised: he had a pastoral concern for those to whom the defeat of an argument for God's existence amounted to the defeat of God's existence, but he also thought that his main position was still defensible. Anscombe had exposed a chink in his armour; she had not utterly stripped it away. He was prepared publicly to admit that there was a 'serious hitch' in the original edition of *Miracles*, which 'ought to be rewritten,'[13] and in 1960 he did rewrite it, taking into consideration Anscombe's criticisms.[14] She later commented that the rewrite demonstrated Lewis's 'honesty and seriousness' as a philosopher. Wilson appears to know nothing of it, for nowhere in his biography of Lewis does he mention this second edition. His two-pronged contention that Lewis abandoned apologetics because he had failed at it and then withdrew into fantasy as a compensatory substitute meets the evidence on neither score.

In order to show how *The Lion, the Witch and the Wardrobe* was Lewis's imaginative response to the Socratic Club debate we need not rehearse Anscombe's criticisms, which were narrowly focussed on particular paragraphs of chapter 3 that dealt with theories of causation. (They are well represented in Victor Reppert's defence of the argument from reason, *C. S. Lewis's Dangerous Idea*). What we need to do is to summarise the main argument that Lewis was trying to advance in *Miracles* as a whole; it was this that he continued to defend. As touched upon in chapter 2 above, Lewis's central point in *Miracles* (in both the first and second editions) was that if the human mind gives access to truth about the world it must be because our thinking is not merely cerebral biochemistry, not simply a process going on inside our own heads, but a participation in a cosmic *logos*. The naturalistic alternative refutes itself, in Lewis's view, for the reason given by Haldane: 'If my mental processes are determined wholly by the motions of atoms in my brain, I have no reason to suppose that my beliefs are true . . . and hence I have no reason for supposing my brain to be composed of atoms.'[15]

Since this position is self-refuting, Lewis concludes that it cannot be true: human thinking must rather be a sharing in a 'supernatural Reason.' By 'supernatural' Lewis means that human thought, when true, is not simply dependent upon the interlocked system of natural causes and natural effects. Rational knowledge is not caused by effects; rather it is the consequence of grounds, being determined only by the truth it knows, not by digestion or heredity or the weather or any other non-rational, naturalistic causation. The ultimate ground of reason itself is the great I AM, that 'eternal, self-existent, rational Being, whom we call God.' Although human reason is dependent on Divine Reason, the two are distinct: 'human thought is not God's but God-kindled.' Whereas Descartes famously concluded, 'I think, therefore I am,' we might sum up Lewis's position with the dictum: 'I AM, therefore I think.' This view of human rationality is what Barfield termed 'participant knowledge'; it has affinities with what Michael Polanyi, an occasional speaker at the Socratic Club, would have called 'personal knowing.'[16]

This is the briefest of summaries of the first few chapters of *Miracles,* and it must be borne in mind that they are not set forth as Lewis's complete anthropology.[17] He is not arguing that reason constitutes the *imago Dei,* or that imagination and will are unimportant in comparison with reason.[18] He is simply contending that 'rationality is the little tell-tale rift in Nature which shows that there is something beyond or behind her.' And properly understood, the rift is not so little, but can be regarded as a 'miracle' of a kind,[19] for Lewis states (with a certain hyperbole):

> The discrepancy between a movement of atoms in an astronomer's cortex and his understanding that there must be a still unobserved planet beyond Uranus, is already so immense that the Incarnation of God Himself is, in one sense, scarcely more startling.[20]

That an unobserved planet, namely Neptune, over two and half billion miles from Earth, can make its presence known to the mind of John Couch Adams, sitting thinking in the Cambridge observatory in 1845, is 'in one sense' no less startling than the coming down to earth of the Son of God. Both rational thought and the incarnation of Christ make present to human beings realities that are otherwise intangible. Of course, there is a vast difference both of degree and kind between the ministrations of 'supernatural Reason' and the incarnation of the Divine Reasoner, but there is nevertheless an analogy. Reason enters our natural being, according to *Miracles,* 'like the arrival of a king among his own subjects,' like a 'lawful sovereign' who 'saves and strengthens' the whole human system, psychological and physical: similarly, God has the jurisdiction of 'a sovereign' over the whole of nature, rational souls included. Acknowledging the former king is a significant step toward acknowledging the latter King on whom the former depends. Naturalists, on the other hand, live in 'a democratic universe'[21] in which 'logic, hitherto the king whom events in all possible worlds must obey, becomes merely subjective.'[22] In naturalism, rational thought is on the same level as every other action of the human brain—or for that matter of the human body; it is qualitatively the same as emotion or sensation: all three are equally caused by naturalistic effects.

Once he had completed this philosophical groundwork about the 'miraculous' nature of human thought, Lewis moved onto theological territory and presented his arguments for 'the grand miracle,' the incarnation of Christ. For, of course, he did not just want to argue in *Miracles* for a cosmos that was irradiated with the kindling of Divine Reason, he wanted to show that the kindler Himself had entered the cosmos at the annunciation. Since reason (that supernatural creature) could be united with a person (a natural creature) in the mind of every human thinker, it need come as no surprise—rather, it should appear entirely harmonious and in order—that God (the supernatural creator) should be united with a person (the human Jesus) in Christ.

From *Miracles* to Narnia

At this point we return to Carpenter's question: 'What kind of mind was it that could switch from rigorous theological argument to children's fantasy?' And the answer is: a mind that thought both rationally and imaginatively. Lewis, I submit, turned to romance not as a retreat from apologetics after his debate with Anscombe, but precisely as a way of explaining his case to himself in imaginative form. He had made a brief and provisional adjustment of his intellectual position as soon as he could, in a note in *The Socratic Digest*,[23] but it would be another twelve years before he published the second edition of *Miracles*.[24] However, in the summer of 1948 he began working on a book 'in the style of E. Nesbit,'[25] that work which became *The Lion, the Witch and the Wardrobe*.

In turning from apologetics to romance, he did not exchange a more complex for a simpler genre. If anything, the change was from simpler to more complex. Lewis was of the opinion that rational argumentation was too rudimentary for the task of conveying Christian truths, that there were 'great disadvantages under which the Christian apologist labours. Apologetics is controversy. You cannot conduct a controversy in those poetical expressions which alone convey the concrete.... And this means that the thing we are really talking about can never appear in the discussion at all.'[26] But the genre of romance allowed, indeed required, 'poetical expressions.' So he transported his ideas about human reasoning and the Divine Reasoner into the imaginative architectonics of the first Chronicle of Narnia.

Miracles had been Lewis's apologetic attempt at showing that 'Naturalism gives us a democratic, Supernaturalism a monarchical, picture of reality.'[27] In *The Lion, the Witch and the Wardrobe*, as demonstrated in chapter 3 above, he imagines an entire world by means of the monarchical imagery of Jupiter. Whereas *Miracles* had *argued* that the human mind in the act of knowing is illuminated by the Divine Reason, the first Chronicle *shows* us that it is illuminated by Divine Reason—as represented by Jupiter. (Jovial influence, as Ficino wrote, is especially attracted by discursive reason.[28]) When the children stumble through the wardrobe into Narnia they do not instantly know where they are; they are literally and metaphorically in the dark:

> 'O-o-oh!' said Susan suddenly. And everyone asked her what was the matter.
>
> 'I'm sitting against a tree,' said Susan, 'and look! It's getting light—over there.'
>
> 'By Jove, you're right,' said Peter, 'and look there—and there. It's trees all round. And this wet stuff is snow. Why, I do believe we've got into Lucy's wood after all.'[29]

Peter's 'By Jove' sounds like a casual expression. It is. It has a very different meaning from Ransom's 'By Jove' at the beginning of *Perelandra*. Ransom, both as a philologist and interplanetary traveller, knew the significance of what he was saying; Peter does not. For him 'By Jove' is an empty metaphor. He does not recognise that, in the Narnian world that he has just entered, it is indeed by Jove (Jove properly understood as the Enjoyable 'mask' of God in this story) that he is able to see light and know it as such. However, although Peter has no *savoir* knowledge of Jove, his *connaître* knowledge is already beginning to operate. His soul (Spirit Sense 1) and his reason (Spirit Sense 2) are sufficiently in tune with this Jovial world for him to ask Lucy to lead the way, to trust the red-breasted robin, and accept the help of the beavers. When he hears the name of Aslan his Spirit (Sense 3) comes alive and rejoices: he feels suddenly 'brave and adventurous.' He discovers a Contemplatable version of Jove, an incarnation of Jupiter, in the form of the kingly Lion.

In *Miracles* Lewis had argued that Christ's miracles 'proclaim that He who has come is not merely a king, but *the* King, [Nature's] King and ours' and that His incarnation demonstrates the arrival of a cosmic 'spring,' 'spring-time,' 'summer is coming,' converting human beings from mere mortals into spirits who can 'ride' nature and who, as a result, will be able eternally to 'gallop with the King.' In *The Lion*, he presents the same set of ideas with the advent of 'the King of the Wood . . . the King of the Beasts' whose coming brings about 'spring,' a 'magic spring,' turning the land from January to May and transforming Peter from a mere schoolboy into a sovereign horseman and huntsman. Peter's brother, Edmund, on the other hand, wants to become a king on his own terms. He is resentful, discontented, mistrustful, and fearful about getting lost; his soul and his reason are out of harmony with the Narnian world. It comes as no surprise that he shrinks back from the name of Aslan with a sensation of 'mysterious horror.' After Edmund deserts his siblings, Lucy recalls that he had even asked whether the Witch could turn Aslan into stone. 'So he did, by Jove,' says Peter.

Edmund's ability to be sceptical is itself supported 'by Jove,' though of course he does not acknowledge this dependence. He would rather cut off the bough upon which he sits than submit to the King of the Wood. Edmund resembles the naturalist who tries to use reason in a way that denies human reason and the Divine Reasoner on whom it relies. Only when the consequences of this choice become unavoidably evident and he realises that the Witch is about to slit his throat does the true nature of his world come rushing in upon his mind in the form of Aslan's troops who hurry to his rescue.

Thus, within the overarching Jovial symbolism of the book, Lewis portrays a kingdom in which both his argument from *Miracles* and its detractors have a place; he has imaginatively presented to himself the situation with which he was confronted at the Socratic Club. This is not to suggest that Edmund somehow represents Elizabeth Anscombe: she was a devout Catholic and critiqued Lewis's case because she felt it did not give sufficient regard to certain philosophical technicalities, not because she was at odds with theism or Christianity. But Edmund may be understood, in a sense, as a representative of those whom Lewis regarded as taking the privileges of idealism (and, by implication, theism and Christianity) whilst denying its logic. Edmund, before his rescue, is like Robin's wife and the painter in 'The Man Born Blind': able to see, but unable to account for sight and, in fact, spiritually committed to a position that prevents a convincing account from being given.

The original edition of *Miracles* was the only one of Lewis's works that he reworked after public criticism and may rightly be called his least successful book. *The Lion, the Witch and the Wardrobe*, in contrast, is widely regarded as his greatest achievement, the one title in the Lewisian corpus which is likely to enjoy a permanent place in the canon of English literature. The difference between the two books suggests that Lewis was right when he claimed that the imaginative faculty was, in him, older and more continuously operative than his rational side. He was more poet than apologist. Patrick sums it up by saying: 'when Lewis moves on to poetic ground, imagination carries reason with it and the perplexities of his metaphysics move into the background.'[30]

The Lion, the Witch and the Wardrobe may be taken then, in a sense, as one large metaphor, a metaphor for the human situation vis-à-vis reason and the Divine Reasoner. It is an example of a 'true, imaginative metaphor' which, according to Barfield, 'expresses and may communicate participant knowledge.'[31] Readers participate in a story which is the romance equivalent of the philosophical and theological argument advanced in *Miracles*; they Enjoy in his fiction that vision of the world which Lewis had tried to make Contemplatable in his apologetics.

Anscombe had reminded Lewis of the generic deficiency of apologetics, that rational argumentation can never convey the concrete realities of spiritual experience. Recounting the debate to his friend Dyson, Lewis used imagery that was all about 'the fog of war, the retreat of infantry thrown back under heavy attack,' to which Dyson responded by saying, 'with great sympathy' that Lewis had now 'come to the foot of the Cross.'[32] Sayer was of the view that the debate was indeed 'a humiliating experience, but perhaps it was ultimately good for him.' If it gave rise to *The Lion, the Witch and the Wardrobe*, then the debate certainly did have beneficial effects, for it humbled Lewis into imaginative engagement with the concrete dimensions of his faith and forced him away from serving up easier, thinner, less nourishing abstractions. He already knew of the dangers of abstract argument, as is shown by his poem, 'The Apologist's Evening Prayer.' There he prays to be delivered from 'cleverness' shot forth in public debate on God's behalf: 'From all my thoughts, even from my thoughts of Thee, / O thou fair Silence, fall, and set me free.' The 'fair Silence' that Lewis wove into the Chronicles of Narnia, constructing each story so that it communicated divine presence implicitly and Enjoyably, as well as Contemplatably, may be understood as his enacted answer to that prayer.

In addition to providing a solution to the problem of occasion, the case that I have advanced in this chapter helps explain why Lewis should have started out with the intention of writing just one book. He had not originally conceived the idea of a series that would enable him to portray all seven planets; rather, he had found a way of reimagining *Miracles* using the imagery of Jupiter, because Jupiter's kingly aspect was especially associated with the ideas he had expressed in *Miracles* and because Jupiter was, in any case, his favourite planet, part of the 'habitual furniture' of his mind, out of which he believed an author should write. *The Lion* was thus the first example of that 'idea that he wanted to try out.' *Prince Caspian* and *The 'Dawn Treader'* naturally followed because Mars and Sol were both already connected in his mind with the merits of the Alexander technique.[33] Even after completing *The 'Dawn Treader'* Lewis had not decided to write seven stories (according to his letter to Laurence Krieg), but at some point after commencing *The Horse and His Boy* he resolved to treat all seven planets, for seven such treatments of his idea would mean that he had 'worked it out to the full.'[34]

ELEVEN

The Music of the Spheres

Symbols are the natural speech of the soul, a language older and more universal than words.
—'Edmund Spenser, 1552–99'

In the previous ten chapters I have argued two main theses. First, I have argued that the images Lewis habitually associated with the seven planets underlie the Narnia Chronicles, determining the basic plot of each story, countless points of ornamental detail, and, most significantly (from the theological point of view), the presentation of the Christotypical figure of Aslan so that he focusses and locates—makes Contemplatable—the personality of the presiding planetary spirit that is otherwise only Enjoyable by the characters in the story. This reading, I venture to suggest, addresses the problem of composition so effectively that it may be considered 'definitive'—not in the sense of being beyond interrogation, still less in the sense that it forecloses all further discussion of the septet, but in the sense of establishing a new and more than probable interpretative paradigm within which the books may be assessed.

And second, I have advanced an explanation about the origin of the series, connecting it with Lewis's determination to re-state the burden of *Miracles* in imaginative form. This argument is put forward in the belief that it addresses the problem of occasion in a convincing and plausible fashion, though without the same level of conclusiveness as I think can be claimed for the solution of the problem of composition.

In this chapter we turn to the problem of reception: why, given the problems of occasion and composition, have the books become such popular favourites, the first of them especially so? Even before *The Lion* received the sharp boost in public notice provoked by Andrew Adamson's 2005 feature film, it was voted among the ten most popular novels of all time in the United Kingdom, according to a major national survey undertaken by the British Broadcasting Corporation.[1] Sales figures are hard to come by (the Wade Center estimates combined sales of 3.5 million copies annually in thirty-three languages) and, in any case, prove little about actual reading habits; but if we look at the field-research conducted by Hall and Coles, which compared lists of children's fa-vourite authors compiled in 1971 and 1994, we find that 'C. S. Lewis maintains a remarkably consistent place over the two decades.' In the 1994 survey, Lewis was named 'more or less equally' by boys and girls, and 'roughly equally' across the three age-groups of the survey (ten-, twelve-, and fourteen-year olds).[2] And it is not just to the tastes of childhood that the books appeal; adults read and re-read the Narniad with equal, if not greater, avidity. For example, the current two most senior figures in the Church of England are both admirers of the series: the Archbishop of Canterbury, Rowan Williams, has professed an 'enthusiasm' for Lewis in general and a 'love' for the Chronicles in particular and has ad-dressed the Oxford Lewis Society under the title, 'A Theologian in Narnia'; the Archbishop of York, John Sentamu, has named the Narniad as the one work (after the Bible and the complete works of Shakespeare) that he would take with him if cast away on a desert island. It is evident that the Chronicles have acquired something of a classic status and are able to attract an unusually wide spectrum of readers: old and young, male and female, simple and learned. But what accounts for this fact?

The first thing to point out by way of an answer is that, given the suggested solutions to the problems of occasion and composition, the problem of re-ception is already largely addressed. If the series was written in order to tackle a significant philosophical and theological question (namely, the question about naturalism, which had accompanied Lewis since his 'Great War' with Barfield in the 1920s), and if it was founded on symbols that Lewis considered to be 'of permanent value' and that over the whole course of his life he had gradually become intimately familiar with, both in his professional career and in his work as a poet and writer of fiction, then it should be less surprising that the Chro-nicles have been so well received—less surprising, that is, than if we suppose them to be the sorts of books that Wilson and Tolkien assume them to be.

For instance, if we take Wilson's line and imagine that they were the pro-ducts of a mind in psychological shock, a mind groping back to childhood after a painful intellectual misadventure, it is difficult to see why so many readers have found the Chronicles to be eminently genial and relaxed and generous-spirited—'an outpouring of charity,' as Hooper puts it.

And if we take Tolkien's line and imagine that they were composed in a hasty and slapdash manner, it is difficult to see why so many readers have found them to be imaginatively rewarding and engaging and endlessly suggestive—

'the most sustained achievement in fantasy for children by a twentieth century author,' according to Carpenter and Prichard.

The Socratic Club theory of their origins and the donegalitarian theory of their composition do not, of course, mean that the books were necessarily going to win large audiences, but these theories surely do a good deal more to account for the problem of reception than Wilson's and Tolkien's perspectives.

However, it may be maintained that the problem of reception is still not 'solved.' After all, for fifty years and more, no one actually recognised their Socratic Club origins or their donegalitarian scheme. Have not generations of readers read the Chronicles without becoming cognizant in the slightest degree that they had anything to do with the case that Lewis tried to make in *Miracles* or with his lifelong absorption in the imagery of the seven heavens?

All depends on one's definition of cognizance. We have seen how, for Lewis, there were two kinds of cognitive experience: 'looking at' and 'looking along.' In the latter, the beam of knowledge is invisible: it provides a comprehensive, as distinct from an apprehensive, mode of understanding. If Lewis has successfully rendered the arguments of *Miracles* and the symbolism of the spheres into an Enjoyable form, it would not follow that they ceased either to exist or to exert influence upon readers, only that their existence and influence would be of a different order. The order in question would be a pupillary symbolical one, an order which engages the reader in a fuller, more life-like way than the magistral methods of abstract discourse can achieve. Lewis thought that 'symbolism exists precisely for the purpose of conveying to the imagination what the intellect is not ready for'[3] and that poetic archetypes were 'like words—the words of a language which speaks the else unspeakable.'[4] By casting *Miracles* and the planets into the genre of romance he deliberately circumvented conscious intellectual apprehension, and that was all to the good, for 'an influence which cannot evade our consciousness will not go very deep.'[5] In this he was following his master, George MacDonald, who wrote: 'It is not the things we see the most clearly that influence us the most powerfully.'[6]

By choosing to communicate in this way, Lewis aimed to inform his readers by means of a kind of capillary action, because 'the fairy way of writing . . . builds a bridge between the conscious and the unconscious mind.'[7] In *The Uses of Enchantment*, Bettelheim confirms Lewis's understanding of how the fantasy genre achieves its effects: 'There is general agreement that myths and fairy tales speak to us in the language of symbols representing unconscious content. Their appeal is simultaneously to our conscious and unconscious mind.'[8] This is not to imply that Lewis's readers suddenly find themselves believing the argument of *Miracles* or understanding the qualities of the planets without realising it; but it is to suggest that the first circle of cognition may have been successfully penetrated. Lewis thought that the human person could be usefully pictured as three concentric circles: at the centre was the will; surrounding the will was the reason; and outside the reason was the circle of the imagination. Communicating successfully and powerfully to this outer ring was the first step in addressing the whole person, for 'our higher faculties certainly receive something ... from our lower.'[9]

Watson assesses the situation well when he writes: 'There is a potent intellectual myth that to conceptualise is to understand, and for the first time; and the story-teller's task, as Lewis saw it, is to help us to climb out of that imprisoning assumption.'[10] In story-telling mode, Lewis constructs the Chronicles so that they communicate his argument from *Miracles* and the characters of the planets, even if not in a conceptual and Contemplatable fashion. And it makes especially good sense to communicate in this way, because the very things he is trying to communicate are themselves best understood through Enjoyment, not Contemplation. Let us take the two things in turn.

Imaginative Reception of the Argument of *Miracles*

The Pevensies' ability to think, know, and reason (in *The Lion*) is located within and supported by the Jovial *logos* that permeates the Narnian universe as it is presented in that opening book; and so on with respect to the Martial *logos* in *Prince Caspian*, the Solar *logos* in *The 'Dawn Treader,'* et cetera. The characters cannot step outside the cosmic *logos* that irradiates each story for the reason Lewis gives elsewhere: 'the critique of a chain of reasoning is itself a chain of reasoning.'[11] And not just their reason (Spirit, Sense 2), but also their soul (Spirit, Sense 1) and in due course their *novitas* (Spirit, Sense 3) are located within the prevailing planetary power, for each planet, as a symbol of Christ, represents 'the all-pervasive principle of concretion or cohesion whereby the universe holds together' (Lewis's paraphrase of Colossians 1:17, in *Miracles*). What arises on the basis of the children's relation to the presiding planetary spirit in each story is not a particular state or act of their conscious existence, but their whole conscious existence.

And this may help explain why Lewis kept the scheme secret. He was wanting to portray symbolically the human predicament that he had portrayed conceptually in *Miracles*. There he had written:

> The fact which is in one respect the most obvious and primary fact, and through which alone you have access to all the other facts, may be precisely the one that is most easily forgotten—forgotten not because it is so remote or abstruse but because it is so near and so obvious. And that is exactly how the Supernatural has been forgotten.[12]

Miracles uses a variety of images to symbolise this natural human forgetfulness, including transparent windows, native grammar, and breathing. When we see a window-pane, rather than seeing through it, it is probably because it is dirty; when we consciously have to make verbs agree with nouns it is because we are speaking a foreign language; and when we become aware of the noise of our breathing it is because of illness or over-exertion. Clean windows, mother tongues, and healthy lungs do not draw attention to themselves: they work best when they are noticed least. As a result we can quite easily overlook them and act as if they were of no importance. Lewis quotes Aristotle to the same effect: 'For as bats' eyes are to daylight so is our intellectual eye to those truths which are, in their own nature, the most obvious of all.'[13]

And it is not just in *Miracles*, but throughout his writings, that Lewis points out this natural human tendency to be oblivious to the obvious. In *Mere Christianity* he writes: 'Since that [divine] power, if it exists, would not be one of the observed facts but a reality which makes them, no mere observation of the facts can find it.' In *The Problem of Pain* he writes: 'You may reply, as a Christian, that God (and Satan) do, in fact, affect my consciousness in this direct way without signs of "externality." Yes: and the result is that most people remain ignorant of the existence of both.' In *Letters to Malcolm* he writes: 'We may ignore, but we can nowhere evade, the presence of God. The world is crowded with Him. He walks everywhere *incognito*.' In 'The Weight of Glory' he declares that, 'In [the Christian] Christ *vere latitat*—the glorifier and the glorified, Glory Himself—is truly hidden.'[14] And in what he regarded as his best work, *Till We Have Faces*, he has Orual complain, 'Nothing that's beautiful hides its face. Nothing that's honest hides its name.' Of course, she is utterly wrong. Kallistos Ware suggests that the *leitmotif* of *Till We Have Faces* 'is the hiddenness of the Divine,'[15] and this judgement may be equally well applied to Lewis's general theological vision: he is continually preoccupied with God's unperceived ubiquity and propinquity.

Correlatively, the major feature of his spirituality is the exercising of Enjoyment consciousness in order to experience that hidden divinity. Coming to know God, for Lewis, is not like 'learning a subject' but like 'breathing a new atmosphere,'[16] and it is of the highest significance that the word 'atmosphere', which is his preferred term for the kappa element in romance, should also serve for his description of the nature of the Christian life. As a story's inner meaning is cryptic, so, Lewis believes, is one's spiritual state. Standing sentinel at the door of one's mind in order to check up on one's spiritual life is the surest way to inhibit it. When Lewis himself became a Christian in *Surprised by Joy* there was no part of him 'left over or outside the act,' no officious spectator observing the transformation from a distance. He had entered into joy. No longer was joy merely something he could hold, like the tin-lid toy garden that mysteriously evoked Milton's 'enormous bliss of Eden';[17] it was something that held him, like the enclosure at Whipsnade Zoo, full of beauty, above, below and all around—'almost Eden come again.'[18]

Attempting to portray this omnipresent and largely uncontemplatable divine presence in the Narniad, Lewis turned to the image provided by the music of the spheres, that music which (in Eliot's words) is 'heard so deeply that it is not heard at all.'[19] And attempting to portray human participation in that silent music, he turned to the image provided by Herbert's poem about thoughts which work 'like a noiseless sphere.'[20] Of course, nothing is to be rested on these specific links to Eliot and Herbert; they are intended as illustrative, not evidential. What I wish to submit is that, in moving from *Miracles* to the Chronicles, Lewis trod an imaginative path that involved these or similar steps. By some such route he arrived at his depiction of children who do not realise that they and their thoughts and their actions are surrounded and upheld by a mighty creative and sustaining spirit. Through their ignorance, Lewis symbolises what he believed to be our common human condition: unawareness of the supernatural. He could not have disclosed that this was his intention without pulling down the whole imaginative edifice around him.

Although this book is the first to have consciously outlined what Lewis was trying to achieve in this regard, other critics seem to have sensed it unconsciously. For instance, Como has perceived that the best explanation of the secret of Lewis's appeal is that his writings communicate, in Pope's words, 'Something, whose truth convinced at sight we find, / That gives us back the image of our mind.'[21] Franz Rottensteiner is of the opinion that 'The fantastic setting is as important as the story, for the beauty of Narnia...is perhaps designed to awaken an unrecognized desire in the reader, which may be turned into a mystic experience of divine presence.'[22] Peter Schakel thinks that 'readers encounter in Narnia a bright shadow, a divine aura, a world aglow with a divine spirit.'[23] Natasha Giardina acknowledges that the Narniad taught her 'what experiencing the divine was all about' despite the fact that 'this aspect *never* registered while I was reading the story' and even though she was 'never particularly religious.'[24] These critics intuit something of Lewis's underlying purpose in the Narniad, his symbolising of the operation of the human spirit in the divine presence. And I strongly suspect that many other critics and readers who have not articulated any similar perception have nevertheless been affected in similar ways as they have read the books and responded instinctively to their poetic harmonies. As Farrer argues in another context: 'Our ignorance of what we are does not make us cease to be, and our unawareness of the profound levels of our imagination neither abolishes them nor prevents them from acting upon our wills, nor, even, on the wills and minds of others.'[25]

This, then, is our first suggested solution to the problem of reception: readers have sensed that Narnia presents a vision of human life lived in harmony with the spiritual realm, even though this presentation is never directly stated for our hearing.

Imaginative Reception of the Characters of the Planets

The second suggested solution has to do with the nature of the planetary symbols themselves. Lewis was of the view that the planets 'need to be lived with imaginatively, not merely learned as concepts.'[26] In his chapter on 'The Heavens' in *The Discarded Image* he had presented them conceptually: his scholarly overview of the planets provided information regarding how they were understood and written about in medieval and renaissance times. But he wanted to do more than just transmit information. He thought that 'the planetary characters need to be seized in an intuition . . . we need to know them, not to know about them, *connaître* not *savoir*.'[27] And given that he elsewhere wrote that 'the arts depend on turning *savoir* into *connaître* as far as possible,'[28] it would appear that it was just this purpose that he had in mind in his various imaginative attempts at communicating the planets' characteristics. In 'The Planets' and the Ransom Trilogy he went some way toward helping his readers acquire a *connaître*-like knowledge of the planets, but the cognitive relationship in these two works was still essentially one of Contemplation—we know (*savoir*) what it is that we are expected to know (*connaître*). In the Chronicles, by way of contrast, he makes his readers Enjoy the planets completely; he enables his readers to live inside the discarded mindset in a way that escapes our conscious attention.

Of the characters of the planets, Venus and Saturn were most successfully still thriving in the modern imagination, he thought; the Venereal 'world-wide dream of the happy garden' was one of 'the deep unfailing sources of poetry in the mind of the folk,'[29] and Saturn likewise remained 'one of our archetypes.'[30] However, changes in outlook had made it harder for modern students to understand Jupiter and Mercury, which meant that the need for intuitive reception of their qualities was all the greater. This is where Lewis, the self-proclaimed dinosaur who read as a 'native' texts that his students had to read as foreigners, felt he had a vocation. If the all-but-extinct thing 'infused its quality into some other thing which we can get inside, then this other, more penetrable, thing would now be the only medium through which we can get back to the experience itself. Such a 'more penetrable thing' might be provided by a work of plastic or literary art which we can still appreciate,'[31] for 'it is either in art, or nowhere, that the dry bones are made to live again.'[32]

The archetypes communicated by each Chronicle feed what Lewis called 'the primitive or instinctive mind.'[33] He was not a convinced Jungian, but, when he tried to account for the popularity of fairy-tales and fantasy, he admitted that Jung's explanation was one of the theories that was most often in his mind: 'For Jung, fairy tale liberates Archetypes which dwell in the collective unconscious.'[34] Lewis had a high view of archetypes in general (he thought, for instance, that people were born knowing Circe and Alcina),[35] and he was interested, in particular, in the literary use of 'archetypal patterns.'[36] Giants, dragons, paradises, gods, and the like are 'the expression of certain basic elements in man's spiritual experience.' Such symbols, in Lewis's view, were able to reach a broader audience and touch deeper parts of an audience than realistic novels because they spring from a more fundamental source. 'The work of Jung and Freud, and the practice of many modern poets and prose writers, has taught us [that] . . . symbols are the natural speech of the soul, a language older and more universal than words.'[37] And if he considered symbols in general to have this power, it is to be expected that he would view the seven astrological archetypes, those 'spiritual symbols of permanent value,' as even more potently communicative.

Indeed, in *Perelandra*, Lewis gives a speculative account of the planetary gods' continuing power in the modern imagination that supports just this notion. He explains:

> There is an environment of minds as well as of space. The universe is one—a spider's web wherein each mind lives along every line, a vast whispering gallery where (save for the direct action of Maleldil) though no news travels unchanged yet no secret can be rigorously kept. In the mind of the fallen Archon under whom our planet groans, the memory of Deep Heaven and the gods with whom he once consorted is still alive. Nay, in the very matter of our world, the traces of the celestial commonwealth are not quite lost. Memory passes through the womb and hovers in the air.[38]

Although this account is found within a work of fiction, it seems to be close to Lewis's real belief. George Watson is therefore near the mark when he says that, in *The Discarded Image*, 'in spite of the title, Lewis's message was ultimately one of permanence rather than flux. The gods of the Ancients . . . live in the modern mind as images of eternal potency. They did not vanish with Galileo or Newton.'[39]

Lewis never refers to the writings of Joseph Campbell, Mircea Eliade, or Northrop Frye, who have all, in various ways, supported this view that there are certain foundational archetypes that recur in cultures the world over and throughout history: Superman is for us what Hercules was for the Ancients;

Marilyn Monroe's function in the public mind is, in large part, a reprise of that role performed originally by Aphrodite. Their writings, like the work of Jung himself, help account for why the Chronicles have been so positively received. Lewis's readers are being fed a diet that appeals to long-established and deeply-felt appetites in the human imagination.

Objections

If the arguments mounted in this book are accepted, they effectively address the three problems of occasion, composition, and reception. However, are not certain new problems raised as these are solved? We turn now to consider four questions that this interpretation provokes.

Are the Chronicles Intellectual Constructions?

It may be contended that the claims made here only succeed in turning the Chronicles into very elaborate allegories, allegorical expressions of the planets and of Lewis's case against naturalism. The Chronicles thus become, first and foremost, works of magistral symbolism, in which the author knows exactly what he wants to say and how he wants to say it. Does this not reduce, or at any rate limit, the septet to the status of an intellectual construction? How can the Chronicles continue to be regarded as true works of pupillary and heuristic imagination?

In response, I would argue that, although Lewis consciously and purposefully chose a symbolic orientation for each Chronicle, it does not follow that he thereafter conducted their composition only in a calculatingly conscious and intellectual fashion. On the contrary, it may be said of Lewis, as Lewis said of Spenser, that in the composing of his stories (as distinct from their deliberated projection) he partly 'left the images alone to manifest their own unity, a unity far more subtle than conscious contrivance could ever have achieved.'[40] Lewis was of the view that 'not all that is unconscious in art is therefore accidental,'[41] and it is not hard to conceive how, having settled upon a given planet and having worked his mind into the image-world associated with that planet, he could then have proceeded to write each story in a way that did not involve constant reference back to his 'allegorical' purposes. Lewis's famous distinction between allegory and symbolism in *The Allegory of Love* (allegory is a mode of expression, symbolism is a mode of thought) need not be regarded as absolute. A mode of thought might be the very thing that is being expressed. Lewis, as allegorist, could initially adopt, in a magistral way, a symbolic system and then write within that symbolic system in a pupillary way. So the arguments made in this book do not require us to acknowledge only an allegorising in-tellect at work in the Narniad. Rather, we are claiming that Lewis's allegorising intellect and symbolic imagination were mutually and fruitfully engaged.

Why Is the Scheme Not More Perfect?

It may be objected that, although the donegalitarian interpretation explains a good deal about each book, it does not explain everything. Why, for instance, does the word 'lunatic' appear not only in *The Silver Chair*, but also twice in *The Magician's Nephew* and why does that same book contain the word 'quicksilver,' a Mercurial vestige? Why is 'lead' mentioned in *The 'Dawn Treader'* but not in *The Last Battle*? Why are there 'By Joves' and 'By Gums' outside their 'home' books?[42] If the military events in *Prince Caspian* are deemed to be Martial, why not those in *The Last Battle*?

By way of answer we may make the following points.

First, Lewis held that, symbolically speaking, 'in a certain juncture of the planets each may play the other's part'[43] and that, in any case, 'all the planets are represented in each.'[44] Given the interinanimation of these seven spiritual symbols we should not expect the imagery in each Chronicle to be chemically pure. The claim made in this book is that in each of the stories a certain planet dominates, its imagery is pervasive and governing. We do not mean to sug-gest that it utterly excludes all elements connected to the other six. As the Priest remarks in *Till We Have Faces*: '[the gods] flow in and out of one another like eddies on a river, and nothing that is said clearly can be said truly about them.'

Second, we should remember what Lewis calls, in *Studies in Words*, 'the insulating power of context.' When we see the notice 'Wines and Spirits,' we do not interpret 'Spirits' to mean 'angels, devils, ghosts, and fairies'; the first noun, 'Wines', establishes a context which rules out such an interpretation. Similarly, when we read of combat in *The Last Battle* we should not think of Mars; the context of the fighting which occurs in the final Chronicle—ugliness, coldness, darkness, old age, death, disaster and so on—insulates against a Martial inter-pretation (where the context would be rhythm, hardness, order, gaiety, knightly reticence, etc) and points instead toward a Saturnine construal. It is the mean-ing that matters; the spirit, not the letter. Incidentally, when the word 'war' appears in *The Last Battle*, it is used to refer to the events of *Prince Caspian* ('the War of Deliverance') and then in the olive branch Peter offers to Emeth: 'Sir, I do not know that there need be any war between you and us.' For all its armed struggles, *The Last Battle* is not about war.

The third reason for the 'imperfections' in the donegalitarian scheme is one I hesitate to mention because it ill-becomes a critic to argue, 'I am right because my author is wrong.' Nevertheless, for all its apparent ungraciousness, we can bear in mind that Lewis was unlikely to have been perfectly successful in carrying out his own plan. Indeed, he himself was of the view that he had 'improved as the stories went on.'[45] To err is human. Almost all artistic designs will involve certain small flaws, gaps, paddings, and unintended by-products. In this regard, it is interesting to note how Lewis compares imperfect human plans with the perfect artistry of divine creativity, for he uses a planetary illustration. Whereas human inventions will inevitably admit a certain degree of unwanted instrumentality, God's various creative purposes are simultaneously wholly peculiar and wholly interdependent: all created things are present equally for their own sake and for the sake of everything else. In Lewis's opinion, the fine weather at the evacuation of Dunkirk 'was decreed, and decreed for a purpose, when the world was made—but no more so (though more interestingly to us) than the precise position of every atom in the ring of Saturn.' Lewis concedes that this 'may sound excessive,' but, he goes on, 'in reality we are attributing to the Omniscient only an infinitely superior degree of the same kind of skill which a mere human novelist exercises daily in constructing his plot.'[46]

And fourth, I readily confess that this appraisal of the series is itself far from complete. This is partly unintentional: there are doubtless many pieces of evidence that have escaped my notice because of ignorance and imperceptiveness. But it is also in part intentional. Limitations of space have necessarily involved omission of detailed points, and, as was acknowledged in chapter 3, the more microscopic and atomised a case like this becomes the more it loses focus: the nature of the beast demands a certain distance. Moreover, if, as I maintain, the Chronicles are poetic, not purely intellectual, constructions, it would be impossible for any critic, however well-informed and insightful, to suck out the heart of their mystery. Literary criticism can only go so far.

Should Not the Scheme Remain Secret?

But have I already gone too far? Does not the disclosure of this secret frustrate the author's intention to communicate by means of implicitness? Given that he apparently considered it wise to keep his cards close to his chest, should not his example be respected and followed?

In response, I would concede that, yes, inevitably, explanation necessarily involves something like loss, in any department of criticism. Part of the attractiveness, for example, of Mona Lisa's smile is its enigmatic quality; there is fun to be had in speculating what it means. The art critic who convincingly explained why she was smiling would take something away from the painting. However, the loss would surely be more than compensated for by gain. Knowledge, except where it is illicit, is always a kind of pleasure, and it is hard to see how our responses to Leonardo and to the Mona Lisa would not be enriched if we could read the silent message in her lips. To prefer our former ignorance would be to adopt a Luddite or obscurantist stance. So with the Narniad: its problems of occasion, composition, and reception are, in varying degrees, 'solved' by the arguments mounted in this book, and to that extent the septet no longer yields the pleasure that it used to, the pleasure we derive from thinking, 'There's more going on here than meets the eye.' But at the same time these explanations offer up new pleasures, first at the literary-historical level and second at the theological level. It will be worth mentioning these before we proceed to the fourth and final objection.

THE SEPTET ACQUIRES NEW LITERARY-HISTORICAL DEPTHS

The arguments presented in this book enrich the Narniad from the literary-historical point of view because we can now see more clearly how Lewis was building on the work of his medieval and renaissance forebears. As we pointed out in chapter 2, Lewis had a high view of the pagan gods and he was not averse, in fact he was wholly committed, to using them for literary purposes. He held this view largely because writers he respected had held it before him. 'Gods and goddesses could always be used in a Christian sense' by a medieval or Elizabethan poet; paganism was not just 'plumb wrong' to their minds. The redeemed gods could perform all sorts of good, true, and beautiful tasks, as was recognised by Dante, Sidney, Spenser, and Milton, for all of whom 'the gods are God incognito and everyone is in the secret.'[47] Paganism, in Lewis's view, was 'the religion of poetry through which the author can express, at any moment, just so much or so little of his real religion as his art requires.' He coined the term 'transferred classicism' for those poets who imagined their Christianity under classical forms, where 'God is, in some degree, disguised as a mere god' and the reader enjoys seeing 'how well Christianity could produce the councils, catalogues, Mercuries, and battlepieces of ancient epic.'[48] This practice of using mythological untruths to hint at theological truths lasted as late as the composition of Milton's *Comus* (1634) and was, for most poets and in most poems, by far the best method of writing poetry which was religious without being devotional.

As a good medievalist, Lewis, in his fiction and poetry (and even his apologetics), was likewise not concerned to keep pagan deities separate from the deity of his believed religion. He was ever prepared to present God '*sub figuris vilium corporum*.'[49] Although he recognised that the gods had declined from deity to hypostasis and from hypostasis to decoration, he did not consider this a history of sheer loss: 'decoration may let romance in.'[50] He argues that, although the gods 'died into allegory,' they rose again into a world of romantic imagining, a world of myth and fancy, for 'gods, like other creatures, must die to live.' And in the Chronicles he causes the seven planetary deities to enjoy a most sophisticated resurrection, not just using them as a 'top dressing' (as he did for example with Bacchus, Silenus, and Pomona, in *Prince Caspian*, deploying them within his *dramatis personae*), but by turning their characteristic qualities into stories through his newly-minted donegalitarian technique.

In this manner, he gave a contemporary twist to the medieval practice of using cosmological material. One thing that Lewis particularly admired in Dante was his presentation of the best cosmological thought of his day, his acting as a medieval version of Sir James Jeans or Sir Arthur Eddington. The medieval cosmos, he thought, was perhaps the greatest work of art the Middle Ages produced, and Dante's presentation of it was only the most perfect of the various versions on offer. 'They wrote it, they sang it, painted it and carved it. Sometimes a whole poem or a whole building seems almost nothing but verbalized or petrified cosmology.'[51]

We do not have space to examine any of the songs and paintings which Lewis was referring to, but when speaking of the poems which verbalized this cosmology, Lewis had in mind not just the *Commedia*, but also the *De Mundi Universitate* of Bernardus Silvestris where the 'journey through the various planetary levels is well described.'[52] He had in mind Chaucer and Henryson, in whose *Knight's Tale* and *Testament of Cresseid*, the 'character and influence of the planets are worked into' the story-line.[53] And he had in mind Spenser's *Faerie Queene*, which is both 'a representation of, and hymn to, the cosmos as our ancestors believed it to be. There has been no delight (of that sort) in "nature" since the old cosmology was rejected. No one can respond in just that way to the Einsteinian, or even the Newtonian, universe.'[54]

As for the buildings that petrified this cosmology, Lewis is thinking of the old sacristy of San Lorenzo, Florence, in which the constellations depicted on the cupola above the altar are there not for mere decoration, but because they are in the right position for 9 July 1422 when the altar was consecrated. He also mentions the Salone at Padua, which is designed so that at each sunrise the beams will fall on the Sign in which Sol would then ride. 'Just as the planets are not merely present in the Testament of Cresseid but woven into the plot, so in the buildings the cosmological material is sometimes woven into what we may call the plot of a building.'[55]

It is in connection with 'the plot of a building' that Lewis came nearest to disclosing the donegalitarian secret. (This is the second of the hints we mentioned in the opening chapter.) One of his correspondents, Professor William Kinter, had suggested that Lewis's publications could be laid out to form a kind of literary cathedral. Lewis wrote back saying, 'It's fun laying out all my books as a cathedral. Personally I'd make *Miracles* and the other "treatises" the cathedral school: my children's stories are the real side-chapels, each with its own little altar.'[56] *Each with its own little altar.* If the whole series was 'about Christ' in a simple sense, surely the seven books would constitute one large altar dedicated to him. Since the septet is actually 'about Christ' as understood '*sub specie Apollinis*'[57] and the other six gods, each Chronicle constitutes its own peculiar understanding and representation of the divine nature.

And so the pagan gods rise to new life in the seven heavens of Narnia. Lewis's professional expertise as a literary historian and his theological imagination as a Christian writer are aptly united. Norman Cantor in his survey of the great medievalists of the twentieth century is quite right to note that Lewis's fictional works cannot be separated from his scholarly writing; rather, they show how he sought 'to transmute [his] medieval learning into mythopoetic fiction, fantasy literature for a mass audience that communicated the sensibility of medieval epic and romance.'[58] Dante, Chaucer, Henryson, and others had Christened the planetary gods in works of considerable complexity and subtlety, for 'intricacy is a mark of the medieval mind.' Lewis, by adopting and adapting their methods, shows himself to be an heir of their line. Like them, he presents us with a work of art that 'cannot be taken in at a glance, something that at first looks planless though all is planned.'[59]

THE SEPTET ACQUIRES NEW THEOLOGICAL DEPTHS

As well as opening up new literary-historical depths in the Chronicles, the interpretation being offered here serves to illuminate the Narniad from the theological point of view, showing how it is linked to Lewis's characteristic interest in theosis.

Far from Lewis having a 'Talmudic emphasis on the divine transcendence,'[60] as Barfield contends, his tendency was to stress how nature was (in Farrer's term) 'diaphanous' of God's presence and how man might participate in the divine supra-personality. Yes, of course, he believed that 'God is further from us' than any other being, but he also believed that God is 'nearer to us' than any other being.[61] Following Richard Hooker, he thought of God as both 'unspeakably transcendent' and 'unspeakably immanent';[62] but it was the latter quality that he tended to focus upon. He wrote in *Letters to Malcolm*: 'There is no question of God "up there" or "out there"; rather, the present operation of God "in here," as the ground of my own being, and God "in there," as the ground of the matter that surrounds me, and God embracing and uniting both in the daily miracle of finite consciousness.'[63] The conferral of God's common grace on all people by virtue of His creative and sustaining power was but a foretaste of the even greater indebtedness available through *novitas*. For human beings are 'potential gods and goddesses';[64] 'the Son of God became a man to enable men to become sons of God.'[65]

This theological disposition is worked out in each of the Chronicles as the children, who by the common grace of 'nature' are already part of a planetary world, become more so by special grace as they follow the planetary deity's leading. Thus, in *The Lion* they become monarchs under sovereign Jove; in *Prince Caspian* they harden under strong Mars; in *The 'Dawn Treader'* they drink light under searching Sol; in *The Silver Chair* they learn obedience under subordinate Luna; in *The Horse and His Boy* they come to love poetry under eloquent Mercury; in *The Magician's Nephew* they gain life-giving fruit under fertile Venus; and in *The Last Battle* they suffer and die under chilling Saturn. Ware perceptively points out how interested Lewis was in 'interpenetration,'[66] and Payne remarks that his poetic vision amounted to a 'mysticism' which 'consists of the knowledge of an indwelling Christ and the practice of the Presence of God within and without.'[67] In consort with Henryson's Cupid, who says to the planets, 'ye are all sevin <u>deificait</u>, / <u>Participant</u> of devyne <u>sapience</u>,'[68] Lewis's septet presents participatory deification, not of the planets in the divine nature, but of the children in the divine nature as it is understood by means of the planets.

The representation of the divine nature in the Narniad is Lewis's principal achievement, from the perspective of theological imagination. Aslan has previously been thought to be simply 'a Christ figure,' a particular individual character moving about a neutral stage, and John Hick has noted how 'many today have had the scope of their theological imaginations enlarged by C. S. Lewis' allegory of Narnia with the numinous figure of Aslan, who is the divine Logos incarnate as a mighty lion.'[69] The arguments presented here show that the Christology of the books is more sophisticated than Hick realises. Aslan in each book is not just incarnate as an identifiable, locatable character; he is also discarnate as the Word who sustains the cosmos of each romance. He is present in two modes at once.

The local manifestation of his character may thus be taken as symbolic in a way which critics and theologians have often held to be ideal. This kind of symbol is what Coleridge called *tautegory*, 'a Symbol ... characterized by a translucence of the Special in the Individual or of the General in the Especial or of the Universal in the General.... It always partakes of the Reality which it renders intelligible; and while it enunciates the whole, abides itself as a living part in that Unity, of which it is the representative.'[70] Coleridge's tautegory is very close to Rahner's *real symbol*. To Rahner, a real symbol 'does not divide as it mediates but unites immediately, because the true symbol is united with the thing symbolized, since the latter constitutes the former as its own self-realisation.'[71] And Rahner's view is echoed by Farrer, who writes: 'a symbol endeavours, as it were, to *be* that of which it speaks.'[72] Within the subcreated world of Narnia the depiction of Aslan accords well with these three definitions of symbol. In *The Lion*, for example, Aslan is the especial presence of Jupiter in a generally Jovial world; he is constituted by Jove as Jove's own self-realisation; he *is* that of which he symbolically speaks.

And across the series Aslan performs this role seven times over so that the One is radiated through the Many. Lewis's technique is the opposite of Hardy's in *The Dynasts*, a play that consists of 'the invention of a whole pantheon to symbolise the non-existence of God.'[73] Lewis's 'dynasts seven' are a planetary pantheon deployed in order to symbolise the paradoxical existence of a God who is simultaneously both near and far, both speaking and silent. Ingeniously applying the imagery of Psalm 19, which he considered the greatest poem in the psalter and one of the finest lyrics in the world, Lewis portrayed the divine nature as at once utterly proximate and utterly remote.

> The heavens declare the glory of God:
> and the firmament sheweth his handywork...
> There is neither speech nor language:
> but their voices are heard among them.
> Their sound is gone out into all lands
> and their words into the ends of the world.[74]

How may a speechless tongue be heard? How may wordlessness communicate a message? How is it that the planets (like Count Moltke) can be 'silent in seven languages'? The Narniad may be understood as Lewis's imaginative answer to these questions as, following St. Paul's example (Romans 10:18), he hears the voice of Christ in the music of the spheres.

In this connection, it is interesting to see how closely the character of Aslan is linked to the Narnian heavenly bodies. After the founding of Narnia, Aslan announces to his new creation all the things that he is giving it, a list that concludes with the discrete sentence: 'I give you the stars and I give you myself.' And in *The Silver Chair*, when the wanderers are lost in the Underworld, they remember the 'sun and moon and stars and Aslan himself.' It seems natural, within Narnia, to pass from consideration of the heavenly bodies to consideration of the Christ-figure, and this should not surprise us once we understand that Lewis is using the sun and moon and wandering stars to represent Christ under seven veils, seven kinds of iconography: King, Commander, Light, Son, Word, Life, Mystery. Lewis has fashioned, within the genre of romance, a menorah of Christological titles. Aslan is presented, like Hamlet's father, with

> ...the front of Jove himself,
> An eye like Mars, to threaten and command,

A station like the herald Mercury
New-lighted on a heaven-kissing hill,
A combination and a form indeed,
Where every god did seem to set his seal.[75]

And this variety of titles is itself of theological significance. An image of Christ, in Lewis's view, is only 'a model or symbol, certain to fail us in the long run and, even while we use it, requiring correction from other models.'[76] To that extent it is no different from an image of the cosmos. The Einsteinian model of the cosmos has not completely supplanted the Newtonian model; nor did the Newtonian model improve upon the Ptolemaic model in absolutely every respect. At any rate, Lewis suggests that the Newtonian model (with its metaphors of 'laws' and of physical bodies 'obeying rules') is a good deal more anthropomorphic than the Ptolemaic model with its characteristic metaphor of 'kindly enclyning.' Cosmologies, like Christologies, are fallible human constructs, and must therefore be approached with due provisionality. The Lewis who wrote, 'My idea of God is not a divine idea,'[77] could also write, and from much the same perspective, 'No Model [of the universe] is a catalogue of ultimate realities.'[78] Insofar as an image of God becomes divine it becomes demonic and then the true God, in mercy, shatters it: 'He is the great iconoclast.'[79] Likewise, 'it is not impossible that our own [Einsteinian] Model will die a violent death, ruthlessly smashed by an unprovoked assault of new facts'; therefore let us continually bear in mind those 'considerations that may induce us to regard all Models in the right way, respecting each and idolising none.'[80]

Lewis's favourite model of the universe was that of Richard Hooker to whom he affords pride of place at the climax of his chapter on prose in the Golden Period in *English Literature in the Sixteenth Century*. There he writes: 'Every system offers us a model of the universe; Hooker's model has unsurpassed grace and majesty. . . . Few model universes are more filled—one might say, more drenched—with Deity than his,' for '"every effect proceeding from the most concealed instincts of nature" manifests His power.' Enamoured of this theological vision, Lewis sought to recreate it in the Narniad, where even what is concealed from the reader manifests the divine character being depicted.

Why Did Lewis Not Disclose the Secret?

A final objection remains to be considered. If this disclosure has such beneficial effects, exposing literary-historical and theological depths to the septet, why did Lewis not reveal the secret himself? Admittedly, it might have been unwise to flag up the scheme in advance of publication, or early in the reception history, but why did he not divulge it after ten years, say, or in his final illness, or at least in his will? Was such persistent caution really necessary?

To which I would reply that there is a huge difference between what an author does and what a critic does. The same revelation may have very different effects depending upon who makes it and under what circumstances. Undressing oneself and being undressed by someone else, though they may result in an identical state of nakedness, are not identical processes. Lewis chose to tell Arthur Greeves, with regard to 'The Quest of Bleheris,' that its 'inner meaning' was carefully hidden; and he felt it was necessary to provide explanatory chapter headlines in later editions of *The Pilgrim's Regress*. But with the Chronicles of Narnia and their kappa element he was content to wait silently and patiently. He was of the belief that 'what the reader is made to do for himself has a particular importance'[81] and he evidently considered the planetary secret to be something that should be won, not given away. The very process of winning it would engender in the discoverer certain responses that could not arise if the design were announced by the designer.

At this point I am forced to speak personally, and I must say that the making of this discovery has struck me as something analogous to a scientific breakthrough or even a religious revelation. Science and religion are often (and often unreflectively) opposed, as if they were incommensurable modes of discourse. Lewis thought otherwise, and I think I see the fruits of that thought both in the donegalitarian technique that this book has outlined and in Lewis's determination not to tell anyone about it.

For Lewis, all knowledge, except the most basic, was metaphorical.[82] A paradigm shift in science, such as the Copernican revolution, is understood and communicated metaphorically just as much as a conversion in religion, such as that which befell Saul on the Damascus Road. The new metaphors are accepted because they seem to account for the facts (to 'save the appearances') more adequately than the old metaphors. From that point of view, they liberate their discoverers to live in the world more fully and intelligently. However, once accepted, these metaphors also constrain; they channel thoughts and expectations in certain ways.

In connection with scientific progress, the cosmology that a given generation accepts has immense consequences for its thoughts and emotions, and there is always a 'mythology which follows in the wake of science,'[83] a mythology that feeds into our understanding of ourselves and the way we imaginatively interpret the world and our place in it. Garrett Green makes the point well: 'From Galileo and Newton to Einstein and Stephen Hawking, the reigning scientific models of the cosmos have provided the larger culture with powerful analogies and metaphors that shape its epistemology, its poetry, its politics, and its religion . . . many of the leading postmodernist ideas borrow much of their imagery and not a little of their social prestige from scientific notions of relativity, uncertainty, and incommensurability.'[84]

Lewis was particularly alive to the cultural consequences of scientific paradigm shifts because of his intimate scholarly acquaintance with the Copernican revolution. His *magnum opus* begins with a fourteen-page treatment of 'the new astronomy' which was pioneered by Nicolas of Cusa, theorised by Copernicus, and verified by Kepler and Galileo. He concludes that what proved important about the new astronomy was not the mere alteration in our map of space but the methodological revolution which verified it:

> By reducing Nature to her mathematical elements it substituted a mechanical for a genial or animistic conception of the universe. The world was emptied, first of her indwelling spirits, then of her occult sympathies and antipathies, finally of her colours, smells, and tastes. (Kepler at the beginning of his career explained the motion of the planets by their *anima motrices;* before he died, he explained it mechanically.) The result was dualism rather than materialism. The mind, on whose ideal constructions the whole method depended, stood over against its object in ever sharper dissimilarity. Man with his new powers became rich like Midas but all that he touched had gone dead and cold. This process, slowly working, ensured during the next century the loss of the old mythical imagination: the conceit, and later the personified abstraction, takes its place. Later still, as a desperate attempt to bridge a gulf which begins to be found intolerable, we have the Nature poetry of the Romantics.[85]

The important parts of this passage are the references to 'the mind, on whose ideal constructions the whole method depended' and the 'mythical imagination.' The isolation of the one and the loss of the other were not necessary or logical consequences of Copernicus's theory: they were the unscientific or non-scientific collateral effects caused by his scientific advance. Lewis might be thought to be drawing here upon the ideas of Max Weber whose theory of 'disenchantment' bears some striking similarities to this account, but Lewis never mentions Weber in his writings and there is little to suggest that he had read him. If Lewis is indebted to anyone in particular for the picture he paints of a disenchanted cosmos, it is to Owen Barfield, who had written in *Poetic Diction*:

> Science deals with the world which it perceives but, seeking more and more to penetrate the veil of naive perception, progresses only towards the goal of nothing, because it still does not accept in practice (whatever it may admit theoretically) that the mind first creates what it

perceives as objects, including the instruments which Science uses for that very penetration. It insists on dealing with 'data,' but there shall no data be given, save the bare percept. The rest is imagination. Only by imagination therefore can the world be known. And what is needed is, not only that larger and larger telescopes should be constructed, but that the human mind should become increasingly aware of its own creative activity.[86]

Barfield goes on to argue that Newton with his 'gravity' (originally 'weight') and Kepler with his 'focus' (originally 'hearth') were developing meaning, not discovering 'fact.' These terms were as much part of their 'instruments' as the material instruments themselves; they were concepts applied to percepts in new ways which were judged to be illuminating, but which were functions of the imagination rather than 'objective' tools. Scientific and poetic knowledge are therefore indistinguishable in kind. The scientific method does not give us a new way of knowing, only a new way of testing.

To Lewis (as to Barfield), scientists in the modern period were too often naturalistic in their worldview, apt to commit the error of removing their own minds and their thinking processes from the total picture of the world that they were trying to understand and inhabit. This error necessarily de-spiritualises the universe, for the rational mind is itself spiritual, dependent upon the *logos* that saturates the universe and which, in turn, depends upon God Himself. The universe, perceived within such a naturalistic paradigm, becomes 'all fact and no meaning.'[87] The incessant spiritual orchestration that accompanies it, that actually constitutes it, and that is normally inaudible, is now also considered incredible. The cosmos therefore comes to be regarded as nothing more than a very elaborate machine when in reality it is tingling with life; a star comes to be seen as no more than a huge ball of flaming gas when in reality the gas is 'not what a star is but only what it is made of.'[88] And so Kerby-Fulton is right to state that 'for Lewis there is an analogy between the alienation of modern man and the post-Newtonian view of the universe' and to point out that his thought here echoes that of Blake, who famously prayed (in his letter to Thomas Butts): 'May God us keep / From single vision and Newton's sleep.' In Lewis's regretful view, for all that contemporary star-gazers had in common with their sixteenth-century forebears they might as well be staring at a completely different sky.

Lewis was fascinated by the fact that identical phenomena could be perceived in diametrically opposite ways. In *The Pilgrim's Regress*, the country looks different to John on his homeward journey from how it had looked on the outward leg; in *The Great Divorce*, the overarching conceit of the novel is the inability of self-imprisoned souls correctly to perceive the nature of heaven and the saints; and in *Till We Have Faces*, Orual's blindness to Psyche's palace is the central alteration Lewis makes to Apuleius's myth. 'Spiritual things,' he wrote (quoting St. Paul), 'are spiritually discerned.'[89] When a Russian cosmonaut claimed not to have found evidence of God in outer space, Lewis's response was, 'Much depends on the seeing eye.'[90]

The seeing eye that has stared through telescopes in the post-Copernican period has typically been an eye with 'single vision,' one which notices matter and mechanism and little or nothing else. The old 'genial' universe, teeming with spiritual significance, purpose, and relation, has become, like Nelson's ships, invisible; the new model universe, with the sun glaring at its centre, puts those fugitive qualities in the shade. Having successfully superseded the geocentric model, the new cosmology has turned out to be also a Trojan Horse for a rationalist mythology. Athene now rules; Demeter has been cast out.

In Lewis's poem 'Reason,' he reincorporates Demeter into the methodology of belief. Right belief, he thought, came about through the union of clear-eyed Athene (reason) with the dark, warm, 'dim exploring touch' of Demeter (imagination). Maid and mother must be thus combined before one can conceive the universe aright, let alone envisage the God who made it.

Not that he believed divinity to be in the eye of the beholder. On the contrary, he believed the eye of the beholder to be in the divinity, for human sight and insight were created, sustained, and redeemed (or not redeemed) by God. Why some people, like Moses, could talk to God face to face, while others had to descry Him through a glass darkly or not at all, was a deep and painful mystery to Lewis. Yet if that was God's way, there was no point trying to be wiser than God. 'Verily, thou art a God that hidest thyself,' declares Isaiah (Isa. 45:15); 'Unto them that are without, all these things are done in parables, that seeing that may not see,' says Christ (Mark 4:11). And since only through Christ is the veil of blindness removed (2 Cor. 3:14), the Christian may relax: God cannot be revealed if He chooses to remain hidden. Hence Lewis's poem, 'The Apologist's Evening Prayer': 'From all my proofs of Thy divinity, / Thou, who wouldst give no sign, deliver me.'[91] These sorts of considerations, it may be supposed, provided him with a reason to keep silence about his Narnian secret: he was following an example given by the divine Author.

But perhaps that is to overstate the seriousness of Lewis's intentions. Maybe he was just conducting a playful literary experiment, curious to know whether his readers would recognise the Chronicles' symbolic structure, that structure in which, with consummate irony, a wilfully discarded image of the cosmos is used to symbolise God's wilfully concealed presence. 'How long will it take them?' Lewis may have wondered to himself. 'What, if anything, will cause the scales to fall from their eyes?' This leads us to the subject of the final chapter.

TWELVE

Coda

The heaven remembering throws sweet influence still on earth.
—'My Heart Is Empty' (lines 19–20)

The medieval planetary geists that animate the Chronicles of Narnia remained unrecognised for over half a century. Many better minds than mine have studied these books in the five decades since their publication without identifying the cosmological theme, and so it may be of interest to the reader to know how the discovery was made. I had not been looking for the books' governing idea: the thing was entirely unexpected and fortuitous. Nevertheless it is of some personal importance to me to explain how it came about.

Before I do so, it may be worth trying to account for the fact that no one had previously discerned their symbolic scheme, and here I ought to preface my remarks by saying that I had been reading Lewis for thirty years and studying him for nearly half that time, before happening upon this imaginative blueprint. The comments that I am about to make are intended partly as criticisms of my own previous writing on Lewis; they are not meant to apply only to the work of my colleagues in this field.

There are three main explanations for the overlooking of this matter in the half century since the Narniad was originally published.

The first has to do with Owen Barfield, who unwittingly laid something of a false trail across the field of Lewis studies by repeatedly drawing attention to Lewis's emphasis upon God's transcendence (see chapter 2, note 56). Given his status as 'the wisest and best'[1] of Lewis's unofficial counsellors, Barfield's views have received close attention. Most of that attention has been fully deserved, but in this one respect Barfield's testimony is highly subjective and, indeed, ironic, given that his own *Poetic Diction*, with its theory of 'participant knowledge,' was extremely influential on his friend. There were good reasons for Lewis to have emphasised divine transcendence in his private conversations with the anthroposophist Barfield, but it does not follow that there was a similar emphasis in his overall theological outlook. This book has argued that, among other things, the planetary imagery that informs the Chronicles expresses something of divine immanence. Barfield's opinions would not incline researchers to suppose that Lewis was especially interested in immanence.

The second reason is that the books' secret was already considered open. It was always known that the Narniad had more than one level of meaning. Scholars were familiar with the second level—the Christian 'suppositions'—about which Lewis spoke freely. Many were not looking for a third stratum of significance. It is not as though the Chronicles were utterly incomprehensible without this donegalitarian key, and many readers were content to accept that the septet's apparent lack of homogeneity was evidence of hasty writing, not a sign of an unidentified inner meaning. Since Tolkien dismissed the Narniad as a mishmash it is hardly surprising that many critics have done the same.

And the final reason is that those critics who *were* looking for a third level (I myself once made a desultory attempt to link the Chronicles to Shakespearean plays) may not have been as open to the subject of astrology as his work really requires, for, as I have pointed out, astrology, a subject disdained by academics, tends to be given a doubly wide berth by Christian academics. Since most Lewis scholars have been Christian or well-disposed to the Christian tradition, there was an in-built improbability that researchers would fully understand his most successful work.

For instance, even where astrology is explicit in Lewis's work, it has received surprisingly little attention. The Ransom Trilogy is infused throughout with astrological symbolism, but in the only major study of that trilogy, *Planets in Peril* by David C. Downing, there is only a single chapter on its medieval and renaissance background, and very little of that is concerned with astrology. Some of the other chapter headings indicate where the author's principal interests lie: ' "Smuggled Theology": The Christian Vision of the Trilogy'; ' "Souls Who Have Lost the Intellectual Good": Portraits of Evil'; 'Ransom and Lewis: Cosmic Voyage as Spiritual Pilgrimage.' In the last volume of the trilogy Dimble predicts that there will be no mention of the planets when newspapers give their accounts of what has happened; the same could nearly be said of critical treatments of the story itself.

And in studies of Lewis's poetry, where astrology abounds, the avoidance mentality meets us again. The pioneering study of Lewis's poetic legacy by Don W. King repeatedly overlooks astrological symbolism. For instance, in discussing 'Break, Sun, my Crusted Earth,' King takes the metaphor in the title as a 'mining metaphor' when it is clearly an astrological one. In discussing the conclusion of *Dymer*, he focusses on Balder and makes no reference to the inclusion of 'Saturnian years.' In discussing 'Thou Only Art Alternative to God,' he inexplicably omits the word 'Venus' in his quotation of the last line.

If this is the situation apropos the outright and obvious astrology in Lewis's work, it is to be expected that the fundamental but implicit astrology of the Narnia Chronicles would escape detection all the more.

In *An Experiment in Criticism*, Lewis ponders 'who loves Dante as a poet and who loves him as a Thomist.' A similar question could be asked in the field of Lewis studies: 'Who loves him as a writer and who loves him as a Christian?' His status as a Christian too often causes Pavlovian reactions of approval among his co-religionist readership;[2] his interest in astrology gets overlooked in the rush to lionise him. As in all schools of study, there is a tendency to concentrate on those elements in the author's writings that harmonise best with critics' existing interests, rather than a willingness to swallow him *tout à fait*. This inevitable predisposition is mentioned not for the purpose of denigrating Lewis scholarship, but simply to help explain the length of time it has taken for his planetary plan to be discovered. The analysis given in this book may have been a long time coming, but it is not to be mistrusted on that account.

Robert Houston Smith and Nancy-Lou Patterson are the only two critics known to this author who have already seen parallels between the Chronicles and the planets: Houston Smith has noticed the Lunar divide in *The Silver Chair*; Patterson has seen something of the Saturnine influence in *The Last Battle*. However, they have not pursued these leads within those stories nor stepped outside those particular texts to see whether such planetary symbolism is to be found across the septet. A third critic, Peter Milward, recognises the importance of Jupiter in Lewis's imagination and comes close to finding the donegality of *The Lion, the Witch and the Wardrobe*: 'he was indeed a jovial man; and these qualities of his I later recognised . . . in his character of the kingly animal Aslan.'[3] As it happens, none of these critics provided the spark for the research that led to this book: their observations were not discovered until it was into its stride. Nevertheless, they provide a sort of unwitting and retroactive corroboration of its findings.

Before leaving the subject of Lewis's other critics, we must mention Sammons and Foster among those of his readers who have paid attention to his sidereal preoccupations;[4] also Oliver, who holds that the medieval model is 'foundational to Lewis's theology.'[5] Even taken together, their studies do not amount to a satisfactory treatment of the subject, and it is a remarkable oversight, for celestial interest is certainly a major feature of the total Lewis landscape—necessarily, for Lewis thought that, by definition, 'if you have religion it must be cosmic.'[6] His characteristic approach to religion, with its lack of interest in sectarian and denominational questions, is itself partly attributable to his preoccupation with the extra-mundane dimension, for he thought that those who 'stare long at the night sky are less likely than others to be ardent or orthodox partisans.'[7]

If I am right and there has been a reluctance to touch the subject of astrology in Lewis's oeuvre, it will be worth assessing the degree of credence he actually accorded it.

Did Lewis Believe in Astrology?

The modern distinction between astronomy and astrology is not one that clearly existed before the end of the sixteenth century, as Lewis himself observed.[8] Given his immersion in pre-Copernican categories, it may be somewhat unfair to apply that distinction to his own habits of thought. However, if we do, we find that he was interested in both disciplines.

He was a keen amateur astronomer who had a telescope on the balcony of his bedroom and enjoyed visiting the Oxford observatory.[9] He knew about such things as Venus's albedo and was conversant with the broad outlines of the work of such figures in astronomy and physics as Schiaparelli, Ball, Jeans, Eddington, Schrödinger (his Magdalen colleague), and Hoyle,[10] as well as that of more speculative writers such as Dunne, Abbott, Hinton, and Ouspenski.[11] He was not at all like 'the modern educated man' he scorns, who, 'though 'interested in astronomy,' knows neither who the Pleiades were nor where to look for them in the sky.'[12]

As for astrology, the foregoing chapters have shown that Lewis's imaginative fascination with it was life-long and deep. His teenage interest in Scott's novel *Guy Mannering* was piqued simply because its subtitle was 'The Astrologer.' The story, as it turned out, was a disappointment and over forty years later he was still complaining about how badly Scott described the planets.[13] However, he never lost his taste for the subject, and the value he attached to the image of the music of the spheres may be seen in the way he described the final moments of his married life: 'Even after all hope was gone, even on the last night before [Joy's] death, there were 'patins of bright gold.'[14] The quotation is from Shakespeare's *The Merchant of Venice* (V, I, 58ff), where Lorenzo says:

Sit Jessica. Look how the floor of heaven
Is thick inlaid with patins of bright gold:
There's not the smallest orb which thou behold'st
But in his motion like an angel sings,

Still quiring to the young-eyed cherubins;
Such harmony is in immortal souls;
But whilst this muddy vesture of decay
Doth grossly close it in, we cannot hear it

But aside from an imaginative and aesthetic appreciation of the heavens, did Lewis entertain a more literal belief in astrology?

As George Watson has observed, Lewis was endlessly counter-suggestible. He was far more open-minded than his occasional 'bow-wow dogmatism' (his own self-critical term) might suggest, and it occurred to him that the objects of medieval and renaissance thought that it was his job to study might have a concrete reality. Noting of Paracelsus and Ficino that they both admitted the possible existence of aquatic elemental spirits, he adds, 'and who knows, perhaps in this as in so many things the ancients knew more than we.'[15] Those 'many things' may well have included astrological influence, for elsewhere he wrote 'we presume' that the galaxies cannot think,[16] as though he were open to the idea that they might be capable of thought. When wondering why there were many men of genius born in the latter half of the sixteenth century, he remarks that 'the Elizabethans themselves would have attributed it to Constellation'; he sounds somewhat dejected when he goes on, 'I must be content with trying to sketch some of the intellectual and imaginative conditions under which they wrote.'[17] He concedes that 'the stars lost their divinity as astronomy developed,' but maintains that 'it is not the greatest modern scientists who feel most sure that the object, stripped of its qualitative properties and reduced to mere quantity, is wholly real. Little scientists, and little unscientific followers of science, may think so. The great minds know very well that the object, so treated, is an artificial abstraction, that something of its reality has been lost.'[18] So, when Lewis thanked 'all good stars'[19] for fortunate events, it was not for him an entirely empty phrase.

On the other hand, he once stated (albeit in an article that was never published in his lifetime) that he did not believe in 'the astrological character of the planets' as they appear in his Ransom Trilogy.[20] He described the night sky as 'inanimate,'[21] and, in a letter to a Mr Anderson, he calls astrology 'an aberration of the human mind.'[22] The epistolary context of this remark is hard to ascertain because we have only Lewis's side of the correspondence, but it would seem likely that he is reining in Mr Anderson from an excessively eager interest in the subject, not absolutely ruling out the possibility of sidereal influence. Usually, in his public writings, he is aiming to jolt his readers out of what he regards as a likely over-materialistic world-view and make them consider the rich and mysterious potencies with which the universe may be teeming. He is doing something more than merely telling a story when, in *The Last Battle*, he has Roonwit assert: 'If Aslan were really coming to Narnia the sky would have foretold it . . . all the most gracious stars would be assembled in his honour.'

This general perspective on astrology—wondering what may be possible and refusing to adopt hard and fast negative positions—is perhaps the most we can say of Lewis's position on the matter. We could do worse than equate Lewis with his own protagonist, Ransom, who 'found it night by night more difficult to disbelieve in old astrology: almost he felt, wholly he imagined, 'sweet influence' pouring or even stabbing into his surrendered body.'[23] In fact, Lewis virtually admits that that is his own view. After having seen an unusual conjunction of the planets one night, he wrote to his brother that he now 'understood what is at the back of all astrology,' namely, 'the difficulty of believing that anything so splendid is without significance.'[24]

In conclusion, if we cannot say that he believed in astrology, we can say that he found it difficult to disbelieve. He once noted how the Venetian Franciscan, Francesco Giorgi, in his *De Harmonia Mundi Totius* (1525), had 'made his religion entirely absorb his astrology.'[25] Lewis's own attitude could be characterised in the same way: he did not uncritically accept the practice, but nor did he utterly disown it; rather, as if it were a fellow sinner, he 'baptised it'[26] and put it to use in theologically imaginative ways.

The Discovery

Now to the discovery that led to this book, and first, it is worth noting that any 'Eureka' moment, however unplanned, inevitably has a history. In this case it consisted of thirty years' exposure to the texts in question, ten years' teaching Lewis to undergraduates, three years' living at The Kilns, Lewis's Oxford home,[27] and eighteen months' work on this doctoral research, which originated under the provisional title, 'C. S. Lewis and the Word: Christ, Scripture and Language.'

As for the moment itself, it occurred in 2003 as I was nearing the end of my ordination training, and in retrospect I am able to see that it was prompted by two things. A friend, Christopher Holmwood, gave me the soundtrack to the Royal Shakespeare Company's production of *The Lion, the Witch and the Wardrobe*. As one does when one first acquires a new piece of music, I listened to it several times in just a few days. Although I did not think highly of every number in this composition, there were one or two tracks that I felt interpreted parts of the story extremely well. More pertinent, though, was the simple fact of immersing myself in an orchestral and mostly non-verbal rendering of Lewis's work. Without knowing it, I was attuning my mind to the musicality of the tale, the 'symphonic treatment of the images,' by which Lewis set so much store.

Within the week came my regular termly meeting in Cambridge with the Rt Revd Simon Barrington-Ward, the former Bishop of Coventry, to whom I used to go in order to discuss my progress in ordination training and to receive spiritual direction. Bishop Simon knew Lewis well; he worked at Magdalene College, Cambridge, during the time when Lewis was there as Professor of Medieval and Renaissance Literature.[28] The two men used to go walking together and spoke with one another at quite a close personal level despite the difference in their ages. After Lewis had resigned his Fellowship and been elected an Honorary Fellow of Magdalene he wrote to the Master and Fellows of the College making a specific request of his young friend:

> The ghosts of the wicked old women in Pope 'haunt the places where their honour died'. I am more fortunate, for I shall haunt the place whence the most valued of my honours came.
>
> I am constantly with you in imagination. If in some twilit hour anyone sees a bald and bulky spectre in the Combination Room or the garden, don't get Simon to exorcise it, for it is a harmless wraith and means nothing but good.[29]

In my meeting with Bishop Simon on this occasion he was helping me to understand what Lewis meant by 'wordless prayer,' a significant theme of *Letters to Malcolm* and one that had occupied much of the first year of my doctoral research. In order to do this he opened up Archimandrite Sophrony's biography of Father Silouan, *The Monk of Mount Athos*, and read aloud the passage describing Silouan's meeting with the Russian ascetic, Father Stratonicos. Although this passage had nothing directly to do with Lewis, let alone his understanding of medieval cosmology, it illustrated well the subject of wordlessness which in turn (as it later transpired) proved to illuminate the planetary theme of the Chronicles.

Stratonicos, a wise and eloquent monk, full of his own intelligence, has nothing to say when Silouan, in all simplicity, asks him how the perfect speak: he suddenly realises that he does not know the first thing about perfect speech. But his inability to speak allows him to hear, and into his humbled silence Silouan plants the message that 'The perfect never say anything of themselves.... They only say what the Spirit suffers them to say.'[30] Spiritual utterances in prayer, so Silouan suggests, are not just human words directed to a spiritual listener with spiritual intent; they are a participation in (one might say an Enjoyment of) the Holy Spirit himself. Silouan's point, I saw, was essentially the same as that made by Lewis in *Letters to Malcolm*: 'In prayer, God speaks to God.'

This account of Silouan's exchange with Stratonicos made an extraordinarily deep impact on me. There was a momentous charge in the words I was hearing and the atmosphere in the room suddenly became somehow intense and palpable. It was a most unusual experience and I went back to my theological college, Ridley Hall, in a kind of daze. Exactly what had happened to me, I did not know, but I felt it to be of tremendous import.

Before going to sleep that night, I lay reading 'The Heavens,' Chapter V of *The Discarded Image*, when the thought occurred to me that it would be useful to compare and contrast Lewis's academic understanding of the subject with his poetic treatment of the same, so I took up my copy of his collected poems and began reading 'The Planets.' The phrase 'winter passed / And guilt forgiven' sprang from the page, demanding attention. I had come across the passing of winter and the forgiving of guilt elsewhere in Lewis's writings: those things formed the centrepiece of his first Narnia tale. Could there be a link somehow between poem and Chronicle? That thought was the stray spark connecting Jupiter to *The Lion* in my mind, and one by one the other planet-to-book relationships began to be lit up in its train.

As the whole pattern swam into my ken I revisited my conversation with Simon Barrington-Ward. Silouan had mentioned to Stratonicos the notion of irradiated utterance, the Holy Spirit speaking through human prayers; here in Lewis's fiction was an imaginative version of a similar sort of thing, spiritual symbols irradiating stories. I immediately and instinctively knew, though it took much longer to understand with clarity, that Lewis had cryptically designed the Chronicles so that the seven heavens spoke through them like a kind of language or song. He had translated the planets into plots, and the music of the spheres could be heard silently sounding (or tingling, as he would have said) in each work. I recalled that he liked to compare literary images with musical themes and that he thought that both should be richly expressive of mood, existing 'in every possible relation of contrast, mutual support, development, variation, half-echo, and the like.'[31] The Narniad, I now started to see, was a literary equivalent of Holst's *Planets Suite*; each one of the seven heavens gave the key to a different Chronicle. I did not shout 'Eureka!' and run naked down the street like Archimedes, but I did jump from my bed in a state of undress and began to pull books from my shelves, chasing links from work to work.

Simon Barrington-Ward himself deserves the last word. When I told him of the discovery of this 'kappa element' he recognised it straightaway as the sort of thing that Lewis would do. What I have called the donegalitarian technique was characteristic of Lewis, he thought, because of its playfulness and also because of its secretiveness. He perceived long ago that Lewis had a high estimation of the tangential, the tacit, the implicit. Writing about his old colleague shortly after his death, Barrington-Ward maintained that the secret of his personality and of his writings was a kind of hiddenness or shyness.[32] It was through being 'oblique,' he said, that Lewis brings home to us 'the great realities.' 'Indirectly, not by a frontal assault,' the burden of his works is imparted. 'Gradually, almost insensibly,' we come to share his feeling—his feeling for what? 'For the majestic order that runs through all things, *L'amor che move il sole e l'altre stelle.'*

LIST OF ABBREVIATIONS

AGO   *A Grief Observed*
AMR   *All My Road Before Me: The Diary of C. S. Lewis, 1922–1927*
AOL   *The Allegory of Love*
AOM   *The Abolition of Man*
AT   *Arthurian Torso*
B   *Boxen*
CP   *Collected Poems* (1994)
DI   *The Discarded Image*
DT   *The Dark Tower*
EC   *Essay Collection*
EIC   *An Experiment in Criticism*
EL   *English Literature in the Sixteenth Century*
FL   *The Four Loves*
GD   *The Great Divorce*
GMD   *George MacDonald: An Anthology*
HHB   *The Horse and His Boy*
LB   *The Last Battle*
LCSL   *Letters of C. S. Lewis* (1966)
LTM   *Letters to Malcolm*
LWW   *The Lion, the Witch and the Wardrobe*
M   *Miracles*
MC   *Mere Christianity*
MN   *The Magician's Nephew*

NP	*Narrative Poems*
OSP	*Out of the Silent Planet*
OTOW	*Of This and Other Worlds*
PC	*Prince Caspian*
Per	*Perelandra*
PH	*The Personal Heresy*
POP	*The Problem of Pain*
PPL	*A Preface to 'Paradise Lost'*
PR	*The Pilgrim's Regress*
PRCON	*Present Concerns*
ROP	*Reflections on the Psalms*
SBJ	*Surprised by Joy*
SC	*The Silver Chair*
SIL	*Spenser's Images of Life*
SIW	*Studies in Words*
SL	*The Screwtape Letters*
SLE	*Selected Literary Essays*
SMRL	*Studies in Medieval and Renaissance Literature*
TAH	*Timeless at Heart*
THS	*That Hideous Strength*
TWHF	*Till We Have Faces*
VDT	*The Voyage of the 'Dawn Treader'*

NOTES ✑

CHAPTER I

1. Plato, *The Republic*, Book II.
2. Alasdair MacIntyre, *After Virtue: A Study in Moral Theory* (London: Duckworth, 1985) 216.
3. Sarah Zettel, 'Why I Love Narnia: A Liberal, Feminist Agnostic Tells All,' in Shanna Caughey (ed.), *Revisiting Narnia: Fantasy, Myth and Religion in C. S. Lewis' Chronicles* (Dallas: BenBella Books, Inc., 2005) 181–190.
4. George Sayer, *Jack: C. S. Lewis and His Times* (San Francisco: Harper & Row, 1988) xvii.
5. Owen Barfield, 'Introduction,' in Jocelyn Gibb (ed.), *Light on C. S. Lewis* (London: Geoffrey Bles, 1965) ix–xxi: xxi.
6. Malcolm Muggeridge, 'The Mystery,' in Stephen Schofield (ed.), *In Search of C. S. Lewis* (South Plainfield, NJ: Bridge Publishing, 1983) 127–128.
7. Stephen Medcalf, 'Language and Self-Consciousness: The Making and Breaking of C. S. Lewis's Personae,' in Peter J. Schakel & Charles A. Huttar, (eds.), *Word and Story in C. S. Lewis* (Columbia: University of Missouri Press, 1991) 109–144.
8. See 'Posturing' (CP 103) and 'Legion' (CP 133).
9. 'Jack tried to justify his delay in traveling to Ireland during the long vacation of 1919 by lying.... In the pre-Christian stage of his life, Jack did not hesitate to write whatever he thought necessary to keep his father happy.' Sayer, *Jack*, 88–90.

'My relations to my father help to explain (I am not suggesting that they excuse) one of the worst acts of my life. I allowed myself to be prepared for confirmation, and confirmed, and make my first Communion, in total disbelief,' SBJ 130.

10. Sayer, *Jack*, 238.

11. Sayer, *Jack*, 198.

12. He told Sayer that his marriage 'should be kept secret' and it was, from 23 Apr to 24 Dec 1956. See Sayer, *Jack*, 221–223.

13. See George Sayer, 'Jack on Holiday,' in James T. Como (ed.), *C. S. Lewis at the Breakfast Table and Other Reminiscences* (London: Collins, 1980) 208; A. N. Wilson, *C. S. Lewis, A Biography* (London: Collins, 1990) 209. Cf. letter to Sheldon Vanauken, 15 Dec 1958.

14. Sayer, *Jack*, 209.

15. Sayer, *Jack*, 238.

16. CLII 483. Cf. letters to Sir Henry Willink, 23 Jan 1957 and 3 Mar 1962.

17. Letter to Laurence Whistler, 4 Mar 1962.

18. See Alan Bede Griffiths, 'The Adventure of Faith,' in James T. Como (ed.), *C. S. Lewis at the Breakfast Table and Other Reminiscences* (London: Collins, 1980). He wrote under the name 'N. W. Clerk' to Mrs John R. Rolston, 14 May 1962.

19. Humphrey Carpenter. *The Inklings: C. S. Lewis, J.R.R. Tolkien, Charles Williams, and Their Friends* (London: Allen & Unwin, 1978) 226.

20. Sayer, *Jack*, 189.

21. 'I had rather the feeling that, having got the story written down and out of his mind, the rest was someone else's job, and that he wouldn't interfere.' Letter of Pauline Baynes to Walter Hooper, 15 Aug 1967, quoted in Walter Hooper, *C. S. Lewis, A Companion and Guide* (London: HarperCollins, 1996) 406.

22. Sayer, *Jack*, 189.

23. Letter to Margaret Douglas, 31 Dec 1947.

24. Lionel Adey, *C. S. Lewis: Writer, Dreamer & Mentor* (Grand Rapids, MI: Eerdmans, 1998) 192.

25. Tolkien's work is 'consistent and plausible,' 'elaborately prepared,' and shows 'careful pacing.' Lewis's work is 'uneven,' 'hastily written,' and borrows 'indiscriminately from other mythologies and narratives' for 'Lewis threw in any incident or colouring that struck his fancy'. Carpenter, *Inklings*, 224–227. Carpenter gives no evidence or examples to support these opinions.

26. Wilson, *Biography*, 225–226. Wilson's acquaintance with the Chronicles is slight. For instance, he points out, as evidence of the Edwardianism of the stories, that the children say 'Crikey!' (221). In fact, the word 'Crikey' never appears in the septet.

27. 'But for the encouragement of C. S. L. I do not think that I should ever have completed or offered for publication *The Lord of the Rings*.' Letter of Tolkien to Clyde S. Kilby, 18 Dec 1965.

28. E.g., he criticises, *inter alia*, MC, GD, EL, SIW, and SL. See J.R.R. Tolkien, *The Letters of J.R.R. Tolkien*, ed. Humphrey Carpenter with the assistance of Christopher Tolkien (London: Allen & Unwin, 1981) 59–62; 71; 125–129; 302; 371. See also Sayer, *Jack*, 189.

29. Letter to Anthony Boucher, 5 Feb 1953.

30. Steven P. Mueller, 'Translated Theology: Christology in the Writings of C. S. Lewis,' in Angus J.L. Menuge (ed.), *C. S. Lewis, Lightbearer in the Shadow-lands: The Evangelistic Vision of C. S. Lewis* (Wheaton, IL: Crossway Books, 1997) 279–302: 291.

31. Doris T. Myers, *C. S. Lewis in Context* (Kent, OH: Kent State University Press, 1994) xiii, 112–181.

32. Doris T. Myers, 'Growing in Grace: The Anglican Spiritual Style in the Narnia Chronicles,' in David Mills (ed.), *The Pilgrim's Guide: C. S. Lewis and the Art of Witness* (Grand Rapids, MI: Eerdmans, 1998) 185–202.

33. Peter J. Schakel, *Reading with the Heart: The Way into Narnia* (Grand Rapids, MI: Eerdmans, 1979) xiii.

34. Charles A. Huttar, 'C. S. Lewis's Narnia and the "Grand Design,"' in Peter J. Schakel (ed.), *The Longing for a Form, Essays on the Fiction of C. S. Lewis* (Kent, OH: Kent State University Press, 1977) 130.

35. M. A. Manzalaoui, 'Narnia: The Domain of Lewis's Beliefs,' in David Graham (ed.), *We Remember C. S. Lewis: Essays and Memoirs* (Nashville: Broadman & Holman Publishers, 2001) 14.

36. 'Tasso,' SMRL 117.

37. Letter to Anne Jenkins, 5 Mar 1961.

38. Chad Walsh, *The Literary Legacy of C. S. Lewis* (London: Sheldon Press, 1979) 147.

39. '[Aslan] is an invention giving an imaginary answer to the question, "What might Christ become like if there were a world like Narnia and He chose to be incarnate and die and rise again in *that* world as He actually has done in ours?" This is not allegory at all....This...works out a *supposition*,' letter to Mrs Hook, 29 Dec 1958.

40. Charles Wrong, 'A Chance Meeting' in James. T. Como (ed.), *C. S. Lewis at the Breakfast Table and Other Reminiscences* (London: Collins, 1980) 107–114: 113.

41. 'It All Began with a Picture...,' EC 529.

42. SIL 137–140.

43. Letter to Charles Brady, 16 Nov 1956.

44. See Walter Hooper, 'To the Martlets,' in Carolyn Keefe (ed.), *C. S. Lewis: Speaker and Teacher* (London: Hodder & Stoughton, 1971) 49–83.

45. 'Hamlet: The Prince or the Poem?,' SLE 88–105: 104.

46. 'Abecedarium Philosophicum,' *The Oxford Magazine*, LII (13 Nov 1933) 298.

47. 'The Anthropological Approach,' SLE 301–311: 310.

48. SIL 115, Lewis's ellipsis. Cf. AOL 276; letter to Janet Spens, 8 Jan 1934.

49. 'Hamlet: The Prince or the Poem?,' SLE 101–102.

50. 'On Stories,' EC 498–504.

51. SBJ 174; Walter Hooper, *C. S. Lewis, A Companion and Guide* (London: HarperCollins, 1996) 577.

52. 'Meditation in a Toolshed,' EC 607.

53. SBJ 175.

54. 'Edmund Spenser, 1552–1599,' SMRL 137.

55. 'Hamlet: The Prince or the Poem?,' SLE 104–105.

56. Letters to Arthur Greeves, 16 May and 11 July 1916.

57. Letter to Arthur Greeves, 18 July 1916.

58. As regards language, 'hastilude,' 'gentilesse,' 'estres,' 'pajock,' 'seneschal,' 'cantrips,' and 'dromonds' are among the medieval (or at any rate medieval-sounding) words which help establish the desired atmosphere. As regards clothing, note the 'silk and cloth of gold . . . snowy linen glancing through slashed sleeves . . . silver mail shirts and jewelled sword hilts . . . gilt helmets and feathered bonnets' in PC. As regards polity, note that Narnia is a medieval monarchy in which sovereigns have real power under the law, and Bracton's definition of kingship ('The King is under the Law for it is the Law that maketh him a King,' see EL 48) is put into the mouth of King Lune in HHB. As regards geography, Narnia is a flat, not spherical, world (see VDT). As regards cosmology, the Narnia planets are said, in SC, to have 'influences.' And as regards cartography, note Lewis's letter to Pauline Baynes (5 Jan 1951) in which he asks for her map of Narnia to look 'more like a medieval map than an Ordnance Survey,' with winds blowing in the corners and dolphins sporting in the sea. For more on this subject, see Mary Frances Zambreno, 'A Reconstructed Image: Medieval Time and Space in The Chronicles of Narnia,' in Shanna Caughey (ed.), *Revisiting Narnia: Fantasy, Myth and Religion in C. S. Lewis' Chronicles* (Dallas: BenBella Books Inc., 2005) 253–265.

59. SIL 43.

60. SIL 82.

61. SIL 140.

62. SIL 7.

63. AOL 356.

64. Sir Philip Sidney, *The Complete Works of Sir Philip Sidney*, ed. A. Feuillerat, 4 vols. (Cambridge: Cambridge University Press, 1912–26), iii, 45. Cf. SIL 14.

65. '[T]he immense importance of what is not said, which delights us in Mr de la Mare': 'The Novels of Charles Williams,' EC 573; Irene Forsyte is 'one of the very few heroines whose beauty is made convincing, though it is never described,' AMR 105.

66. 'The Fantastic Imagination,' in George MacDonald, *The Complete Fairy Tales*, ed. U.C. Knoepflmacher (London: Penguin, 1999) 5–10: 9f.

67. SIW 317; SBJ 63; AOL 229; 'Imagery in the Last Eleven Cantos of Dante's Comedy,' SMRL 81; 'The Literary Impact of the Authorised Version', SLE 142; LTM 79; 'William Morris', SLE 226.

68. SMRL 52.

69. Sayer, *Jack*, 191.
70. Letter to Joan Lancaster, 7 May 1954; letter to Pauline Baynes, 24 May 1956.
71. DI 185.
72. E.g. 'seven brothers' (PC 69, 70), 'seven days' (SC 57; HHB 60, 66), 'seven feet tall' (MN 61), 'seven figures' (LB 109), 'seven friends' (VDT 20; LB 46), 'seven hours' (MN 126), 'Seven Isles' (PC 99; VDT 21, 134; SC 54; HHB 158), 'seven Kings and Queens' (LB 126), 'seven lords' (PC 57; VDT 40, 96, 159, 180), 'seven people' (LB 46, 47), 'seven years' (VDT 134, 150, 152), 'us seven' (LB 89), 'seven hundred nobles' (MN 57), 'seventh' day (HHB 174), 'seventh in descent' (LB 51), 'seventh son' (LB 153).
73. John Donne, *Donne's Sermons, Selected Passages with an Essay by Logan Pearsall Smith* (Oxford: Clarendon Press, 1919) 160.

CHAPTER 2

1. 'Imagination and Thought in the Middle Ages,' SMRL 51. See DI 113—120; POP 40.
2. DI 119.
3. EL 4.
4. Letter to his father, 28 Oct 1922. Cf. Ransom's whole frame is set 'tingling' when the Oyarsa speaks (Per 181); translunary beauty is like a 'tingling spear' in the poem 'An Expostulation: Against Too Many Writers of Science Fiction'; 'the cold, tingling, almost unbreathable, region of the aerial spirits' ('A Note on *Comus*,' SMRL 180). We should be alive to the astrological connotations of the word even in passages that do have not an explicit astrological connection: e.g. Dymer's body 'tingled' as he awoke from joyless conventionality (*Dymer*, I, ix, line 2, NP 9); Lewis accepts the 'feathery, impalpable, tingling invitation' to joy ('Hedonics,' EC 687); Lewis's ears 'tingled' under a frosty sky on the evening his imagination was baptised (SBJ 145). Cf. Tolkien's Quenya coinage, *tingilyë*, for a twinkling star.
5. Letter to Roger Lancelyn Green, 28 Dec 1938.
6. SBJ 34.
7. OSP 35. Cf. John Milton, *Comus*, lines 976–978.
8. DI 100. Lewis often uses the word 'space' himself in its modern, neutral, astronomical sense, but sometimes he clearly intends to load the term with negative meaning, as when Ransom declares 'space' to be 'the wrong word'; see also the poem 'Prelude to Space.' For this reason, it is better not to refer to *Out of the Silent Planet*, *Perelandra*, and *That Hideous Strength* as 'The Space Trilogy', but rather as 'The Ransom Trilogy' or 'The Cosmic Trilogy.'
9. Medieval cosmology assimilates a body of astronomical doctrines which represents, largely, the systematization of the work of Aristotle (384–322 B.C.) and Hipparchus of Alexandria (190–120 B.C.) by the Greco-Egyptian astronomer, Claudius Ptolemaeus (c. A.D. 100–170).

10. DI 110. Cf. 'On Being Human,' lines 33–34 (CP 48–49): 'I know the senses' witchery / Guards us, like air, from heavens too big to see.'

11. Letter to Arthur Greeves, 8 Nov 1931.

12. 'Is Theology Poetry?,' EC 10–21.

13. Letter to the Revd Henry Welbon, 18 Sept 1936 (Wade Center; not included in CLII or CLIII).

14. M 72.

15. Lewis's conversion to this point of view is recounted in his letter to Greeves, 18 Oct 1931.

16. SIL 14.

17. EL 619; 'Imagination and Thought in the Middle Ages,' SMRL 55. Lewis probably knew the view of John of Damascus (c.655–c.750) who wrote in his *Orthodox Faith* (Book 2, chapter 7) that 'the stars do not cause anything to happen,' but would have followed Aquinas, who cites this passage in his *Sentences* (Book 2) and explains it away by arguing that the Damascene denied the possibility of planetary influence unassisted by God. John's real purpose, according to Aquinas, was to prevent idolatry, not to deny the reality of influence.

    Tertullian (c.160–c.225) allowed that astrology was valid, but that it had changed with Christ's nativity: 'Astrology now ... is the science of the stars of Christ.' See Alexander Roberts and James Donaldson (eds). *Ante-Nicene Library* (1867), Vol. XI: Tertullian, I, page 152.

    For a discussion of Augustine's views on the subject, see L. Thorndike, *A History of Magic and Experimental Science* (1923), Vol. I, chapter xxii: 'Augustine on Magic and Astrology'.

18. Worship of the planets is repeatedly outlawed in the Bible: e.g., Deut. 4:19; 2 Kgs. 17:16; 21:3; 23:5; Job 31:26f; Jer. 8:2; 19:13.

19. Aquinas opposes the idea that influences cause anything more than propensities or tendencies (*Summa*, Ia, CXV, Art. 4), following Augustine who casts no doubt upon the fact of stellar influence but believes it can be overcome by man's free will and the grace of God (*De Civ. Dei*, V, 7.). Cf. Dante's *Purgatorio*, XVI, 67–81.

20. See DI 103.

21. Matt. 2:1–10. Cf. Gen. 1:14; Jer. 10:2; Matt. 24:29. Interpreting the significance of the stars is depicted negatively in Isa. 47:13 and Dan. 1:20; 2:27; 4:7; 5:7, but more, it seems, because it was practised by heathens for godless ends than because such astrological enquiry was considered evil *per se*.

22. See, e.g., 1 Kgs. 22:19; Job 38:7; Ps. 19:2; 148:2f; cf. Isa. 40:26. The Sun and the Moon are, of course, ubiquitous in the scriptures. Of the other five planets (or the gods associated therewith), all are mentioned or alluded to in the Bible: Mercury (Acts 14:12; Rom. 16:14); Venus (Jer. 7:18; 44:17, 25); Mars (Acts 17:19, 34); Jupiter (Acts 14:12, 13); Saturn (Amos 5:26). Fritz Hommel points to the fact that the Hebrew root which denotes the verb 'to swear' is the same as that which denotes 'seven' and claims that this fact establishes a connection

between swearing an oath and the seven planets. See *The Jewish Encyclopedia*, Vol. XI (New York: Funk & Wagnalls, 1905) 528. Cf. Gen. 21:28–32.

23. Austin Farrer, 'Inspiration: Poetical and Divine,' in Charles C. Conti (ed.), *Interpretation and Belief* (London: SPCK, 1976) 47.

24. The other four planets give the other four days of the week their names as follows: Mars, Tuesday (the Norse god *Tyr* was the equivalent of the Roman Mars; cf. French *Mardi*); Mercury, Wednesday (Norse *Wodin*; cf. French *Mercredi*); Jupiter or Jove, Thursday (Norse *Thor*; cf. French *Jeudi*); and Venus, Friday (Norse *Frigg*; cf. French *Vendredi*).

25. 'The Alliterative Metre,' SLE 23f; originally entitled 'A Metrical Suggestion.'

26. AOL 45.

27. 'Bluspels and Flalansferes: A Semantic Nightmare,' SLE 251–265.

28. AOL 48.

29. 'Edmund Spenser, 1552–99,' SMRL 137.

30. See 'The Vision of John Bunyan,' SLE 149.

31. SIL 112.

32. 'Edmund Spenser, 1552–99,' SMRL 137. Cf. 'When allegory is at its best, it approaches myth, which must be grasped with the imagination, not with the intellect,' PR 19. For more on this, see Paul Piehler, 'Myth or Allegory? Archetype and Transcendence in the Fiction of C. S. Lewis,' in Peter J. Schakel & Charles A. Huttar (eds.), *Word and Story in C. S. Lewis* (Columbia: University of Missouri Press, 1991), 199–212.

33. EC 783–786. The title is an allusion to Christ's healing of the sightless man at the pool of Siloam (John 9:1–40). There is an extant draft of the story, entitled 'Light' (Bodleian Library: MS. Facs. c.158).

34. Owen Barfield, 'Owen Barfield's response to John Fitzpatrick's essay on "The Man Born Blind,"' *CSL: The Bulletin of the New York C. S. Lewis Society*, Vol. 14, No. 8 (June 1983) 5. Cf. Owen Barfield, 'Introduction,' in Jocelyn Gibb, (ed.). *Light on C. S. Lewis* (London: Geoffrey Bles, 1965) xviii.

35. John Fitzpatrick, 'The Short Stories: A Critical Introduction,' *CSL: The Bulletin of the New York C. S. Lewis Society*, Vol. 14, No. 6 (Apr 1983) 1–5: 3.

36. 'Meditation in a Toolshed,' EC 609.

37. SBJ 168. Cf. Barfield, Owen. *Owen Barfield on C.S. Lewis*, ed. G.B. Tennyson (Middletown, CT: Wesleyan University Press, 1989) 150.

38. 'Transposition,' EC 277.

39. These words provided Lewis with the title of Chapter III of the original edition of *Miracles* (1947). In the second edition (1960) he revised them to 'The Cardinal Difficulty of Naturalism.'

40. '*De Futilitate*,' EC 676.

41. M 33.

42. SBJ 168.

43. 'Is Theology Poetry?,' EC 20.

44. Letter to N. Fridima, 15 Feb 1946.

45. Christopher Derrick, *C. S. Lewis and the Church of Rome: A Study in Proto-Ecumenism* (San Francisco: Ignatius Press, 1981) 213.

46. George Herbert, *The Temple and A Priest to the Temple* (London: Dent, undated) 54–55. An alternative source, if Lewis needed a source, is the fifteenth century *Epitre d'Othée* of Christine de Pasan in which the planets' children are illustrated in such a way that they resemble the apostles receiving the gifts of the Holy Spirit.

47. Corbin Scott Carnell, *Bright Shadow of Reality: C. S. Lewis and the Feeling Intellect* (Grand Rapids, MI: Eerdmans, 1974) 98.

48. THS 289. Ransom forbids Merlin from kneeling to the planets (THS 320) with the words, 'See thou do it not!,' an allusion to Rev. 19:10; 22:9.

49. Paul Fiddes, 'C. S. Lewis the Myth-Maker,' in Andrew Walker & James Patrick, (eds.), *A Christian for All Christians: Essays in Honour of C. S. Lewis* (London: Hodder & Stoughton, 1990) 132–155: 138. Cf. Deut. 32:8.

50. Dorothy L. Sayers complimented Lewis on the passage, saying that 'the arrival of the gods is grand' (letter of 3 Dec 1945) and Lewis replied, 'I am so glad you like the descent of the gods' (6 Dec 1945), a response that was more than mere politeness, for chapter 15 is centrally important to the novel's (and the trilogy's) whole purpose; in the abridged version of THS, *The Tortured Planet*, Lewis left the description of the descent virtually unchanged. Patterson opines that the passage 'is one of Lewis's most breathtaking and audacious achievements, and these richly sensual images adorn the structure of his narrative with a splendour worthy of their medieval prototypes.' Likewise, Downing calls the passage 'a brilliant prose poem.' Despite a general consensus on the excellence of the style in this chapter, voices have been raised in objection to its theological implications. Wolfe, for instance, thinks that it represents less a moment of grace than a kind of 'possession' in which the characters 'behave more like puppets than apostles': see Gregory Wolfe, 'Essential Speech: Language and Myth in the Ransom Trilogy,' in Peter J. Schakel, & Charles A. Huttar, (eds.), *Word and Story in C. S. Lewis* (Columbia: University of Missouri Press, 1991) 58–75: 75. Haldane, alluding to Shakespeare's *Measure for Measure* (III, i, 9), disapproves of 'Mr. Lewis's saints who are *"Servile to all the skyey influences"*': J.B.S. Haldane, 'Auld Hornie, F.R.S.,' *The Modern Quarterly* (Autumn 1946) 32–40: 38. It is true that the characters who are downstairs in the kitchen of St. Anne's during the descent of the gods do seem to be somewhat 'possessed.' However, upstairs, Ransom specifically warns Merlin against servility when he reminds him that the planetary intelligences 'are our fellow servants' (THS 320).

51. M 176.

52. 'Transposition,' EC 274. Cf. EL 460–461 and letters to Cecil Harwood (28? Oct 1926) and Edward Dell (4 Feb 1949).

53. LTM 23.

54. MC 129.

55. LTM 71.

56. Barfield's contention that Lewis 'always emphasised the chasm between Creator and creature, rather than anything in the nature of participation' is far from accurate. See Owen Barfield, *Owen Barfield on C. S. Lewis*, ed. G.B. Tennyson (Middletown, CT: Wesleyan University Press, 1989) 111; cf. 11, 65, 78, 133. His tendency to focus on Lewis's presentation of God's transcendence arises, I suspect, in part because of the nature of the disagreement between him and Lewis about anthroposophy. As Adey defines it, 'Anthroposophical training reunites the human ego, 'of the same nature and essence as the divine,' with the external world from which it has become separated, a cosmos no less spiritual than material': Lionel Adey, *C. S. Lewis' 'Great War' with Owen Barfield* (Wigton: Ink Books, 2002) 20. For Lewis, this did not allow for a full doctrine of creation *ex nihilo*: he wrote to Daphne Harwood (another Anthroposophist), 'I don't think the conception of *creatureliness* is part of your philosophy at all' (letter of 6 Mar 1942). Given this disagreement, it is to be expected that Barfield would have been especially sensitive to any statement Lewis made, either in personal conversation or in his published works, regarding the 'chasm' between Creator and creature. And it is true that, in his works of apologetics Lewis did sometimes emphasise transcendence, claiming to do so for the deliberate strategic purpose of counteracting pantheism (see 'Rejoinder to Dr Pittenger,' TAH 114). However, at other times his concern was to counteract deism (LTM 76) and to emphasise the potential for participation: see, e.g., 'The thing that matters is being actually drawn into that three-personal life ... being pulled into God, by God, while remaining [oneself],' MC 139.
57. MC 149.
58. LTM 85.
59. 'The gift of the Holy Spirit ... can't usually be—perhaps not ever—experienced as a sensation or emotion': letter to Genia Goelz, 15 May 1952.
60. Letter to Mary Willis Shelburne, 20 Feb 1955.
61. Letter to Genia Goelz, 20 June 1952.
62. LTM 77.
63. PPL 87.
64. E.g., 'The Phoenix,' CP 135.
65. Wesley. A. Kort, *C. S. Lewis Then and Now* (Oxford: Oxford University Press, 2001) 15.
66. GMD 128; also used in the epigraph to AOL, chapter VII.
67. James T. Como, 'A Look into Narnia,' *CSL: The Bulletin of the New York C. S. Lewis Society*, Vol. 15, No. 9 (July 1984) 4.
68. PPL 132.
69. PPL 133.
70. Letter to Arthur Greeves, 13? Jan 1930. He thought that the *Paradiso* represented 'the highest point that poetry has ever reached' ('Shelley, Dryden and Mr Eliot,' SLE 203).
71. 'Donne and Love Poetry in the Seventeenth Century,' SLE 107.

72. DI 120.

73. 'Imagery in the Last Eleven Cantos of Dante's "Comedy",' SMRL 78.

CHAPTER 3

1. EIC 82.

2. MN 38. The reason for its being named in MN will be explored in chapter 8.

3. SLE 24.

4. DI 105–106.

5. SBJ 171.

6. Statius's 'Jupiter, if I mistake not, comes far closer than that of the *Aeneid* to the god of strict monotheism, the transcendent Creator.... This Jove is clearly the Creator of the universe': 'Dante's Statius,' SMRL 99–100; cf. DI 34. Chaucer 'equates Jupiter with the Prime Mover' (Lewis's underlining in his copy of Bennett's edition of *The Knight's Tale* now in the Wade Center): Geoffrey Chaucer, *The Knight's Tale*, ed. J.A.W. Bennett (London: Harrap, 1954) 19. Dante speaks of the true God under the Pagan name of Jupiter in *Purgatorio* VI, 118: see 'Dante's Statius,' SMRL 99. In AOL 273 Lewis draws attention to the 'very important marginal gloss' found in Lydgate's *Reason and Sensuality* which helps explain the *significacio* of the gods wherever they appear in medieval poetry: 'Jubiter apud poetas accipitur multis modis; aliquando pro deo vero et summo sicut hic...aliquando capitur pro planeta, aliquando pro celo, aliquando pro igne vel aere superiori, aliquando eciam historialiter accipitur pro rege Crete' ['Jupiter is handled among the poets in a variety of ways, sometimes in the place of the true and most powerful God (as here)... sometimes for the planet Jupiter, sometimes for the sky, sometimes for fire or the aether, sometimes even historically for the King of Crete']: see Lewis's copy of Lydgate now in the Wade Center, complete with various underlinings made in his hand. Spenser's 'king of gods, the best of planets, the *fortuna major*, is...*ex officio* a vicegerent and "idole" of the Almighty': 'Neoplatonism in the Poetry of Spenser,' SMRL 152. 'You need not *speculate* about [Shakespeare's] Jove standing for God: changes from "God" in Quarto to "Jove"...in Folio run through most of the plays which exist in both texts and were certainly made in obedience to the "Act to Restrain Abuses of Players" (1606) which forbade the mention of any Divine Name on the stage': letter to Violet Toy, 1 Aug 1944. '[I]n Milton and many others, Jove is often Jehovah incognito': 'Neoplatonism in the Poetry of Spenser,' SMRL 152.

7. In his university lectures, Lewis described the jovial character as 'cheerful and festive; those born under Jupiter are apt to be loud-voiced and red-faced.' He would then pause and add: 'It is obvious under which planet I was born!'— which always produced a laugh. See Roger Lancelyn Green & Walter Hooper, *C. S. Lewis: A Biography*, revised & expanded edition (London: HarperCollins,

2002) 146. As it happens, Lewis was indeed astrologically as well as temper-amentally Jovial; his birthday, November 29th, falls under the sign of Sagittarius, ruled by Jupiter. This aspect of his personality was in part inherited from his father, who was 'often the most jovial and companionable of parents' (SBJ 38). Milward remembers Lewis's 'sturdily jovial manner' and detects 'a hidden connection with both the outward appearance and the inner character of Lewis himself'; see Peter Milward, *A Challenge to C. S. Lewis* (London: Associated University Presses, 1995) 79, 104.

8. AOL 197.

9. See Lewis's much-marked copy of Henryson's poetry now in the Wade Center. Robert Henryson, *The Poems of Robert Henryson*, ed. W.M. Metcalfe (Paisley: Alexander Gardner, 1917) 143–168.

10. 'Donne and Love Poetry in the Seventeenth Century,' SLE 113.

11. SBJ 157.

12. 'Talking about Bicycles,' EC 689–692. Cf. AMR 399.

13. PPL 137.

14. AOL 271.

15. Stephen Medcalf, 'Language and Self-Consciousness: The Making and Breaking of C. S. Lewis's Personae,' in Peter J. Schakel & Charles A. Huttar (eds.). *Word and Story in C. S. Lewis* (Columbia: University of Missouri Press, 1991) 143–144.

16. SBJ 189. Lewis may have genuinely misremembered and confused it with a later trip to Whipsnade when the bluebells were in flower; see his letter to his brother of 14 June 1932. It may have been a deliberate mistake made on the grounds of artistic licence, designed to portray himself more fully as a votary of Novalis's Blue Flower (see SBJ 12).

17. See George Watson, *Never Ones for Theory? England and the War of Ideas* (Cambridge: Lutterworth Press, 2000) 45.

18. See letter to Dom Bede Griffiths, 20 Dec 1961.

19. Lewis had already written one work of fiction five years earlier, namely PR, but it was allegorical and autobiographical rather than novelistic and entirely fictional; it also did not sell at all well: hence 1938 as the date of his 'emergence as a writer of fiction.' Even in PR we find Jovial imagery. God is portrayed likening himself to Jove by implication when he asks John if he has not heard the story of Semele, who demanded to see Jupiter in his unveiled majesty and was consumed when he granted her request (PR 217). Cf. Ovid, *Metamorphoses*, Book III.

20. 'There is no conscious connection between any of the phonetic elements in my "Old Solar" words and those of any actual language. I am always playing with syllables and fitting them together (purely by ear) to see if I can hatch up new words that please me. I want them to have an emotional, not intellectual, suggestiveness: the heaviness of *glund* for as huge a planet as Jupiter,' letter to Mrs Hook, 29 Dec 1958. Given that at least one of Lewis's other planetary

names, Viritrilbia, is an apparent portmanteau of existing English words (see below, chapter 7), I suspect that 'glund' may be not unconnected with 'glad' and 'jocund,' two important words in Lewis's Jovial lexicon.

21. Maleldil is the Christ-figure (and sometimes, as here it seems, the God-figure) of the trilogy. 'Local habitation' is an allusion to Shakespeare's *A Midsummer Night's Dream* (V, i, 17). For more on attributing to God 'a throne and a local habitation,' see M 81, an example of the frequent Jovial imagery in that book.

22. The tower is the centrepiece of the N.I.C.E.'s plans (THS 23; cf. 288). The time-travel element consists in Merlin's appearance in the twentieth century from the age of Arthur.

23. Per 16; cf. 68. Ransom longs to return to Malacandra and enjoy another evening 'when Jupiter was rising, too bright to look at' (Per 17).

24. The language of Weston and Devine, however, is empty. When they say 'By Jove' (OSP 12, 147; THS 38) they mean nothing by it.

25. Per 185–186.

26. In THS, in addition to the increasingly Jovial Ransom and his divine archetype, Maleldil, whom the eldils regard 'as their king', Lewis presents a demoniac anti-king (see note 30 in this chapter) and various kingly supernumeraries, including the 'old British under-kings,' 'unheard-of kings' of the Pre-Roman and Pre-British past, and George VI whom Merlin describes as 'this Saxon king of yours who sits at Windsor.' Merlin himself is said to look like a 'carving of a king.'

27. ROP 103–104.

28. THS 146. Cf. Ransom's joke about making MacPhee and Grace Ironwood 'marry one another.'

29. The reason for Martial Mark's submission to Venus is discussed below in chapter 4.

30. The 'demoniac' Venus operates under that demoniac Jupiter who is alluded to in various places throughout the book. Straik prophesies his arrival: 'A king cometh . . . who shall rule the universe with righteousness and the heavens with judgment. . . . It is a man—or a being made by man—who will finally ascend the throne of the universe.' This anthropic, usurping spirit of kingliness is represented by the logo of the N.I.C.E., 'a muscular male nude grasping a thunderbolt,' a parody of Jove's bolt. In reality the N.I.C.E. king turns out to be less than human, is indeed anti-human: 'monstrous, improbable, the huge shape of the elephant thrust its way into the room . . . its ears standing stiffly out like the devil's wings. . . . Something more than danger darted from the sight into Mark's brain. The pride and insolent glory of the beast, the carelessness of its killings, seemed to crush his spirit even as its flat feet were crushing women and men. Here surely came the King of the world.'

31. Cf. Tolkien's use of these means. When Aragorn arrives at Gondor 'the joy and wonder of the City was a music of trumpets and a ringing of bells.' J.R.R. Tolkien, *The Return of the King* (London: Allen & Unwin, 1984) 123. In his

own myths, Tolkien renames the planets in his invented language of Quenya as follows: Isil (Luna), Elemmírë (Mercury), Eärendil (Venus), Anar (Sol), Carnil (Mars), Alcarinquë (Jupiter), Lumbar (Saturn). His understanding of the more than merely material significance of stars had a part to play in Lewis's conversion (see Carpenter, *Inklings*, 43).

32. THS 326–327.

33. Letter to Cecil and Daphne Harwood, 11 Sept 1945.

34. THS 380.

35. E.g., 'Dante's Similes,' SMRL 73. For more on this, see chapter 9.

36. Rowan Williams, '*That Hideous Strength*: A Reassessment,' address to the Oxford Lewis Society, 5 Oct 1988 (Lewis Society recordings archive).

37. Brut, the first king of Britain in mythical history, was a descendant of Aeneas of Troy and called his British capital Troynovant; cf. SMRL 24; DI 179. As part of Brut's line, Jane is reminiscent of Spenser's Britomart: 'from thy wombe a famous Progenie / Shall spring, out of the auncient Trojan blood,' *Faerie Queene*, III, iii, 22 (SIL 25). Ruth Pitter, whom Lewis said he would have liked to have married, was another descendant: 'I always thought the Pitters (*diespiter* and all that) descended from Jove, through Aeneas and Brute,' letter to Pitter, 4 Jan 1954; cf. Sayer, *Jack*, 211.

38. Letter to Mary Willis Shelburne, 26 Jan 1954.

39. 'The Small Man Orders His Wedding,' lines 41–56 (CP 46–47).

40. 'Edmund Spenser, 1522–99,' SMRL 130. Cf. 'The intense desire for posterity (who will people not only earth but heaven) and the astrological connexion of this with the 'thousand torches flaming bright' above the house-tops add not only a public but almost a cosmic solemnity to the poem,' EL 373.

41. We will consider only the appearances of Jupiter or Jove; for brevity, Thor and Zeus must be left out of account.

42. 'Le Roi S'Amuse' (CP 37–38), his most complex poem. The rhyme scheme of each stanza is: AB, AB, CCD, EF, EF, GGD, HHI, JJKKI.

43. 'From the Latin of Milton's *De Idea Platonica Quemadmodum Aristoteles*.' See *English*, V, 30 (1945) 195; not included in CP.

44. 'The Planets,' lines 79–101 (CP 28).

45. See letter to Barfield: 'Isn't Jupiter splendid these nights?' (6 Sept 1938); letters to his brother: 'the most beautiful night I've ever seen—full moon, and Jupiter, not, as when you were here, over Adders [Addison's Walk] but over the tower and under the moon' (24 Nov 1939); 'the sky [above The Kilns] was blazing "with few, but with how splendid stars" [a line from James Elroy Flecker], Jupiter among them' (31 Dec 1939); 'Did you happen to see the moon (first quarter), Jupiter and Venus, all in a line?' (18 Feb 1940); letter to Ruth Pitter: 'It was beautiful, on two or three successive nights about the Holy Time [i.e., the Christmas just passed], to see Venus and Jove blazing at one another, once with the Moon right between them: Majesty and Love linked by Virginity—what could be more appropriate?' (2 Jan 1953).

46. Pliny the Elder, *Natural History*, 2.169a. For more on this great sea-trading people, see Ezek. 26–28.
47. 'Prologue,' lines 1–13 (CP 163).
48. That is, the earliest in which Jupiter is treated positively. See the discussion of 'Quam Bene Saturno' in chapter 9.
49. See Lewis's copy of Seznec, now in the Wade Center, Wheaton College. Jean Seznec, *The Survival of the Pagan Gods: The Mythological Tradition and Its Place in Renaissance Humanism and Art*, trans. Barbara F. Sessions (New York: Pantheon, 1953) 162.
50. AT 149–150.
51. 'The Turn of the Tide,' lines 69–70 (CP 63–65).
52. LWW 110–114.
53. His kingship is referred to in only two of the other six books: VDT 122; HHB 140.
54. PPL 118.
55. LWW 165.
56. AOL 345.
57. THS 360–361.
58. Letter to Carol Jenkins, 22 Jan 1952.
59. 'Neoplatonism in the Poetry of Spenser,' SMRL 160.
60. It may be asked why Aslan continues to appear as a lion at all in the other, non-Jovial books. Three answers may be given. First, 'all the planets are represented in each' (THS 316). Second, Jupiter is especially liable to make his presence felt outside his own domain because his is the wisdom which governs the stars. Third, there are limits to the flexibility of any symbol-system. Nevertheless, as we will demonstrate below, in the other six Chronicles Aslan takes on the properties of the other planets even while he (usually) maintains his leonine form.
61. SIL 138.
62. Lewis was well acquainted with the works of Bruno, mentioning them in AOL, EL, and DI. He also very carefully read Ernst Cassirer's *The Individual and the Cosmos*; his copy of that book now at the Wade Center brims with his marginalia. Cassirer writes: 'Bruno's *Spaccio* develops in all directions that ethical-allegorical language which seeks to shed light on the relationships of the inner world by using figures of the visible, spatial cosmos. The forces that move the inner man are viewed as cosmic potencies; virtues and vices are viewed as constellations. In this view, *Fortezza* (valour) assumes the place of honour': Ernst Cassirer, *The Individual and the Cosmos in Renaissance Philosophy*, trans. Mario Domandi (Mineola, NY: Dover, 2000) 74–75. Cf. what Lewis says about fortitude as the master of the four cardinal virtues (MC 73).
63. Cassirer, *The Individual and the Cosmos in Renaissance Philosophy* 74.
64. Robert Henryson, 'The Testament of Cresseid,' lines 181–182.
65. See 'Hermione in the House of Paulina' (CP 32); cf. letter to Greeves of 5 Sept 1931; POP 132. He reworks the image in MC (Book 4, Chapter 5), where 'tin

soldiers' (a significant metal) serve the same function as Shakespeare's puta-
tive stone statue. It is interesting that tin soldiers await redemption, whereas
'lead soldiers'—that is, Saturnine soldiers—await damnation by being 'melted
down into their Master [Satan]' (see Per 160).

66. M 100.

67. Roger Lancelyn Green & Walter Hooper, *C. S. Lewis: A Biography*, revised &
expanded edition (London: HarperCollins, 2002) 307.

68. Peter J. Schakel, *Reading with the Heart: The Way into Narnia* (Grand Rapids,
MI: Eerdmans, 1979) 140.

69. James George Frazer, *The Golden Bough: A Study in Magic and Religion*
(London: Macmillan, 1922) 148; Lewis underlined these words in his copy,
now in the possession of the Wade Center.

70. 'I have never concealed the fact that I regarded him as my master; indeed I fancy
I have never written a book in which I did not quote from him,' GMD xxxvii.

71. George MacDonald, *An Expression of Character: The Letters of George Mac-
Donald*, ed. Glenn Edward Sadler (Grand Rapids, MI: Eerdmans, 1994) 133.

72. PH 114; cf. 144.

73. Admittedly, Lewis subtitled *That Hideous Strength* 'a modern fairy-tale for
grown-ups', but its fairy-tale elements are largely obscured by its novelistic
qualities.

74. Letter to Patricia Hills, 10 Mar 1959, quoted in Walter Hooper, *C. S. Lewis, A
Companion and Guide* (London: HarperCollins, 1996) 581; not included in
CLIII.

75. Letter to Patricia Hills, 10 Mar 1959.

76. EL 49.

77. Philip Pullman, *The Amber Spyglass* (London: Scholastic, 2001) 548. Cf. Philip
Pullman, 'The Republic of Heaven,' *The Horn Book Magazine* (Nov/Dec 2001)
655–667.

78. 'Equality,' EC 666–668: 668.

79. Richard Harries, 'C. S. Lewis and Philip Pullman: Myth and Competing
Moralities,' address given to the conference 'Reasons of the Heart: Myth,
Meaning and Education,' University of Edinburgh, Sept 2004.

80. Letter to Mary Willis Shelburne, 10 July 1953.

81. As opposed to 'pale and interesting.' See her letter to Lewis of 3 Dec 1945, *The
Letters of Dorothy L. Sayers, Vol. Three, 1944–1950: A Noble Daring*, chosen and
edited by Barbara Reynolds (Cambridge: The Dorothy L. Sayers Society,
1988) 177.

82. Rowan Williams, '*That Hideous Strength*: A Reassessment,' address to the
Oxford Lewis Society, 5 Oct 1988 (Lewis Society recordings archive).

83. Wesley A. Kort, *C. S. Lewis Then and Now* (Oxford: Oxford University Press,
2001) 147.

84. See MC 53–58; cf. LTM 106; letter to Mr Young, 31 Oct 1963.

85. Doris Myers, *C. S. Lewis in Context* (Kent, OH: Kent State University Press,
1994) 126.

86. SIL 99.
87. See letters to E. R. Eddison, 29 Apr 1943; Owen Barfield, 17? May 1943; and Laurence Harwood, 22? Dec 1944.
88. M 136.
89. M 146. The Incarnation leads to 'spring' (M 127), 'spring-time' (M 128), the first 'snowdrop' (M 145); 'Summer is coming' (M 146).
90. 'The Grand Miracle,' EC 3–9.
91. Austin Farrer, *The Glass of Vision* (Westminster: Dacre Press, 1948) 92.
92. SBJ 189.
93. Lewis's determination to keep the secret was resolute; so much so that he told one of his correspondents, a Mrs Roy Kieper, in a letter of 5 Aug 1961, that 'the background [of Narnia] has no hidden meaning.' Was this a lie, a white lie, or the truth? I think it can be seen as all three. It is a lie because as this chapter has shown (and as the subsequent six chapters will confirm) the Narnia Chronicles are saturated with hidden meaning in their background, foreground and middle ground. It is a white lie because Lewis had very good reasons for withholding this information from Mrs Kieper, which will be discussed in chapter 11. It is the truth on two counts. First, because Mrs Kieper presumably did not enquire whether the Narnian background had the sort of hidden meaning we are here discussing. So when Lewis tells her it contains no hidden meaning, he may have meant 'hidden meaning' in the same sense she meant it—probably in the sense of a hidden Biblical allegory, which is how most readers have always approached the septet. (He gets Aslan off the hook in a similar way in LB 160 when Peter is unable to understand how he can have returned to Narnia. Digory tells him: 'When Aslan said you could never go back to Narnia, he meant the Narnia you were thinking of.') Second, there is, in a sense, no *hidden* meaning in the Chronicles. All the meaning is on display. It remains hidden in effect only because readers 'look along' it, rather than at it.
94. DI 109.
95. 'It All Began with a Picture,' EC 529.
96. 'Neoplatonism in the Poetry of Spenser,' SMRL 152.
97. That is, the presentation of Aslan's character is not so much based upon Lewis's general understanding of Christ as upon his particular understanding of Jove as a Christologically potent symbol.
98. Lewis first heard *The Planets Suite* (or part of it) at a concert in 1935; see W. H. Lewis, *Brothers and Friends: The Diaries of Major Warren Hamilton Lewis*, ed. Clyde S. Kilby and Marjorie Lamp Mead (San Francisco: Harper & Row, 1982) 169. Ten years later he heard a gramophone recording and 'was greatly moved by it,' though he thought 'Jupiter the weakest'; see letter to Arthur Greeves, 26 Dec 1945; cf. letter of 13 May 1946. In a letter to Sister Penelope of 31 Jan 1946, discussing the *Suite* in connection with 'The Descent of the Gods,' Lewis wrote: 'About Holst's *Planets*, I heard Mars and Jupiter long ago and greatly admired them but have heard the complete work only

within the last six weeks. But his characters are rather different from mine, I think. . . . On Jupiter . . . I think his is more "jovial" in the modern sense of the word. The folk tune on which he bases it is not regal enough for my conception. But of course there is a general similarity because we're both following the medieval astrologers. His is, anyway, a rich and marvellous work.' Holst's Jupiter is named 'the Bringer of Jollity' and it may be worth noting that the words 'jollification' and 'jolly' both appear in *The Lion*, but never again in the Narniad ('jolly' reappears as an intensifier, but never adjectivally). Seven years after the end of the First World War Holst made the central melody of his Jupiter movement into a hymn-tune, 'Thaxted,' and fitted to it the words of Sir Cecil Spring-Rice's poem 'The Two Fatherlands,' written in 1918. Once established as the melody to this hymn ('I Vow To Thee My Country'), the folk tune that Lewis had found insufficiently regal for his conception became linked with a patriotic, royally-sanctioned view of England. It was sung at the wedding of the Prince and Princess of Wales in 1981 and at the Princess's funeral in 1997.

99. Not that Holst's seven planets are identical with the medieval seven. He omits Sol and Luna, replacing them with Uranus (discovered 1781) and Neptune (discovered 1846).

100. SIL 116–117. Cf. 'On Stories,' EC 495.

101. See, e.g., letters to Arthur Greeves, 24 July 1917; Warren Lewis, 9 June 1919; Roger Lancelyn Green, 15 Sept 1953; Rhona Bodle, 3 Oct 1956.

102. SBJ 147.

103. 'The Day with a White Mark,' lines 3–4 (CP 42–43).

104. EL 78; cf. LTM 18.

105. LWW 164.

CHAPTER 4

1. OTOW 10.

2. Letter to Arthur Greeves, 30 May 1916.

3. DI 198.

4. SBJ 151.

5. 'The Planets,' lines 57–79 (CP 27–28).

6. See Don W. King, 'Lost but Found: The "Missing" Poems of C. S. Lewis's *Spirits in Bondage,*' *Christianity and Literature*, Vol. 53, No. 2 (Winter 2004) 163–201.

7. 'The Queen of Drum,' IV, 135–136 (NP 158). See also IV, 29 where the General, or Fuhrer, is described as 'the firstborn of necessity.'

8. DI 116–117.

9. Letter to John Chapman, 29 Aug 1956.

10. '*De Descriptione Temporum,*' SLE 12.

11. Letter to Arthur C. Clarke, 20 Jan 1954.

12. This is partly why Lewis sets his satirical short story 'Ministering Angels' on Mars: men on a masculine planet are doubly in need of the relief which only women can bring (see EC 849–857).

13. TWHF 195. Cf. 'There is, hidden or flaunted, a sword between the sexes till an entire marriage reconciles them,' AGO 42f.

14. Per 185.

15. OSP 89. Cf. 'it will not be necessary' for the Malacandrian Oyarsa to kill the visitors from Thulcandra (OSP 143).

16. Letter to William Kinter, 27 Nov 1951.

17. Letter to Victor M. Hamm, 11 Aug 1945.

18. Cato the Elder: *De Agricultura* 83, *De Re Rustica* 141.

19. James George Frazer, *The Golden Bough: A Study in Magic and Religion* (London: Macmillan, 1922) 577ff. See Lewis's much-marked copy in the Wade Center.

20. Austin Farrer, *Saving Belief: A Discussion of Essentials* (London: Hodder & Stoughton, 1964) 68.

21. Ransom learns war fully in the sphere of Venus (THS 274) and it is his 'long struggle in the caves of Perelandra' which comes back to him when Mars descends in THS. We might have expected this to happen on Malacandra, and to explain this apparent inconsistency we must recall that 'in a certain juncture of the planets each may play the other's part' (letter to A.K. Hamilton Jenkin, 4 Nov 1925); also that the trilogy is largely concerned with the acquisition of true masculinity and true femininity. Mythologically, Lewis seems to be suggesting that masculinity is only fully learnt in relation to femininity. Deep in the 'caves' of Venus, stricken with pain, as the Malacandrian Oyarsa had foretold (OSP 166), Ransom overcomes the Un-man, giving of himself for the life of the planet, and so realises what it is to be a man.

22. Virgil, *Aeneid*, VI, 557–8: 'The sound of savage blows with the noise of dragged iron chains.'

23. 'Martyr,' of course, means 'witness' (see letter to Sister Penelope, 19 Feb 1944), and Straik's use of 'witness' (78) is probably intended to connote a martyr's religious fervour. Jane calls Mrs Dimble a 'martyr' (76), who denies it. Merlin does not sound likely to be 'a martyr' (332) according to the imperceptive Frost. Fairy Hardcastle announces that Alcasan is to be 'made into a martyr' (98). Cf. Weston's 'expected martyrdom' (OSP 155).

24. William Blacker, 'The Boyne Water' (a poem about the Battle of the Boyne), line 19.

25. Site of Arthur's twelfth victory in battle where the Saxon advance into Britain was finally halted.

26. Virgil's name for Mars: *Aeneid*, VIII, 630.

27. 'About Holst's *Planets*, I heard Mars... long ago and greatly admired [it]... But his characters are rather different from mine, I think. Wasn't his Mars brutal and ferocious?' letter to Sister Penelope, 31 Jan 1946. Cf. 'Mars, of course, bowls one over,' letter to Arthur Greeves, 26 Dec 1945. See also Warren Lewis's diary entry (7 Feb 1935) after he and his brother attended a

performance of the *Planets*: 'we both thought Mars was the best... "the finest piece of anti-war propaganda I have struck" said J[ack].' W. H. Lewis, *Brothers and Friends: The Diaries of Major Warren Hamilton Lewis*, ed. Clyde S. Kilby and Marjorie Lamp Mead (San Francisco: Harper & Row, 1982) 169.

28. Rowan Williams, '*That Hideous Strength*: A Reassessment,' address to the Oxford Lewis Society, 5 Oct 1988 (Lewis Society recordings archive).

29. AOL 76.

30. See George Watson, 'The Art of Disagreement: C.S. Lewis (1898–1963),' *The Hudson Review* (1995) 229–239: 233. Cf. 'In the *Odyssey* those loves [of Mars and Venus] were little more than a merry tale; by Spenser's time they had come to symbolize the victory of beauty over strength and peace over war': 'Spenser's Cruel Cupid,' SMRL 164–165. See also AMR 95; EIC 18, 19; SIL 50, 78, 104; Alastair Fowler, 'C. S. Lewis: Supervisor,' *Yale Review*, Vol. 91, No. 4 (Oct 2003) 64–80.

31. Donald E. Glover, *C. S. Lewis: The Art of Enchantment* (Athens, OH: Ohio University Press, 1981) 148.

32. Doris Myers, *C. S. Lewis in Context* (Kent, OH: Kent State University Press, 1994) 132.

33. Cf. 'It has been assumed without discussion that if you... want to understand some 'ideology' (such as medieval chivalry...), you must listen not to those who lived inside it, but to sociologists': 'Meditation in a Toolshed,' EC 608.

34. See Walter Hooper, (ed.). *C. S. Lewis: A Companion and Guide* (London: HarperCollins, 1996) 422.

35. 'Glozelle' means 'liar' according to Lionel Adey in *C. S. Lewis: Writer, Dreamer & Mentor* (Grand Rapids, MI: Eerdmans, 1998) 189. Cf. 'the liar made lord': 'The Planets,' line 73 (CP 28).

36. Originally a marshal was someone who looked after horses (mares), with no link to Mars. That a field-marshal should now be a military rank is a linguistic coincidence. Lewis is perhaps playfully creating his own 'mistaken philological connection.'

37. Cf. '[The Little Master] was sensible enough not to condemn individual Chess whom he really liked. And none did he like better than Samuel Macgoullah, a knight,' B 100. See also, 'the shiny red / Chessknight' who only loosely 'resembles stallions when they stamp and neigh': 'The Genuine Article,' lines 7–8 (CP 77–78). The chess piece in PC has ruby eyes, reminiscent of the cross pricked out with rubies in Canto XIV of *Paradiso*, in the heaven of Mars.

38. DI 10.

39. 'A fine armour is almost part of the personality of the knight who wears it' and fine or shabby appearance can amount to 'an almost spiritual significance,' EL 279. Cf. Sopespian's exclamation about Edmund: 'What mail he wears! None of our smiths could make the like,' PC 153.

40. SIW 115.

41. EL 151.

42. PC 135. See also LWW 145, 146; VDT 84, 87.

43. PC 167–168.
44. Of Chaucer's *Compleynt of Mars* Lewis wrote, 'the astronomical allusions are, I confess, too hard for me,' AOL 170. Likewise, this author cannot explain the Martial significance, if any, of the names Tarva or Alambil, nor even those of Caspian and Miraz.
45. Peter J. Schakel, *The Way into Narnia: A Reader's Guide* (Grand Rapids, MI: Eerdmans, 2005) 50.
46. AT 159.
47. Lewis seems to have acquired some Turkish from his reading of Lane's translation of *The Arabian Nights*: see letter to Carol Jenkins, 22 Jan 1952, where he reports that 'Aslan' is 'Turkish for Lion.'
48. PPL 64.
49. 'On Punishment: A Reply by C. S. Lewis,' EC 707.
50. 'Necessitas ultimum et maximum telum est' (Necessity is the last and strongest weapon), Titus Livy, *Annales* IV, 28.
51. 'Twas a cruel necessity' (the beheading of Charles I). Yet Cromwell also said, in a speech to Parliament in 1654, 'Necessity hath no law. Feigned necessities, imaginary necessities, are the greatest cozenage men can put upon the Providence of God, and make pretences to break known rules.'
52. 'So spake the Fiend, and with necessity, / The tyrant's plea, excused his devilish deed,' John Milton, *Paradise Lost*, IV, 393.
53. 'Necessity is the plea for every infringement of human freedom. It is the argument of tyrants,' William Pitt the Younger, speech on the India Bill, 1783.
54. See letter to Dom Bede Griffiths, 5 Oct 1938, where Lewis alludes to Augustine's *De Civitate Dei*, Book XIX, ch. 12.
55. 'The Necessity of Chivalry' is Lewis's title for the essay first published as 'Notes on the Way,' *Time and Tide*, Vol. XXI (17 Aug 1940) 841; reprinted EC 717–720. Cf. PRCON 9.
56. SBJ 9.
57. MC 105. Reepicheep, it will be remembered, is 'a gay and martial mouse,' PC 73; Malacandra makes his children 'gay, light, nimble, and alert,' THS 325.
58. Peter Hollindale and Zena Sutherland in Hunt, Peter (ed.). *Children's Literature, An Illustrated History* (Oxford: Oxford University Press, 1995) 274–275.
59. Lewis held that the retributive element in punishment was the *sine qua non* of justice; see 'The Humanitarian Theory of Punishment,' EC 698–709.
60. 'Why I Am Not A Pacifist' (EC 281–293). For more on his understanding of the ethics of war, see 'Private Bates' (EC 604–606) and 'Is English Doomed?' (EC 434–436).
61. 'Talking about Bicycles,' EC 691.
62. EL 153. Cf. letter to the Editor of *Theology* (27 Feb 1939) and to Stephen Schofield (23 Aug 1956).
63. PC 135.
64. HHB 187; cf. MN 129.

65. PC 136.
66. 'Christianity and Culture,' EC 80.
67. PC 125. There is, however, at least one unfortunate consequence of making PC unlike 'last time'. The need to avoid repeating LWW explains one of the main problems of PC, the unsatisfactory dramatic trajectory of the eponymous character. Peter tells Caspian, 'I haven't come to take your place, you know, but to put you into it' (148); however, there is no coronation scene at the end of the book. Coronation (which provided a suitable climax to the previous story, with its Jovial theme) is inappropriate to the Martial donegality, and therefore we are merely told in passing that Caspian 'was now King' (182). (Incidentally, this reinforces the point made in chapter 1 about the letter Lewis wrote to Anne Jenkins: if the 'restoration' theme mentioned in that letter were truly the fundamental governing idea of the book, surely Lewis would have provided a scene in which Caspian was triumphantly restored to his throne.) That there is no coronation instils—or rather compounds—a damaging doubt as to who is the main character of the story. Already, Caspian has been relegated to the role of spectator at the single combat and prevented from avenging his father himself, because he is 'wounded' (150). Adding to the sense that Caspian is passive and distant is the fact that it is Trumpkin, rather than Caspian, who tells the Pevensies the prince's history. Caspian seems to be little more than a puppet, moved about by other characters: Dr Cornelius, Glenstorm, Nikabrik, Peter. As well as these problems, PC suffers from abrupt cutting between different plot-lines in chapter 14 and has a group of uninteresting and confusing characters in the form of the Telmarines: the good ones want to stay in Narnia, but of those who want to leave some are 'decent', some cowardly; too many distinctions among a set of characters who are so minor. Most seriously, the motifs of knightliness and martyrdom are not thrown into sufficient relief. Peter's courage, Lucy's witness, and Caspian's own story never come to a truly crucial point; they are resolved too easily. In the other books the cruxes are more clearly defined, usually by tears: in LWW they flow at the death of Aslan; in VDT they flow at the undragoning of Eustace and the attempted abdication of Caspian; in SC pain is a necessary part of overcoming the witch's enchantment and tears flow for the death of Caspian; in HHB Shasta cries when he meets Aslan in the mountain-pass; in MN Digory and Aslan weep for his mother; in LB Tirian and the others weep for the loss of Narnia. In PC we do not feel enough real pain or grief on the part of Peter or Lucy, nor even on the part of Caspian, who, though homeless, concussed and bitten, is hardly shown to suffer as a result of these experiences. Lucy becomes 'tremulous' (129) when she witnesses to Aslan, and Peter recognises that he might not win the combat (165), but that is it. Colin Manlove is surely correct to hold the view that, in comparison with the other books, PC represents a 'weakness of inspiration': *The Chronicles of Narnia: The Patterning of a Fantastic World* (New York: Twayne, 1993) 44. Lewis reports

that it sells much less well than the other six stories: see his letter to Kathleen Raine, 7 Nov 1963.

68. PC 125–126.
69. PC 126.
70. THS 325.
71. PC 133.
72. SIL 134–135.
73. GMD 85, MacDonald's italics. Lewis is quoting MacDonald's sermon 'The Truth in Jesus,' from *Unspoken Sermons*, of which Lewis wrote: 'My own debt to this book is almost as great as one man can owe to another,' GMD xxxiv.
74. Acts 17:28.

CHAPTER 5

1. DI 106.
2. By Aristarchus of Samos (c.310–c.280 B.C.). See Sir Thomas Heath, *Aristarchus of Samos: The Ancient Copernicus* (Oxford: Clarendon Press, 1913).
3. However, the placement of the Sun in the middle of the seven planets was held to indicate a certain special nobility, like the heart's position in the middle of the body, or like a wise king in the middle of his kingdom. For more on this see Edward Grant, *Planets, Stars, and Orbs: the Medieval Cosmos, 1200–1687* (Cambridge: Cambridge University Press, 1994) 220–235.
4. AOL 342.
5. E.g. Ps. 84:11; Mal. 4:2; 2 Cor. 4:6; Rev. 21:23; 22:5.
6. 'Dante's Similes,' SMRL 71.
7. 'Spenser's Cruel Cupid,' SMRL 167.
8. SBJ 20. The quotation is from Henry Wadsworth Longfellow's 'Tegnér's Drapa,' lines 1–3.
9. He frequently touched on whether Gawain was properly understood as a Solar deity (e.g., 'The Anthropological Approach,' SLE 301); discusses 'infra-solar deities' ('Genius and Genius,' SMRL 170); disagrees with Ellrodt's equation of Adonis with Sol in *The Faerie Queene* ('Neoplatonism in the Poetry of Spenser,' SMRL 156), but notes the Solar origin of Amoret and Belphoebe (SIL 48).
10. 'Religion Without Dogma?' EC 165.
11. 'Myth Became Fact,' EC 142.
12. See ROP 89.
13. DI 106. Cf. DI 26–27; EL 12.
14. We shall therefore omit:
    i) 'Descend to Earth, Descend, Celestial Nine,' a heroic narrative poem inspired by Wagner which dates to 1912–1913. See Don W. King, *C. S. Lewis,*

Poet: The Legacy of his Poetic Impulse (Kent, OH: Kent State University Press, 2001) 245–265. The Rhine maidens give Alberich, king of the Nibelung, a vision of the Rhinegold, hoping thus to direct his attention away from them, but they foolishly disclose the gold's dread power:

> . . . who would the Rhinegold gain
> Must first curse love before his hands may hold
> The glistening and so much desired gold.
> And he, should he but gain the pile he wants
> (If there be truth in legendary vaunts)
> If to a RING he forge it by the art
> Of goldsmith, then to rule shall be his part;
> Whoe'er the treasure keeps and wears the RING
> Shall rule the world, an everlasting king. (I, 84–92)

    ii) 'To a Friend,' lines 10–12 (CP 118–119): 'the noon / That nourishes Earth can only sear / And scald the unresponding Moon.'

    iii) 'On Being Human,' lines 9–11 (CP 48–49): 'the meaning of / Arboreal life, how from earth's salty lap / The solar beam uplifts it.'

    iv) 'Solomon,' lines 10–12 (CP 60–61): 'Like the unbearable noon-day in the glare of its power, / So solemn and so radiant was Solomon to behold, / Men feared his immense forehead and his beard of gold.'

    v) 'The Turn of the Tide,' line 71 (CP 63–65): 'Monsters in the Sun.' These monsters are salamanders, a kind of lizard, in whom Lewis had a persistent interest. Cf. 'The Salamander' (CP 86–87) and letter to Valerie Pitt, 1 Mar 1949.

15. Perhaps an allusion to the palm tree under which Apollo was born on the isle of Delos.
16. See SIL 48 for his discussion of Spenser's treatment of Sol's progenitive power.
17. 'The Planets,' lines 38–67 (CP 27).
18. See Lewis's Arden edition of *Hamlet* in the library of Magdalene College, Cambridge. Lewis has underlined I, i, 162: 'no planets strike' and also marked the editor's note on the word 'strike': 'blast, esp. of planetary influence. *Coriolanus*, II, ii, 117: 'struck Corioli like a planet.' Furness quotes Florio's *Dict*: "Assiderare: to blast or *strike* with a planet." ' Cf. his own use of 'moonstruck,' SL 112; also the probable word-play in 'From where I stood that beam of light, with the specks of dust floating in it, was the most striking thing in the place' ('Meditation in a Toolshed,' EC 607) and again in 'There is a striking difference between this Model [of the universe] . . . and the Christian picture,' DI 120.
19. Plutarch in *Moralia* maintains that 'Apollo' signifies unity on the basis that *pollon* means 'many' and the prefix *a*- negates it ('The E at Delphi,' 393c).
20. 'Noon's Intensity,' CP 128.
21. 'Transposition,' EC 267–278.
22. 'Scazons,' CP 132.

23. This observation courtesy of Andrew Cuneo. Alchemy, according to Burck-hardt, was 'the art of the transmutations of the soul. In saying this I am not seeking to deny that alchemists also knew and practised metallurgical proce-dures such as the purification and alloying of metals; their real work, however, for which all these procedures were merely the outward supports of "opera-tional" symbols, was the transmutation of the soul. The testimony of the al-chemists on this point is unanimous.' Titus Burckhardt, *Alchemy* (London: Penguin, 1972) 23.

24. SBJ 135. Cf. 'Re-Adjustment,' CP 116.

25. See chapter 3, note 87.

26. THS 201. See Bacon's *Sylva Sylvarum, or a Naturall Historie in ten Centuries* (1627), Century IV.

27. AOM 46–47.

28. EL 13.

29. See Robert Boyle, *The Sceptical Chymist* (London: J. M. Dent & Sons, 1949). Lewis's copy of this work in the Wade Center is well marked, underlined and annotated, including the following passage: 'And though gold is, of all metalls, that, whose mercury [i.e., essence] chymists have most endeavoured to extract, and which they do the most brag they have extracted; yet the experienced Angelus Sala, in his spagyrical account of the seven terrestrial planets (that is the seven metalls) affords us this memorable testimony, to our present purpose; "Quanquam (saies he) etc. experientia tamen (quam stultorum magistram vo-camus) certe comprobavit, mercurium auri adeo fixum, maturum, et arcte cum reliquis ejusdem corporis substantiis conjungi, ut nullo modo retrogredi possit"' (101) ['And yet nevertheless experience (what we call the teacher to dunces) has demonstrated that the essence of gold is so securely, vigorously, and tightly joined together with the remaining elements of the same body that it is in no way capable of retrogression']; Lewis's underlining.

   'The fact of the matter is, Newton was an alchemist, and his major interest in chemistry, in his earlier years, centred on the possibility of transmuting metals.... Why should Newton not be an alchemist? All his contemporaries, even Boyle, Locke, and Hooke were.' More, Louis Trenchard. *Isaac Newton, A Biography* (New York: Scribner, 1934) 158f.

30. 'The World's Last Night,' EC 47.

31. The words 'gold,' 'golden,' 'gilded' and 'gilding' appear no fewer than thirty-five times and the words 'sun,' 'sunrise,' 'sunshine,' 'sunlight,' 'sunlit,' 'sundown,' 'sunny' and 'sunset' come nearly sixty times in a book with 189 pages. In other words, through the use of 'gold' and 'sun' (or variants thereof) alone, almost every second page contains a reference to Solar influence.

32. PPL 44. Cf. Robin's question, 'Is that what Milton was talking about?': 'The Man Born Blind,' EC 783–786: 784.

33. Robert Henryson, 'The Testament of Cresseid,' *The Poems of Robert Henryson*, ed. W. M. Metcalfe (Paisley: Alexander Gardner, 1917) 151, line 199 (Wade Center; Lewis's underlining).

34. VDT 98.
35. VDT 100.
36. Aslan's image on Peter's shield in LWW is red, 'as bright as a ripe strawberry,' appropriate for Jupiter. However, the image is also red on Rilian's shield in SC, where Lewis might have made it silver, and on the banner carried by Lord Peridan in HHB, where he might have made it mercury-coloured. The redness suggests Jupiter's reign not just in his own sphere, but as king over the whole universe, his wisdom being that which 'dominates the stars.' The only place outside VDT where Aslan's image is golden is on the banner that is lowered at the end of SC following the death of Caspian. For discussion of the presence of gold in SC, see chapter 6.
37. DI 92. The Dominical sayings that Lewis mentions are Luke 13:4 and John 9:13 (sic, a misprint for 9:3).
38. VDT 81–82.
39. William Shakespeare, *The Tempest*, V, i, 50.
40. SIW 113.
41. John Henry Newman, *The Scope and Nature of University Education* (1852), IV, quoted in SIW 131.
42. SIW 127.
43. VDT 137.
44. Homer, *Hymn to Apollo*, lines 358–362 (trans. Hugh G. Evelyn-White).
45. 'Is romantic yearning an appetite for heaven, or is it the ultimate refinement of covetousness? One cannot but respect his sense of responsibility in voicing his doubt about what so deeply moved him.' Austin Farrer, 'The Christian Apologist' in Jocelyn Gibb (ed.), *Light on C. S. Lewis* (London: Geoffrey Bles, 1965) 23–43: 40.
46. VDT 183–185.
47. AT 99, 103, 197; cf. M 112; LTM 31.
48. '*De Audiendis Poetis*,' SMRL 1–17: 8. Cf. letter to Vera Gebbert, 20 Sept 1952.
49. 'Christianity and Culture,' EC 82.
50. Coriakin is a fallen star, expelled from the heavens and sent down to Narnia as a punishment. Cf. the pseudepigraphical Book of Enoch, 18:13–16, the narrative concerning the imprisonment of certain stars that had 'transgressed the commandment of the Lord.' Shooting stars were often called 'fire-dragons' in the Middle Ages, according to Lewis's letter to Anne and Martin Kilmer, 7 Aug 1957. It is possible that, as part of his Sauroctonus theme, Lewis conceived of Coriakin and Ramandu because he wanted Caspian and the other protagonists to encounter and to go beyond yet another kind of dragon.
51. DI 144.
52. VDT 143.
53. GMD xxxix.
54. ROP 75.
55. EL 535; the quotation is from Donne's 'A Valediction Forbidding Mourning,' line 24.

CHAPTER 6

1. EL 489. As a boy, he enjoyed Wells's *The First Men in the Moon* (letter to his father, 28 Feb 1909). Near the end of his life, he was interested to know whether Kepler's *Somnium* (1634), which tells of a young man's journey to the Moon where he exchanges ideas with the Moon-men, the Selenites (Selene is the Greek goddess of the Moon), would ever be translated ('Unreal Estates' EC 530).

2. Letter to Katharine Farrer, 3 Feb 1954. Cf. 'A Confession,' line 15 (CP 15): 'I've never known / The moon look like a hump-backed crone.'

3. EL 316.

4. DI 108–109.

5. See, e.g., letters to Arthur Greeves, 18 Oct 1916: 'the room was full of moon-light, bright bright as anything. It is too cold to sit looking at the glorious night but it is beautiful!'; and 9 May 1940: 'the blackout has given me so many beautiful sights of Oxford in moonlight that, for purely selfish reasons, I shouldn't mind if it continued for ever.'

6. See, e.g., letter to Greeves, 30? June 1916; MC 68, 118; PC 86; EIC 77.

7. Luna's association with wateriness arises from her effect upon earth's tides. Her dryness featured in Lewis's dream-life, as he records in a letter to his father, 30 Mar 1927, a theme taken up in, 'Forms of Things Unknown,' set on the Moon, where the Hydra petrifies all visitors (EC 882–888). Cf. letter to his brother, 17 Jan 1932.

8. A term used in the Bible. Among those whom Jesus heals in the Gospel According to Matthew are σεληνιαζομένους (lunatics), Matt. 4:24; cf. Matt. 17:15, Ps. 121:6. Lewis had food for thought on this relation between Lunar influence and madness from his meeting with W. B. Yeats. In a letter to Greeves, ? June 1921, he reports how Yeats 'talks very well and not unlike his own printed prose: one sentence came almost directly out of 'Per Amica Silentia Lunae' . . . 'ah yes—So-and-so: he went in for magic too, but his brain wasn't strong enough and he went mad'—'at that time I was going through what are known as Lunar meditations.'

9. DI 109.

10. SIL 62.

11. 'There is no Oyarsa in Heaven who has not got his representative on Earth. And there is no world where you could not meet a little unfallen partner of our own black Archon, a kind of other self. That is why there was an Italian Saturn as well as a Heavenly one, and a Cretan Jove as well as an Olympian. It was these earthly wraiths of the high intelligences that men met in old times when they reported that they had seen the gods. It was with those that a man like Merlin was (at times) conversant. Nothing from beyond the Moon ever really descended,' THS 316–317.

12. Ransom is forewarned of these last days when Tor tells him that he and the Oyarsa of Malacandra 'shall fall upon your moon, wherein there is a secret evil,

and which is as the shield of the Dark Lord of Thulcandra—scarred with many a blow. We shall break her. Her light shall be put out,' Per 196–7; cf. Matt. 24:29. For references to her boundary status, see Per 8, 18, 135.

13. J.B.S. Haldane, 'Auld Hornie, F.R.S.' *Modern Quarterly* (Autumn 1946) 32–40. See Lewis's 'Reply to Professor Haldane,' OTOW 97–109.

14. Lewis did not live to see Neil Armstrong's small step and so it is impossible to say whether he would have regarded it as a giant leap for mankind. His prognostications of space travel were invariably pessimistic. He thought the Moon would be 'contaminated' by human contact (letter to Sister Penelope, 21 Oct 1946); cf. 'Religion and Rocketry' (EC 231–236) and 'Cross-Examination' (EC 557). At a 'sentimental, or perhaps aesthetic' level he objected to the colonisation of the Moon: 'The immemorial Moon—the Moon of the myths, the poets, the lovers—will have been taken from us for ever. Part of our mind, a huge mass of emotional wealth, will have gone. Artemis, Diana, the silver planet belonged in that fashion to all humanity: he who first reaches it steals something from us all': 'The Seeing Eye,' EC 63. However, he acknowledged that only 'a dull clod' could look at the Moon through a telescope without asking what it must be like to live there ('On Science Fiction,' EC 453) and he described the news of Yuri Gagarin's pioneering trip into space as 'exciting' (letter to Alastair Fowler, 17 Apr 1961). One who knew Lewis well remarked that 'it was a pity that [he] could not have lived a few more years until the moon landing. ... How thrilled [he] would have been if he could have seen the rock and dust brought back from the moon!' Fred W. Paxford, 'He Should Have Been a Parson,' in David Graham, (ed.), *We Remember C. S. Lewis: Essays and Memoirs* (Nashville: Broadman & Holman, 2001) 119–128: 126f.

15. THS 273.

16. THS 175–176.

17. Rowan Williams, '*That Hideous Strength*: A Reassessment,' address to the Oxford Lewis Society, 5 Oct 1988 (Lewis Society recordings archive).

18. THS 176.

19. William Shakespeare, *Othello*, V, ii, 111–112: 'It is the very error of the moon, / She comes more near the earth than she was wont, / And makes men mad.'

20. As with Sol, it is not easy to know when Lewis is using the specifically Ptolemaic Luna and when he is using the post-Copernican Moon. I err on the side of caution and therefore do not include, for example, 'A Confession' in this list (see note 2 above). The Moon there is 'a riddle,' which has something in common with the cheating, confusing quality of Luna, but otherwise it savours little of the planet astrologically considered.

21. Cf. 'The Planets,' line 107 (CP 29): 'fancy fails us,' i.e., the influence of Luna's sphere no longer reaches us.

22. 'The Queen of Drum,' V, 138 (NP 168).

23. John Betjeman wrote in a letter to Lewis of 13 Dec 1939: 'I don't see how anyone who has looked at the moon can think of it as 'cruising monthly' in a light canoe.' See John Betjeman, *Letters, Vol. I, 1926–1951*, ed. Candida Lycett

Green (London: Methuen, 1994) 251. His dismissal of the image is attributable more to his enduring vendetta against his former tutor than to considered poetic judgement, and the letter may never in fact have been sent.

24. 'The Planets,' lines 1–13 (CP 26).

25. Her name is significant. 'Jill' is a form of 'Gillian,' from 'Julian(a),' a name very popular in the Middle Ages, especially in the diminutive forms *Gill* and *Jill*. *Gillot* or *Jillet* became a designation for a changeable or flighty girl, whence probably *jilt*. 'Pole' comes from the Old English *pol*, meaning pool, and denotes someone living near a pool or pond. 'Jill Pole' might therefore be translated 'changeable water-dweller.'

26. It is worth noting that this atmosphere affects England as much as Narnia. In LWW, PC and VDT there is nothing clearly Jovial or Martial or Solar about the episodes set in England. But in SC and MN the English scenes are respectively Lunar and Venereal. (There are no scenes set in England in HHB; and in LB the English scenes are brief and either visionary or couched in reported speech.) This may account for why Lewis thought he had got better at the books as the series went on; see letter to Pauline Baynes, 24 May 1955.

27. Lewis may be glancing at *Paradiso* II, 31, where Dante the Pilgrim is enclosed by a cloud in the Moon's circle.

28. The name comes from the work of John Studley, a versifier and translator of 'the Drab Age,' treated in EL 255–256. Studley renders 'Tacitae Stygis' (from Seneca's *Hippolytus*, line 625) as 'Stygian puddle glum.'

29. The quest is different from the quests in the other books: Puddleglum, Jill and Eustace are looking for a person rather than a place, and they do not know where he is located. In LWW and PC the main journey of the story is to Aslan's How; in VDT to the Utter East; in HHB to Narnia and the North; in MN to the western garden and back again. There is no quest in LB.

30. Per 158.

31. Per 157.

32. Per 155.

33. VDT is its nearest rival with four: England, Narnia (i.e., Narnian territories: the Islands which Caspian claims kingship over), the Country-under-Wave, and Aslan's Country.

34. He described it as being among 'those great contrasts which have bitten deeply into my mind . . . air and ether, the low world and the high,' SBJ 125.

35. See DI 199.

36. Robert Houston Smith, *Patches of Godlight: The Pattern of Thought of C. S. Lewis* (Athens, GA: University of Georgia Press, 1981) 98–99.

37. There is a similar sparing and chiasmic use of the sun. We are greeted by (a) a 'blaze of sunshine,' like 'the light of a June day [pouring] into a garage when you open the door.' Then (b) images of weak or fading sunlight: Jill is blown west into the sun, which had been overhead but now is 'getting lower,' producing 'sunset light'; Glimfeather arrives but is 'not quite myself till the sun's down'; 'the sun had set and the air was growing cool,' leaving 'the red remains

of the sunset'; we see 'a morning sun,' 'pale winter sunlight,' a 'sunless river,' a 'sunless sky,' another morning scene in which 'the sun was shining' on wet snow, 'pale sunlight.' Then (c) complete sunlessness for nearly eighty pages while the adventurers are underground. Then back to (b) 'morning sunlight' and 'winter sunshine.' And finally back to (a) 'a great brightness of midsummer sunshine.'

38. A pun on Chaucer's 'Parlement of Foules.' Owls hate 'broad, blazing sunlight' (SC 55).

39. Cynthia (that is, Luna) is '<u>haw</u>,' according to the 'Testament of Cresseid.' Lewis underlined the word and wrote 'pale' in the margin of his copy (now in the Wade Center). Robert Henryson, *The Poems of Robert Henryson*, ed. W.M. Metcalfe (Paisley: Alexander Gardner, 1917) line 257, page 153.

40. SIW 180.

41. See John D. Cox, 'Epistemological Release in *The Silver Chair*,' in Peter J. Schakel (ed.), *The Longing for a Form, Essays on the Fiction of C. S. Lewis* (Kent, OH: Kent State University Press, 1977).

42. See EL 316. Lewis marked Seznec's mention of Spenser's horses in a marginal note on page 293 of his copy of Jean Seznec, *The Survival of the Pagan Gods: The Mythological Tradition and its Place in Renaissance Humanism and Art*, trans. Barbara F. Sessions (New York: Pantheon, 1953) now in the Wade Center.

43. Diana, the huntress, is associated with Luna because moonlight allows night-time hunting. Jill becomes 'like a hunted animal...as long as the pack was after her, she must run till she dropped' (118). Cf. the Queen of Drum who, after offering herself to the Moon, runs faster 'Than when the toilsome chase began' (V, 142).

44. William Shakespeare, *Romeo and Juliet*, II, ii, 4–8.

45. 'What we see him doing at the end of *The Silver Chair* is really quite stunning. I cannot imagine a betrayal of one's faith more complete than this last picture of Christ at the playground, putting weapons into the hands of children.' John Goldthwaite, *The Natural History of Make-Believe: A Guide to the Principal Works of Britain, Europe and America* (Oxford: Oxford University Press, 1996) 241–242. '"Experiment House"...is presumably a school developed on humanistic, rational, non-Christian principles. *Aslan leads a punitive attack on this school*: he specifically directs a process of physical assault.' David Holbrook, *The Skeleton in the Wardrobe, C. S. Lewis's Fantasies: A Phenomenological Study* (Lewisburg: Associated University Presses, 1991) 23–24; his italics.

46. DI 186.

47. James T. Como, *Branches to Heaven: The Geniuses of C. S. Lewis* (Dallas: Spence, 1998) 137.

48. SC 201.

49. 'Before the starry threshold of Jove's court / My mansion is, where those immortal shapes / Of bright aerial spirits live insphered / In regions mild of calm and serene air, / Above the smoke and stir of this dim spot / Which

men call Earth,' John Milton, *Comus*, lines 1–5. Lewis, of course, knew these lines, and the reference to 'wreaths of smoke' is an allusion to them. See his 'A Note on *Comus*,' SMRL 180; cf. SBJ 125. He conducted a correspondence with B. A. Wright about *Comus*, entitled 'Above the Smoke and Stir,' in the *Times Literary Supplement* in 1945.

50. Deut. 6: 6–7. The full Shema is 6: 4–9.

51. Wilson, *Biography*, 137.

52. Austin Farrer, 'The Christian Apologist,' in Jocelyn Gibb, (ed.), *Light on C. S. Lewis* (London: Geoffrey Bles, 1965) 41.

53. Henry Vaughan, 'Peace,' lines 1–2.

54. SBJ 190, alluding to Walter Hilton's *The Scale of Perfection*, II.

55. POP 103.

56. PPL 73.

57. Dante, *Paradiso*, I, 88ff.

58. Dante, *Paradiso*, III, 18.

59. Doris Myers, *C. S. Lewis in Context* (Kent, OH: Kent State University Press, 1994) 154.

60. 'Hamlet: The Prince or the Poem?,' SLE 102. Rilian is not only dressed in black 'like Hamlet' (SC 133), but directly borrows from *Hamlet* when he calls the adventurers 'the more deceived,' a phrase Ophelia uses of herself (III, i, 120). See '*De Audiendis Poetis*' (SMRL 1–17: 8) for more on lunacy in *Hamlet* and why 'Hamlet's lunacy will not be noticed in England.'

61. Her pretension to Solar status is suggested in the first description given of her: '[Rilian and Drinian] rested till it came to high noon: and at noon Drinian looked up and saw the most beautiful lady he had ever seen.' Cf. Rilian's description of her as an 'all but heavenly Queen.'

62. John Milton, *Comus*, line 977; quoted OSP 35.

63. E.g., 'Christianity and Literature,' EC 415; POP 140; MC 149.

64. See letter to Dom Bede Griffiths, 21 Dec 1941.

65. FL 61.

66. DI 20.

67. PPL 79; cf. *Paradise Lost*, VI, 719.

68. Alister McGrath, *Bridge-Building: Effective Christian Apologetics* (Leicester: IVP, 1998) 248–249.

69. Cf. 'With whatever sense of unworthiness, with whatever sense of audacity, we must affirm that we know a little of the higher system which is being transposed': 'Transposition,' EC 274.

70. 'French Nocturne,' line 13 (CP 168). Cf. the various mentions of fancy in SC (32, 151, 206).

71. Lewis was reworking 'Anselm and Descartes . . . I have simply put the 'Ontological Proof' in a form suitable for children,' letter to Nancy Warner, 26 Oct 1963.

72. That the witch turns into a serpent is taken by Spufford as evidence of Lewis's 'misogyny': see Francis Spufford, *The Child that Books Built* (London: Faber &

Faber, 2002) 102. Spufford overlooks the fact that the witch's womanly form is only an appearance: in reality the enemy is a serpent. Rilian is relieved that 'the foul Witch took to her serpent form at the last. It would not have suited well either with my heart or with my honour to have slain a woman' (SC 158f).

73. 'The Funeral of a Great Myth,' EC 22–32: 32.
74. FL 109.
75. Matt. 6:33.
76. FL 122.
77. 'Christianity and Culture,' EC 82.
78. Paul Fiddes, 'C. S. Lewis the Myth-Maker,' in Andrew Walker, & James Patrick, (eds.). *A Christian for All Christians: Essays in Honour of C. S. Lewis* (London: Hodder & Stoughton, 1990) 132–155: 147.
79. POP 140. The quotation is from George MacDonald's *Unspoken Sermons: Third Series*, 11, 12.
80. '"Originality" in the New Testament is quite plainly the prerogative of God alone; even within the triune being of God it seems to be confined to the Father' ('Christianity and Literature,' EC 416).
81. MC 129.
82. POP 139.
83. 'French Nocturne,' line 16 (CP 168).
84. William Shakespeare, *Troilus and Cressida*, I, iii, 85–92.
85. William Shakespeare, *Troilus and Cressida*, I, iii, 133–134.
86. PPL 74.
87. Phil. 2:6.
88. PPL 75.

CHAPTER 7

1. 'The most articulate being I have ever known,' was the verdict of George Watson; see his 'The Art of Disagreement: C. S. Lewis (1898–1963),' *The Hudson Review* (Summer 1995), 231. Emrys Jones has described him as being 'unfailingly eloquent on every single occasion I met him'; he 'used words with lexicographical precision' (Lewis Foundation Summer Colloquium, Oxford, 18 July 2002). For further evidence of his remarkable fluency see Leo Baker's 'Near the Beginning,' in James T. Como, *C. S. Lewis at the Breakfast Table and Other Reminiscences* (London: Collins, 1980) 6–7. The young Lewis was 'an intolerable chatterbox' (SBJ 15); and as an adult he admitted (letter to his father, 29 July 1927) that 'I love to "ride the cork on the ocean of eloquence"' and that "Talking too much is one of my vices" (letter to Mary Willis Shelburne, 15 Apr 1956). He knew Norse, Old and Middle English, Latin, Greek, French, Italian, and some German and Old Welsh.
2. At the age of sixteen he was described by his tutor as 'the most brilliant translator of Greek plays I have ever met' (Roger Lancelyn Green, & Walter

Hooper, *C. S. Lewis: A Biography*, revised & expanded edition (London: HarperCollins, 2002) 28); a year later he was being compared to Addison, Landor, and Macaulay. (W.H. Lewis, *The Lewis Papers: Memoirs of the Lewis Family, 1850–1930* (unpublished: Wade Center) Vol. V, 74). His writing skill was recognised by the award of the Chancellor's English Essay Prize at Oxford in 1921, by the Gollancz Memorial Prize (for AOL) in 1937, and by the Carnegie Medal (for LB) in 1956. His pen was swift: by the time of his death he had published 38 titles, about 200 essays or articles, 72 poems, 2 short stories, 40 book reviews, 64 letters, and edited or prefaced 11 other volumes; his juvenilia, diaries, private correspondence and unpublished writings ran to thousands of pages.

3. SBJ 38.
4. DI 109.
5. DI 108.
6. In Lewis's copy of *Love's Labour's Lost*, now in the library of Magdalene College, Cambridge, is the following underlining: 'The words of <u>Mercury are harsh after the songs of Apollo</u>' (V, ii, 919–920). Lewis annotates it: 'MERCURY & APOLLO. Hart explains "the best prose is harsh after verse." *Eloquence* v. *Poetry* almost certainly right.'
7. DI 107–108.
8. PH 20–21.
9. PH 21.
10. DI 163.
11. AT 171.
12. See William Shakespeare, *The Winter's Tale*, IV, iii, 24–26.
13. For his love of definition, see, e.g., the seven-fold definition of 'romantic' in PR 9–12; the five-fold definition of 'spirit' in M 173–177. For his interest in 'families' of words, see EIC 89: 'We are driven to speak of the 'colour,' 'flavour,' 'texture,' 'smell' or 'race' of words.' For homophones, see, e.g., 'some sum' (THS 104); 'poor paw' (VDT 78). For homonyms, see, e.g., the different meanings of 'ransom' (Per 135). For synonyms, see his amusing letter to Barfield, 17? May 1943, where he asks, 'Why can I never say anything *once*?' For onomatopoeias, see, e.g., 'Narnian Suite' (CP 20–21).
14. See his letter to Pitter, 24 July 1946, about uniting form and content in poetry. In his fiction, the paragraph in Per (202) beginning, 'And now, by a transition which he did not notice' is an example of such a union. In his apologetics, LTM is a prime example, where the epistolary relationship with Malcolm reflects the prayer relationship with God; cf. letter to Greeves, 24 Dec 1930. In his scholarship it is most obviously evident in the *con amore* passage about Richard Hooker in EL 462f, beginning, 'The style is, for its purpose, perhaps the most perfect in English.' As Lewis says of Hooker's phrase-making, so it may be said of his own: 'The structure mirrors the real movement of his mind.'
15. 'Shelley, Dryden and Mr. Eliot,' SLE 201.
16. Percy Bysshe Shelley, *The Witch of Atlas*, lines 613–616.

17. See EL 104. The Tower's shadow (the 'shadow of that hideous strength') is said to be more than six miles in length. The tower planned by the N.I.C.E. is to be so tall that it 'would make a quite noticeable addition to the skyline of New York' (THS 23; cf. 288).

18. Lewis invented the name 'Viritrilbia' for its 'vibrating, tintillating quality,' appropriate, he thought, 'for the subtlety of Mercury'; see letter to Mrs Hook, 29 Dec 1958. Astronomically, Mercury is the lightest and swiftest of the six planets other than the Sun. It weighs 0.055 units of Earth mass (Venus 0.815; Mars 0.107; Jupiter 318.0; Saturn 95.2) and revolves round the Sun once every 88 days (Venus 225 days; Mars 687 days; Jupiter 12 years; Saturn 29 years).

19. THS 228–229.

20. EL 525.

21. EL 14.

22. Francis Bacon, *The Advancement of Learning*, ed. Michael Kiernan (Oxford: Clarendon Press, 2000) 120.

23. THS 100. In *The Meaning of Meaning* (1923), Ogden and Richards had argued that everything could be said with under one thousand words by substituting descriptive phrases for particular terms. They established rules for classifying words so as to ensure that each signifier stood for only one referent and they used these rules to invent 'Basic English,' a collection of 850 English words covering the needs of everyday life. Richards believed that Basic English could be used for teaching English as a second language and spent several years in China trying to put his theories into practice.

24. See Doris Myers, *C. S. Lewis in Context* (Kent, OH: Kent State University Press, 1994).

25. Owen Barfield, *The Rediscovery of Meaning and Other Essays* (Middletown, CT: Wesleyan University Press, 1977) 64; cf. 123. See also Owen Barfield, *Poetic Diction, A Study in Meaning* (Hanover, NH: Wesleyan University Press, 1984), a work which deeply influenced Lewis (see SBJ 161).

26. 'Bluspels and Flalansferes: A Semantic Nightmare,' SLE 265.

27. THS 321–322. Thoth was the Egyptian god of record-keeping, calculation, calendars, and orderly practices in general, whom the Greeks later identified with Hermes. One of Hermes' titles is *Argeiphontes*, 'the slayer of Argos.'

28. Humphrey Carpenter. *The Inklings: C. S. Lewis, J.R.R. Tolkien, Charles Williams, and Their Friends* (London: Allen & Unwin, 1978) 220.

29. Owen Barfield, 'Introduction,' in Jocelyn Gibb (ed.), *Light on C.S. Lewis* (London: Geoffrey Bles, 1965) xvi.

30. 'A Reply to Professor Haldane,' OTOW 97.

31. G.K. Chesterton, *The Well and the Shallows* (London: Sheed & Ward, 1935) 10.

32. AOL 173.

33. Joe R. Christopher, *C. S. Lewis* (New York: Twayne, 1987) 93.

34. E.g., John 6:26; 10:38; cf. M 136–167.

35. Heb. 1:3; cf. MC 131–141.

36. See LTM 81.
37. 'The Psalms,' EC 218. Cf. the two chapters on 'second meanings' in ROP (Chapters X and XII).
38. AT 125.
39. LTM 86.
40. George Orwell, *Nineteen Eighty-Four* (London: Penguin, 1983) 49.
41. Orwell reviewed THS for *The Manchester Evening News* (15 Aug 1945) 2. He wrote: 'One could recommend this book unreservedly if Mr. Lewis had succeeded in keeping it all on a single level. Unfortunately, the supernatural keeps breaking in.' George Orwell, *The Complete Works of George Orwell*, ed. Peter Davison, Vol. XVII (London: Secker & Warburg, 1986–1998) 250–251. Kath Filmer-Davies is of the view that Lewis's novel 'clearly influenced Orwell's own *Nineteen Eighty-Four*': see her essay, 'Fantasy' in Thomas L. Martin, (ed.). *Reading the Classics with C. S. Lewis* (Grand Rapids, MI: Baker Academic, 2000) 285–296: 293.
42. E.g., in the character of Ampleforth (whose name connotes the well-known Catholic school in Yorkshire) who is liquidated for retaining the word 'God' in an edition of the poems of Kipling. See George Orwell, *Nineteen Eighty-Four* (London: Penguin, 1983) 199.
43. James Patrick, 'The Heart's Desire and the Landlord's Rules: C. S. Lewis as a Moral Philosopher' in Mills, David (ed.). *The Pilgrim's Guide: C. S. Lewis and the Art of Witness* (Grand Rapids, MI: Eerdmans, 1998) 81.
44. See 'A Reply to Professor Haldane,' OTOW 107–109.
45. 'Poetry is failing us, or we it, if after our reading we do not find ourselves changed; not with temporary change . . . but with a permanent alteration of our possibilities as responsive individuals in good or bad adjustment to an all but over-whelming concourse of stimulations.' I. A. Richards, *Poetries and Sciences* (London: Routledge & Kegan Paul, 1970) 47. Whether Lewis thought that Richards had wittingly or unwittingly volunteered for the role of devil on the shoulder of language is not clear, but he was of the view that Richards's theories were spiritually debilitating. He wrote: 'The whole school of critical thought which descends from Dr Richards bears such deep marks of its anti-Christian origins that I question if it can ever be baptised': 'Christianity and Culture,' EC 82f.
46. 'Re-Adjustment,' line 7 (CP 116).
47. 'On Stories,' EC 503.
48. That the Sun should be the 'sire' of Mercury is mythologically confusing, for Mercury was the son of Jupiter, not Sol. But this may be explained by the frequent overlap of Solar and Jovial qualities. Mercury, in the modern cosmos, is the planet nearest the Sun.
49. Cf. the 'wreathèd wand' of 'The Planets,' line 19. This is the caduceus with which Mercury (or the kerykeion with which Hermes) healed the sick and led the dead to the other world. 'Mercury conducts pious *animae* to the happy dwellings,' according to Horace's *Odes* (I, x, 17); see SIW 271.

50. 'The Birth of Language,' CP 24–25. For more on the background to the poem, see letter to Ruth Pitter, 24 July 1946, and Owen Barfield's note 'On the Text of "The Birth of Language"' in Charles A. Huttar's essay, 'A Lifelong Love Affair with Language: C. S. Lewis's Poetry' in Peter J. Schakel, & Charles A. Huttar (eds.), *Word and Story in C. S. Lewis* (Columbia: University of Missouri Press, 1991) 86–108: 107f. Cf. letter to Barfield, 25 May 1946.
51. Letter to Rhona Bodle, 24 June 1949. Cf. SIL 115.
52. 'The Planets,' lines 13–27 (CP 26).
53. Roger Lancelyn Green, & Walter Hooper, *C. S. Lewis: A Biography*, revised & expanded edition (London: HarperCollins, 2002) 310.
54. Mercury also rules Virgo, and this connection may have led Lewis to the two storylines of challenged but preserved virginity: Aravis has to escape from a forced marriage to Ahoshta; Susan is subjected to the unwanted attentions of Rabadash. I am indebted to Emily Younger for this observation.
55. Letter to Arthur Greeves, 12 Oct 1915.
56. Homer, *Iliad* 3.237, 'Castor, tamer of horses, and Pollux, the fine boxer.'
57. AT 149. Castor and Pollux were the sons of Leda and Jupiter; he seduced her in the form of a swan. 'Leda's twin-born progeny' find their way into Lewis's poem 'After Aristotle' (CP 94–95). He would have known that Paul's ship in the Acts of the Apostles had these 'Dioscuri' as its figurehead (Acts 28:11), and this perhaps explains his own variation on this Mercurial theme in the minor detail of the Splendour Hyaline's prow shaped like a 'swan's head' (recalled in PC 99). 'Hyaline' means 'transparent like glass,' and Mercury's inhabitants are likewise vitrified, according to Sterne in *Tristram Shandy* (Vol. I, chapter 23) and Godwin in *Enquiry Concerning Political Justice* (Book V, section 1). Cf. the water 'clear as glass' in Aslan's footprint (HHB 142).
58. Letter to his brother, 11 Apr 1940.
59. SIL 7. Cf. OSP 129 where Mercury is depicted as a 'winged figure' carrying a trumpet, in the sculpture of the solar system.
60. Martha C. Sammons, *A Guide Through Narnia* (London: Hodder & Stoughton, 1979) 153.
61. EL 266.
62. EL 304.
63. EL 347.
64. Aravis thus appears to represent 'Philology' (i.e. Literature), squired by Mercury (Shasta): their coupling is Lewis's version of Martianus Capella's *De Nuptiis Philologiae et Mercurii*; see DI 107. Under his Greek name of Hermes, Mercury had the title *Kriophoros* ('ram-bearer'), which may explain why Shasta and Aravis name their son 'Ram'; Rabadash's battering-ram may be meant as a punning perversion of the same. Another of Hermes' titles is *Propulaios* ('before the gates'), which helps account for the title of chapter 3, 'At the Gates of Tashbaan,' and Shasta's long wait outside the city gates, which lasts from chapter 6 to chapter 9. Hermes was also credited with inventing the flute; 'flute players' are the only musicians mentioned by the Narnians (HHB 65, cf. PC 99).

65. AOL 252.
66. 'The Queen of Drum,' V, 151 (NP 168).
67. HHB 139.
68. HHB 139–140.
69. Letter to Sister Penelope, 20 Feb 1943.
70. SIW 271; see note 49 above.
71. Alister McGrath, *The Renewal of Anglicanism* (London: SPCK, 1993) 95.
72. LTM 13; cf. 18, 30, 65, 87.
73. 'Footnote to All Prayers,' lines 11–12 (CP 143).
74. 'The Apologist's Evening Prayer,' lines 9–10 (CP 143).
75. M 97.
76. Letter to Arthur Greeves, 18 Oct 1931.
77. Matt. 6:7–8.
78. PR 248.
79. Gal. 4:6; cf. LTM 22.
80. LTM 71.
81. LTM 63.
82. LTM 72.
83. George Steiner, *After Babel: Aspects of Language and Translation* (Oxford: Oxford University Press, 1998) 116.
84. LTM 83; cf. 'Behind the Scenes,' EC 710–713.
85. 'The Ecstasy,' lines 37–38 (CP 51).
86. See letter to Warfield Firor, 17 Aug 1949.
87. Cf. Rev. 8:1.
88. According to the OED, the various meanings of 'bree' include the eye-lid or the superciliary ridge (cf. the reference to Bree's eyelids and his supercilious manner, HHB 168), pottage, to scare or terrify, water or sea, and disagreement. 'Bree' is also the name of a village in Tolkien's Middle-Earth.
89. Eutyches (c. 378–454), a monk of Constantinople, affirmed that there was only one nature in Christ 'after the union' and denied that His manhood was consubstantial with ours.
90. Martha C. Sammons, *A Guide Through Narnia* (London: Hodder & Stoughton, 1979) 133.
91. Dante, *Paradiso*, VI, 14–15. Despite his Eutychian views, Justinian is received into Paradise where he is shown to the pilgrim in Mercury's sphere and is seen singing 'twin-lustred with his two-fold luminance' (VII, 5).
92. Andrew Walker, 'Scripture, revelation and Platonism in C.S. Lewis,' *Scottish Journal of Theology* 55 (1), 2002, 19–35: 34.
93. Mary Warnock, 'Religious Imagination,' in James P. Mackey (ed.), *Religious Imagination* (Edinburgh: Edinburgh University Press, 1986) 142–157: 154.
94. Lyle H. Smith, 'C.S. Lewis and the Making of Metaphor,' in Peter J. Schakel, & Charles A. Huttar (eds.), *Word and Story in C. S. Lewis* (Columbia: University of Missouri Press, 1991) 11–28: 27.
95. HHB 140.

96. After his torture in the Objective Room, Mark realises 'the night must be nearly ended' (THS 270).
97. PPL 41.
98. Lee D. Rossi, *The Politics of Fantasy: C. S. Lewis and J.R.R. Tolkien* (Epping: UMI Research Press, 1984) 33. Lewis's taste for equivocation was more discriminating than that of Shakespeare, whose penchant for punning (according to Johnson) was his fatal Cleopatra for whom he lost the world and was content to lose it. Lewis disliked bad puns (letter to Greeves, 20 June 1916), but still makes a few of them himself, e.g., 'traits/trays' (letter to Ruth Pitter, 22 Sept 1949), 'mews/news' (letter to Martin, 24 Apr 1958). His better puns include 'Vascular da Gama' (Green & Hooper, op. cit. 124), 'experimental husbands' ('On Obstinacy in Belief,' EC 211), and 'you must have had a pretty beastly time' (VDT 84); he also enjoyed reapplying malapropisms, e.g., 'the alligator of love' (letter to Barfield, 28 June 1936), 'nice derangement' (DI 195). But his main paranomasiacal interest was in jolting dead or dormant metaphors back to literal life: e.g., 'below the belt' (VDT 30); 'saving the bacon' (SC 76); 'old wives' tale' (PR 101); 'all being well' (PR 247); 'for pity's sake' ('The Saboteuse,' CP 52f); 'bleeding charity' (GD 32); 'absolute hell' (MC 70); 'damned nonsense' (MC 41).
99. Michael Edwards, 'C. S. Lewis: Imagining Heaven,' *Literature and Theology*, 6 (June 1992) 107–124: 108.
100. AOL 45, quoting from *Religio Medici* by Sir Thomas Browne (Pt. 1, para 13).
101. E.g., Matt. 16:18.
102. Augustine, *Sermones* CXC.
103. One of Lewis's favourite maxims, taken from Thomas à Kempis's *The Imitation of Christ* (Book 2, ch. 10). Cf. FL 9; LTM 89.
104. Terms used by Lewis to describe how God is seen in Hooker's 'model of the universe,' see EL 459–460, a passage which can usefully be read as Lewis's theological self-portrait.

CHAPTER 8

1. George Herbert, 'Sonnet I,' line 4.
2. George Herbert, 'Jordan (I),' line 15.
3. Austin Farrer, *The Glass of Vision* (Westminster: Dacre Press, 1948) 118.
4. 'What Chaucer really did to *Il Filostrato*,' SLE 28.
5. Letter to Arthur Greeves, 20 Feb 1917.
6. However, he had already acquired a musical interest in this symbolic region, listening to Charles Gounod's 'Bright Star of Eve' and Wagner's 'Venusburg music.' See letter to his brother, 22 Dec 1914, and letters to Greeves, 4 May 1915, 11 May 1915.
7. See letter to Greeves, 5 May 1919. This was probably his copy of the 'Mirror of Venus' referred to in his diary in 1923: see W.H. Lewis, *The Lewis Papers:*

Memoirs of the Lewis Family, 1850–1930, 11 vols. (unpublished: Wade Center), entry in Lewis's diary, 26 May 1923. Whether it was the painting by Velázquez or Titian or Burne-Jones or another artist is not known. It might have been Bronzino's 'Allegory of Venus and Cupid' which later hung in his rooms at Magdalen: see Derek Brewer, 'The Tutor: A Portrait,' in James T. Como (ed.), *C. S. Lewis at the Breakfast Table and Other Reminiscences* (London: Collins, 1980) 56. There he also had Tintoretto's 'The Origin of the Milky Way,' see Peter Bayley, 'From Master to Colleague' in Como, *Breakfast Table*, 77.

8. 'I have nearly finished the Venus poem and am full of ideas for another... about Helen, whom Simon Magus... found living as a very earthly person in Antioch and gradually recalled to her who she was and took her up to Zeus again, reborn: on their way they had to fight 'the Dynasties' or planets,' letter to Greeves, 5 May 1919. Cf. letter to Leo Baker, 25 Feb 1921.

9. 'Every night Venus grows more spectacular. It is true *Chaucerian* weather!' (letter to his brother, 21 Apr 1940); 'Do you ever notice Venus these mornings at about quarter past seven? She has been terrifically bright lately, almost better than Jupiter' (letter to Laurence Harwood, 31 Dec 1946). Roger Lancelyn Green recalls Lewis seeing Venus above Addison's Walk and exclaiming 'Perelandra!' with 'a passionate longing in his voice'; he then went on to quote Tennyson's 'Locksley Hall Sixty Years After,' the passage about Venus which ends with the lines: 'Might we not in glancing heavenward on a Star so silver-fair / Yearn, and clasp the hands and murmur, 'Would to God that we were there'?' Roger Lancelyn Green, & Walter Hooper, *C. S. Lewis: A Biography*, revised & expanded edition (London: HarperCollins, 2002) 201f.

10. See AMR 297, 346, 395.

11. Lewis comments on the significance that Jung found in Faust's cry, 'The Mothers! The Mothers!' in 'Psycho-analysis and Literary Criticism,' SLE 298.

12. See George Sayer, *Jack: C. S. Lewis and His Times* (San Francisco: Harper & Row, 1988) 251.

13. '[When I was] about 9... my Mother died, and there has never really been any sense of security and snugness since. That is, I've not quite succeeded in growing up on that point: there is still too much of 'Mammy's little lost boy' about me,' letter to Phyllis Sandeman, ? Dec 1953.

14. See Green and Hooper, *C. S. Lewis* 308–314. The surviving draft of what became MN was written immediately after LWW. That the two works were originally entangled in the womb of Lewis's imagination is suggested by his comment about 'a cupboard which one had hitherto valued as a place for hanging coats [that] proved one day, when you opened the door, to lead to the garden of the Hesperides' ('Different Tastes in Literature,' EC 468). According to Lilly's *Christian Astrology* (1659, Vol. I, chapters ix and xii), both Jupiter and Venus have a particular influence upon wardrobes.

15. For a treatment of which, see W.D., Norwood, Jr. 'C. S. Lewis' Portrait of Aphrodite,' *Southern Quarterly*, VIII (1970) 237–272. Norwood's analysis of

TWHF 'has as its basis this very point: that the goddess Ungit—Aphrodite, as she is identified by the Fox, or Venus—is one "face" of the true God; i.e., she is God in his aspect of Love,' op. cit. 255. AGO also contains much material pertaining to this theme, e.g., its frequent references to mothers (10, 19, 24, 30, 41), its reference to Joy Lewis as 'H' (suggesting Helen, her first name); A. L. Rowse even thinks that the title is modelled on Fry's *Venus Observed* (*The Diaries of A.L. Rowse*, ed. Richard Ollard (London: Penguin, 2003) 365). Finally, Lewis's short story, 'After Ten Years' (EC 864–881), indicates continuing rumination on the subject of the beautiful female and the loss thereof, here typified by Helen of Troy.

16. DI 107.
17. SIL 16.
18. AOL 225.
19. SIL 50f; cf. EL 374f.
20. AOL 121.
21. SIW 225.
22. 'Hero and Leander,' SLE 70.
23. EL 498–9. Cf. 'Hero and Leander,' SLE 59.
24. SIL 51.
25. SIL 49; cf. EL 375.
26. SIL 49.
27. AOL 332.
28. SIL 16.
29. 'The Philosopher,' lines 12–13 (CP 186).
30. 'Death in Battle,' lines 1–4 (CP 223).
31. AMR 314. Cf. SBJ 140, 165; also NP 4 where Lewis mentions the 'Hesperian or Western Garden' system of imagery which he 'mainly derived from Euripedes, Milton, Morris, and the early Yeats.' The Hesperides were the daughters of Hesperus, god of the evening star, who guarded the grove of immortality-giving apple trees in Hera's western orchard and who occasionally plucked fruit for themselves. Not trusting them, Hera placed in the garden an unsleeping, hundred-headed dragon named Ladon.

 The apple is also central in the myth of the marriage of Peleus and Thetis at which Eris (Strife) threw a golden apple into the midst of the guests. It bore the inscription 'For the fairest.' Hera, Athene, and Aphrodite quarrelled over it and finally made Paris the arbiter of their dispute. They each offered him bribes, Aphrodite's being Helen, wife of Menelaus, ruler of Sparta. Paris gave the apple to Aphrodite and abducted Helen.
32. 'The Landing,' CP 41–42. Cf. 'To a Friend,' lines 5–9 (CP 118–119).
33. 'Lilith,' CP 109; cf. letter to Barfield, 19 June 1930; letter to Greeves, 1 Sept 1933; THS 62–63. See also Screwtape's letter to Wormwood: 'You will find, if you look carefully into any human's heart, that he is haunted by at least two imaginary women—a terrestrial and an infernal Venus' (SL 104).

34. SBJ 137.
35. Lewis would have acknowledged that 'discreditable' expressions of Venus (in his case he means masturbation and his early intense, possibly adulterous, relationship with Mrs Moore) were not full tests of *sehnsucht*. Marriage, on the other hand, was. However, this, too, could not test it to destruction. See AGO 9: 'We both knew we wanted something besides one another.'
36. Cf. Psyche, 'slim and straight as a sceptre,' TWHF 40. As the Martial spear partly symbolised the penis (see chapter 4), so the Venereal 'secret sceptre' should be understood partly as a symbol of the clitoris.
37. 'The Planets,' lines 27–38 (CP 26–27).
38. An allusion to Rev. 2:28. Cf. letter to Oliver Chase Quick, 18 Jan 1941; Per 200.
39. Lewis probably had in mind Shelley's 'Ode to the West Wind' and possibly Masefield's 'The West Wind.' The west wind has an obvious connection to the western Garden of the Hesperides. 'Westwind himself' becomes Psyche's husband in TWHF.
40. 'The Weight of Glory,' EC 104.
41. 'Five Sonnets,' lines 43–45 (CP 141).
42. 2 Cor. 12: 2: 'I know a man in Christ who . . . was taken up to the third heaven.' In Jewish writings both before and after Christ, the conception of seven heavens is found. See *The Testament of Levi* 2:7; *Assumption of Isaiah* 6:13; Babylonian Talmud *Hagigah* 12b. Cf. 1 Kgs 8:27; Eph. 4:10.
43. He returns permanently to Perelandra at the end of THS, joining Arthur in Avalon, which in that book is variously called Abhalljin and Aphallin. 'Abhal' means *apple* in Gaelic.
44. As regards sweetness, Lewis gives us 'a light wind, full of sweetness,' 'sweet heather,' 'sweet new scents,' 'sweet night breezes.' As regards laughter, he tells us that Perelandrian thunder is 'the laugh, rather than the roar, of heaven'; Ransom suffers 'a real schoolboy fit of the giggles'; the Green Lady bursts 'into laughter—peal upon peal of laughter till her whole body shook with it'; 'her sudden laughter'; she 'laughed for a whole minute on end'; 'the King laughed . . . Ransom laughed . . . the Queen laughed as well. And the birds began clapping their wings and the beasts wagging their tails.' As regards Venus's metal, he mentions a 'copper-coloured floor,' a 'copper-coloured ridge,' 'copper-coloured heather,' the 'coppery-green of the water,' the 'coppery sea.' And as regards warmth and wetness, Ransom's first experience of the planet is of 'unconsciously' swimming in an ocean which is 'as warm as a shallow bay with sandy bottom in a sub-tropical climate'; he is 'naked yet warm'; 'the darkness was warm'; there is 'warm splendour' all over Perelandra, the planet on which 'the lands swim'; the Green Lady, Ransom speculates, has 'a marine ancestry'—naturally, because she is the foam-born goddess.
45. Euripides, *Hippolytus*, 1:742; cf. TWHF 17.
46. 'Spenser's Cruel Cupid,' SMRL 166. For more on Hesperian apples see letter to Ruth Pitter, 5 Mar 1955.
47. EL 103.

48. THS 322–323.
49. Ransom says: 'I have long known that this house [St. Anne's] is deeply under [Venus's] influence.' St. Anne is traditionally thought to have been the mother of the Virgin Mary, that is, mother of The Holy Mother. However, Lewis claimed to have selected 'St. Anne's' 'merely as a plausible and euphonious name,' not for any deeper reason (letter to William Kinter, 30/7/54). If this is an accurate recollection on Lewis's part, the choice was a happy one.
50. When the bears begin eating everything comestible in the kitchen, Ransom says, 'Sine Cerere et Baccho, Dimble' (375), alluding, inaccurately, to the comedy Eunuchus (IV.v.6) by the Roman dramatist Terence (2nd century B.C.). He meant, 'Sine Cerere et Libero friget Venus': 'without Ceres and Libero [= Bacchus], Venus freezes,' i.e., without food and drink, love is cold. It is for this reason that 'food and wine' await Mark and Jane at the Lodge. Cf. God 'is Bacchus, Venus, Ceres all rolled into one,' M 118.
51. Doris Myers, C. S. Lewis in Context (Kent, OH: Kent State University Press, 1994) 10.
52. See his undated letter 'to a friend,' LCSL 208. Williams's work is alluded to twice in the course of the story (THS 194, 370).
53. AT 101.
54. A phrase borrowed from William Wordsworth, Prelude, XIV, 226.
55. AT 102.
56. AT 149.
57. DI 99.
58. Letter to Paul Elmer More, 23 May 1935.
59. SIW 257; cf. MN 77.
60. C. S. Lewis, Il Nipote del Mago, Traduzione di Giorgina Vivanti (Torino: Paravia, 1960).
61. FL 92.
62. AOL 237; FL 92. 'Aphrodite the laughing' is Homer's formula epithet for the goddess in the Iliad and Odyssey. In Lewis's view, modern discussions of 'the act of Venus' (his term for sexual intercourse), 'sandpapered most of the Homeric laughter off her face' (LTM 16). See also TWHF 29–30: Orual laughs more during Psyche's early days than 'in all my life before ... I laughed because [Psyche] was always laughing. She laughed before the third month.'
63. Myers, C. S. Lewis in Context, 174.
64. MN 110–111. Cf. 'The animals, like our own dogs in similar circumstances, dimly understood that there was merriment afoot; all manner of gambolling, wing-clapping, snorting, and standing upon hind legs began to be displayed. And still the Green Lady laughed' (Per 48).
65. The presence of policemen may be a joke twice over. First, because policemen are commonly nicknamed coppers. Second, because Venus guides 'the amerouse constablerye' (Lewis made this underlining in his copy of John Lydgate's The Assembly of Gods: or The Accord of Reason and Sensuality in the Fear of Death, Vol. I, page 40, line 1470, now in the Wade Center).

66. Jadis, though she has the beauty of Venus, does not possess Venereal fertility. Her 'infernal' nature manifests itself in the exact opposite, a love of death, so that she speaks the Deplorable Word in order to destroy Charn. The donegalitarian interpretation of her character helps explain why she is so different from the Jadis of LWW; there she is a Hans Andersen–like Snow Queen because she represents the wintriness that Joviality is going to counteract.

67. He has, by this time, become 'a nicer and less selfish old man than he had ever been before,' suggesting that he is, like Cunizza and Rahab, whom Dante put in the sphere of Venus, now penitent of his lawless love.

68. It is interesting to see how he suggested a Jovial element in the surviving unfinished draft of MN. In that manuscript to which Hooper has given the title 'The Lefay Fragment,' Digory and Polly plan to explore a river on an oaken raft. That it is made from oak, Jove's tree, suggests again that Venus is not going to be left without vestiges of the kingly planet.

69. FL 91.

70. PR 110; FL 85. Cf. Lewis's argument that virginity ought to be lost 'in obedience to Venus' rather than 'in obedience to the lure of the caucus' ('The Inner Ring,' EC 724). See also his argument that unchastity is an evil, not because coitus is an evil, but because it is good and must be honoured: 'Foamborn Venus . . . golden Aphrodite . . . Our Lady of Cyprus . . . I never breathed a word against you' ('We Have No 'Right to Happiness',' EC 390, Lewis's ellipses).

71. Letter to James Higgins, 2 Dec 1962. Cf. letter to Ruth Pitter, 8 Jan 1952.

72. Such a thing 'embarrasses and nauseates me' ('On Science Fiction,' EC 460). Not that he was averse to depicting sexuality in the Narniad, as Philip Pullman has alleged (see Pullman, Philip. 'The Dark Side of Narnia,' *The Guardian*, 1 Oct 1998). There are marriages, and fruitful marriages, depicted in the Chronicles: e.g., between Caspian and Ramandu's daughter (VDT 188); between Cor and Aravis (HHB 188); Bree and Hwin also get married, but not to each other (HHB 188); and there is a teasing suggestion of a budding romance between Lucy and Tirian at the end of LB (134, 136, 137).

73. Frank's name is itself suggestive of Venereal activity. Lewis was struck by Spenser's description of the act of love: 'franckly each paramor his leman knowes' (AOL 316, 332, quoting *Faerie Queene*, III, vi, 41); and he writes approvingly of the 'singularly fresh and frank account of Arthur's meeting with Gloriana' (AOL 332f). 'The god of love, in the *Romance of the Rose*, says that the servant . . . must be . . . *frans* [frank]' and Lewis quotes Shakespeare's line 'bearing with frank appearance their purposes towards Cyprus' (SIW 124).

74. Helen's name connotes Helen of Troy, that avatar of beauty, whom Lewis habitually links with Venereal imagery.

75. Charles A. Huttar, 'C. S. Lewis's Narnia and the "Grand Design",' in Peter J. Schakel, (ed.) *The Longing for a Form, Essays on the Fiction of C. S. Lewis* (Kent, OH: Kent State University Press, 1977) 125.

76. THS 323.

77. MN 108.
78. It it used three times in TWHF: Psyche is rescued by Westwind's 'beautiful arms which seemed to burn me (though the burning didn't hurt)' (121); when she takes the cup in his palace: 'again, that burning, though without pain' (123); and when Orual encounters Psyche at the end of the story, 'I knew that she was a goddess indeed. Her hands burned me (a painless burning) when they met mine' (317).
79. See Peter J. Schakel, *The Way into Narnia: A Reader's Guide* (Grand Rapids, MI: Eerdmans, 2005) 101.
80. SIL 129.
81. SIL 56.
82. Lewis's mother died before he was ten: 'With my mother's death all settled happiness, all that was tranquil and reliable, disappeared from my life. There was to be much fun, many pleasures, many stabs of Joy; but no more of the old security. It was sea and islands now; the great continent had sunk like Atlantis' (SBJ 23). Intriguingly, the rings that Uncle Andrew uses to send people between the worlds are made from dust found in a secret box left to him by his godmother, Mrs Lefay, and 'the box was Atlantean; it came from the lost island of Atlantis' (MN 24). It does not seem fanciful to draw a connection here: Lewis likens the loss of his mother to the disappearance of Atlantis; he has Digory's mother saved from death by means of dust retrieved from Atlantis.
83. SIL 56.
84. Digory, a highly unusual name, meaning 'almost lost,' is taken from the anonymous Middle English poem, *Sir Degaré*. Degaré's story, like Digory's, involves restoration of his relationship with his parents. Degaré (unlike many medieval heroes) was born illegitimately and abandoned by his mother. Digory also is without his father, who is away in India, and has to face up to the expected loss of his mother (through her imminent, approaching death). Both Degaré and Digory reclaim their natal parents before the end of their stories. See Anne Laskaya, & Eve Salisbury (eds.), *The Middle English Breton Lays* (Kalamazoo, MI: Medieval Institute Publications, 1995) 89–144. Digory's surname, 'Kirke' (he is not named in LWW), which in LB will allow Lewis to suggest something of his old Saturnine tutor, Kirkpatrick, here possibly connotes maternal influence by cross-reference to 'Mother Kirk' (PR 100 *et seq*).

Polly is a form of 'Molly,' which is a form of 'Mary,' the archetypal mother, with whom Lewis associated 'warmth and wetness and fecundity' (PR 232). Polly's surname, 'Plummer,' is perhaps meant to suggest a grower of plums: cf. the description of the Wood between the Worlds as 'rich as plum-cake.' Mrs Dimble, the most Venereal character in THS, complains that the N.I.C.E. have destroyed all her plum trees.
85. Alfred Lord Tennyson, 'Locksley Hall Sixty Years After,' line 185. See note 9 above.
86. John Milton, *Comus*, lines 394ff; cf. SIL 24. See also Per 39.

87. PPL 51.
88. Letter to Charles Williams, 22 Feb 1939.
89. M 142; cf. 118.
90. 'Neoplatonism in Spenser's Poetry,' SMRL 155.
91. 'Priestesses in the Church?' EC 400–401.
92. LTM 54f.
93. TWHF 283.
94. 'Priestesses in the Church?,' EC 398.
95. See letter to Alastair Fowler, 22 Nov 1960.
96. SIL 42.
97. SIL 16.
98. Letter to Alastair Fowler, 22 Nov 1960.
99. *The Faerie Queene*, III, vi, 12; IV, x, 47. Cf. AOL 342; SIL 43.
100. Cf. Edmund Spenser, *An Hymne in Honour of Beautie*, lines 50–56, quoted in SIL 44:

> For through infusion of celestiall powre,
> The duller earth it quickneth with delight,
> And life-full spirits privily doth powre
> Through all the parts, that to the lookers sight
> They seeme to please. That is thy soveraine might,
> O Cyprian Queene, which flowing from the beame
> Of thy bright starre, thou into them doest streame.

101. Job 38: 4a, 7; cf. Per 97.
102. POP 41.
103. When Pullman was seven his father died in a plane crash. He later discovered that his parents had been preparing to divorce at the time of his father's death. For further details see Nicholas Tucker, *Darkness Visible: Inside the World of Philip Pullman* (Cambridge: Icon Books, 2003).
104. Public meeting, St Andrew's Church, North Oxford, 16 June 2002. For more on this and Pullman's other criticisms of the Narniad, see Michael Ward, 'Philip Pullman's Attack on Narnia: A Defense,' *Mars Hill Review*, No. 21 (2003) 127–135.

CHAPTER 9

1. 'Quam Bene Saturno.' W. H. Lewis. *The Lewis Papers: Memoirs of the Lewis Family, 1850–1930* (unpublished: Wade Center) Vol. 4, 51–52.
2. ROP 85. Cf. Isa. 7:14, 15; 9:7; 11:6–8; 35:1.
3. ROP 90. Cf. 'De Audiendis Poetis,' SMRL 4.
4. *Dymer*, IX, 35 (NP 90).
5. Don W. King. *C. S. Lewis, Poet: The Legacy of his Poetic Impulse* (Kent, OH: Kent State University Press, 2001) 179.

6. 'The Planets,' lines 101–122 (CP 28–29).
7. DI 117. 'Mope' is an instructive word. Cf. 'far from moping I am spoiling for a fight [after the death of Charles Williams],' letter to Barfield, 18 May 1945; and 'One meets young people who make the threat of [the H-bomb] a reason for poisoning every pleasure and evading every duty in the present. Didn't they know that, Bomb or no Bomb, all men die (many in horrible ways)? There is no good moping or sulking about it': 'Willing Slaves of the Welfare State,' EC 746–747.
8. DI 105.
9. 'Hero and Leander,' SLE 58–59.
10. 'Dante's Similes,' SMRL 73.
11. SBJ 171.
12. 'Christanity and Literature,' EC 414. Cf. letter to Mr Lucas, 6 Dec 1956.
13. 'The World's Last Night,' EC 42–53. The quotation is from the thirteenth of Donne's *Holy Sonnets*.
14. See his diary entry for 17 Aug 1922 (*Lewis Papers*).
15. A. E. Housman, *Last Poems* (1922), 'The Chestnut Casts His Flambeaux': 'We for certainty are not the first / Have sat in taverns while the tempests hurled / Their hopeful plans to emptiness, and cursed / Whatever brute and blackguard made the world.' See '*De Futilitate*,' EC 677; cf. EIC 126.
16. SBJ 170.
17. William Shakespeare, *A Midsummer Night's Dream*, II, ii, 138–139: 'The heresies that men do leave / Are hated most of those they did deceive.'
18. It is not clear why the descent of Saturn should be singled out for special mention in the dialogue between Ransom and Merlin (THS 274). A possible explanation is that, being the Intelligence of the furthermost planetary sphere, Saturn might be taken to include the lower planets and thus imply the descent of all the gods.
19. THS 325–326.
20. THS 318.
21. E.g., the political idealist must reckon with the fact that after all has been done to improve the lot of mankind, 'the race and the planet themselves must one day follow the individual into a state of being which has no significance—a universe of inorganic homogeneous matter moving at uniform speed in a low temperature' ('William Morris,' SLE 230); 'It is sobering and cathartic to remember . . . the . . . astronomical processes which may, in the long run, make many of our hopes . . . ridiculous' ('On Science Fiction,' EC 455).
22. E.g., no 'social or biological development on this planet will delay the senility of the sun' ('The Weight of Glory,' EC 99); 'entropy is the real cosmic wave, and evolution only a momentary tellurian ripple within it' ('Dogma and the Universe,' EC 123); 'organic life is only a lightning flash in cosmic history' ('*De Futilitate*,' EC 670); cf. 'Is Theology Poetry?' EC 14.
23. E.g., 'the planet will one day be uninhabitable' ('My First School,' EC 596); 'The astronomers hold out no hope that this planet is going to be permanently

inhabitable. The physicists hold out no hope that organic life is going to be a permanent possibility in any part of the material universe. Not only this earth, but the whole show, all the suns of space, are to run down' ('On Living in an Atomic Age,' EC 362).

24. SIW 304. The comment contradicts Donne's sonnet 'Death, be not proud' with its concluding assertion: 'Death, thou shalt die.' SIW appeared in September 1960, a few months after the death of Lewis's wife. Cf. his ruminations on the lack of true tragic dignity in human sufferings (e.g., 'The Funeral of a Great Myth,' EC 32; also EIC 78).

25. *Lewis Papers*, Vol. 4, 64–65.

26. In the *Theogony* of Hesiod, Cronos swallows his children, only to disgorge them later. Galileo, when he first saw round projections on either side of Saturn in July 1610, mistook them for a pair of close 'companions.' Two years later he was astonished to find that they had vanished. He wondered if the planet, like its mythological counterpart, had 'devoured his own children.' (See Dava Sorbel, *The Planets* (London: Fourth Estate, 2005) 177.) That these projections were part of a ring surrounding the planet was not discovered until 1655, by the Dutch astronomer Christiaan Huygens.

27. Lewis evidently picked up this brand of bitter humour from his tutor. On the outbreak of the Second World War he announced to his friends, 'Well, at any rate we now have less chance of dying of cancer.' Humphrey Carpenter, *The Inklings: C. S. Lewis, J.R.R. Tolkien, Charles Williams, and Their Friends* (London: Allen & Unwin, 1978) 69.

28. SBJ 120.

29. When Stuart Barton Babbage, an RAF chaplain, sermonised about the Christian's inner peace in relation to the fact of death, Lewis disagreed: 'No, he said, death is dreadful and we are right to fear it . . . [It] is not a very little thing and it is horrible.' Babbage recalls that Lewis distrusted his 'easy assurance in the presence of death. My attitude, he implied, was sentimental rather than serious.' See Carolyn Keefe (ed.), *C. S. Lewis: Speaker and Teacher* (London: Hodder & Stoughton, 1971) 92–93. Cf. letter to Edward Dell, 5 Mar 1961.

30. Holst's literal orchestration of the same subject matter was one of Lewis's favourites. When he heard the *Planets Suite* in 1935 he thought Saturn 'the best,' along with Mars (see W. H. Lewis, *Brothers and Friends: The Diaries of Major Warren Hamilton Lewis*, ed. Clyde S. Kilby and Marjorie Lamp Mead (San Francisco: Harper & Row, 1982) 169). Apparently the complete work was not performed on that occasion (cf. letter to Sister Penelope, 31 Jan 1946). He only heard the full piece ten years later when he still thought Saturn 'the best,' but this time included Uranus and Neptune alongside it (letter to Arthur Greeves, 26 Dec 1945). Holst himself likewise declared the Saturn movement to be his favourite and remarked that 'Saturn brings not only physical decay, but also a vision of fulfilment' (see Dava Sorbel, *The Planets*, 175).

31. Lee D. Rossi, *The Politics of Fantasy: C. S. Lewis and J.R.R. Tolkien* (Epping: UMI Research Press, 1984) 75. Determining exactly when the narrator is

present is a nice question. There are three main methods by which the author can make his presence felt: (i) the authorial 'I'; (ii) conversely, the address to 'you,' the reader; (iii) reference to 'this,' the story itself. Lewis uses all three methods, but relies on (i) and (iii) as introductory options. The narrator thus appears in each of the other six books on the very first page: LWW 9 (using technique iii); PC 11 (a variant of iii); VDT 7 (i); SC 11 (iii); HHB 11 (iii); MN 9 (iii). In LB he delays appearing till the end of the fourth chapter, page 47 (i).

32. Peter J. Schakel, *The Way into Narnia: A Reader's Guide* (Grand Rapids, MI: Eerdmans, 2005) 104.

33. Doris Myers, *C. S. Lewis in Context* (Kent, OH: Kent State University Press, 1994) 178.

34. EL 356.

35. John Lydgate, *The Assembly of Gods: or the Accord of Reason and Sensuality in the Fear of Death*, Vol. I, ed. Oscar Lovell Triggs (London: Kegan Paul, 1896) page 39, line 1438. Lewis underlined these words in his copy of Lydgate now in the Wade Center.

36. Typescript of SC, page 121 (Bodleian Library). Cf. page 178 where Jill says 'I wonder is what's his name—Saturn—flooded out now.' To which Eustace replies, 'I shouldn't think the water has reached Saturn's cave yet.' This is the only Narnia typescript to have survived.

37. AOL 285.

38. Nancy-Lou Patterson, 'The Host of Heaven: Astrological and Other Images of Divinity in the Fantasies of C. S. Lewis, Part 1,' *Mythlore*, 25 (Autumn 1980) 19–29: 26.

39. LB 142–143.

40. That is, deaths among the 'good' characters. As befits romance, enemies are despatched with ease and there are very few fatalities among the heroes of the earlier stories. In LWW, apart from Aslan himself, none of the good characters dies, although after the final battle 'Edmund is covered in blood . . . his face a nasty green colour'; those who are petrified or wounded are depetrified or healed very quickly. In PC Caspian's army has 'the worst' of the early fighting, 'the best of the Bears had been hurt, a Centaur terribly wounded, and there were few in Caspian's party who had not lost blood'; Caspian's father is murdered off-stage before the story begins, but no one else among the Old Narnian forces dies except Nikabrik, who is a traitor. In VDT a man is lost overboard during the storm and Reepicheep is translated (which may be counted as a death). In SC Rilian's mother is killed by the serpent, a Talking Stag is killed by the Harfang giants and Caspian dies as an old man. In HHB a Narnian giant is downed at the Battle of Anvard, 'shot through the eye,' but we are not told if it is a mortal wound; a knight starves himself to death in order to save Cor. In MN a couple of policemen are felled by Jadis, but it is not clear whether these are fatalities or not; 'old Great-Uncle Kirke' dies. In sum there are nine clear deaths amongst the 'good' characters in these six books;

three of them (Aslan, Reepicheep, and Caspian) are major characters, two of whom depart without violence and all three of whom are shown to enjoy resurrection.

41. AOL 62.

42. 'The signe of Capricorn, / The hous appropred to Satorne,' AOL 205.

43. See what he has to say about the 'dark answers' of Calvin's *Institutio* (EL 43). Cf. AGO 28; 'Two Ways with the Self,' EC 298; 'The Empty Universe,' EC 636. Consider also his position on the Euthyphro dilemma: POP 88; ROP 54–55.

44. Lewis would rather skirt Dualism (see MC 44–47; letter to Dom Bede Griffiths, 20 Dec 1961) than allow that God was somehow either immoral or amoral.

45. See M 129.

46. See PR 229.

47. AMR 186. *Dymer* IX, 4–5 (NP 82). Per 140; THS 337. POP 90–91; FL 111; ROP 106; LTM 46–47. 'The World's Last Night,' EC 45; 'The Efficacy of Prayer,' EC 241. AT 154–155. Letters to Mr Offer, 9 May 1944; Edith Gates, 2 May 1945; Mrs Jessup, 13 Nov 1952; Mary Willis Shelburne, 20 Feb 1955 and 21 July 1958. AGO 8; 26–27. Under the heading 'Eli, Eli,' Lewis quotes from MacDonald's *Unspoken Sermons*, First Series, 'The Eloi,' GMD 18.

48. LB 45.

49. 'The Seeing Eye,' EC 61.

50. GMD 21.

51. Cf. 'On Obstinacy in Belief,' EC 206–215. It makes reference to the phrase 'Dilly, dilly, come and be killed' (EC 214) as does LB 102.

52. GMD 18.

53. Cf. ROP 55, 71; AOM 60.

54. Contemplation in Alexander's sense and contemplativeness in the Saturnine sense are, of course, to be distinguished.

55. AOL 96.

56. Tasting the water is an Enjoyment experience: 'Such was their thirst that it seemed the most delicious drink they had ever had in their lives, and while they were drinking they were perfectly happy and could not think of anything else.' Cf. 1 Cor. 10:4; Exod. 17:6.

57. See letter to Mary Neylan, 26 Mar 1940.

58. Cf. AOM 22.

59. 'Dangers of National Repentance,' EC 295.

60. Letter to Paul Elmer More, 23 May 1935.

61. T. S. Eliot, 'The Wasteland,' line 22.

62. Cf. POP 101.

63. M 135. Cf. FL 111.

64. PR 248.

65. Letter to Dom Bede Griffiths, 5 Nov 1954. Cf. TWHF 82.

66. The Stellatum and the Primum Mobile receive no treatment in the Narniad.
67. EL 89; Lewis's italics.
68. LB 164.
69. Kathleen Raine, 'From a Poet,' in Jocelyn Gibb (ed.), *Light on C. S. Lewis* (London: Geoffrey Bles, 1965: 102–105) 102.
70. Franzen, Jonathan. *The Corrections* (London: Fourth Estate, 2001) 161. The novel describes Lewis as a 'Catholic propagandist' (161; cf. 167, 232–233).
71. See Carpenter's discussion of this subject in Carpenter, Humphrey. *The Inklings: C.S. Lewis, J.R.R. Tolkien, Charles Williams, and Their Friends* (London: Allen & Unwin, 1978) 218–224.
72. 'One of the most vile moments in the whole of children's literature, to my mind, occurs at the end of *The Last Battle*, when Aslan reveals to the children that "The term is over: the holidays have begun" because "There was a real railway accident. Your father and mother and all of you are—as you used to call it in the Shadowlands—dead." To solve a narrative problem by killing one of your characters is something many authors have done at one time or another. To slaughter the lot of them, and then claim they're better off, is not honest storytelling: it's propaganda in the service of a life-hating ideology.' Philip Pullman, 'The Dark Side of Narnia,' *The Guardian* (1 Oct 1998) 6.
73. Public meeting, St. Andrew's Church, North Oxford, 16 June 2002. For more on this and Pullman's other criticisms of the Narniad, see Michael Ward, 'Philip Pullman's Attack on Narnia: A Defense,' *Mars Hill Review*, No. 21 (2003) 127–135.
74. For instance, since Lewis elsewhere paints Kirkpatrick as Saturn and himself as Jupiter, what should we conclude about the victories of Jupiter over Saturn in LWW and LB? Is not the healing of Digory's mother in MN at least partly a compensatory fantasy for the loss of Lewis's own mother early in his life?
75. Rowan Williams, *Lost Icons: Reflections on Cultural Bereavement* (Edinburgh: T. & T. Clark, 2000) 17.
76. See, e.g., letter to Arthur Greeves, 17 Dec 1932; also SC 202–203; EIC 70–73.
77. See 'On Three Ways of Writing for Children,' EC 507.
78. Joy Davidman, *Smoke on the Mountain: An Interpretation of the Ten Commandments in Terms of To-day* (London: Hodder & Stoughton, 1955) 7.
79. SL 153–155.
80. AT 181.
81. PPL 137.
82. See Robert Graves, *Goodbye to All That, An Autobiography* (London: Jonathan Cape, 1929). Lewis uses the phrase in M 26. For a discussion of this subject in relation to Tolkien's work, including Lewis's assessment thereof, see John Garth, *Tolkien and the Great War: The Threshold of Middle-earth* (London: HarperCollins, 2003) 287–313.
83. See letter to Dom Bede Griffiths, 20 Dec 1946.
84. See AMR 283, 286, 281; *De Futilitate*, EC 680. Cf. letter to Peter Bide, 14 June 1960.

85. 'De Futilitate,' EC 680.
86. See letter to Dorothy L. Sayers, 30 June 1949.
87. PPL 137.
88. 'The Alliterative Metre,' SLE 24.
89. AT 143.
90. Letter to A.K. Hamilton Jenkin, 4 Nov 1925.
91. G.W.F. Hegel, *Phenomenology of Spirit*, trans. A.V. Miller (Oxford: Clarendon Press, 1977) 19.
92. Letter to Joyce Pearce, 20 July 1943.
93. See letter to Martin Kilmer, 22 Jan 1957. Goldthwaite is mistaken when he identifies Lewis's 'summary damnation of Susan.' John Goldthwaite, *The Natural History of Make-Believe: A Guide to the Principal Works of Britain, Europe and America* (Oxford: Oxford University Press, 1996) 236. Susan does not appear in LB and no statement is made about her eternal destiny.
94. EL 296.
95. 'Meditation in a Toolshed,' EC 608.
96. 'What the Bird Said Early in the Year,' line 11 (CP 85).
97. 'Imagery in the Last Eleven Cantos of Dante's *Comedy*,' SMRL 91. For the pilgrim's review of his journey through the spheres, see Dante, *Paradiso*, Canto XXII, 133–150. Sayers and Reynolds comment that the pilgrim 'retraces with his gaze (for it is endowed with supernatural acuity and power) the course he has taken through the seven planetary spheres, until it rests at last upon the puny semblance of our little globe. Allegorically, it is after passing through a period of spiritual contemplation (the Heaven of Saturn) that man can see the world in its true proportions.' "Cf. the final two words of LTM."

CHAPTER 10

1. 'On Three Ways of Writing for Children,' EC 510.
2. E.g. 'When you 'have an idea' could you tell anyone exactly *how* you thought of it?,' 'It All Began with a Picture,' EC 529; 'the types of relation between conscious and subconscious are as various as those between man and wife,' letter to George Rostrevor Hamilton, 17 June 1946; 'the fool rejoices in his own consciousness, instead of the life of that consciousness,' GMD 102; cf. PPL 136; EL 113, 558.
3. The debate took place on 2 Feb 1948. For more on the Socratic Club, see Walter Hooper, 'Oxford's Bonny Fighter,' in James T. Como, (ed.), *C. S. Lewis at the Breakfast Table and Other Reminiscences* (London: Collins, 1980) 137–185; and Christopher W. Mitchell, 'University Battles: C. S. Lewis and the Oxford University Socratic Club,' Angus J.L. Menuge, (ed.), *C. S. Lewis, Lightbearer in the Shadowlands: The Evangelistic Vision of C. S. Lewis* (Wheaton, IL: Crossway Books, 1997) 329–351.
4. Carpenter, *The Inklings*, 217.

5. Wilson, *Biography*, 220.
6. See 'On Fairy-Stories' in J.R.R. Tolkien, *The Monsters and the Critics and Other Essays* (London: HarperCollins, 1997) 109–161.
7. AGO 11.
8. AMR 432. By 'Christina Dreams,' Lewis means wishful-thinking, fantasies with purely psychological causes; see AMR 20,
9. Letter to Arthur Greeves, 30 May 1916.
10. POP 87.
11. Letter to Don Giovanni Calabria, 5 Jan 1953.
12. G.E.M. Anscombe, *Metaphysics and the Philosophy of Mind* (Minneapolis: University of Minnesota Press, 1981) 10.
13. 'Rejoinder to Dr Pittenger,' TAH 110–117. Cf. letters to Kenneth Brewer, 9 May 1962 and 15 June 1962.
14. 'Lewis refurbished but did not abandon it.... Philosophically, this representation of reality is eminently defensible. It is traditional, and within certain limits can claim as authorities Plato, Plotinus, Dionysius, and in part St. Augustine and St. Thomas, as well as Leibniz and Berkeley.' James Patrick, 'C. S. Lewis and Idealism,' in Andrew Walker, & James Patrick, (eds.), *A Christian for All Christians: Essays in Honour of C. S. Lewis* (London: Hodder & Stoughton, 1990) 156–173: 162. Alvin Plantinga's *Warrant and Proper Function* (New York: Oxford University Press, 1993) defends a version of the argument from reason (216–237) and notes its similarity to Lewis's case in the final footnote of the book.
15. M 19. The quotation is from J.B.S. Haldane, *Possible Worlds and Other Essays* (London: Chatto & Windus, 1927) 209.
16. Polanyi's name appears on the list of Socratic speakers in 1952 and 1953. Polanyi thought well of Lewis's writings; several Lewis titles are to be found in his library now in the Regenstein Library, University of Chicago (Boxes 57 & 58): SBJ, POP, AOM, GD and '*De Descriptione Temporum*.' He refers sympathetically to AOM in one of his own works; see Michael Polanyi, and H. Prosch, *Meaning* (Chicago, 1975) 28.
17. See M 33. However, he did occasionally equate reason with the essence of humanity. See his poem 'Le Roi S'Amuse,' where Jove creates 'Stern Athene' (who represents Reason) and, with her, 'Man.'
18. Nevertheless, it is one of his favourite arguments in defence of the existence of God: e.g., 'What is behind the universe is more like a mind than it is like anything else we know,' MC 30. Wayne Shumaker writes: 'The demonstration of the permeation [of the universe with mind] was the most basic part of Lewis's total purpose [in the Ransom Trilogy], since his world view rests on a conviction that behind the apparently mechanical processes of the universe are both Divine awareness and Divine purpose. The Empirical Bogey ("the great myth of our century with its gases and galaxies, its light years and evolutions, its nightmare perspectives of simple arithmetic" [Per 164]) had to be

overborne by images with contrary implications. But how image Divine Mind, which, although totally present at every point in space and therefore immanent in every setting and event, is nonmaterial and therefore nonsensory?' Wayne Shumaker, 'The Cosmic Trilogy of C. S. Lewis' in Peter J. Schakel (ed.), *The Longing for a Form, Essays on the Fiction of C. S. Lewis* (Kent, OH: Kent State University Press, 1977) 51–63: 55.

19. M 47.
20. M 114–115.
21. M 31.
22. 'The Poison of Subjectivism,' EC 657.
23. See 'Reply—Note,' *The Socratic Digest*, No. 4 (1948) 15–16.
24. Incidentally, before the revised edition appeared, Lewis's publisher planned to bring out an abridged version. When he learned this, Lewis wrote back: 'By Jove, of course there must be a note showing that the paper-back *Miracles* is the abridgement.' See letter to Jocelyn Gibb, 22 Feb 1958.
25. Chad Walsh, *C. S. Lewis: Apostle to the Skeptics* (New York: Macmillan, 1949) 10.
26. 'The Language of Religion,' EC 261.
27. M 11.
28. See D. P. Walker, *Spiritual and Demonic Magic from Ficino to Campanella* (London: The Warburg Institute, 1958) 15. Lewis was well-acquainted with Ficino's works; see, e.g., 'The Empty Universe' (EC 636) and EL *passim*.
29. LWW 53.
30. James Patrick, 'C. S. Lewis and Idealism,' in Andrew Walker & James Patrick (eds.), *A Christian for All Christians: Essays in Honour of C. S. Lewis* (London: Hodder & Stoughton, 1990) 156–173: 173.
31. Owen Barfield, *Poetic Diction, A Study in Meaning* (Hanover, NH: Wesleyan University Press, 1984) 37.
32. Carpenter, *Inklings*, 217.
33. Chivalry was one of the first things Lewis thought of when discussing the advantages of 'looking along the beam'; see above, chapter 4, note 33. VDT, with its Solar donegality, has an obvious connection with 'Meditation in a Toolshed,' a connection that Lewis makes explicit when a shaft of light falls on the ship as it escapes from the Dark Island, and Lucy looks 'along the beam' (VDT 143).
34. See letter to Laurence Krieg, 23 Apr 1957. Three of the stories (PC, VDT, HHB) were completed before LWW was published on 16 Oct 1950; hence the closing sentence of LWW sets up the reader to expect sequels, 'it was only the beginning of the adventures of Narnia.' SC was completed by Mar 1951. Green had had part of an early draft of MN read to him by Lewis on 14 June 1949; he read the complete MS in Feb 1954. In the meantime, Lewis told his publisher on 11 Mar 1953 that he had 'just finished' LB. See Walter Hooper, *C. S. Lewis, A Companion and Guide* (London: HarperCollins, 1996) 401–405.

CHAPTER 11

1. 'The Big Read' was the name given to the survey conducted by the BBC in 2003. Available: http://www.bbc.co.uk/arts/bigread/vote/

2. In the samples, 54 children named him as their favourite author in 1971, compared with 53 in 1994. This put him eighth in a table of thirteen authors in 1971, but second in a table of the same thirteen in 1994. Enid Blyton, who tops the rankings in both years, fell from 1,604 mentions in 1971 to 498 in 1994. Hall, Christine & Coles, Martin. *Children's Reading Choices* (London: Routledge, 1999) 45–46.

3. Letter to Sister Penelope, 25 Mar 1943.

4. PPL 57.

5. 'The Literary Impact of the Authorised Version,' SLE 142.

6. George MacDonald, 'The Imagination: Its Functions and Its Culture,' in *Orts* (London: Sampson Low, Marston, Searle, & Rivington, 1882) 28.

7. AOL 210.

8. Bruno Bettelheim, *The Uses of Enchantment: The Meaning and Importance of Fairy Tales* (London: Thames & Hudson, 1976) 36.

9. DI 103–104.

10. George Watson, *Never Ones for Theory? England and the War of Ideas* (Cambridge: Lutterworth Press, 2000) 91.

11. PPL 11.

12. M 45.

13. Aristotle, *Metaphysics*, II, i. See M 43.

14. 'The Weight of Glory,' EC 106. The phrase *vere latitat* is borrowed from one of the sacramental hymns of Thomas Aquinas which begins: 'Adoro te devote, latens Deitas, / quae sub his figuris vere latitas' ('I worship thee with reverence, hidden Deity, / thou who hidest truly in these shapes').

15. Kallistos Ware, 'God of the Fathers: C. S. Lewis and Eastern Christianity,' in David Mills (ed.), *The Pilgrim's Guide: C. S. Lewis and the Art of Witness*, 58.

16. ROP 95; cf. letters to Edward Lofstrom, 10 June 1962, and Keith Manship, 13 Sept 1962. See also: 'because [Jill] was moving at the same pace as the breath, there was no wind' (SC 31); 'the door into life generally opens behind us,' GMD 126; Mark 'was not thinking in moral terms at all; or else (what is much the same thing) he was having his first deeply moral experience' (THS 299); 'the ethical category is self-destructive' (EL 187); 'The real work must be, of all our works, the most secret. Even as far as possible secret from ourselves. Our right hand must not know what our left is doing' (FL 123); Screwtape attempts to 'smuggle into his [patient's] mind the gratifying reflection "By jove! I'm being humble," and almost immediately pride—pride at his own humility—will appear' (SL 71); 'The moment good taste knows itself, some of its goodness is lost' (SBJ 86); 'it is the self you really are and not its reflection in consciousness that matters most' (letter to Edith Gates, 23 May 1944); 'Eros fled when Psyche turned the lamp upon him' ('Sir Walter

Scott,' SLE 215); 'the real thing must always be the background of one's mind' (letter to Arthur Greeves, 3 May 1920).

17. SBJ 19.
18. SBJ 190.
19. PPL 61, a rare example of Lewis referring to Eliot's poetry with apparent approbation. See T. S. Eliot, 'The Dry Salvages,' V, 27f.
20. George Herbert, 'Conscience,' line 8, Lewis's underlining. See his copy of George Herbert, *The Temple and a Priest to the Temple* (London: Dent, undated), now in the Wade Center, page 105. He refers to the poem in LTM 37 and his letter to Katharine Farrer, 3 Feb 1954.
21. James T. Como (ed.), *C. S. Lewis at the Breakfast Table and Other Reminiscences* (London: Collins, 1980) xxxiv.
22. Franz Rottensteiner, *The Fantasy Book, an Illustrated History from Dracula to Tolkien* (London: Thames & Hudson, 1978) 126.
23. Peter J. Schakel, *The Way into Narnia: A Reader's Guide* (Grand Rapids, MI: Eerdmans, 2005) 34.
24. Natasha Giardina, 'Elusive Prey: Searching for Traces of Narnia in the Jungles of the Psyche,' in Shanna Caughey (ed.), *Revisiting Narnia: Fantasy, Myth and Religion in C. S. Lewis' Chronicles* (Dallas: BenBella Books Inc., 2005) 33–43.
25. Farrer, Austin. *A Rebirth of Images: The Making of St John's Apocalypse* (Westminster: Dacre Press, 1949) 13.
26. DI 173.
27. DI 109.
28. Letter to Dom Bede Griffiths, 14 Sept 1936.
29. AOL 119–120.
30. DI 106.
31. 'De Audiendis Poetis,' SMRL 11.
32. 'The Anthropological Approach,' SLE 305.
33. AOL 312.
34. 'On Three Ways of Writing for Children,' EC 509.
35. Letter to William Kinter, 30 July 1954.
36. See PPL 48, 52, 59.
37. 'Edmund Spenser, 1552–99,' SMRL 137.
38. Per 187.
39. Watson, *Never Ones For Theory?* 87.
40. SIL 139.
41. AOL 203.
42. PC 18, 34; SC 32, 89, 130, 152; LB 164; LWW 114; SC 18.
43. Letter to A.K. Hamilton Jenkin, 4 Nov 1925.
44. THS 316. Cf. Williams's doctrine of coinherence in the houses of the zodiac: 'each is in all' (AT 149).
45. Letter to Pauline Baynes, 24 May 1956.
46. M 179; cf. MC 43–44, 141.
47. EL 342.

48. See his review of Lord David Cecil's *The Oxford Book of Christian Verse* in *The Review of English Studies*, XVII, 65 (Jan 1941) 95–102: 99f.
49. 'Rejoinder to Dr Pittenger,' TAH 116.
50. AOL 75.
51. 'Imagination and Thought in the Middle Ages,' SMRL 60.
52. AOL 95.
53. DI 198.
54. 'Neoplatonism in the Poetry of Spenser,' SMRL 162. Cf. letter to Colin Eccleshare, 28 Dec 1962.
55. DI 201.
56. Letter to William Kinter, 28 Mar 1953.
57. On honeymoon in Greece with his dying wife, Lewis found it hard not to pray to Apollo the Healer; 'but somehow one didn't feel it would have been very wrong—would only have been addressing Christ *sub specie Apollinis*,' letter to Chad Walsh, 23 May 1960. Elsewhere he wrote that he 'would gladly believe that the gesture of homage offered to the moon was sometimes accepted by her Maker,' ROP 69. And in *Perelandra*, Ransom wonders whether 'there might, if a man could find it, be some way to renew the old Pagan practice of propitiating the local gods of unknown places in such fashion that it was no offence to God,' Per 170.
58. Norman F. Cantor, *Inventing the Middle Ages: The Lives, Works, and Ideas of the Great Medievalists of the Twentieth Century* (Cambridge: Lutterworth Press, 1991) 208.
59. DI 194.
60. Owen Barfield, *Owen Barfield on C. S. Lewis*, ed. G. B. Tennyson (Middletown, CT: Wesleyan University Press, 1989) 65.
61. See POP 29.
62. EL 460.
63. LTM 81.
64. 'The Weight of Glory,' EC 105.
65. MC 150, quoting Athanasius, *The Incarnation of the Word of God*, 54, 3. Cf. letter to Clyde Kilby, 20 Jan 1959.
66. Kallistos Ware, 'God of the Fathers: C. S. Lewis and Eastern Christianity' in David Mills, (ed.). *The Pilgrim's Guide: C. S. Lewis and the Art of Witness*, 63.
67. Leanne Payne, *Real Presence: The Christian Worldview of C. S. Lewis as Incarnational Reality* (Grand Rapids, MI: Baker Books, 2002) 142.
68. 'The Testament of Cresseid,' Robert Henryson, *The Poems of Robert Henryson*, ed. W. M. Metcalfe (Paisley: Alexander Gardner, 1917) 143–168, lines 288–289. Lewis underlined these words in his copy of Henryson now in the Wade Center.
69. John Hick, *The Metaphor of God Incarnate* (London: SCM Press, 1993) 90.
70. Coleridge, Samuel Taylor. *Lay Sermons (the Statesman's Manual and Blessed Are Ye that Sow Beside All Waters)*, ed. R.J. White (London: 1972) 30. In Lewis's copy of Coleridge's *Aids to Reflection* in the Wade Center the word

'tautegorical' is underlined: S. T. Coleridge, *Aids to Reflection and the Confessions of an Inquiring Spirit* (London: George Bell, 1890), Aphorisms on Spiritual Religion, Aphorism VII, 136.

71. Karl Rahner, *Theological Investigations 4* (London: Darton, Longman & Todd, 1966) 252.

72. Austin Farrer, *A Rebirth of Images: The Making of St John's Apocalypse* (Westminster: Dacre Press, 1949) 19.

73. Letter to Janet Spens, 18 Apr 1938.

74. Ps. 19:1, 3–4 (Coverdale); cf. ROP 49, 56, 70. Lewis is alluding to Psalm 19 in THS 320 when the gods descend; in Ransom's Blue Room are heard 'tingling sounds that were clearly not voices though they had articulation.' The allusion is even clearer in OSP 35, where Ransom says to himself, 'Space was the wrong name. Older thinkers had been wiser when they named it simply the heavens— the heavens which declared the glory.'

75. William Shakespeare, *Hamlet*, III, iv, 55ff. See 'Variation in Shakespeare and Others,' SLE 74–87.

76. FL 115.

77. AGO 55.

78. DI 222.

79. AGO 55.

80. DI 222.

81. 'Imagery in the Last Eleven Cantos of Dante's *Comedy*,' SMRL 78–93: 81.

82. 'When we pass beyond pointing to individual sensible objects, when we begin to think of causes, relations, of mental states or acts, we become incurably metaphorical. We apprehend none of these things except through metaphor': 'Bluspels and Flalansferes: A Semantic Nightmare,' SLE 263.

83. OSP 35.

84. Garrett Green, *Theology, Hermeneutics, and Imagination* (Cambridge: Cambridge University Press, 2000) 15.

85. EL 3–4.

86. Owen Barfield, *Poetic Diction, A Study in Meaning* (Hanover, NH: Wesleyan University Press, 1984) 28.

87. 'Transposition,' EC 277.

88. VDT 159.

89. 'Transposition,' EC 273.

90. 'The Seeing Eye,' EC 58–65: 61.

91. 'The Apologist's Evening Prayer,' lines 5–6 (CP 143). See Matt. 12:39.

CHAPTER 12

1. Lewis's words of dedication to Barfield on the title page of AOL. The two men met in 1919 and had a close, sparring, intellectual relationship until some time shortly after Lewis's Christian conversion. From that point on, Barfield felt

that 'something was broken. So, thereafter, broadly speaking, anything Lewis knew about my ideas and opinions he got only from my books, not from conversation with me' (*Owen Barfield on C. S. Lewis*, 106). And the same was true in reverse: 'I really know no more of what [Lewis] thought after his conversion than can be gathered from his published writings' (*Owen Barfield on C. S. Lewis*, 79).

2. Lindskoog, who considered herself 'mentally "married"' to Lewis is an example of this kind of reader: see Kathryn Lindskoog, 'Reactions from Other Women,' in Stephen Schofield (ed.), *In Search of C. S. Lewis* (South Plainfield, NJ: Bridge Publishing, 1983) 77–88: 82. See also Perry Bramlett, *C. S. Lewis: Life at the Center* (Macon, GA: Peak Road, 1996). It ought to be added that certain reactions of disapproval among Lewis's non-Christian audience seem to be motivated by an equal but opposite Pavlovian response. The uncritical hostility demonstrated toward him by Pullman, Goldthwaite, and Holbrook, among others, reflects what appears to be an *a priori* opposition to Christianity and/or the Church.

3. Peter Milward, *A Challenge to C. S. Lewis* (London: Associated University Presses, 1995) 104.

4. Martha C. Sammons, *A Guide Through C. S. Lewis's Space Trilogy* (Westchester, IL: Cornerstone Books, 1980) 41–57. Brett Foster, 'An Estimation of an Admonition: The Nature of Value, the Value of Nature, and the Abolition of Man,' *Christian Scholar's Review*, 1998, Vol. XXVII (No. 4) 416–435: 423.

5. Naomi Glenn Oliver, 'The Higher and Lower Mediums of Meaning in Three Models Presented by C. S. Lewis: The Medieval, Modern and Incarnational Models' (Ph.D. diss., Drew University, 1992).

6. 'Unreal Estates,' EC 533.

7. 'On Science Fiction,' EC 456.

8. See EL 619.

9. 'He was much interested in astronomy. Once, when letting a friend and me out of college late at night, he pointed out to us the extremely rare conjunction of five planets all brilliantly visible in a circle in the sky at once': Derek Brewer, 'The Tutor: A Portrait,' in James T. Como (ed.), *C. S. Lewis at the Breakfast Table and Other Reminiscences* (London: Collins, 1980) 41–67: 48. 'He was very interested in the stars and moon and liked a trip to the observatory': Fred W. Paxford, 'He Should Have Been a Parson,' in David Graham (ed.), *We Remember C. S. Lewis: Essays and Memoirs* (Nashville: Broadman & Holman Publishers, 2001) 119–128: 126f. See also *CSL: The Bulletin of the New York C. S. Lewis Society*, Vol. 8, No. 11 (Sept 1977) 16; and his letter to Edward Allen, 3 Apr 1952.

10. Giovanni Virginio Schiaparelli (1835–1910), prolific Italian astronomer and cartographer of Mars: see Per 20, 25.

Sir Robert Ball (1840–1913), Andrews Professor of Astronomy, Trinity College, Dublin, and author of thirteen books on popular astronomy: see SBJ 57.

Sir James Jeans (1877–1946), mathematician, astronomer, and theoretical physicist who taught at Princeton University (1905–1909) and Cambridge University (1904–1905, 1910–1912); Sir Arthur Eddington (1882–1944), father of modern theoretical astrophysics: see MC 54; 'Dante's Similes,' SMRL 75; 'Historicism,' EC 631; letter to Margaret Sackville Hamilton, 23 Sept 1952; letter to Dorothy L. Sayers, 25 June 1957; POP 74.

Erwin Schrödinger (1887–1961), Nobel Prize-winning physicist and colleague of Lewis's at Magdalen College, Oxford, 1933–1938: see OSP 12.

Sir Fred Hoyle (1915–2001), Plumian Professor of Astronomy, Cambridge University, 1958–1972: see letter to Genia Goelz, 15 May 1952; 'Religion and Rocketry,' EC 231; 'The Seeing Eye,' EC 64.

11. J. W. Dunne (1866–1949), aeronautical engineer and designer of military aircraft, whose *An Experiment with Time* (1927) outlined a new model of multi-dimensional time: see THS 130; letter to Margaret Sackville Hamilton, 23 Sept 1952; Daniel Morris, 'Encounter in a Two-Bit Pub' in Graham, *We Remember C. S. Lewis* 112.

Edwin A. Abbott (1838–1926), clergyman, biographer of Bacon, and author of *Flatland* (1884), a satire about multi-dimensional geometry; Charles H. Hinton (1853–1907), mathematician and author of numerous works on multi-dimensionality, including *The Fourth Dimension* (1904); P. D. Ouspenski (1878–1947), Russian mathematician and mystic, whose works include *Tertium Organum* (1911) and *A New Model of the Universe* (1931): see Graham, *We Remember C. S. Lewis* 112.

12. EL 62.
13. Letter to Arthur Greeves, 25 Oct 1916; cf. 'Sir Walter Scott,' SLE 215; EIC 31.
14. Letter to Chad Walsh, 18 Oct 1960.
15. SIL 129.
16. 'Imagination and Thought in the Middle Ages,' SMRL 52.
17. EL 2; cf. 323.
18. AOM 42f.
19. E.g., letter to Laurence Harwood, 26 Jan 1963.
20. 'Reply to Professor Haldane,' OTOW 99.
21. LTM 58.
22. Letter to Francis Anderson, 23 Sept 1963.
23. OSP 34. He takes a less litotic line in 'Infatuation' (CP 87–90).
24. Letter to his brother, 18 Feb 1940.
25. D. P. Walker, *Spiritual and Demonic Magic from Ficino to Campanella* (London: The Warburg Institute, 1958) 115 (Lewis's underlining in his copy of Walker now in the Wade Center).
26. His position with respect to astrology in general is the same as that of Mrs Dimble with respect to Venus in particular (THS 314).
27. I was employed by The C. S. Lewis Foundation as resident warden, 1996–1999.

28. He was Chaplain of Magdalene College, Cambridge, 1956–1960, and Dean, 1963–1969. He and I are not related.
29. Letter to the Master and Fellows of Magdalene College, Cambridge, 25 Oct 1963.
30. Archimandrite Sophrony, *The Monk of Mount Athos, Staretz Silouan 1866–1938*, trans. Rosemary Edmonds (New York: St. Vladimir's Seminary Press, 1973) 38–40.
31. SIL 116.
32. Barrington-Ward, Simon. 'The Uncontemporary Apologist,' *Theology*, LXVIII (Feb 1965) 103–108.

BIBLIOGRAPHY

Adey, Lionel. *C.S. Lewis' 'Great War' with Owen Barfield*. Wigton: Ink Books, 2002.

————. *C.S. Lewis: Writer, Dreamer & Mentor*. Grand Rapids, MI: Eerdmans, 1998.

————.'Medievalism in the Space Trilogy of C.S. Lewis,' *Studies in Medievalism*, Vol. 3, No. 3 (Winter 1991) 279–289.

Allen, Don Cameron. *The Star-Crossed Renaissance: The Quarrel about Astrology and Its Influence in England*. New York: Octagon Books, 1966.

Avis, Paul. *God and the Creative Imagination: Metaphor, Symbol and Myth in Religion and Theology*. London: Routledge, 1999.

Bacon, Francis. *The Advancement of Learning*, ed. Michael Kiernan. Oxford: Clarendon Press, 2000.

Barbour, Brian. 'Lewis and Cambridge,' *Modern Philology*, Vol. 94, No. 4 (May 1999) 439–484.

Barfield, Owen. *Owen Barfield on C.S. Lewis*, ed. G.B. Tennyson. Middletown, CT: Wesleyan University Press, 1989.

————. 'Owen Barfield's response to John Fitzpatrick's essay on "The Man Born Blind",' *CSL: The Bulletin of the New York C.S. Lewis Society*, Vol. 14, No. 8 (June 1983) 5.

————. *Poetic Diction, A Study in Meaning*. Hanover, NH: Wesleyan University Press, 1984.

————. *The Rediscovery of Meaning and Other Essays*. Middletown, CT: Wesleyan University Press, 1977.

Barkman, Adam. 'C.S. Lewis and the Enduring Relevance of Monarchy,' *CSL: The Bulletin of the New York C.S. Lewis Society*, Vol. 37, No. 4 (July-Aug 2006) 1–15.

Barr, Stringfellow. *The Mask of Jove, A History of Graeco-Roman Civilization from the Death of Alexander to the Death of Constantine*. New York: Lippincott, 1966.

315

Barrington-Ward, Simon. 'The Uncontemporary Apologist,' *Theology*, LXVIII (Feb 1965) 103–108.

Bennett, J.A.W. (ed.). 'The Humane Medievalist: An Inaugural Lecture.' Cambridge: Cambridge University Press, 1965.

Betjeman, John. *Letters, Vol. I, 1926–1951*, ed. Candida Lycett Green. London: Methuen, 1994.

Bettelheim, Bruno. *The Uses of Enchantment: The Meaning and Importance of Fairy Tales.* London: Thames & Hudson, 1976.

Bevan, Edwyn. *Symbolism and Belief.* London: Allen & Unwin, 1938.

Beversluis, John. *C.S. Lewis and the Search for Rational Religion.* Grand Rapids, MI: Eerdmans, 1985.

Bramlett, Perry. *C.S. Lewis: Life at the Center.* Macon, GA: Peak Road, 1996.

Brown, Devin. *Inside Narnia: A Guide to Exploring The Lion, the Witch and the Wardrobe.* Grand Rapids, MI: Baker Books, 2005.

Brown, Hanbury. *Man and the Stars.* Oxford: Oxford University Press, 1978.

Burckhardt, Titus. *Alchemy.* London: Penguin, 1972.

Campbell, David C. & Dale E. Hess. 'Olympian Detachment: A Critical Look at the World of C.S. Lewis's Characters,' *Studies in the Literary Imagination*, Vol. XXII, No. 2, Georgia State University, Atlanta, GA (Fall 1989) 199–215.

Cantor, Norman F. *Inventing the Middle Ages: The Lives, Works, and Ideas of the Great Medievalists of the Twentieth Century.* Cambridge: Lutterworth Press, 1991.

Carnell, Corbin Scott. *Bright Shadow of Reality: C.S. Lewis and the Feeling Intellect.* Grand Rapids, MI: Eerdmans, 1974.

Carpenter, Humphrey. *The Inklings: C.S. Lewis, J.R.R. Tolkien, Charles Williams, and Their Friends.* London: Allen & Unwin, 1978.

Carpenter, Humphrey & Mari Prichard (eds.). *The Oxford Companion to Children's Literature.* Oxford: Oxford University Press, 1987.

Cashford, Jules. *The Moon: Myth and Image.* London: Cassell Illustrated, 2003.

Cassirer, Ernst. *The Individual and the Cosmos in Renaissance Philosophy*, trans. Mario Domandi. Mineola, NY: Dover, 2000.

———. *Individuo e Cosmo nella Filosofia del Rinascimento*, traduzione di Federico Federici. Firenze: La Nuova Italia, 1927.

Caughey, Shanna (ed.). *Revisiting Narnia: Fantasy, Myth and Religion in C.S. Lewis' Chronicles.* Dallas: BenBella Books Inc., 2005.

Chapman, Allan. *Gods in the Sky, Astronomy from the Ancients to the Renaissance.* London: Channel 4 Books, 2002.

Christensen, Michael J. *C.S. Lewis on Scripture.* London: Hodder & Stoughton, 1979.

Christopher, Joe R. *C.S. Lewis.* New York: Twayne, 1987.

Coleridge, S.T. *Aids to Reflection and The Confessions of an Inquiring Spirit.* London: George Bell & Sons, 1890.

———. *Lay Sermons (the Statesman's Manual and Blessed are ye that sow beside all waters)*, ed. R.J. White. London: 1972.

Como, James T. *Branches to Heaven: The Geniuses of C.S. Lewis.* Dallas: Spence, 1998.

———. (ed.). *C.S. Lewis at the Breakfast Table and Other Reminiscences*. London: Collins, 1980.

Cuneo, Andrew P. 'Selected Literary Letters of C.S. Lewis.' D.Phil. diss., University of Oxford, 2001.

Daigle, Marsha A. 'Dante's *Divine Comedy* and the Fiction of C.S. Lewis.' Ph.D. diss., University of Michigan, 1984.

Danielson, Dennis Richard (ed.). *The Book of the Cosmos: Imagining the Universe from Heraclitus to Hawking*. Cambridge, MA: Perseus Publishing, 2000.

Dante Alighieri. *The Divine Comedy Vol. II: Purgatory*, trans. Mark Musa. London: Penguin, 1985.

———. *The Divine Comedy Vol. III: Paradise*, trans. Dorothy L. Sayers & Barbara Reynolds. London: Penguin, 1962.

Davidman, Joy. *Smoke on the Mountain: An Interpretation of the Ten Commandments in Terms of To-day*. London: Hodder & Stoughton, 1955.

Derrick, Christopher. *C. S. Lewis and the Church of Rome: A Study in Proto-Ecumenism*. San Francisco: Ignatius Press, 1981.

Donne, John. *Donne's Sermons, Selected Passages with an Essay by Logan Pearsall Smith*. Oxford: Clarendon Press, 1919.

Downing, David C. *Planets in Peril, A Critical Study of C.S. Lewis's Ransom Trilogy*. Amherst: University of Massachusetts Press, 1992.

Dreyer, J.L.E. *History of the Planetary Systems from Thales to Kepler*. Cambridge: Cambridge University Press, 1906.

Duriez, Colin. *J.R.R. Tolkien and C.S. Lewis: The Story of Their Friendship*. Stroud: Sutton Publishing, 2003.

Eade, J.C. *The Forgotten Sky: A Guide to Astrology in English Literature*. Oxford: Clarendon Press, 1984.

Edwards, Bruce L. (ed.). *The Taste of the Pineapple: Essays on C.S. Lewis as Reader, Critic and Imaginative Writer*. Bowling Green, OH: Bowling Green State University Popular Press, 1988.

Edwards, Michael. 'C.S. Lewis: Imagining Heaven,' *Literature and Theology*, 6 (June 1992) 107–124.

Farrer, Austin. *The Glass of Vision*. Westminster: Dacre Press, 1948.

———. *Interpretation and Belief*, ed. Charles C. Conti. London: SPCK, 1976.

———. *A Rebirth of Images: The Making of St John's Apocalypse*. Westminster: Dacre Press, 1949.

———. *The Revelation of St. John the Divine*. Oxford: Clarendon Press, 1964.

———. *Saving Belief: A Discussion of Essentials*. London: Hodder & Stoughton, 1964.

Filmer, Kath. *The Fiction of C.S. Lewis: Mask and Mirror*. London: Macmillan, 1993.

Fitzpatrick, John. 'The Short Stories: A Critical Introduction,' *CSL: The Bulletin of the New York C.S. Lewis Society*, Vol. 14, No. 6 (Apr 1983) 1–5.

Foster, Brett. 'An Estimation of an Admonition: The Nature of Value, the Value of Nature, and *the Abolition of Man*,' *Christian Scholar's Review*, Vol. XXVII, No. 4 (1998) 416–435.

Fowler, Alastair. 'C. S. Lewis: Supervisor,' *Yale Review*, Vol. 91, No. 4 (Oct 2003) 64–80.

Frazer, James George. *The Golden Bough: A Study in Magic and Religion.* London: Macmillan, 1922.

Freeland, Guy & Anthony Corones. *1543 And All That: Image and Word, Change and Continuity in the Proto-Scientific Revolution.* Dordrecht: Kluwer Academic Publishers, 2000.

Funkenstein, Amos. *Theology and the Scientific Imagination: from the Middle Ages to the seventeenth century.* Princeton: Princeton University Press, 1986.

Garth, John. *Tolkien and the Great War: The Threshold of Middle-earth.* London: HarperCollins, 2003.

Gibb, Jocelyn (ed.). *Light on C.S. Lewis.* London: Geoffrey Bles, 1965.

Gibson, Evan K. *C.S. Lewis, Spinner of Tales: A Guide to His Fiction.* Grand Rapids, MI: Eerdmans, 1980.

Gilbert, Douglas & Clyde Kilby. *C.S. Lewis: Images of his World.* Grand Rapids, MI: Eerdmans, 1973.

Gilchrist, James K. *A Morning After: C.S. Lewis and World War I.* New York: Peter Lang, 2005.

Glover, Donald E. *C.S. Lewis: The Art of Enchantment.* Athens, OH: Ohio University Press, 1981.

Goffar, Janine. *C.S. Lewis Index: Rumours from the Sculptor's Shop.* Riverside, CA: La Sierra University Press, 1995.

Goldthwaite, John. *The Natural History of Make-Believe: A Guide to the Principal Works of Britain, Europe and America.* Oxford: Oxford University Press, 1996.

Graham, David (ed.). *We Remember C.S. Lewis: Essays and Memoirs.* Nashville: Broadman & Holman Publishers, 2001.

Grant, Edward. *Planets, Stars, and Orbs: the Medieval Cosmos, 1200–1687.* Cambridge: Cambridge University Press, 1994.

Green, Garrett. *Theology, Hermeneutics, and Imagination.* Cambridge: Cambridge University Press, 2000.

Green, Roger Lancelyn & Walter Hooper. *C.S. Lewis: A Biography,* revised & expanded edition. London: HarperCollins, 2002.

Gresham, Douglas. *Lenten Lands: My Childhood with Joy Davidman and C.S. Lewis.* London: HarperCollins, 1988.

Griffin, William. *C.S. Lewis: The Authentic Voice.* Tring: Lion Publishing, 1986.

Guroian, Vigen. *Tending the Heart of Virtue: How Classic Stories Awaken a Child's Moral Imagination.* Oxford: Oxford University Press, 1998.

Haigh, John D. 'The Fiction of C.S. Lewis.' Ph.D. diss., University of Leeds, 1962.

Haldane, J.B.S. 'Auld Hornie, F.R.S.,' *The Modern Quarterly* (Autumn 1946) 32–40.

———. *Possible Worlds and Other Essays.* London: Chatto & Windus, 1927.

Hall, Christine & Martin Coles. *Children's Reading Choices.* London: Routledge, 1999.

Harries, Richard. 'C.S. Lewis and Philip Pullman: Myth and Competing Moralities,' address to the conference 'Reasons of the Heart: Myth, Meaning and Education,' University of Edinburgh, Sept 2004.

———. *C.S. Lewis: The Man and his God.* London: Collins, 1987.

Harrison, H.M. *Voyager in Space and Time: The Life of John Couch Adams, Cambridge Astronomer.* Lewes: Book Guild, 1994.

Harwood, Laurence. 'Memories of my Godfather,' address to the Oxford Lewis Society, 4 Mar 1997. Lewis Society recordings archive.

Hazlerig, James Alvin. 'Recovering the Discarded Image: The Function of Medievalism in Two Cycles by C.S. Lewis.' M.A. diss., Stephen F. Austin State University, 1992.

Heath, Sir Thomas. *Aristarchus of Samos: the ancient Copernicus.* Oxford: Clarendon Press, 1913.

Henryson, Robert. *The Poems of Robert Henryson,* ed. W.M. Metcalfe. Paisley: Alexander Gardner, 1917.

Hegel, G.W.F. *Phenomenology of Spirit,* trans. A.V. Miller. Oxford: Clarendon Press, 1977.

Herbert, George. *The Temple and a Priest to the Temple.* London: Dent, undated.

Hick, John. *The Metaphor of God Incarnate.* London: SCM Press, 1993.

Hieatt, A. Kent. *Short Time's Endless Monument: The Symbolism of the Numbers in Edmund Spenser's "Epithalamion."* New York: Columbia University Press, 1960.

Hillegas, Mark R. (ed.). *Shadows of Imagination: The Fantasies of C.S. Lewis, J.R.R. Tolkien, and Charles Williams.* Carbondale and Edwardsville: Southern Illinois University Press, 1979.

Holbrook, David. *The Skeleton in the Wardrobe, C.S. Lewis's Fantasies: A Phenomenological Study.* Lewisburg: Associated University Presses, 1991.

Holmer, Paul. *C.S. Lewis, The Shape of His Faith and Thought.* London: Sheldon Press, 1976.

Holst, Imogen. *Gustav Holst: A Biography.* London: Oxford University Press, 1969.

———. *The Music of Gustav Holst.* London: Oxford University Press, 1951.

Holyer, Robert. 'Imagination and Faith: A Response to Mary Warnock,' *Theology* (May 1989) 181–187.

Honda, Mineko. *The Imaginative World of C.S. Lewis: A Way to Participate in Reality.* Lanham, MD: University Press of America, 2000.

Hooper, Walter. *C.S. Lewis, A Companion and Guide.* London: HarperCollins, 1996.

———. *Past Watchful Dragons: A Guide to C.S. Lewis's Chronicles of Narnia.* London: Collins, 1980.

Howard, Thomas. *C.S. Lewis, Man of Letters: A Reading of His Fiction.* Worthing: Churchman Publishing, 1987.

Hulan, David. 'Narnia and the Seven Deadly Sins,' Proceedings of the Narnia Conference, Los Angeles, CA, 12 Nov 1969. Unpublished: Wade Center, Wheaton College, IL, 21–23.

Hunt, Peter. *An Introduction to Children's Literature.* Oxford: Oxford University Press, 1994.

———. (ed.). *Children's Literature, An Illustrated History.* Oxford: Oxford University Press, 1995.

———. (ed.). *International Companion Encyclopedia of Children's Literature.* London: Routledge, 1996.

Hunt, Peter & Millicent Lenz. *Alternative Worlds in Fantasy and Fiction*. London: Continuum, 2001.

Huttar, Charles A. (ed.). *Imagination and the Spirit*. Grand Rapids, MI: Eerdmans, 1971.

Jacobs, Alan. *The Narnian: The Life and Imagination of C.S. Lewis*. London: SPCK, 2005.

Jaki, Stanley L. *God and the Cosmologists*. Edinburgh: Scottish Academic Press, 1989.

Johnson, Francis R. *Astronomical Thought in Renaissance England: A Study of English Scientific Writings from 1500 to 1645*. Baltimore: The Johns Hopkins Press, 1937.

Kay, Richard. *Dante's Christian Astrology*. Philadelphia: University of Pennsylvania Press, 1994.

Keefe, Carolyn (ed.). *C.S. Lewis: Speaker and Teacher*. London: Hodder & Stoughton, 1971.

Kerby-Fulton, Kathryn. '"Standing on Lewis's Shoulders": C.S. Lewis as Critic of Medieval Literature,' *Studies in Medievalism*, Vol. 3, No. 3 (Winter 1991) 257–278.

Kilby, Clyde S. *The Christian World of C.S. Lewis*. Abingdon: Marcham Manor Press, 1965.

King, Don W. *C.S. Lewis, Poet: The Legacy of his Poetic Impulse*. Kent, OH: Kent State University Press, 2001.

———. 'Narnia and the Seven Deadly Sins,' *Mythlore*, 10.4 (Spring 1984) 14–19.

———. 'Lost but Found: The "Missing" Poems of C.S. Lewis's *Spirits in Bondage*,' *Christianity and Literature*, Vol. 53, No. 2 (Winter 2004) 163–201.

Klibansky, R., E. Panofsky & F. Saxl, *Saturn and Melancholy: Studies in the History of Natural Philosophy, Religion, and Art*. New York: Basic Books, 1964.

Kort, Wesley A. *C.S. Lewis Then and Now*. Oxford: Oxford University Press, 2001.

Kuhn, Thomas S. *The Structure of Scientific Revolutions*. Chicago: Chicago University Press, 1962.

Lakoff, George & Mark Johnson. *Metaphors We Live By*. Chicago: University of Chicago Press, 2003.

Laskaya, Anne & Eve Salisbury (eds.). *The Middle English Breton Lays*. Kalamazoo, MI: Medieval Institute Publications, 1995.

Lewis, C.S. *The Abolition of Man* (Glasgow: Collins, 1984).

———. *The Allegory of Love: A Study in Medieval Tradition*. Oxford: Oxford University Press, 1958.

———. *All My Road Before Me: The Diary of C.S. Lewis, 1922–1927*, ed. Walter Hooper. London: HarperCollins, 1991.

———. *Boxen, The Imaginary World of the Young C.S. Lewis*, ed. Walter Hooper. London: Collins, 1985.

———. *Collected Letters, Volume I*, ed. Walter Hooper. London: HarperCollins, 2000.

———. *Collected Letters, Volume II*, ed. Walter Hooper. London: HarperCollins, 2004.

———. *Collected Letters, Volume III*, ed. Walter Hooper. London: HarperCollins, 2006.

———. *The Collected Poems of C.S. Lewis*, ed. Walter Hooper. London: Fount, 1994.

———. *The Dark Tower and Other Stories*, ed. Walter Hooper. London: Collins, 1977.

———. *The Discarded Image*. Cambridge: Cambridge University Press, 1964.

———. *English Literature in the Sixteenth Century, Excluding Drama.* Oxford: Clarendon Press, 1954.

———. *Essay Collection*, ed. Lesley Walmsley. London: HarperCollins, 2000.

———. *An Experiment in Criticism.* Cambridge: Cambridge University Press, 1961.

———. *The Four Loves.* Glasgow: Collins, 1991.

———. *George MacDonald: An Anthology.* San Francisco: HarperCollins, 2001.

———. *The Great Divorce: A Dream.* Glasgow: Collins, 1982.

———. *A Grief Observed.* London: Faber & Faber, 1966.

———. *The Horse and His Boy.* Glasgow: Fontana Lions, 1980.

———. *The Last Battle.* Glasgow: Fontana Lions, 1981.

———. *Letters*, edited with a memoir by W.H. Lewis, revised and expanded edition, ed. Walter Hooper. London: Fount, 1988.

———. *Letters: C.S. Lewis - Don Giovanni Calabria*, trans. & ed. Martin Moynihan. London: Collins, 1989.

———. *Letters to An American Lady*, ed. Clyde S. Kilby. London: Hodder & Stoughton, 1969.

———. *Letters to Children*, ed. Lyle W. Dorsett & Marjorie Lamp Mead. London: Collins, 1985.

———. *The Lion, the Witch and the Wardrobe.* Glasgow: Fontana Lions, 1982.

———. *The Magician's Nephew.* Glasgow: Fontana Lions, 1981.

———. *Mere Christianity.* Glasgow: Collins, 1990.

———. *Miracles: A Preliminary Study.* Glasgow: Collins, 1980.

———. *Miracles: A Preliminary Study.* London: Geoffrey Bles, 1947.

———. *Narrative Poems*, ed. Walter Hooper. London: HarperCollins, 1994.

———. *Of This and Other Worlds*, ed. Walter Hooper. London: Collins, 1982.

———. *Out of the Silent Planet.* London: Pan, 1983.

———. *Perelandra.* London: Pan, 1983.

———. *The Pilgrim's Regress: An Allegorical Apology for Christianity, Reason and Romanticism.* Glasgow: Fount, 1980.

———. *Prayer: Letters to Malcolm.* London: Collins, 1983.

———. *A Preface to Paradise Lost.* Oxford: Oxford University Press, 1984.

———. *Present Concerns: Ethical Essays*, ed. Walter Hooper. Glasgow: Collins, 1986.

———. *Prince Caspian: The Return to Narnia.* Glasgow: Fontana Lions, 1981.

———. *The Problem of Pain.* Glasgow: Collins, 1983.

———. *Reflections on the Psalms.* Glasgow: Collins, 1984.

———. *Rehabilitations and Other Essays.* London: Oxford University Press, 1939.

———. 'Review: *The Oxford Book of Christian Verse*,' *The Review of English Studies*, XVII (Jan 1941) 95–102.

———. *The Screwtape Letters.* Glasgow: Collins, 1982.

———. *Selected Literary Essays*, ed. Walter Hooper. Cambridge: Cambridge University Press, 1980.

———. *The Silver Chair.* Glasgow: Fontana Lions, 1981.

———. *Spenser's Images of Life*, ed. Alastair Fowler. Cambridge: Cambridge University Press, 1967.

————. *Studies in Medieval and Renaissance Literature*, ed. Walter Hooper. Cambridge: Cambridge University Press, 1966.

————. *Studies in Words*. Cambridge: Cambridge University Press, 1990.

————. *Surprised by Joy: The Shape of My Early Life*. Glasgow: Collins, 1982.

————. *That Hideous Strength: A Modern Fairy-Tale for Grown-Ups*. London: Pan, 1983.

————. *They Stand Together: The Letters of C.S. Lewis to Arthur Greeves (1914–1963)*, ed. Walter Hooper. London: Collins, 1979.

————. *Till We Have Faces: A Myth Retold*. Glasgow: Collins, 1985.

————. *Timeless at Heart*. Glasgow: Collins, 1987.

————. *The Voyage of the 'Dawn Treader'*. Glasgow: Fontana Lions, 1981.

Lewis, W.H. 'The Lewis Papers: Memoirs of the Lewis Family, 1850–1930,' 11 vols. Unpublished: Wade Center, Wheaton College, IL.

————. *Brothers and Friends: The Diaries of Major Warren Hamilton Lewis*, ed. Clyde S. Kilby & Marjorie Lamp Mead. San Francisco: Harper & Row, 1982.

Lilly, William. *Christian Astrology*, third edition. Exeter: Regulus Publishing Co., 1985.

Lindskoog, Kathryn. *The Lion of Judah in Never-Never Land: The Theology of C.S. Lewis Expressed in His Fantasies for Children*. Grand Rapids, MI: Eerdmans, 1973.

Lippmann, Friedrich. *The Seven Planets*, trans. Florence Simmonds. London: Asher & Co., 1895.

Lydgate, John. *The Assembly of Gods: or The Accord of Reason and Sensuality in the Fear of Death*, Vol. I, ed. Oscar Lovell Triggs. London: Kegan Paul, 1896.

Lynch, William F. *Christ and Apollo: The Dimensions of the Literary Imagination*. Wilmington, Del: ISI Books, 2004.

Lyne, R.T.R. 'C.S. Lewis and his Arden Shakespeare,' *Magdalene College Magazine & Record*, New Series No. 42. (1997–98) 48–52.

MacDonald, George. *An Expression of Character: the Letters of George MacDonald*, ed. Glenn Edward Sadler. Grand Rapids: Eerdmans, 1994.

————. *The Complete Fairy Tales*, ed. U.C. Knoepflmacher. London: Penguin, 1999.

————. *Orts*. London: Sampson Low, Marston, Searle, & Rivington, 1882.

————. *Phantastes, A Faerie Romance*. Grand Rapids, MI: Eerdmans, 2000.

Macdonald, Michael H. & Andrew A. Tadie. *G.K. Chesterton and C.S. Lewis: The Riddle of Joy*. London: Collins, 1989.

MacIntyre, Alasdair. *After Virtue: A Study in Moral Theory*. London: Duckworth, 1985.

Mackey, James P. (ed.). *Religious Imagination*. Edinburgh: Edinburgh University Press, 1986.

Manlove, C.N. *C.S. Lewis: His Literary Achievement*. London: Macmillan, 1987.

————. *The Chronicles of Narnia: The Patterning of a Fantastic World*. New York: Twayne, 1993.

Markley, Robert. *Dying Planet: Mars in Science and the Imagination*. Durham: Duke University Press, 2005.

Marshall, Cynthia (ed.). *Essays on C.S. Lewis and George MacDonald: Truth, Fiction, and the Power of Imagination*. Lampeter: Edwin Mullen Press, 1991.

Martin, Thomas L. (ed.). *Reading the Classics with C.S. Lewis.* Grand Rapids: Baker Academic, 2000.

Mascall, E.L. *Christian Theology and Natural Science.* London: Longmans, Green & Co., 1956.

Mastrolia, Arthur. *C.S. Lewis And The Blessed Virgin Mary: Uncovering A "Marian Attitude"* Lima, OH: Fairway Press, 2000.

Matthews, Kenneth. 'C.S. Lewis and the Modern World.' Ph.D. diss., University of California, Los Angeles, 1983.

May, Stephen. *Stardust and Ashes: Science Ficion in Christian Perspective.* London: SPCK, 1998.

McGrath, Alister E. *Bridge-Building: Effective Christian Apologetics.* Leicester: IVP, 1998.

————. *The Renewal of Anglicanism.* London: SPCK, 1993.

McIntyre, John. *Faith, Theology and Imagination.* Edinburgh: The Handsel Press, 1987.

McLuhan, Marshall. *Understanding Media: The Extensions of Man.* London: Routledge & Kegan Paul, 1964.

Menuge, Angus J.L. (ed.). *C.S. Lewis, Lightbearer in the Shadowlands: The Evangelistic Vision of C.S. Lewis.* Wheaton, IL: Crossway Books, 1997.

Mills, David (ed.). *The Pilgrim's Guide: C.S. Lewis and the Art of Witness.* Grand Rapids: Eerdmans, 1998.

Milward, Peter. *A Challenge to C.S. Lewis.* London: Associated University Presses, 1995.

Montgomery, John Warwick (ed.). *Myth, Allegory and Gospel: An Interpretation of J.R.R. Tolkien, C.S. Lewis, G.K. Chesterton, Charles Williams.* Minneapolis: Bethany Fellowship Inc., 1974.

Moodie, C.A.E. 'C.S. Lewis: Exponent of Tradition and Prophet of Postmodernism?' D.Th. diss., University of South Africa, 2000.

More, Louis Trenchard. *Isaac Newton, A Biography.* New York: Charles Scribner's Sons, 1934.

Morris, Francis J. 'Metaphor and Myth: Shaping Forces in C.S. Lewis's Critical Assessment of Medieval and Renaissance Literature.' Ph.D. diss., University of Pennsylvania, 1977.

Morris, Francis J. & Ronald C. Wendling. 'Coleridge and 'the Great Divide' between C.S. Lewis and Owen Barfield,' *Studies in the Literary Imagination*, 12, No. 2 (Fall, 1989) 149–159.

Myers, Doris. *C.S. Lewis in Context.* Kent, OH: Kent State University Press, 1994.

Newell, Roger J. 'Participatory Knowledge: Theology as Art and Science in C.S. Lewis and T.F. Torrance.' Ph.D. diss., University of Aberdeen, 1983.

Nicolson, Marjorie Hope. 'The "New Astronomy" and English Literary Imagination,' *Studies in Philology*, XXXII (1935) 428–462.

————. 'The Telescope and Imagination,' *Modern Philology*, XXXII (1935) 233–260.

————. *Voyages to the Moon.* New York: Macmillan, 1948.

North, John David. *Chaucer's Universe.* Oxford: Clarendon Press, 1988.

————. *Stars, Minds and Fate: Essays in Ancient and Medieval Cosmology.* London: Hambledon, 1989.

Norwood, W.D., Jr. 'C.S. Lewis' Portrait of Aphrodite,' *Southern Quarterly*, VIII (1970) 237–272.

Nuttall, A.D. 'Lewis, Hume and Miracles,' address to the Oxford Lewis Society, 25 Oct 1988. Lewis Society recordings archive.

Oliver, Naomi Glenn. 'The Higher and Lower Mediums of Meaning in Three Models Presented by C.S. Lewis: The Medieval, Modern and Incarnational Models.' Ph.D. diss., Drew University, 1992.

Orr, M.A. *Dante and the Early Astronomers*. London: Allan Wingate, 1956.

Orwell, George. *Nineteen Eighty-Four*. London: Penguin, 1983.

———. *The Complete Works of George Orwell*, ed. Peter Davison. London: Secker & Warburg, 1986–1998.

Patrick, James. *The Magdalen Metaphysicals: Idealism and Orthodoxy at Oxford, 1901–1945*. Mercer University Press, 1985.

Patterson, Nancy-Lou. 'The Host of Heaven: Astrological and Other Images of Divinity in the Fantasies of C.S. Lewis, Part 1,' *Mythlore*, 25 (Autumn 1980) 19–29.

———. 'The Host of Heaven: Astrological and Other Images of Divinity in the Fantasies of C.S. Lewis, Part 2,' *Mythlore*, 26 (Winter 1981) 13–21.

Payne, Leanne. *Real Presence: The Christian Worldview of C.S. Lewis as Incarnational Reality*. Grand Rapids, MI: Baker Books, 2002.

Pietrusz, Jim. 'Rites of Passage: The Chronicles of Narnia and the Seven Sacraments,' *Mythlore*, 54 (Summer 1988) 61–63.

Poe, Harry Lee & Rebecca Whitten Poe. *C.S. Lewis Remembered* (Grand Rapids, MI: Zondervan, 2006).

Polanyi, Michael & H. Prosch. *Meaning*. Chicago: University of Chicago Press, 1975.

Principe, Lawrence. *The Aspiring Adept: Robert Boyle and his alchemical quest: including Boyle's 'lost' Dialogue on the transmutation of metals*. Princeton, NJ: Princeton University Press, 1998.

Pullman, Philip. *The Amber Spyglass*. London: Scholastic, 2001.

———. 'The Dark Side of Narnia,' *The Guardian* (1 Oct 1998) 6.

———. 'The Republic of Heaven,' *The Horn Book Magazine* (Nov/Dec 2001) 655–667.

Pyles, Franklin Arthur. 'The Influence of the British Neo-Hegelians on the Christian Apology of C.S. Lewis.' Ph.D. diss., Northwestern University, 1978.

Rahner, Karl. *Theological Investigations 4*. London: Darton, Longman & Todd, 1966.

Reppert, Victor. *C.S. Lewis's Dangerous Idea: In Defense of the Argument from Reason*. Downers Grove, IL: InterVarsity Press, 2003.

Richards, I.A. *Coleridge on Imagination*. London: Kegan Paul, 1934.

———. *Poetries and Sciences*. London: Routledge & Kegan Paul, 1970.

Robson, W.W. *Critical Essays*. London: Routledge & Kegan Paul, 1966.

Rossi, Lee D. *The Politics of Fantasy: C.S. Lewis and J.R.R. Tolkien*. Epping: UMI Research Press, 1984.

Rottensteiner, Franz. *The Fantasy Book, An Illustrated History from Dracula to Tolkien* (London: Thames & Hudson, 1978).

Rowse, A.L. *Glimpses of the Great*. Lanham, MD: University Press of America, 1985.

The Diaries of A.L. Rowse, ed. Richard Ollard. London: Penguin, 2003.

Sammons, Martha C. *"A Far-Off Country", A Guide to C.S. Lewis's Fantasy Fiction.* Lanham, MD: University Press of America, 2000.

———. *A Guide Through C.S. Lewis's Space Trilogy.* Westchester, IL: Cornerstone Books, 1980.

———. *A Guide Through Narnia.* London: Hodder & Stoughton, 1979.

Sayer, George. *Jack: C.S. Lewis and His Times.* San Francisco: Harper & Row, 1988.

Sayers, Dorothy L. *The Letters of Dorothy L. Sayers, Vol. Three, 1944–1950: A Noble Daring,* chosen and edited by Barbara Reynolds. Cambridge: The Dorothy L. Sayers Society, 1988.

Schakel, Peter J. *Imagination and the Arts in C.S. Lewis.* Columbia: University of Missouri Press, 2002.

———. (ed.) *The Longing for a Form, Essays on the Fiction of C.S. Lewis.* Kent, OH: Kent State University Press, 1977.

———. *Reading with the Heart: The Way into Narnia.* Grand Rapids, MI: Eerdmans, 1979.

———. *Reason and Imagination in C.S. Lewis: A Study of 'Till We Have Faces'.* Grand Rapids, MI: Eerdmans, 1984.

———. *The Way into Narnia: A Reader's Guide.* Grand Rapids: Eerdmans, 2005.

Schakel, Peter J. & Charles A. Huttar. (eds.). *Word and Story in C.S. Lewis.* Columbia: University of Missouri Press, 1991.

Schofield, Stephen (ed.). *In Search of C.S. Lewis.* South Plainfield, NJ: Bridge Publishing, 1983.

Seznec, Jean. *The Survival of the Pagan Gods: The Mythological Tradition and its Place in Renaissance Humanism and Art,* trans. Barbara F. Sessions. New York: Pantheon, 1953.

Sidney, Sir Philip. *The Defence of Poesie,* ed. Albert Feuillerat. Cambridge: Cambridge University Press, 1923.

Smilde, Arend. 'Sweetly Poisonous in a Welcome Way, Reflections on a Definitive Biography: *C. S. Lewis: A Biography* (1990) by A. N. Wilson.' Online. Available: http://www.solcon.nl/arendsmilde/cslewis/reflections/e-definitivebiography.htm

Smith, Robert Houston. *Patches of Godlight: The Pattern of Thought of C.S. Lewis.* Athens, GA: University of Georgia Press, 1981.

Sobel, Dava. *The Planets.* London: Fourth Estate, 2005.

Sophrony, Archimandrite. *The Monk of Mount Athos, Staretz Silouan 1866–1938,* trans. Rosemary Edmonds. New York: St. Vladimir's Seminary Press, 1973.

Spufford, Francis. *The Child that Books Built.* London: Faber & Faber, 2002.

Steiner, George. *After Babel: Aspects of Language and Translation.* Oxford: Oxford University Press, 1998.

Taliaferro, Charles. 'A Narnian Theory of the Atonement,' *Scottish Journal of Theology,* Vol. 41 (May 1988) 75–92.

Thorson, Stephen. 'Knowing and Being in C.S. Lewis's "Great War" with Owen Barfield,' *CSL: The Bulletin of the New York C.S. Lewis Society,* Vol. 15, No.1. (Nov. 1983) 1–8.

Tillyard, E.M.W. *The Elizabethan World Picture.* London: Chatto & Windus, 1960.

Tillyard, E.M.W. & C.S. Lewis. *The Personal Heresy, A Controversy*. London: Oxford University Press, 1965.

Tolkien, J.R.R. *The Letters of J.R.R. Tolkien*, ed. Humphrey Carpenter with the assistance of Christopher Tolkien. London: Allen & Unwin, 1981.

———. *The Monsters and the Critics and Other Essays*. London: HarperCollins, 1997.

———. *The Return of the King*. London: Allen & Unwin, 1984.

Trupia, Robert C. 'Learning Christian Behavior: The Way of Virtue in *The Chronicles of Narnia*,' *The Lamp-Post*, 11.4 (Nov 1988) 3–8.

Tucker, Nicholas. *Darkness Visible: Inside the World of Philip Pullman*. Cambridge: Icon Books, 2003.

Tynan, Kenneth. *The Diaries of Kenneth Tynan*, ed. John Lahr. London: Bloomsbury, 2001.

Underhill, Evelyn. *The Letters of Evelyn Underhill*, ed. Charles Williams. London: Longmans, Green & Co., 1943.

Urang, Gunnar. *Shadows of Heaven: Religion and Fantasy in the Writing of C.S. Lewis, Charles Williams and J.R.R. Tolkien*. London: SCM Press, 1971.

Van Buren, Paul M. *The Edges of Language, An essay in the logic of a religion*. New York: Macmillan, 1972.

Walker, Andrew. 'Scripture, revelation and Platonism in C.S. Lewis,' *Scottish Journal of Theology*, Vol. 55 (2002) 19–35.

Walker, Andrew & James Patrick (eds.). *A Christian for All Christians: Essays in Honour of C.S. Lewis*. London: Hodder & Stoughton, 1990.

Walker, D.P. *Spiritual and Demonic Magic from Ficino to Campanella*. London: The Warburg Institute, 1958.

Walsh, Chad. *C.S. Lewis: Apostle to the Skeptics*. New York: Macmillan, 1949.

———. *The Literary Legacy of C.S. Lewis*. London: Sheldon Press, 1979.

Ward, Michael. 'Philip Pullman's Attack on Narnia: A Defense,' *Mars Hill Review*, No. 21 (2003) 127–135.

———. 'Planet Narnia,' *The Times Literary Supplement* (25 Apr 2003) 15.

———. 'Through the Wardrobe: A Famous Image Explored,' *Seven: An Anglo-American Literary Review*, Vol. 15 (1998) 55–71.

———. 'Where Dreams Don't Come True: How To Read *The Voyage of the 'Dawn Treader*,' address to the Oxford Lewis Society, 10 Mar 1998. Lewis Society recordings archive.

Watson, George. 'The Art of Disagreement: C.S. Lewis (1898–1963),' *The Hudson Review*, XLVIII (Summer 1995) 229–239.

———. (ed.). *Critical Essays on C.S. Lewis*. Aldershot: Scolar Press, 1992.

———. *Never Ones for Theory? England and the War of Ideas*. Cambridge: Lutterworth Press, 2000.

Watson, Victor (ed.). *The Cambridge Guide to Children's Books in English*. Cambridge: Cambridge University Press, 2001.

White, William Luther. *The Image of Man in C.S. Lewis*. Nashville: Abingdon Press, 1969.

Williams, Charles & C.S. Lewis. *Arthurian Torso*. London: Oxford University Press, 1952.

Williams, Rowan. 'A Theologian in Narnia,' address to the Oxford Lewis Society, 9 Nov 1999. Speaker's own notes (copy in this author's possession).

———. *Lost Icons: Reflections on Cultural Bereavement*. Edinburgh: T & T Clark, 2000.

———. '*That Hideous Strength*: A Reassessment,' address to the Oxford Lewis Society, 5 Oct 1988. Lewis Society recordings archive.

Wilson, A.N. *C.S. Lewis, A Biography*. London: Collins, 1990.

Wind, Edgar. *Pagan Mysteries in the Renaissance*. London: Faber & Faber, 1958.

Withycombe, E.G. *The Oxford Dictionary of English Christian Names*. Oxford: Oxford University Press, 1977.

Wojciechowski, M. 'Seven Churches and Seven Celestial Bodies,' *Biblische Notizen*, 45 (1988) 48–50.

Worsley, Howard. 'Popularized Atonement Theory Reflected in Children's Literature,' *The Expository Times*, Vol. 115, No. 5 (Feb 2004) 149–156.

Zerubavel, Eviatar. *The Seven Day Circle*. New York: Macmillan, 1985.

Zipes, Jack (ed.). *The Oxford Companion to Fairy Tales*. Oxford: Oxford University Press, 2000.

Zogby, Edward Gabriel. 'C.S. Lewis: Christopoesis and the Recovery of the Panegyric Imagination.' Ph.D. diss., Syracuse University, 1974.

GENERAL INDEX ❧

BIBLICAL INDEX

Printed in the United Kingdom by
Lightning Source UK Ltd., Milton Keynes
139671UK00001BB/2/P

9 780195 313871